Doctrine is Life

The study of Robert D. Preus

Doctrine is Life

The Essays of Robert D. Preus
on Justification
and the Lutheran Confessions

EDITED BY KLEMET I. PREUS

CONCORDIA PUBLISHING HOUSE · SAINT LOUIS

To my mother, Donna Preus—faithful companion
and wife of 48 years to Robert D. Preus

Introductory chapter and essay introductions
copyright © 2006 Concordia Publishing House
3558 S. Jefferson Ave.
St. Louis, MO 63118-3968
1-800-325-3040 • www.cph.org

Manufactured in the United States of America

Library of Congress Cataloging-in-Publication Data

Preus, Robert D., 1924–1995
   Doctrine is Life : The Essays of Robert D. Preus on Justification and the Lutheran Confessions / edited by Klemet I. Preus.
      p. cm.
   ISBN-13: 978-0-7586-1266-3
   ISBN-10: 0-7586-1266-4
   1. Justification (Christian theology). 2. Lutheran Church—Creeds. 3. Lutheran Church—Doctrines. I. Preus, Klemet I. II. Title.
   BT764.3.P74 2006
   230′.41—dc22
                                                      2006013917

1 2 3 4 5 6 7 8 9 10   15 14 13 12 11 10 09 08 07 06

Contents

PREFACE

IN EARLY AUTUMN 2001, I had the privilege of sitting in the backyard of the Rev. Matthew Harrison in his suburban St. Louis home, drinking lemonade, admiring the fall colors, and talking theology with my host. Brother Harrison was basking in the short-lived adulation associated with his translation and editing of *The Lonely Way: Selected Essays and Letters of Hermann Sasse*, which Concordia Publishing House had just released. As he shared the intricacies of the translation task, the felicitous proactivity of Concordia Publishing House, and the justifiable sense of humility at having stood, as it were, on the shoulders of a giant, it occurred to us that something of the same could be done with the writings of Robert Preus.

I frankly don't remember if it was his brainchild or mine, but I went away from that relaxing afternoon confident that a book on the writings of Robert Preus was a great idea. It would require no translation for the English reader, which, with my paucity of language skills, uniquely qualified me for the task. I was fairly well-acquainted with the literature and was convinced that the new generation of pastors entering the Lutheran ministry, as well as serious systematic theologians and historians throughout the church, would be interested in such a work. Subsequently, Harrison's encouragement was equaled by that of the good people at Concordia, and I soon found myself joyfully immersed in Preus's writings.

As I read, it occurred to me that much of my own life had been shaped not only by the parenting predilections of Robert Preus and by his orthodox Lutheran theology but also by the often bizarre geographic quest for knowledge that he had undergone throughout his professional life, often with his growing brood of children in tow. In 1950 and 1951, when I was just a toddler, I lived for a year in Edinburgh, Scotland, with my parents and my older brother. I have no recollections of that time, but I am reliably informed that my first words were characterized by that lilting brogue that Americans find so charming. The reason for this overseas visit was my father's study at the university there. He subsequently earned his first doctorate, the thesis for which became the basis for his book *The Inspiration of Scripture*.

In the summer of 1963, Robert and Donna Preus packed up their nine children and moved for a year to Norway. There we lived on the island of Nesøya, which was part of the archipelago dotting the western Oslo Fjord. The island was connected to the mainland by a single bridge near the little town of Sandvika, about 20 miles south of Oslo. The house, as I recall, had one sink, which was in the kitchen and spurted water at a gushing speed that precluded anything such as hand washing, tooth brushing, or shaving. There were no bathtubs, showers, or indoor toilets. The downstairs featured a small kitchen and spacious living and dining rooms. Upstairs were two large bedrooms and a couple of rather large closets that also functioned as bedrooms. I was a child of 13 years at the time and was assigned a bed in the walk-through closet. The little home stood on the side of a hill that banked gently down toward the peaceful and temperate waters of the fjord, which afforded summer swimming, winter skating, and year-long beauty.

Six of the kids were enrolled in the Norwegian public schools. At the age of 13, I was directed to learn Norwegian, make friends, and take a shower after gym class every day—orders I gladly and pointedly obeyed. I was too young really to reflect upon the reasons why we were in such an idyllic setting. It was simply a twelve-month adventure the likes of which most children only dream. I still remember it vividly as one of the best years of my life. Later I learned that the Universitetsbibliotek at the University of Oslo provided my father the chance to do the research necessary for his second book, *The Theology of Post-Reformation Lutheranism, Volume One*. I never asked my mother at the time how she felt.

Five years later my father was at it again. Mom and Dad, now with ten kids, moved to France for a year. We lived in two apartments on the sixth and tenth stories of a seventeen-story apartment building. The sixth-floor apartment was rented from Dr. John Warwick Montgomery, redoubtable scholar, Francophile, Christian apologist, and prolific author whose countless books were packed into his small library and throughout the flat, much like the many small German homes crowding the streets and avenues in the Alsatian town of Strasbourg that we called home that year. Four brothers occupied the sixth-floor dwelling, safely distant from the oversight of parents. It was a different kind of adventure but memorable nonetheless. I was 19 at the time, and with newfound European friends, I found myself exploring the various villages and towns of northwestern France, sampling the wine and generally soaking up the culture.

This time I understood why we were here. Dad was earning his second doctoral degree at the University of Strasbourg and doing the research that resulted in his third book, *The Theology of Post-Reformation Lutheranism, Volume 2*. This time I was also aware, albeit somewhat distractedly, that my mother was a remarkably good sport to endure and even encourage her husband's scholarly pursuits. Apparently Robert Preus found that the writing of books was accomplished for him more easily in Europe than in the New World. Fortunately for his wife, if not for serious theology students, Robert Preus stopped writing books after the French experience.

Whether this hiatus in book writing was caused by the press of administrative duties or his inability to get his growing family to Europe is anyone's guess. Preus's production of scholarly journal writings continued unabated, however, until his death in 1995. These writings were effected largely in his study at home or at the lake in northeastern Minnesota, a veritable Eden, albeit with mosquitoes, whose distractions were resisted by Preus in deference to that higher calling that every pastor/theologian knows—the doing of theology. I can remember as a teenager listening to the endless clickety-clack of the circa-1930 typewriter on which my father would work, isolating himself for days at a time, it seemed, and emerging periodically from his work for nutritional sustenance or the pleasant company of his wife of 48 years, Donna.

While Preus's books are still readily available to the interested reader, his journal writings have not been so easily accessed. These volumes provide that easy access to the most notable of these many writings. They contain more than twenty-five articles produced over five decades and from a host of ecclesiastical and theological contexts. From these writings the reader will gain not only an appreciation of the keen theological mind of Robert Preus but a taste of the times in which he lived. Especially helpful are the lessons Preus provides on the manner in which theology is done in the heat of controversy. Throughout his writings, a spirit of devotion to the Scriptures and the Lutheran Confessions is manifested that transcends European libraries, tranquil summer cottages, and even the times in which he lived. For his devotion and the theology that emanated from it the church can be thankful.

Robert Preus had a long and distinguished ministry. In 1948 as a pastor in North Dakota he commenced his ministry. Preus also served parishes in Boston and northwestern Minnesota before his teaching ministry began in 1957. For eighteen years Preus served as professor of philosophy, systematic theology, and the Lutheran Confessions at Concordia Seminary, St. Louis. In 1974 Preus became president of Concordia Theological Seminary in Springfield, Illinois. The seminary moved to Ft. Wayne, Indiana, in

1976. He served as professor and president of that institution until 1993. For almost forty years Preus taught hundreds of students at the seminaries in St. Louis and Ft. Wayne. His influence upon confessional Lutheranism within the LCMS was long and profound.

ACKNOWLEDGMENTS

I need to thank some people who helped in the production of this book. My brother Daniel, former executive director at Concordia Historical Institute, and Martin Noland, who succeeded him, gave me free reign of that important facility. Robert Preus chose not to seal his files upon his death, and a treasury of important historical and theological data was made available to the public in the late 1990s through the institute.

At Concordia Publishing House, Laura Lane, who began the production process, was helpful in getting me started, while Dawn Weinstock, the indefatigable and always cheerful production editor of scholarly works at Concordia Publishing House, held my hand through the completion process. Mark Sell, senior editor of Academic, Professional, and Consumer Books at Concordia, championed the cause, while Fritz Baue and Paul McCain also offered helpful encouragement.

I want especially to acknowledge two women in my life whom I love. My wife, Janet, both motivated me and left me alone to work, despite her loving instincts to the contrary. Consequently, she enjoys my deepest admiration. And my mother, Donna Preus, to whom this book is dedicated, provided my father, Robert, the opportunity to learn and write. She was his soul mate of fifty years, and there is little doubt that the church owes her a tremendous debt of thanks for that which her husband has given.

Robert Preus summarized the convictions of his own ministry in the oft-repeated phrase, borrowed from an old Norwegian woman in northern Minnesota, "Doctrine is life." He taught and wrote over a forty-five-year career because he believed that the content of his teaching gave eternal life in Christ to those who believed it.

Robert Preus and the Purpose of Theological Scholarship

Robert Preus was a scholar. He produced four books and nearly countless journal articles during his lifetime and had at least three in the hopper before his death. His erudition is also manifest from the articles contained in this volume. Preus's scholarly interests were somewhat vast within the broad confines of Lutheranism. He wrote extensively on the doctrine of the Scriptures—their inspiration, inerrancy, power, unity, authority, proper interpretation, and relevance for the church. He was an expert on the Lutheran Confessions and gave to the church systematic presentations of their subscription, hermeneutics, and relevance for today. His earliest writings betray his original interest in the article of conversion and the new birth. He was an avid defender of divine monergism, carefully walking the path "between Calvinism and synergism."[1] In the late 1960s, questions of Christian fellowship occupied his thoughts,[2] while in his latter years his monograph on "The Doctrine of the Call in the Confessions and Lutheran Orthodoxy"[3] enjoyed wide readership and posthumous

---

1 Robert Preus, "The Significance of Luther's Term *Pure Passive* as Quoted in Article II of the Formula of Concord," *Concordia Theological Monthly* XXIX, no. 8 (August 1958): 561.

2 Robert Preus, "To Join or Not to Join: A Study of Some of the Issues in the Question of Joining with the America Lutheran Church in Pulpit and Altar Fellowship," presented at the February 13–16, 1968, North Dakota District Convention at Grand Forks, North Dakota (published by the North Dakota District Office).

3 Robert Preus, "The Doctrine of the Call in the Confessions and Lutheran Orthodoxy," *Luther Academy Monograph* 1 (April 1991).

republication. He even wrote on the subject of "clergy burnout."[4] And, of course, his "preoccupation" with the article of justification permeated his writings from first until last. Through it all, he presented and applied the teachings of Martin Luther, Philip Melanchthon, the Lutheran Confessions, the orthodox Lutheran fathers, C. F. W. Walther, and, of course, the Scriptures. His scholarship is beyond question.

But what drove the man so tirelessly? No one studies this much on such a wide variety of subjects over four decades unless he is motivated by something more than mere knowledge of the subject matter. And few write so prolifically just because they want to add to the body of research. Preus was never content with knowledge for the sake of knowledge. Rather, he is an example of the most noble and worthy purposes of theological scholarship. "Doctrine is life," said Preus.[5] He simply wanted to teach the church the doctrine of Christ, hoping that others would learn of him who brings eternal life to those who believe.

Preus was first and foremost a teacher. "The burden of the ministry is to teach. Oversight, rule, ministry, preaching, pastoring, leading, the various duties inherent in the ministry are all realized through the teaching of the gospel."[6] In fact, claimed Preus, "preaching and teaching the Gospel: the two terms are interchangeable."[7] Whether he spoke in the classroom or wrote in his study, Preus always taught. The two activities were not different in substance. So his writings were, to him, no different than his lectures and no different than a pastor's sermons. In fact, his writings became sermons to the church on topics of importance. His writings took on a somewhat devotional tone as he hid poorly his own faith in both the objects and the conclusions of his scholarly pursuits. It was not uncommon for Preus to exhort his readers to faith precisely in his topics of discussion, whether it be the Word of God[8] or the chief article.[9] Preus would even

---

4 Robert Preus, "Clergy Mental Health and the Doctrine of Justification," *Concordia Theological Quarterly* 48, nos. 2–3 (April–June 1984): 113–22.

5 Robert Preus, *Preaching to Young Theologians* (St. Louis: Luther Academy, 1999), 66.

6 Preus, "Doctrine of the Call" (1991), 14.

7 Preus, "Doctrine of the Call" (1991), 15.

8 Robert Preus, "The Power of God's Word," *Concordia Theological Monthly* XXXIV, no. 8 (August 1963): 453–65. "Only when we seize and are seized by the Word of God do we know the exceeding greatness of His power toward us who believe (Eph. 1:219). And only when our faith stands in God's power do we discover what the Word of God really is (I Cor. 2:5)" (453).

9 Robert Preus, "Perennial Problems in the Doctrine of Justification," *Concordia Theological Quarterly* 45, no. 3 (July 1981): 163–84. Robert Preus, "The Doctrine of Justification in the Theology of Classical Lutheran Orthodoxy," *The Springfielder* XXIX, no. 1 (Spring 1965): 24–39.

pray,[10] quote hymns,[11] or begin with a Trinitarian invocation.[12] His "dogmatic bias" was no less defensible than that of the apostles, and he made no attempt to hide it:

> Of course [the apostles] have a dogmatic bias. Who would not when he had seen the risen Christ? Of course they were believing Christians and not merely objective historians. But faith and history do not oppose each other. How can one report a historical event if he does not believe it? And profound interpretation does not vitiate or cast doubt upon the reality and historicity of the event interpreted. A religious aim may well influence the presentation of facts, but this does not change the facts themselves. There is nothing wrong with facts being explained by one who has experienced them and been deeply affected by them.[13]

Having thus absolved himself of the charge of undue passion, Preus was free to teach the truth.

And teach he did, addressing himself to virtually every issue that confronted the church during the second half of the twentieth century. In the writings of Robert Preus, three didactic principles manifest themselves: the coherence principle, the correspondence principle, and the confessional principle.

COHERENCY

Throughout his writings, Preus demonstrated a relentless adamancy to present doctrine that was utterly consistent with itself. Truth must cohere. It must contain no inner contradictions or logical flaws. Truth is one. Preus's insistence on coherence within a theological system is seen in his understanding of both formal and material principles. Preus found the coherency principle in the Bible itself.

Scripture, the formal principle of theology, must have meaning that is inherent in the words of the Bible itself. If you have to provide clarity from somewhere else or through some principle besides *sola scriptura*, then your theology does not cohere. So, for example, Preus could never pit the

---

10 Robert Preus, "Confessional Lutheranism in Today's World," *Concordia Theological Quarterly* 54, nos. 2–3 (April–June 1990): 113.

11 Preus, "Confessional Lutheranism in Today's World," 103

12 Robert Preus, "Walther and the Scriptures," *Proceedings of the Thirty-eighth Convention of the Texas District of The Lutheran Church—Missouri Synod*, Austin, Texas (April 3–7, 1961): 30–57.

13 Robert Preus, "Biblical Hermeneutics and the Lutheran Church Today," *Proceedings, Twentieth Convention of the Iowa District West of The Lutheran Church—Missouri Synod* (August 21–26, 1966): 47.

analogy of faith or the article of justification against the exegetical meaning of a text no matter how firmly he held to its centrality. Systematic theologian that he was, Preus could value and apply the analogy of faith, "analogical exegesis," as he called it, which was "tracing a theological theme or article of faith throughout the Scriptures."[14] After all, such tracing is precisely what systematicians do. And Preus himself engaged in tracing.[15] Conceding that an analogical approach to Scripture would never do violence to the meaning of a given text or pericope,[16] Preus never allowed for a type of "canon within the canon of Scripture." He even disagreed with the redoubtable Hermann Sasse for using the article on justification as a type of "norm within the norm" of the Holy Scriptures.[17] Preus didn't think it was necessary. The clear meaning of any scriptural text could not violate the central article. Lutheran theology is too coherent for that. Why protect the absolute authority of Scripture with a "canon within the canon" as if the Bible is only meaningful when justification remains central? Preus taught that justification was the central article of the faith not so he could understand the Bible but because the clear and understandable teaching of the Bible is that justification is central. Through his coherence principle, he avoided the inevitable circular reasoning of Sasse. (If the key to understanding the Bible is the doctrine of justification, and the Bible is unclear without this article, then from what clear and authoritative source did we get the article in the first place?) If Preus was respectful and deferential to Sasse, whom he knew and considered a friend, he was brusque and impatient with those who denied the coherency of Scripture by postulating that a biblical text could have different meanings at different times or that somehow the analogy of faith trumped the clear meaning of a text.[18] Such a view did not cohere.

Coherency of biblical meaning suggests coherency in our view of the power of the word as well. To Preus the notion that the Word of God in one form is somehow more powerful than the Word in another was not a consistent view. Preus was quick to assert the lack of coherence.

---

14 Robert Preus "How Is the Lutheran Church to Interpret and Use the Old and New Testaments?" paper delivered at the 1973 Reformation Lectures at Bethany Lutheran College, Mankato, Minnesota.

15 Preus, "Power of God's Word," 453–55.

16 Preus, "How Is the Lutheran Church to Interpret," 9 See also Robert Preus, "The Unity of Scriptures," *Concordia Theological Quarterly* 54, no. 1 (January 1990): 17.

17 Robert Preus, "Luther and the Doctrine of Justification," *Concordia Theological Quarterly* 48, no. 1 (January 1984): 14.

18 Preus, "Biblical Hermeneutics," 47–49. See also Robert Preus, "Can the Lutheran Confessions Have Any Meaning 450 Years Later?" *Concordia Theological Quarterly* 44, nos. 2–3 (July 1980): 105; and Preus, "Unity of Scripture," 4–5.

This stress on the unity of the Word is necessary because of late a curious and subtle distinction has been made between the written Word of Scripture and the *kerygmatic* preaching of the church. According to this distinction, there is somehow more power in the preached Word, while Scripture, the written Word, remains in itself a dead letter. But Scripture knows no such distinction.[19]

Preus argues in two ways. First, he cites the Bible, which calls itself the Word of God and asserts its own power.[20] He also reasons somewhat syllogistically. The Word of God is powerful. Holy Scripture is the Word of God. Therefore Holy Scripture is powerful. It is a valid syllogism. It is, further, a syllogism whose logic is forced upon any theologian who aspires to Preus's belief in the coherence of Scripture.

The power of the Word is questionable neither because of its form nor because of its speaker. So Preus viewed that the ministerial actions of laypeople are equally as valid as those performed by the pastor. Preus even allows the validity of the "ministerial" acts of women "pastors," whom he considered "private persons,"[21] while denying that any women actually held the office of pastor. The political climate of the church in the 1990s, with its ongoing debate about lay ministers and "women pastors," would certainly have tempted Preus to question or deny the validity of actions performed by laypeople. But the coherence principle would not allow it. Certainly he opposed both the practice of lay preachers and the placing of women into the office of pastor. Anyone, however, who hears or reads the Word—whether a pastor, layperson, or personally—can "have joy and comfort to know that God Himself is present speaking to you and mediating to you His Son, His Holy Spirit, His forgiveness and all the riches of His grace."[22]

If coherence applied to the formal principle, Scripture, then even more so did Preus require consistency when presenting the article upon which the church stands or falls. One example will do. Consider Preus's discussion of the expression *per fidem* ("through faith"). In the article of justification, faith is always passive. It only receives the acquittal from God. Only by holding the role of faith in our justification "as pure receptivity"[23] can "the sinner . . . ever be certain of his own forgiveness and salvation."[24] More cosmically, according to Preus, by holding to the *per fidem*, "the

---

19 Preus, "Power of God's Word," 455.

20 Preus, "Power of God's Word," 454.

21 Preus, "Confessional Lutheranism in Today's World," 116.

22 Preus, "Walther and the Scriptures," 48.

23 Preus, "Perennial Problems," 171.

24 Preus, "Doctrine of Justification," 36.

entire Roman Catholic dogmatic structure (whether pertaining to justifi-cation, penance, sacraments, or whatever) breaks down."[25] Further, the *per fidem* vanquishes Arminianism, which characterizes most of American Evangelicalism and the Church Growth Movement.[26] It would seem that the two largest and most influential, albeit heterodox, Christian groups in North America would fold if the simple *per fidem* of Lutheranism were embraced. Preus never shied away from drawing the logical conclusions of his theology, no matter how far-reaching.

On the other hand, if our understanding of the passive role of faith in the article of justification is denied, then all sorts of mischief occurs. "Faith becomes directed toward itself," resulting in "synergism, pietism and reli-gious emotionalism . . . an inordinate interest in the phenomenology of faith . . . [and] Christ and His atoning work" are diminished.[27] The result is "all kinds of subjectivistic aberrations."[28] No wonder Preus was so incredulous when one of his colleagues at Concordia Seminary, St. Louis, Missouri, asserted that we are justified *propter fidem* ("because of faith").[29] No wonder also that he felt compelled to explain Luther's puzzling and offhanded use of the phrase *propter fidem*, a phrase that is, paradoxically, un-Lutheran.[30] For Preus, coherence required these responses.

Coherency in the theological task also moved Preus, especially in his latter years, to discuss the necessary and important relationship between doctrine and practice in the church. Preus complained of a "queer dichotomy and divorce, alien to the Lutheran Confessions, between doc-trine on the one hand and practice and worship on the other."[31] Preus attributed this dichotomy to the Enlightenment, not to the Lutheran Con-fessions, and labeled it a "quasi-docetic self-delusion" in which pastors "give lip-service to the creeds, *pro forma* subscription to the confessions, and reaffirmation of orthodox doctrinal statements, while their practice and worship lapse into Reformed or sectarian or generic forms, discon-nected from their high doctrinal assertions."[32] In the Lutheran Confes-sions, according to Preus, " 'practice' is linked to doctrine, worship, the

---

25 Preus, "Perennial Problems," 172.

26 Robert Preus, "Review Essay, 'Church Growth' as Mission Paradigm, a Lutheran Assessment, by Kurt Marquart," *Logia* III, no. 4 (October 1994): 54.

27 Preus, "Perennial Problems," 176.

28 Preus, "Perennial Problems," 177.

29 "Faithful to Our Calling, Faithful to Our Lord: An Affirmation in Two Parts by the Faculty of Concordia Seminary, St. Louis, Missouri," Part II (St. Louis: n.d.), 20.

30 Preus, "Luther and the Doctrine of Justification," 5, 13.

31 Preus, "Confessional Lutheranism in Today's World," 102.

32 Preus, "Confessional Lutheranism in Today's World," 102.

sacraments, prayer, good works, confession . . . the Ten Commandments . . . and the Lord's day."[33] Hence the "confessions indiscriminately reject false doctrine and false practice . . . and at times the formulation 'our churches teach' introduces matters of practice rather than doctrine."[34] To Preus, "doctrine and practice cannot be separated. Doctrine must result in practice."[35] Luther also "makes no distinction between doctrine and practice."[36] Why such a concern? The coherency principle with which Preus lived and functioned required it. Doctrine and practice cohere. The one entails the other, whether we speak of worship, prayer, Baptism, the Lord's Supper, or, more negatively, the veneration of relics, penance, or the refusal of Anabaptists to serve their government. Preus was frankly alarmed at the advancement of the so-called Church Growth Movement in Lutheran circles in which doctrine is ostensibly confessed while foreign practices are imposed upon the church.

Nowhere is the coherence of doctrine and practice more apparent for Preus than in his discussion of church fellowship. The occasion for his broaching the topic was the anticipated declaration of fellowship between The Lutheran Church—Missouri Synod (of which Preus was a member) and the American Lutheran Church. In 1968 and in 1971, he gave papers to the North Dakota District Convention and the Wyoming District Pastor's Conference respectively in which he first tried to convince the LCMS not to declare fellowship and subsequently tried to talk her into rescinding it.

Preus's logic, again syllogistic, went something like this: The LCMS should declare fellowship only with church bodies that hold to genuine Lutheran doctrine. The ALC does not hold to genuine Lutheran doctrine. Therefore the LCMS should not declare fellowship with the ALC. The logic is valid. If you grant the premises, then you must hold to the conclusion. An analysis of Preus's reason will reveal if he can support the two premises.

Preus held that fellowship should "rest upon the proper basis, viz. agreement in the doctrine of the Gospel and the administration of the Sacrament, i.e. full agreement in Christian doctrine."[37] This view was articulated more clearly after fellowship had been declared: "A declaration of fellowship between these two church bodies [the LCMS and the ALC]

33 Preus, "Confessional Lutheranism in Today's World," 100.

34 Preus, "Confessional Lutheranism in Today's World," 101.

35 Robert Preus, "Luther: Word, Doctrine and Confession," *Concordia Theological Quarterly* 60, no. 3 (July 1996): 199.

36 Preus, "Luther: Word, Doctrine and Confession," 198.

37 Preus, "To Join or Not to Join," 3.

assumed doctrinal consensus between them and therefore also a recognition by the Missouri Synod that the prevailing theology of the ALC was genuinely Lutheran."[38] Elsewhere Preus supported this understanding of the basis for fellowship by citing the Lutheran Confessions. He said:

> In accordance with this model [AC VII], the formula for concord for churches that are divided is very simply to achieve consensus in the doctrine and administration of the sacraments [SD Rule and Norm 1] . . . . In other words, concord in the church consists of consensus, and this consensus is expressed and represented by a formal confession (Epit. Rule and Norm, 3–4). This confession is drawn always and only from the Word of God, Scripture (Tappert, p. 6; SD Rule and Norm, 5, 9). And it is unanimously, that is, with total commitment and without qualification . . . subscribed by the churches (*ibid.* 1, 2, 6, 8). This consensus means that the churches will never depart nor deviate from the formal confessions (Tappert, p. 9; SD XII, 40).[39]

So Preus poses a test:

> If in our studies and in our meetings with representatives and members of the American Lutheran Church we discover a full doctrinal agreement between our Church and the ALC and if in our dealings with the members of the ALC we are able to achieve a "unified evangelical position and practice in areas of church life" (Resolution 3-23 [of the 1967 LCMS convention]), then we can open our arms to the members of the ALC and enter with them into pulpit and altar fellowship with joy and thanksgiving.[40]

Note that Preus cites the Lutheran Confessions and synodical resolutions to prove that there should be consensus in doctrine and practice as a basis for fellowship.

Having then established his first premise, Preus tackles the question of consensus. In Preus's opinion, does such a consensus exist? No. In "To Join or Not to Join," Preus cites as "roadblocks" to fellowship any number of aberrations in the ALC: the problem of that church body's acceptance of Lodge members; its involvement in the ecumenical movement; its fellowship with the LCA; synergism; and the ALC's questioning and open denial of the authority, inspiration, and inerrancy of the Bible.[41] Later, in "Fel-

---

38 Robert Preus, "Fellowship Reconsidered: An Assessment of Fellowship between the LCMS and the ALC in the Light of Past, Present and Future," presented at the Wyoming District (LCMS) Convention, April 13–15, 1971 (Casper, Wyo.: Mount Hope Lutheran Church, 1971), 2.

39 Robert Preus, "The Basis for Concord," *Theologians Convocation: Formula for Concord* (St. Louis: Commission on Theology and Church Relations, November 1977), 23.

40 Preus, "Fellowship Reconsidered," 3.

41 Preus, "To Join or Not to Join," 8–25.

lowship Reconsidered," Preus repeated the same litany of errors apparent in the ALC, then added to the list new "hindrances": the apparent lack of interest in the ALC to address its problems, its recent (1970) decision to ordain women into the office of pastor, and a move toward structural union of all Lutherans. For Preus, even the election of a heterodox or tolerant president of the ALC brought into question the basis for fellowship. When Kent Knutson was elected in 1970 as the second president of the ALC, Preus viewed this as a reason to question both the orthodoxy of the ALC and also, consequently, fellowship with that church.[42] Notice the close coherence of doctrine and practice. All the new "hindrances" mentioned in 1970 are specific actions (or lack of action) on the part of the ALC; they are practices. Having then shown that consensus did not exist and that consensus was required for fellowship, Preus could draw no other conclusion than "the declaration of fellowship with the ALC at Denver was wrong and continues to be wrong."[43] It was really the only consistent position if Preus's theology was to cohere. One can conclude that Preus would have advocated the breaking of fellowship over practices that impacted the evangelical doctrine, even the election of a heterodox synodical president. His practice was required because doctrine and practice belong together. A coherent view of truth requires it.

This somewhat extensive presentation of Preus's view of fellowship is not meant to rehash old decisions about church bodies that no longer exist. Rather, this example illustrates the fact that if our theology is to cohere, then the church must engage in the same type of painstaking analysis over all matters of doctrine and practice that confront her.

Preus's coherency principle is also reflected in his passion for the mission of the church. Preus defined the church's mission as "the single ministry of being the Spirit's instrument in proclaiming the Gospel and administering the sacraments."[44] To Preus the Gospel was not some vague, amorphous message void of cognitive content or lexical meaning. Rather, "[t]he Gospel is doctrine. . . . And this doctrine of the Gospel is a definite, authoritative, cognitive message and proclamation. . . . No wonder our confessions take doctrine so seriously and insist that they believe, teach and confess the pure doctrine . . . . The salvation of souls is at stake."[45] "There is a very explicit and definite content to this Gospel proclamation,"

---

42 Preus, "Fellowship Reconsidered," 12–21.

43 Preus, "Fellowship Reconsidered," 2.

44 Robert Preus, "The Confessions and the Mission of the Church," *The Springfielder* XXXIX., no. 1 (June 1975): 30.

45 Robert Preus, "Confessional Subscription," in *Evangelical Directions for the Lutheran Church*, ed. Erich Kiehl and Waldo Werning (n.p., 1970), 48. See also Preus, "Confessions and the Mission of the Church," 25.

says Preus,[46] who subsequently expresses a "burning desire to retain and proclaim the Gospel content unimpaired and unadulterated."[47] In such a proclamation, there is no cleavage between purity of doctrine and the salvation of souls. Rather, "Christian doctrine and preaching . . . confer upon us sonship, faith in Christ, fellowship with Him and all blessings which we have through Christ."[48] False doctrine, on the other hand, destroys the mission of the church, and those theologians who "pooh-pooh" pure doctrine undermine the church's true mission.[49] Lutherans love the pure doctrine "because of their evangelical concern for lost sinners and their spiritual welfare, their loving concern over tender and terrified consciences[, and] their concern over confused Christians."[50]

Such a view of the church's mission is completely coherent. If the central article of the faith is that God justifies us for Christ's sake by grace through faith, and if people must know this doctrine to be saved, and if this good news is communicated through the doctrine of the Gospel, then cognitive purity of this Gospel is essential to the salvation of souls. One wonders, given the pious logic and coherence of Preus's view, how such evangelical reasoning could ever be doubted. The syllogism is flawless: The Gospel is pure doctrine. The Gospel saves. Therefore pure doctrine saves.

But it does seem to fly in the face of some voices in Lutheranism. Some have suggested that the mission of the church can take place without purity of doctrine or that pastors are either doctrine, oriented or mission, oriented rather than both—a view that Preus would consider somewhat incoherent. Others have "pooh-poohed" (to use Preus's term) the consistent vigilance the church must always exercise to keep her doctrine pure. Still others have resolutely avoided the discussion of doctrine. Such views, far from helpful, simply do not cohere and ultimately undermine the church's mission. Just as tragically, they are a symptom of our age in which propositional truth is considered irrelevant or even harmful. Preus could complain in 1971:

> To me the great threat to our synod today is indifference, indifference often born of frustration, but indifference, none the less . . . indifference to what our brother pastors believe, teach and confess, yes, and indifference to the Gospel; indifference which will not take a stand on the ethical and doctrinal issues that confront our synod and cry for

---

46 Preus, "Confessions and the Mission of the Church," 24.

47 Preus, "Confessions and the Mission of the Church," 24–25.

48 Preus, "Luther: Word, Doctrine and Confession," 192.

49 Preus, "Confessions and the Mission of the Church," 37.

50 Preus, "Confessional Subscription," 48.

solution, lukewarm indifference which plays to the "uncommitted middle" and tries to anticipate what this shapeless group will do or not do; indifference which immobilizes us and saps our strength and will ultimately change us into a different kind of people and into a different kind of synod than we formerly were. For we have changed and we are changing.[51]

Two decades later, confronted with the church's frequent unwillingness to discuss doctrine, Preus again commented: "After a long ministry, I have discovered that when theologians do not want to discuss theology, the church is in trouble."[52] Why such trouble? Because those churches that have stopped discussing doctrine "seem to have lost their bearing and their Lutheran identity."[53] They also lose their ability to carry out the church's mission. Christ's mission is, after all, nothing less than teaching the pure doctrine. It all has to fit together.

Doctrine must cohere.

CORRESPONDENCE

Coherency of doctrine, though vital, is not sufficient of itself for true Christian scholarship and teaching. Doctrine must also correspond to reality. Just as the Scriptures contain no inner contradictions threatening their coherence, so we cannot postulate "cases in which statements of Scripture do not seem to correspond to the apparent data in the external world (astronomy, geography, topography, etc.) or to accepted facts of history. Here is a conflict which is synthetic."[54] Preus was a champion of what other theologians have labeled "the realist principle of theology."[55]

Preus claimed that "the referents of all theological discourse are real. This is a fundamental theological and confessional principle."[56] Such a comment, made in the twilight of Preus's career, is both remarkable and unremarkable. It is remarkable because it so thoroughly opposed the spirit of Preus's times. These were times in which the encroachment of postmodernism in society and the residue of both pietism and neoorthodoxy in

---

51 Preus, "Fellowship Reconsidered" 24.

52 Robert Preus, "A Report," unpublished paper delivered at a conference in St. Louis, Missouri, October 15, 1993. Available in the files of Robert Preus at Concordia Historical Institute (St. Louis), 6.

53 Preus, "Report," 6.

54 Robert Preus, "The Word of God in Theology of Lutheran Orthodoxy," *Concordia Theological Monthly* XXXIII, no. 8 (August 1962): 479.

55 Kurt Marquart, "The 'Realist Principle' of Theology," *Logia* V, no. 3 (1996): 15–17.

56 Preus, "Doctrine of the Call," 29.

the church made Preus's "realist principle" anachronistic at best and politically incorrect at worst. The statement was unremarkable in that Preus had been saying the same thing for almost thirty years. In 1965 he averred that "Scripture, like all cognitive discourse, operates under the rubrics of a correspondence idea of truth."[57] His "realist principle," which Preus attributed to Luther, is nothing more than the fact that theological assertions correspond to reality outside of themselves.

Certainly any truly evangelical scholar would affirm that historical assertions, and much of the Bible is history, refer to things that actually happened in space and time. So Preus contends that "declarative statements of Scripture are, according to their intention, true in that they correspond to what has taken place (for example, historical statements)."[58] Preus applies the same principle to "theological affirmations and other affirmations of fact."[59] To Preus there was no distinction between theological judgments and historical judgments. Both are based on real things if they are to mean anything.[60]

Perhaps Preus's most exhaustive explication of his "realist principle" was presented at the 1973 Reformation Lectures of Bethany College in Mankato, Minnesota.

> History and reality underlay the theology of Scripture. Election was a real decree of God (FC SC XI), not merely a theological construct. The Lord's Supper and Holy Baptism were the results of real historical dominical institution and words (LC IV, 6, 36, 53; V, 4). Our justification before God is a real verdict, not a myth (Apol. IV). The virgin birth, the suffering and death, the miracles, the resurrection of Christ are historical, having real referents in fact. Any theology of a non-event is unthinkable to Luther and our Confessions. The ascension to and the session at the right hand, although not demonstrable by any historical investigation, are real events. The right hand of God is everywhere, as Luther insisted, but it *is* everywhere. The hermeneutical principle underlying such exegetical realism is not a philosophical theory, but a conviction based upon Scripture, that God who has caused all Scripture to be recorded is indeed a living God who invades history, authors it, and reveals himself historically.[61]

---

57 Robert Preus, "Notes on the Inerrancy of Scripture," *Concordia Theological Monthly* XXXVIII, no. 6 (June 1967): 366.

58 Preus, "Notes on the Inerrancy of Scripture," 366.

59 Preus, "Notes on the Inerrancy of Scripture," 366.

60 Preus, "How Is the Lutheran Church to Interpret," Lecture 2, 6.

61 Preus, "How Is the Lutheran Church to Interpret," Lecture 2, 6–7. Cf. also Robert Preus, "Perennial Problems," 175: "According to this classic Christian model, God is real, the creator and sustainer of all that exists; He is really Triune (an immanent,

Theology corresponds to what is real. If it does not, then it is false theology.

The realist principle applies to all articles of faith. Sin is real because "the actuality of the fall as recounted in Gen. 3 is the basis of the actuality of original sin today."[62] The doctrine of the Holy Trinity corresponds to reality, and we need to "accept the historical or in many cases the theologico-ontological (incarnation, Trinity, etc.) referents of biblical assertions. . . . [For] when a biblical assertion in its intended sense has a referent, it is a real referent, whether the referent is a historical occurrence (Christ's resurrection), a state of being (the personal union), an act of God in history (personal justification through faith in Christ), or whatever."[63]

This "realist principle" gives certainty to our theology. According to Preus, "exegesis leads to doctrine."[64] This is a "fundamental" principle of hermeneutics. Pure doctrine, then, depends as much upon the correspondence of biblical assertions to objective reality as it does upon the internal coherence of the biblical witness. You cannot approach the Scriptures with a belief that what they say can be any other kind of truth than truth that corresponds to reality. If you do, then you will not only deny the truth of the Bible, you also will make the whole idea of doctrine impossible. You must approach the Bible as an objective witness to things that are ontologically real. "The nature of Scripture as God's revelation of Himself and His will cannot be ignored or discounted at any point by any method seeking to deal with Scripture in terms of its form or content."[65] When the realist principle is denied, the church is led into a "skeptical *cul de sac*" from which there is no escape.[66] The result is either the reduction "of Christianity to a religion of ideas or truths which are not based upon historical fact or reality" or a retreat into subjectivism. In either event, "one has departed from historic Christianity which is based upon the reality of a living God acting in real history."[67]

Why does Preus insist that the content of our teaching correspond to reality? Preus's primary concern is to protect the material principle—the

---

not just an economic Trinity); the first Adam really fell and his sin was really imputed to the whole human race; the Son of God really became incarnate; He really suffered and died and rose again; the atonement is real; heaven is real; hell is real; forgiveness and justification are real, not just metaphors for something else."

62 Preus, "Biblical Hermeneutics," 36.

63 Preus, "Unity of Scripture," 10.

64 Preus, "How Is the Lutheran Church to Interpret," Lecture 3, 7.

65 Preus, "How Is the Lutheran Church to Interpret," Lecture 3, 3.

66 Preus, "How Is the Lutheran Church to Interpret," Lecture 3, 9.

67 Preus, "How Is the Lutheran Church to Interpret," Lecture 3, 9.

doctrine of justification by grace. Preus reasons this way: The atonement, as every Christian knows, is the basis for God's verdict of justification upon sinners.[68] This atonement must correspond to reality—something that occurred in history—or the very basis of the sinner's favorable relationship with God is unreal and justification becomes a myth. "If there is no real satisfaction made for sin and no real righteousness to be imputed, there can be no justification at all in the realistic Lutheran sense."[69] If statements about Christ are merely "general spiritual truth, religious ideas, symbolic language, eternal truth, experience, myth, or anthropology," then such statements "become deceptive theological blather."[70]

> The Christological language of Scripture refers to reality, whether it refers to God's grace, forgiveness, and salvation in Christ, or whether it refers to Christ's eternal deity and attributes, his historic virgin birth, life, miracles, preaching, death, resurrection, ascension, and future return to judgment. And the effects of Christ's life and death and resurrection are real; God has been reconciled, the world has been redeemed, the sinner will be saved forever through faith in Christ—really and truly.[71]

Not only is the basis of justification real in the historical works of Christ and the atonement but also the verdict of justification itself is real. Preus used the "term 'justification' as . . . St. Paul and our Lutheran confessions employ it—as an event; a real, divine action; a verdict of acquittal which has happened and is happening vis-a-vis the world of concrete sinners."[72] No mere metaphor, justification is a real event each time God speaks it through the Gospel. Preus was fond of citing the orthodox theologians against the Roman Catholics of the day. And citations were not tough for Preus to find because "the entire controversy with the church hinged on one crucial issue, viz. the nature of justification."[73] The Romanists taught that forensic justification had no ontological foundation and was, therefore, not real, but fictional. They did not base the justification of

---

68 Robert Preus "Objective Justification," President's Message (Ft. Wayne, Indiana: n.p.), 3: "Objective justification which is God's verdict of acquittal over the whole world is not identical with the atonement, it is not another way of expressing the fact that Christ has redeemed the world. Rather it is based upon the substitutionary work of Christ, or better, it is part of the atonement itself. It is God's response to all that Christ died to save us [sic]."

69 Preus, "Perennial Problems," 174.

70 Preus, "Unity of Scripture," 8.

71 Preus, "Unity of Scripture," 8.

72 Preus, "Clergy Mental Health," 113.

73 Preus, "Justification in the Theology of Classical Lutheran Orthodoxy," 27–28.

the sinner upon the fact of the atonement and, on this account, could not accept the reality of forensic justification.[74] The Lutherans, notably Quenstedt, whom Preus cited often, having linked justification to the historic and real atonement of Christ, could conclude that "the imputation consists in a real reckoning. According to the judgment of God, the sinner who believes in Christ is absolved of sins and the righteousness of Christ is truly reckoned to him."[75] Preus himself could also preach:

> There is nothing fictional or untrue about this verdict. My justification is as true and valid as Christ's cursed death on the cross . . . . His verdict is effective: it accomplishes what it says. When He pronounces me righteous in Christ, then it is so, all accusations, inner doubts and empirical evidence to the contrary notwithstanding. Nor is God's verdict a mere possibility—to which I add my faith. And it will not be undone, just as Christ's incarnation, suffering and death cannot be undone.[76]

Justification had to be a real verdict based on a real atonement that occurred through real historical events or the Christian could have no certainty of the grace of God.

Further, if both the basis of justification and the verdict of justification are real, then the application of this justification through the Gospel is real. Baptism really washes sins away. The Word really absolves. And especially in the Lord's Supper is the realist principle apparent. Marburg's debate between Luther and Zwingli, Preus reminds us, was not simply a discussion of a single passage or the Reformed inability to accept the absolute authority of the Bible. Zwingli's failure to accept the bodily presence of Christ in the Sacrament resulted in his "failure to relate the Sacrament to justification."[77] One fiction leads to another. One wonders if the converse is also true. If Zwingli could somehow have understood the Sacrament in relation to the verdict of acquittal based on the atonement, perhaps his bizarre *aleosis* could have been avoided. Zwingli never understood that "reality, substance, history, God's acts and commands underlie the assertion and commands of Scripture."[78] And that includes the assertion "this is my body." Lutherans, on the other hand, have a couple of quick ways to assert the realism inherent in the Lord's Supper: "The antidonatism of the doctrine of the Lord's Supper, that the body and blood of

---

74 Preus, "Justification in the Theology of Classical Lutheran Orthodoxy," 30.

75 Preus, "Justification in the Theology of Classical Lutheran Orthodoxy," 31.

76 Preus, *Preaching to Young Theologians*, 15, 37.

77 Preus, "How Is the Lutheran Church to Interpret," Lecture 2, 7.

78 Preus, "How Is the Lutheran Church to Interpret," Lecture 2, 7.

Christ are distributed even by a wicked priest, indicates the same theological realism. . . . The principle of realism is brought out whenever the *manducatio indignorum* [that the impious also eat and drink Christ's body and blood in the Sacrament] is stressed."[79]

To Preus, the reality of justification can be applied to the mundane occurrences and exigencies of life with infallible certainty. One example will do. In an enigmatic little article titled "Clergy Mental Health," Preus asks: "Does the gospel of justification help pastors to cope with the tensions of their office? Does it alleviate clergy stress? Does it mitigate burnout and help the pastor to transcend the causes of it?"[80] Preus answers yes. There is no surprise here. But the manner of his presentation is laced with his reality theme as justification is applied to one narrowly defined human problem—clergy burnout. The human condition is characterized by "two realities," claims Preus.[81] The first is sin. "Sin is a reality which must be repented of." And "guilt is a [second] reality. It is not a subjective reality—merely an experience, a feeling of guilt or estrangement."[82] Thankfully God has two themes that respond to human sinfulness: the grace of God in Christ and the power of God in his Word. "These two themes which pervade the entire Scriptures must be portrayed and applied not as mere ideas, gimmicks or metaphors for something else, but as reality which, if they do not always affect the greatly troubled pastor, are the only real spiritual therapeutics he has."[83] Consequently, the divine cure of the anxious, tired, and "burned out" pastor is something ontologically real.

> The troubled sinner who perceives the objective and forensic nature of justification will not look inwardly to feelings, experience or quality of faith to gain assurance that he or she is right with God. Rather, such a person looks to Christ crucified and risen "for our justification" (Romans 4:25) and to the word which proclaims and confers this justification.[84]

The Gospel of the justification of the sinner before God could properly be applied to just about any human predicament. Its applicability in real situations is as vast and as real as the grace upon which it is based.

---

79 Robert Preus, "Hermeneutics of the Formula of Concord," in *No Other Gospel: Essays in Commemoration of the 400th Anniversary of the Formula of Concord*, ed. Arnold Koelpin (Milwaukee: Northwestern, 1980), 333.

80 Preus "Clergy Mental Health," 113.

81 Preus "Clergy Mental Health," 116.

82 Preus "Clergy Mental Health," 117.

83 Preus "Clergy Mental Health," 118.

84 Preus "Clergy Mental Health," 119.

Heaven is also real. Preus was not merely engaged in some type of lofty academic distinction in asserting that our teaching must correspond to that which is real. The realist principle is crucial for the salvation of sinners. Not only does the Gospel provide present pardon and certainty in the face of real guilt, it also provides eternal and eschatological certainty. The future is just as real as the past, and we can assert it as confidently as we can our own forgiveness, for the statements of Scripture "correspond . . . to what will take place (for example, predictive prophecy)."[85]

The implications of the realist principle were forced upon Preus rather profoundly when he was dismissed from his office as president and professor of Concordia Theological Seminary, Fort Wayne, Indiana, by the Board of Regents in the summer of 1989. At the time, one of his friends urged him to bear his cross quietly and "accept the decision of the Board of Regents without demur," confident that he would "no doubt have further opportunity to teach and write in [his] chosen field of theology." This friend concluded "the entire church will be served better by your accepting this option."[86] Perhaps such counsel would have made sense and actually been prudent had there been no realist principle of theology. Writing two years later, Preus affirmed: "As God, sin, Christ, justification, Word and Sacrament, and the church are real, so is the ministry—and the one who occupies that office. Although one may—wisely or unwisely—consider the ministry *in abstracto*, apart from any consideration of the minister, there is nothing abstract or unreal about the ministry or the minister or the function [of the ministry]."[87]

The historical and ecclesiastical implications of Preus's decision not to accept his dismissal have been analyzed elsewhere. The theological basis for it is often ill-considered. The call into the ministry comes from God and is as real as he is. "It is His call, His office to which He calls, His saving Word which the minister is called to preach, His word of salvation for Christ's sake. With His Word He creates the Church, with His Word He creates the preaching office. And through the preaching office word and office become one."[88] Anything brought into being by God's Word is real—whether the world, the church, or the minister. Preus simply was stuck with reality. It was not a question of what he wanted, his perception of good for the church, or anything else. For him to deny a reality estab-

---

85 Preus, "Notes on the Inerrancy of Scripture," 366.

86 Private correspondence from Waldemar Degner to Robert Preus, July 1, 1989 (from the personal files of Robert Preus housed at Concordia Historical Institute).

87 Preus, "Doctrine of the Call," 28.

88 Preus, "Doctrine of the Call," 6.

lished by God by accepting his own dismissal would be a dangerous thing, for it would be a denial of the correspondence principle of theology. He might as well deny the reality of the church, the Word, or Christ himself.

Theology must correspond.

Confessionalism

The doctrine of the Scriptures is not simply to be analyzed or synthesized. Analysis can ascertain coherence. Synthesis can determine correspondence. The true Christian scholar must also take this Bible doctrine and speak it. He must confess. To Preus confessionalism was as easy as A, B, C, and D. If a man's confession corresponded to the formal written confessions of the church, and the confessions of the church corresponded to the Scriptures, and the Scriptures corresponded to reality, then a man's confession corresponded to reality. Such a notion required utter confidence in a man's confession.

When Robert Preus set forth the teachings of the Gospel, he was always making a confession. "The essential work of the pastor, called to the public ministry of preaching the gospel and administering the sacraments, is simply confession, confession of Christ and his doctrine."[89] To Preus, confession did not begin with the symbols of the Christian faith contained in the Book of Concord. Confession, for the pastor, began with teaching the Scriptures and the willing expression of faith in the evangelical doctrine. A true confession corresponded to and spoke the realities of the biblical truth and was spoken from faith in the doctrines of the Word of God. Preus taught as one who confessed before the world the very content of his teaching. To be confessional, then, is not merely to value the historical documents associated with the reformation of the sixteenth century. It is to speak with confidence the truths of God. "Just as doctrine is certain, as we have seen, one who confesses the doctrine must be certain."[90] And this confidence in both the Word and the corresponding confession of it applied to every Christian. "The creed confessed by the entire church is no more a confession than the simple witnessing of a child about his savior."[91]

At the same time, confessionalism, if it is truly the speaking of the truths of God, will always agree with those symbols or statements that correspond to the teachings of the Scriptures. So subscription to the teachings of the Book of Concord is incumbent upon any teacher who wishes to con-

---

89 Preus, "Luther: Word, Doctrine and Confession," 208.

90 Preus, "Luther: Word, Doctrine and Confession," 211.

91 Preus, "Luther: Word, Doctrine and Confession," 208.

fess the truth of the Bible. In perhaps his most exhaustive definition of confessional subscription, notice that Preus first asserts the necessity of confessing the faith, then concludes with the necessity of confessing the symbols of the church.

> Confessional subscription is a solemn act of confessing in which I willingly and in the fear of God confess my faith and declare to the world what is my belief, teaching and confession. This I do by pledging myself with my whole heart to certain definite, formulated confessions. I do this in complete assurance that these confessions are true and a correct exposition of Scripture. These symbolical writings become for me permanent confessions and patterns of doctrine according to which I judge all other writings and teachers.[92]

The implications of this view of Christian confession are profound, especially for pastors.

First, confession must be ecumenical, that is, it should characterize the teachings of the whole church. It is not enough as an individual to confess Christ, though this is certainly a noble thing. A confessing and confessional pastor finds himself within the fellowship of the church throughout the ages. Consequently, confessing the faith will always involve subscription to the ecumenical creeds. Further, confession means not that Lutherans view the documents of the Book of Concord as uniquely theirs or as defining only the Lutheran Church. Rather, though Lutherans may proudly bear the appellation associated with the great reformer, they will understand that "the Augsburg Confession or the Apology is meant to be ecumenical. That is, an orthodox confession which would represent the whole church."[93] Any true confession must be subscribed with the confidence that no orthodox Christian would hesitate in making the same confession. Lutherans subscribe to their confessional formulas not as mere Lutherans, but as orthodox Christians. They understand the Lutheran Confessions to be generic, basic, simple, clear, obvious, and clearly biblical. "Confessional subscription . . . is a responsible *public* act of confession, done in fellowship and union with the Christian church and indicating that I share unconditionally the 'unanimous and correct understanding' of the church which has steadfastly remained in the pure doctrine."[94]

With this attitude toward confessionalism, Preus was completely unself-conscious in his use of the Lutheran Confessions. Thus in a paper delivered at the 1986 International Council on Biblical Inerrancy, Preus

---

92 Preus, "Confessional Subscription," 46.

93 Preus, "Luther: Word, Doctrine and Confession," 209.

94 Preus, "Confessional Subscription," 46 (*original emphasis*).

cites the Lutheran Confessions repeatedly, though his audience was made up primarily of Calvinists.[95] If a confessional writing is biblical, then even Calvinists should subscribe. And in all of his writings, Preus flits back and forth between citing the Scriptures and citing the Lutheran Confessions because they were both authoritative for all Christians.

Second, confession must be timely. Preus was fond of this statement attributed to Luther:

> If I profess with the loudest voice and clearest exposition every portion of the truth of God except precisely that little point which the world and the devil are at that moment attacking, I am not confessing Christ, however boldly I may be professing Christ. Where the battle rages, there the loyalty of the soldier is proved, and to be steady on all the battlefields besides is more flight and disgrace if it flinches at that point.[96]

The timeliness of Christian confession forced Preus to warn the Missouri Synod against declaring fellowship with the American Lutheran Church in the 1960s. It required him to attack the use of the historical-critical method at Concordia Seminary, St. Louis, Missouri, in the 1970s. In the mid-1980s, Preus was the champion of the doctrine of objective justification against those who questioned it or ignored it. He said:

> The doctrine of objective justification is a lovely teaching drawn from Scripture which tells us that God who has loved us so much that he gave His only Son to be our Savior has for the sake of Christ's substitutionary atonement declared the entire world of sinners for whom Christ died to be righteous (Romans 5:17–9) . . . . Objective justification is not a mere metaphor, a figurative way of expressing the fact that Christ died for all and paid for the sins of all. Objective justification has happened, it is the actual acquittal of the entire world of sinners for Christ's sake.[97]

Because the winners of theological conflict generally write its history, Preus can justly be called a hero for his habit of timely confession throughout the 1960s, the 1970s, and even into the 1980s.

Such praise would, however, be short-lived for Preus because his penchant for doctrinal gadflyism became annoying to some in the church as

---

95 Robert Preus, "The Living God," *Summit III Papers*, International Council on Biblical Inerrancy, ed. Kenneth Kantzer (Walnut Creek, Calif.: n.p.), 1–26.

96 Preus, "Luther: Word, Doctrine and Confession," 197.

97 Preus, "Objective Justification," 3. See also Robert Preus, "Law and Gospel in Early Lutheran Dogmatics," *The Beauty and the Bands* (St. Louis: Luther Academy, 1995), 65–66.

the twenty-first century approached. So in the 1990s Preus was conscientiously unable and happily unwilling to stifle his confession of the pure doctrine when less popular articles of faith required defense. For example, the biblical understanding of the Office of the Ministry was on everyone's mind in 1989 at the Wichita convention of the LCMS. Wichita asserted that laymen could preach and administer the Sacraments, even if not completely trained and neither called nor ordained into the office of the ministry. Preus's response was quick, decisive, and based upon the historical confessions of the church: "The term 'minister' is applied only to pastors with a divine call . . . . According to the theology of our confessions, the idea of a 'lay-minister' is an inconceivable oxymoron, like sheep being shepherds."[98] His outrage was directed specifically at the delegates of the convention. "The majority of delegates at Wichita seemed to think it proper that . . . the resolution could be adopted, even if it flew in the face of the doctrine, practice and church order of the Lutheran Confessions."[99]

In 1991 Preus continued his lambaste of the "Wichita Recension" and wrote "The Doctrine of the Call in the Confessions and Lutheran Orthodoxy," which was delivered in Chicago at the second annual meeting of the Association of Confessional Lutherans and expanded for publication later in the year. There, on the basis of Augsburg Confession XIV and without referring specifically to the convention decision, Preus asserted "preachers without a call are of the devil. They rob legitimately called pastors of their ministry, indeed rob God himself."[100] This bit of doctrinal confession was not greeted with as much enthusiasm as his heroic defense of the authority of the Bible two decades earlier.

In the same document, Preus spoke to the question of the dismissal of a president of a seminary.

> In reference to the "retirement" of presidents and faculty members of seminaries the LCMS has gotten itself into a tangle which for good theological and confessional reasons it never should have gotten into . . . . It is troubling . . . to read . . . that the president of the LCMS . . . said, "That the calls are usually extended according to specific terms, which may ordinarily call for mandatory retirement . . . these calls, though divine, are unlike pastoral calls to parishes because of their limited tenure." . . . The statement as it speaks of "mandatory retirement" of one who has been rightly called into the ministry of the Word

98 Preus, "Confessional Lutheranism in Today's World," 110.

99 Preus, "Confessional Lutheranism in Today's World," 115.

100 Preus, "Doctrine of the Call," 114.

and bases that retirement upon specific terms of the call, introduces a concept foreign to AC XIV.[101]

These assertions certainly did not endear Preus to the synodical power structures. But Christian confession must be made especially when certain articles are under attack, and Preus made the confession.

The most pointed and timely polemics of his waning years dealt with the Church Growth Movement. In a 1994 book review published in *Logia*, Preus warned:

> Today the LCMS is at war with herself again . . . over the material principle, the *sola fide* and the *sola gratia*, the heart of the gospel, what has been called the *solus Christus* and the uniquely Lutheran theology of the cross. Today the enemy infiltrating Missouri's ranks, confusing our pastors and people and turning brother against brother . . . is a movement, a great world movement . . . . It is impressive, respected, exciting, winsome, and popular, a movement to be reckoned with. It is gaining converts, also in the Missouri Synod and other Lutheran synods. We are speaking of the modern Church Growth Movement.[102]

Later in the same brief article, Preus complained that the leaders in Synod ignored his dire warnings of the Church Growth Movement. He also warned "the war will go on in Missouri." So he confessed his faith on precisely that point of doctrine that the church was debating. Confessionalism, to Preus, required no less.

The third implication of Preus's understanding of Christian confession is that confession results in the cross. "To preach the gospel publicly and to confess the Christ and the faith inevitably brings crosses, affliction, and persecution upon the Christian and the church, especially the public minister of the Word. These things happen without fail."[103] Of course, such insights, written after his dismissal as seminary president, should be no surprise. But throughout his life, Preus was no stranger to bearing the cross because of his confession. This was demonstrated clearly at both the beginning and the end of his long ministry. Before he was a pastor, on January 25, 1947, Preus wrote a "confession" through which he announced his intention of leaving the Evangelical Lutheran Church (ELC). On the eve of being placed by that synod into the Office of the Holy Ministry, Preus, a 23-year-old seminarian, sent a letter to the ELC Church Council:

---

101 Preus, "Doctrine of the Call," 44.

102 Preus, "Review Article," 53.

103 Preus, "Luther: Word, Doctrine and Confession," 213.

I wish at this time to confess my personal faith in the Triune God and in Jesus Christ as my only Savior from sin, death, hell and Satan. I, a corrupt miserable, contemptible and helpless sinner claim no responsibility whatsoever as over against the faith which I confess, but I believe with all my heart that it is solely a work and gift of the Holy Spirit in me. At Luther Theological Seminary I have been taught that this my conviction on the important doctrine of conversion is not in accordance with the teaching of the Holy Scriptures but is sectarian, and that, in a sense, my salvation—and indeed that of every other person on earth whether unregenerate or regenerate—depends on me in that I am responsible as over against the acceptance or the rejection of grace.[104]

Preus then recounts his frustrating realization that the ELC not only allowed synergism to be taught but "also defended it and has also given no indication that anything would be done to rectify this deplorable situation." He concludes:

I hereby bring to the attention of the venerable Church Council of the Evangelic Lutheran Church the fact that, for conscience sake, I cannot present myself as a candidate for ordination in the Evangelical Lutheran Church of America. I make this decision only after prayerful and sincere study of God's Word and it is with sorrow and regret that I terminate fellowship with Evangelical Lutheran Church.[105]

So Preus delayed becoming a pastor for the sake of his confession. Less than a year later, having been ordained into the ministry in the Evangelical Lutheran Synod, Preus was serving a small congregation in eastern North Dakota. But in the process he lost prestige, friends, position, and the goodwill of many colleagues. It was good training.

Ironically, 47 years later, in the waning years of his ministry, Preus again found himself suffering. This time rather than voluntarily delaying his ministry for the sake of confession, he fought to retain the Office of the Holy Ministry that had been taken from him, again because of his confession. That office for which he suffered by foregoing he now suffered by pursuing. But it was the same confession that impelled him and the same suffering that attended his confession. Preus rarely whined or complained about the various crosses the Lord saw fit to place upon him. Others, however, observed his pain: "I was struck by the contrast between the youthful zest of his ongoing passion for good theology on the one hand, and the

---

104 Robert Preus, "Vita Submitted to the Church Council of the Evangelical Lutheran Church of America" (in the files of Robert Preus at Concordia Historical Institute).

105 Preus, "Vita."

painful evidence of how the vendetta of officialdom against him had both outwardly aged and inwardly hurt Preus on the other."[106] The church need not thank God for the sufferings of the saints, but she must raise a Te Deum for the confession that sufferings produce.

Conclusion

"Something which has always puzzled me," mused Robert Preus in a 1966 essay delivered to the Iowa West District of the LCMS, "is that the critics of Scripture often search it and master its contents with a zeal which shames us who have the highest and noblest view of it."[107] Preus, a young professor at the time, could not understand a devotion to academic pursuits that did not result in evangelical teaching, confessing the truth, the advancement of the Gospel's mission, coherent and biblical theology, greater faith, or something that would benefit the church. He certainly did not spend his life learning God's Word so he could deny, criticize, or question it. In fact, his tireless pursuit of the theological task served purposes sufficiently lofty to provide readers, even a generation later, with an example of true Christian scholarship.

Robert Preus wrote and taught theology. He applied his analytic and communication skills to the theological task. He taught Christ's doctrine because, to Robert Preus, "doctrine is life." His theology was *coherent*—consistent with itself. His doctrine *corresponded* to the Bible and to the Lutheran Confessions. And his writings were always a *confession* of his faith and the faith of the church.

This theology was loved by his first students and his last. True testimony to a teacher is paid never by those who will not learn or have no opportunity. Rather, the measure of a teacher is in his faithfulness to the subject matter and the testimony of those pupils who truly sat at his feet. The legacy of Robert Preus was theology—his writings. His legacy, in addition, is the many appreciative pastors and students who learned to love his theology. One of Preus's first students summarized the sentiments of two generations of seminarians who studied under Preus:

> My classmates are agreed to a man that dogmatics in the mid-1950s was a completely undistinguished enterprise. That's a polite way of saying it was dull. You read the book. The highlight of the day was a poorly worded quiz. When Preus came to St. Louis in 1957, the change was radical. He had the intellectual capacity to recognize where

---

106 John Stephenson, "Robert Preus, Historian of Theology," *Logia*, Vol. V, no. 3 (Holy Trinity 1996): 14.

107 Preus, "Biblical Hermeneutics and the Lutheran Church Today," 60.

the church was going and the conviction and courage to do something about it. And he did. He gathered a generation of students who caught the contagion of his convictions. From this confessional revival we were born. When students are talking theology outside of the classrooms, you know the enterprise is alive . . . . Now his students are found in the pulpits and classrooms everywhere. They are still doing theology.[108]

I trust those who read the essays in this volume will share these sentiments.

---

108 David P. Scaer, "Commemoration Sermon for Dr. Robert D. Preus," *Logia* 5, no. 3 (Holy Trinity 1996): 10.

JUSTIFICATION BY FAITH:
The Material Principle
of Theology

Justification by grace through faith for Christ's sake is the central article of the Scriptures. It is the material principle of Lutheran theology and, not surprisingly, it was the preoccupation of Robert Preus. His early articles on the subject were presentations of what the Lutheran fathers wrote on the subject. Later in his career, he applied the doctrine to specific situations that the church confronted.

The Justification
of a Sinner before God

As Taught in Later Lutheran Orthodoxy

> "The Justification of a Sinner before God as Taught in Later Lutheran Orthodoxy" is limited to a brief explanation of the theology of John Andrew Quenstedt on this important article of faith. It was published by *The Scottish Journal of Theology* in 1960. (Permission has been granted for reproduction in this collection.)

DURING THE HISTORY OF THE LUTHERAN Church the doctrine of justification has been spoken of commonly and rather loosely as the *articulus stantis et cadentis ecclesiae*. This was certainly the conviction of Luther, as many of his statements testify. The purpose of this study is to examine the teaching of John Andrew Quenstedt, the most prominent and able representative of the later seventeenth-century Lutheran orthodoxy, on this doctrine and to learn how closely the dogmatics of his time approximates the emphasis and terminology of Luther. Quenstedt is the 'book-keeper'—one might say the Aquinas—of Lutheran scholasticism, and he quite accurately sums up the theology of the entire century. It might be said by way of introduction that modern Lutheranism owes much to the dogmaticians of the age of orthodoxy for the manner in which it deals with this doctrine; and for this reason I feel justified in presenting an article of this nature.[1] I propose merely to summarise Quenstedt's treatment of the doctrine of justification, and to offer comments when I deem them necessary.[2] I

---

1 cf. Koeberle, *The Quest for Holiness*, N.Y., 1936; F. Pieper, *Christian Dogmatics*, St. Louis, 1951; Elert, *Der Christliche Glaube*, Hamburg, 1956, pp. 470ff.; et al.

2 All references and quotations from Quenstedt's *Theologia Didactico-Polemica sive Systema Theologicum*, de justificatione, sect. 1, unless otherwise stated.

believe that the reader will find that Quenstedt's presentation is quite well balanced and that it gives the impression of being consistently drawn from Scripture. At least it is obvious that this is Quenstedt's persuasion as he develops the doctrine.

At the outset of his discussion Quenstedt wishes to show his dependence upon Luther by insisting that justification must be considered the central doctrine of theology. He says that the doctrine of justification of a sinner before God 'is the citadel of the whole Christian religion; the nexus by which all members of the body of Christian doctrine are joined together; and should this doctrine be violated, all the remaining articles will be abandoned and overthrown'. Then in characteristic fashion he listens to some of the fine statements of Luther and others on the importance of this article. Luther in his comments on Gen. 21 says (Erl. ed. Lat., 10.137): 'This is the highest article of our faith, and if one should abandon it as the Jews do or pervert it like the Papists, the Church cannot stand nor can God maintain His glory which consists in this, that He might be merciful and that He desires to pardon sins for His Son's sake and to save.'[3] Quenstedt also quotes the classic statement from Chemnitz (*Loci Theologici*, 1653 ed., II, 200): 'This article is in a sense a stronghold and the high fortress of all the doctrine and of the entire Christian religion; if it is obscured or adulterated or set aside, the purity of doctrine in other articles of faith cannot possibly be maintained. But if this article is kept pure, all idolatry, superstitions, and whatever corruptions there are in the other articles of faith tumble down from their own weight.' The final introductory quotation of Quenstedt's is from B. Meisner (Ἀνθρωπολόγιας Sacrae . . . , 3rd ed., Wittebergae, 1663, Decas. III, Disp. XXIV, p. 139): 'This article is the central point of theology according to which all other articles of faith are adjusted; it is the sacred ocean into which all other doctrines flow, it is the treasure chest of our faith which keeps safe and unharmed all the other doctrines.' Quenstedt probably takes these quotations from Gerhard and Meisner who both offer even more statements of Luther on the importance of this doctrine. Both Meisner and Gerhard quote, for instance, the well-known statement of Luther (op. cit., 21.3): 'In my heart one article alone rules supreme, that of faith in Christ, by whom, through whom and in whom all my theological thinking flows back and forth day and night. And still I find that I have grasped this so high and broad and deep a wisdom only in a weak and poor and fragmentary manner.' When K. Barth[4] points out that no one ever followed Luther's emphasis to the

---

3 Quenstedt also cites similar statements of Luther. Erl. ed. Lat., 21.12, 20.

4 *Church Dogmatics*, IV, 1, p. 522.

point of actually planning and organising an evangelical dogmatics around the article of justification he is correct, and his words also apply to Quenstedt. But this does not imply any lessening of emphasis on the centrality of this doctrine.[5] The fact is that no doctrine was made a unifying principle in the dogmatics of the orthodox Lutheran theologians; to attempt such a thing never occurred to them. It is unfortunate, as Barth points out, that the later orthodox Lutherans called the doctrine of justification by faith alone a secondary fundamental doctrine.[6] However, Hollaz meant only to stress the fact that one could be saved without knowing explicitly the doctrine of justification by faith alone in its proper formulation; and this would obtain in the case of many simple Christians who could not adequately express their faith in this manner. But that faith saves Hollaz calls a fundamental article (*articulus fidei constituens*). And the doctrine that Christ is Mediator, the doctrine of the atonement, the doctrine of the justifying grace of God—these also are called *articuli fidei constituentes*. But it can only lead to confusion when Hollaz makes justification a fundamental article and justification by faith alone a secondary article. These two ideas cannot be separated.

Barth says that the *articulus stantis et cadentis ecclesiae* is not the doctrine of justification as such, but its basis and culmination. In saying this he is not going beyond Luther and the later dogmaticians. Luther often speaks merely of the article of Christ as the teaching upon which everything else hangs, and he means by this the teaching concerning the work of Christ.[7] The dogmaticians too when they speak of justification as the article upon which all theology depends are thinking of justification in the wider sense, for in every discussion of the doctrine they include a thorough treatment of its basis (Christ's work) and its aim and effects (*unio mystica*, sonship, peace of conscience, sanctification and eternal life).

Proceeding to the actual presentation of the doctrine Quenstedt begins with a simple word study of the pertinent verbs and their cognates. The words 'to justify' (δικαιοῦν, הִצְדִּיק) in Scripture never signify a justification through infusion of new qualities, but they are used to denote an action whereby God justifies the impious before His bar, in a forensic

---

5 Chemnitz in his *Loci Theologici* devotes no less than 100 folio pages to the doctrine of justification and often calls this the central teaching of Christian theology. Gerhard too is very thorough in his treatment of the doctrine and in his discussion on justification (*Loci Theologici*, Tom. VII) he includes his presentation of the work of Christ.

6 Baier, *Compendium Theologiae Positivae*, prol. I, 33. Hollaz, *Examen Theologicum Acroamaticum*, prol. quaes. 19–24.

7 cf. Erl. Aufl. 50.26–29, 48.18, 40.324ff.

sense. In Scripture the term often means (*a*) a recognition of divine righteousness (*justitiae divinae agnitio*), Ps. 51.4; Luke 7.29. Again it can mean (*b*) that a person is seen to be just be his works (Jas. 2.12). In this case there is no reference to the righteousness which is imputed to faith, but to the fact that a man's faith through which he becomes righteous is shown by his works. The term means (*c*) a devoting of oneself to the study of righteousness, Dan. 12.3. It denotes (*d*) a continuation in righteousness, Rev. 22.11: 'And he that is righteous, let him be righteous still.' This verse either implies an *actus continuatio* in which case we should try diligently to retain the righteousness of faith which we have, or it implies an *actus reiteratio* according to which he who falls into sin should through repentance return to God and be justified again. The word denotes (*e*) a sinfulness which is called by the name of righteousness when compared to worse sin, Ezek. 16–51, Jer. 3.11. The term points sometimes merely to (*f*) the attempt to arrogate to oneself the title of righteous, Luke 10.29, 16.15. It may denote (*g*) a censure or reprehending (*traductio et reprehensio*), Matt. 11.19. This at least represents the opinion of Luther, Brenz, Chemnitz, Hunnius, Osiander, Gerhard and others on this passage. The word may denote (*h*) a liberation from sin, Rom. 6.7, 18, 22. The term points (*i*) to the administrating of justice between contending parties, 2 Sam. 15.4. The word refers finally to (*j*) a forensic act of a judge and of justice (*actus judicialis*), by which a person is judicially declared righteous, Deut. 25.1, Prov. 17.5, Matt. 12.37. 'And in those passages where the justification of a sinner before God is spoken of the word "to justify" is always used in the forensic sense.' This becomes clear when we notice the contrast to this justification, viz. judgment which even Bellarmine grants must be considered a forensic act of God. Christ and the apostles employ the two terms as opposites consistently (John 3.18, 5.24; Rom. 5.19; Acts 10.43). 'We conclude then that the word "to justify" never means in Scripture to pour the quality of righteousness into somebody, but in this connexion it denotes nothing else than to establish righteousness forensically, or to make righteous by an act which is entirely outside man.'

The subject (*subjectum*) of justification, considered as the *terminus a quo*, is sinful man (cf. Rom. 3.23). With these words of the apostle the indisposition of man towards his own justification is graphically described, and that *intensively* by virtue of the extreme misery of man and the total corruption of his faculties, and also *extensively* since all men are subject to the curse of the Law. The apostle describes the *subjectum justificandum* (1) by his common state of corruption in that all have sinned, and (2) by his lacking of glory which he possessed in his original state of integrity and righteousness. However, it cannot be said that man is justified in so far as he is a sinner (*quatenus in statu peccati est*) and is deprived of the glory of God, but sinful man (*homo peccator*) is justified in so far as he is born again and believes. Therefore we say that the *subjectum justificandum*, when justification is considered as a present state (*ratione actus and status praesentis*), is the believer (*homo credens*), for only the believer in Christ is actually (*actu*) justified. Thus Paul says in Rom. 3.22: 'The righteousness of God which is by faith of Jesus Christ unto all and upon all them that believe.' In this passage 'the righteousness of God' is not to be understood as the righteousness which is in God essentially, but it is the righteousness which is from God, which comes to believers, i.e. it is imputed to believers. It is the same righteousness which the apostle speaks of later in Rom. 4.3ff where the perfect obedience of Christ which comes about by His obeying the Law and His suffering comes 'unto all and upon all them that believe'. The pleonasm in this verse emphasises that the righteousness (or obedience of Christ) is always apprehended by those who believe and only by those who believe, cf. Rom. 4.5. In this latter verse Quenstedt points out that ' "the ungodly" are not to be taken as those ungodly who without repentance persist in their ungodliness, but as the ungodly who recognise their ungodliness, desire to be freed from it, and flee with true faith to Christ and His throne of grace'.

The efficient cause of justification is the entire Trinity; for justification is an *opus ad extra* of God. The work of justification is attributed to God the Father in John 3.16–17 and Rom. 8.33. In the last passages the Father is referred to, for it is He who delivered up His Son (v. 32). The work of justification is attributed to the Son in Isa. 53.11: 'By his knowledge shall my righteous servant justify many,' i.e. through faith. Keeping in mind this passage Quenstedt remarks that Christ may be considered the cause of our justification because of His active and passive obedience, for this work of Christ was performed in order to make satisfaction for our unrighteousness and bring righteousness to us again. Thus Christ is called 'the Lord our righteousness', Jer. 23.6. Justification is attributed to the Holy Spirit in 1 Cor. 6.11 where we are told that we 'are justified in the name of the Lord Jesus, and by the Spirit of our God'. And so Quenstedt concludes, 'The work of justification pertains indivisibly to all three Persons, although you notice the mode of operation of each one in the carrying out of this mystery.'

That which moves God to justify us (*causa impulsiva interna*) is His own free grace. But before discussing this Quenstedt refers us to his consideration of the purpose of the vicarious atonement. On the part of God the purpose of the atonement is twofold: (1) to satisfy divine justice, for God will not remit sins without satisfaction; (2) to show His mercy which is manifested most clearly in this, that God gave His Son over to the most shameful death for our sake and accepted His satisfaction for us, and in this, that the Son willingly took our sins and made atonement for them by His death (II, III, II, thesis 41). This second fact is brought out most clearly in such passages as Rom. 5.8, John 3.16, John 15.13 and Eph. 5.25. Commenting on 1 John 3.16 Quenstedt says:

> This is the love of God: rather than banish men eternally from heaven He removed Himself from heaven, clothed Himself with flesh, became the Creature of a creature, inclosed Himself in the womb of the virgin, was wrapped in rags, laid in hay and housed in a barn. Nor does His love stop here; but after a life spent in poverty and adversities this love drives Christ to the ground on Olivet, binds Him in chains, delivers Him to jailors, cuts Him with the lash, crowns Him with thorns, fastens Him with nails to the Cross, and gives Him to drink the cup of bitterness. And finally this love compels Him to die, to die for adversaries and enemies (Rom. 5.6). Continuously and in these sundry ways Christ, who thirsts so greatly for our salvation, declares His love and mercy towards the human race.

That grace as the cause within God which moves Him to justify us by noting that this gracious disposition of God is expressed in two ways in Scripture. (1) κατ' ἄρσιν by removing any false impression that in us there is some cause of justification. This truth is brought out in all those passages which speak of God justifying us freely (δωρεάν, *gratis*), Rom. 3.24. This passage indicates that no power and ability to be justified resides in us, nor do we contribute any work or merit toward this end. That the term conveys this meaning (Luther: *Ohne Verdienst*) is shown also from John 15.25, 'They hated me with a cause' (Luther: *Ohne Ursach*, cf. 1 Sam. 19.5; Ps. 35.19, 69.4 where the Heb. חִנָּם, *gratis*, is used). (2) Scripture expressed God's loving disposition towards us κατὰ θέσιν, by explicitly using the word 'grace' to denote not some gift dwelling in us or some quality infused into us, but the gracious favour of God which is received by believers. In the preceding verses the word 'grace' not only excludes all righteousness of the Law and shows that the righteousness spoken of comes without the Law but the context implies the idea conveyed by the δωρεάν, viz. that this grace is simply gratuitous.

> Our justification is gratuitous therefore in this sense, that God judges us by His mercy and not by His justice. It is gratuitous because God bestows this benefit on us although we are unworthy and far from meriting it and because He bestows it without any intervention of works on our part; and this is in keeping with the clear opposition between grace and works which always obtains, according to the apos-

tle, Rom. 11.6: 'If by grace, then it is no more of works,' Eph. 2.8, 9: 'It is the gift of God: not of works, lest any man should boast.' Hence this grace is also called χρηστότης, φιλανθρωπία, kindness and love, Tit. 3.4–6: kindness by reason of the advantage which it offers us; φιλανθρωπία in reference to object of this grace, namely, men, mercy by reason of our misery by which our Lord allowed Himself to be moved, Gen. 8.21.

The external meritorious cause of our justification is the all-sufficient merit of the obedience of our Mediator. For we are justified 'through the redemption that is in Christ Jesus: whom God hath set forth to be a propitiation through faith in His blood.' The διά here is to be taken in the sense of *propter* (διὰ τῆς ἀπολυτρώσεως) as it is interpreted in other passages. In this verse the meritorious cause of our justification is the ἀπολύτρωσις, the redemption which is the very basis of our justification before God, for this redemption is mediated through the precious blood of Jesus Christ. This same redemption God sets forth as a propitiation for us, and that not merely in the sense of freeing us, but of making satisfaction for us.

Propitiation may also be called the meriting cause (*causa promerens*) of our justification, for the apostle says that God has set forth Christ as a propitiation to be accepted through faith in His blood. The term ἱλαστήριον which Luther translates '*Gnadenstuhl*' means an expiation, a compensation for the guilt of sin, an idea which is expressed in Heb. 11.17. The verb λάσκειν may also mean to placate or pacify, and this is the meaning the ἱλασμός takes on in 1 John 2.2, 4.10.

> Thus God justifies us freely and without any merit on our part and regards only the merit of Christ which is an ἀπολύτρωσις ἱλαστική, ἱλασμός, a bloody and appeasing sacrifice, a redemption and atonement. And so Christ is called in the above passages a ἱλαστήριον because He performed a ἱλασμός, a redemptive expiation and atonement through His blood for us, and by means of this placated God who was angry with sinners.

The *causa media* of justification is from God's side the Word and Sacraments through which the righteousness of Christ is offered to faith. The Word and Sacraments offer and bring the righteousness of Christ and the forgiveness of sins, Luke 24.47. The Word and Sacraments also bring sinners to faith in Christ and His righteousness and keep them and strengthen them in that faith. The *causa media* on the part of man is the so-called *organon* ληπτικόν, the faith which receives these benefits. Again we must listen to Rom. 3.22 which tells us that this righteousness of God is 'by faith of Jesus Christ unto all and upon all them that believe'. Compare also v. 25 where we are told that the benefits are received 'through faith in his blood'. The object of faith here is the blood which must be understood synecdochically for the entire cruel suffering of Christ through His whole life. The διά points out the *causa organica* through which the atoning and propitiatory blood of Christ becomes ours. Thus it is the same thing to say that we are justified, that we receive grace, that we live in Christ, for it is all through faith (πίστει, Acts 26.18; ἐκ πίστεως, Gal. 3.7, 8, 9, 11, 12; διὰ τῆς πίστεως, Rom. 3.30, 31; μετὰ πίστεως, 1 Tim. 1.14; ἐπὶ τῇ πίστει, Phil. 3.9; ἐν πίστει, 1 Tim. 3.13; κατὰ πίστιν, Heb. 11.13).

> On our part it is this faith alone which justifies us and effects (*influit*) our justification. Whatever merely embraces and apprehends to itself the promises of grace, the forgiveness of sins and the merit of Christ does so without any admixture of works. And only that on the part of man which enters into the picture when we consider God justifying him can be said to justify. Thus we are said to be justified by faith exclusively without the deeds of the Law, Rom. 3.28. Eph. 2.8, 9. True, faith is never alone, never all by itself and isolated from good works, and yet faith alone apprehends the merit of Christ, and we are justified by means of faith alone.

Faith is to be considered an organic cause of justification not in so far as it is our act or our acceptance of God's grace (*in se et in sua natura*), but by virtue of the object which it apprehends. Here Quenstedt troubles himself to distinguish between the *causalitas* of faith in the matter of justification and the *ratio causandi* in this matter. The causality of faith in justification consists in this, that faith receives and accepts the grace of God (λαμβάνειν, John 1.12, Rom. 5.17, Gal. 3.14; καταλαμβάνειν, John 1.5; παραλαμβάνειν, John 1.11; δέχεσθαι, Luke 8.13, Acts 8.14; ἀποδέχεσθαι, Acts 2.41, 1 Tim. 1.15). The reason for this causality of faith in justification does not consist in this, that faith is an acceptance and reception (*quatenus est apprehensio*), for a person can apprehend to himself imaginary things or human righteousness; rather it consists in this, the object which faith apprehends, viz. the merit of Christ. And of this St. Paul speaks in Rom. 3.25 where he says that 'the whole justifying power of faith depends on the thing apprehended, on the bloody merit of Christ which is the proper object of justifying faith'. Quenstedt goes on to illustrate with the following interesting analogy:

> When the hand of a starving man seizes bread which is offered to it, it is not this taking of the bread which satisfies the man, for he could seize a piece of mud or a stone or something else which could not satisfy him, but his being satisfied depends on the object which he takes to himself and depends on his eating it, i.e. it depends on the bread.

When the lips of a thirsty man drink water which has been drawn with a bucket from some well, it is not the drinking as such that quenches his thirst, for you can also draw sand or blood with a bucket. No, if his thirst is to be satisfied, the drink which he consumes must have the power to quench thirst. Thus he who hungers and thirsts after righteousness receives it through faith, as the begging hand which receives the bread coming down from heaven (John 6.50–51) and as the vessel of the thirsting soul draws the water springing up into everlasting life (John 4.14); but it is not this receiving and drinking as such which drives away the spiritual hunger and quenches the thirst. Man does not possess anything of such a nature as can accomplish this, e.g. his own merits, his own pretended autonomy, satisfactions which are the inventions of the Synagogue of Rome. No, the whole strength of man's receiving depends on the thing received through faith, the redemption and the blood of Jesus Christ.[8]

The form of justification consists in the fact of certain changes which take place in man. This is not to be understood as though sin were driven out of man completely and righteousness infused or as though one is changed from being inherently unrighteous to being inherently righteous. For want of a better term Quenstedt calls this change a moral change which means that man becomes righteous by a forensic and external action, and this action is not performed in man but in respect to man and outside man (*circa et extra hominem*), and so it is extrinsic and at the same time real and true.

The nature of justification (*forma in specie*) is twofold: (A) It is the forgiveness of sins and the non-imputation of our own righteousness; (B) It is the imputation of the obedience of Christ.[9]

(A) Quenstedt discusses three passages at great length in showing that justification is the remission of sins, or the same thing, the non-imputation of guilt. His first exegesis revolves around Ps. 32.1–2 and Rom. 4.7–8. Here it is his interest to demonstrate that the whole gamut of man's sin and rebellion against God is summed up in the three nouns פֶּשַׁע (*Praevaricatio, quae est gravior a Domino supremo defectio, eaque malitiosa, pertinax, horrenda*), חֲטָאָה which is from חָטָא which means to wander or err, and עָו (*perversitas, iniquitas*), even as the entire story of God's work of redemption and justification are summed up in the three verbs נָשָׂא (*elevavit, condonavit, vel reatum aut poenam ab altero delinquente abstulit, removit,* Num. 14.19), כָּסַה (*tegit, operitur*), and חָשַׁב (*cogitavit, cogitando, reputavit, quandoque cum לְ constructum, significat, aliquid alteri imputavit, aut cogitando annumeravit*

---

8 cf. *Formula of Concord*, Thor. decl. III, 13ff.

9 This agrees with the *Formula of Concordia*, Art. III.

[*Germanice* zurechnen]). Commenting on 2 Cor. 5.19 Quenstedt says that the non-imputation of sins means that God chooses not to punish sins. The basis for this non-imputation is not in the subject, man, for if God had regard only to sinful man He must punish sin. 'The basis is in Christ who made atonement for this sin which is in man and which is not imputed.'

(B) Positively the nature of justification consists in the imputation of Christ's obedience. The first Bible verse for consideration is Rom. 4.5. Three questions may be asked in reference to this passage: (1) What does it mean to impute? (2) To whom is the imputation made? (3) What is imputed? In answer to the first query Quenstedt replies that the word 'to impute' can often be taken in a physical sense as meaning to infuse as when a branch is grafted on to a plant. However, the word is also used as an acceptation, e.g. victory is imputed to Caesar although he is absent. According to the first meaning to impute sin to someone would mean to instil or infuse iniquity into him, which is an unorthodox way to speak. According to the second meaning there may be an imputation of either evil or good. For instance, Scripture says that sin is imputed to the workers of iniquity, Lev. 17.16. Sometimes sin is imputed to a person undeservedly as when adultery was imputed to Susanna. And again sin is imputed *ex gratia* as when our sins were imputed to Christ in His atoning for our sins. Righteousness may also be imputed as well as sin, and that (*a*) *jure et secundum debitum* when the basis of the imputation is in the subject (Rom. 4.4), or (*b*) *injuria* as when a stupid person is reputed to be wise just because he is silent (Prov. 17.27), or (*c*) *ex gratia* when the guilty is absolved because of the merit of another. This last usage is that of Scripture when speaking of our justification. In answer to the second question we need merely repeat the words of the apostle, 'To him that worketh not, but believeth on him that justifieth the ungodly.' The person who does not work is simply the one who does not depend on his works for justification, not one who lacks good works, for works always proceed from faith. The believer, then, is the one to whom this imputation is made, the believer who does not trust in himself. But what does he trust in? In Him 'that justifieth the ungodly', viz. God, 'who promises in the Word of the Gospel that He wishes to be gracious for the sake of Christ's merit and justify the ungodly out of grace, that is, forgive him all his sins and pronounce him righteous, that he may believe and not spurn the grace offered in the promised Word, but seize it and hold on to it with faith'. The ἐπὶ τόν expresses a trust in the mercy of God, a trust which rests firmly in God. The 'ungodly' is not one who was formerly ungodly, but one who is ungodly even now and merits eternal judgment but for this, that God by grace for Christ's sake forgives all his sins, since Christ bore his ungodliness and the sins of the whole world. In answer to the third question, it is righteousness which is imputed, the righteousness of Christ. And this agrees perfectly well with what Paul says here, viz. that 'his faith is counted for righteousness'. Quenstedt says, 'The imputation of the righteousness of Christ and the imputation of faith for righteousness is one and the same. For faith does not justify because of its own character, but because of the value of its object.'

Speaking on Rom. 5.19 Quenstedt notes three things. (1) As to the cause of the condemnation and the salvation spoken of here, the cause of the former is the disobedience of Adam, the cause of the latter is the obedience of Christ. (2) As to the effects of Adam's disobedience and Christ's obedience, the effect of the former is that all men were made sinners, the effect of the latter is that all men are made (*constituuntur*) righteous. (3) As to the dominion which the actions of both these men exert (*utriusque subjecta*), the disobedience of Adam passed upon (*transiit*) all men, the obedience of Christ was performed (*praestita est*) on behalf of all men. Quenstedt warns that we must not press the parallel beyond this point, for then it might be inferred that the righteousness of Christ was passed on to all men without any consideration of their faith or unbelief, just as the sin of Adam is propagated through natural generation. Gerhard[10] uses slightly different language here. He says that just as the offence of Adam brought sin upon all so that all are justly condemned by God unless reconciliation is made, so by the merit of Christ righteousness and salvation were brought to (*propagatur*) all in order that all might be justified by faith. Both the condemnation and the justification were forensic. Later in a footnote, however, Gerhard states exactly what Quenstedt said above.

Quenstedt next offers a very long exegesis of 2 Cor. 5.21 to which I offer only a few brief allusions. He says that this verse leads us to speak either in reference to the person to whom imputation is made or to the thing which is imputed. Here is what he says:

> When we say that our sin is imputed to Christ and Christ's righteousness is imputed to us, then we mean that our sin which is in us and not in Christ is transferred to Christ according to God's decree and determination, that is, it is reckoned as though it were in Christ; on the other hand, the righteousness of Christ which is in Christ and not in us is transferred to us according to God's decree and determination, that is, it is reckoned as though it were in us.

The non-imputation of sin—and this is precisely the forgiveness of sin—is inseparably joined with the imputation of Christ's righteousness.

---

10 *Loci Theologici*, Cotta ed., Tuebingen, 1762, VII, 11.

From the above delineation of Quenstedt's doctrine of justification it seems quite clear that Lutheran orthodoxy made the concerted effort to remain faithful to the teachings of Scripture on the one hand and of Luther and the Lutheran Confessions on the other hand. The question may be asked: just how close were the theologians of Quenstedt's day to the doctrine of Luther? There is no doubt that their terminology differs from Luther's to a marked degree, especially after the *Formula of Concord*. Luther, in speaking of the foreign righteousness which becomes ours through faith, does not shrink from calling it a *justitia extra infusa*,[11] even though he insists that it is a *justitia aliena*. *Gratia infusa* is a term commonly employed by Luther, even in his later writings. He says that when God justifies 'He drives sin out of the heart and drives in grace'.[12] He speaks of the righteousness of God according to the usage of Scripture meaning 'the grace and mercy of Christ poured into us through Christ'.[13] He has of course purged such concepts of their mechanical, Romish meaning, as may be seen from the context of such statements; but the fact remains that after the *Formula of Concord* Lutheran theologians could and did not speak in such a free manner. They repudiate the term 'infused righteousness', and insist that the word 'justify' in Scripture never denotes a justification by the infusion of new qualities into a person (*per infusionem novarum qualitatum*).[14] This does not imply that they are abandoning anything that was taught by Luther; but after Trent and the appearance of Osiander in their own ranks they have concluded that it is simply not possible to baptise some of the questionable Roman terminology still employed by Luther. In their day the *gratia infusa* was irrevocably associated with the synergism of the Roman doctrine of justification.[15] The later dogmaticians do not even like to speak of justification as being an act whereby God makes an unrighteous man righteous, although Luther and the Lutheran confessions freely speak that way. For this was the terminology of Rome and implied that justification was a process like sanctification. Bellarmine, for instance, had said,[16]

> Ordinarily a person is said to be warmed not only when from being cold he is made warm, but when from being warm he is made warmer. Thus too one is said to be justified not only when from being unrigh-

---

11 *Sermo de duplici iustitia*, 1519. WA 2.245–6.
12 Erl. Aufl., 14.204. 1 Advent, 1522.
13 Erl. Aufl., 10.18ff. Sermon on Matt. 9.1–9.
14 cf. *supra*. Also Gerhard, op. cit., VII.8.13.
15 Council of Trent, Sess. 6, Ch. 7 and can. 11.
16 *Disputationes*, Tom. 4, de justificatione, I, III.

teous he is made righteous, but when from being righteous he is made more righteous.

The Lutheran theologians were even hesitant about speaking of justification as a change (*mutatio*), for Roman theology used this terminology often to mean a change which was like a sick person being made well. The Lutherans were wont to abandon any terminology which would imply that justification was a process.

The question in all this is simply whether the later dogmaticians departed in any way from Luther's teaching on justification, or whether they are only defining and refining terms. The accusation has often been made that Lutheran orthodoxy taught an unreal justification with its doctrine of imputed righteousness. Perrone says,[17]

> According to the doctrine of the Protestants it does not happen in justification that sins are really remitted at all, but are merely concealed according to an extrinsic imputation of the righteousness of God or Christ, and thus by the power of this justification there begins to take place in us a certain inner renewal by which man becomes inwardly and formally righteous from sin.

This is a caricature, not only of the doctrine of Luther, but of the later orthodox Lutherans as well. Quenstedt, following Chemnitz, insists that the imputation has an absolutely firm foundation which is not in man who is justified, but in Christ and His work. It is very important for our present discussion that Quenstedt's point of view be made clear on this matter. When we know precisely what he understood by the imputation in justification, we quickly learn that he has not departed from Luther's doctrine of justification on any important point, and we learn that any accusation that the old orthodox teaching made justification merely a legal fiction is unfounded. Therefore I quote Quenstedt at length.

> The imputation consists in a real reckoning. According to the judgment of God the sinful man who believes in Christ is absolved of sins and the righteousness of Christ is truly reckoned to him. Now granted that the reckoning does not work the result that the righteousness of Christ inheres inherently in the believer; the imputation, nevertheless, is not thereby fictitious and imaginary, a mere opinion of a just person, without any actual effect, as the papists maliciously report us as teaching. No, this λογισμός or imputation is earnest and real. It has its gracious foundation in Christ and its termination in us (*ad nos*). It consists in a gracious determination of God and in a real conferring and transferring of Christ's righteousness to the believer. And so when one

---

17 *Praelectiones Theologicae*, ed. 27, Ratisbonae, 1856, II, 229.

believes, he is by this reckoning made and accounted righteous in the judgment of God's mind. And this is a most real judgment of God which from the throne of His grace extends over the sinner who from the Gospel believes in Christ. . . . Those to whom the righteousness of Christ is imputed are truly righteous, although not inherently or by inherence, but imputatively and through an extrinsic designation that they are such, for also from that which is extrinsic a true designation can take place. Therefore it is a vain question, whether we are really righteous by that imputation, or whether we are only regarded as righteous. For God's judgment is according to truth. Wherefore he who is regarded by God as righteous is truly righteous.

This statement of Quenstedt's which is quite typical of all the later dogmaticians[18] places him squarely in the camp of Luther with his emphasis upon the greatness and the reality of God's imputation. It is reminiscent of Luther's words,[19]

This imputation is not a thing of no consequence, but is greater than the whole world, yea, than all the holy angels. Reason cannot see all this, for reason disregards the Word of God; but we (I say) thank God that we have such a Saviour who is able to pass us by and reckon our sin as nothing.

Hence the concern of many modern theologians[20] that the forensic justification be not a fiction is fully met not only by Luther but also by the later dogmaticians. Adolf Hoenecke has summarised their position well,[21]

The position of the dogmaticians is clear. They wish to show that according to Scripture there is a middle ground between the physical infusion of indwelling righteousness and an empty, ineffective, declarative reckoning (as the papists groundlessly charge against the Lutheran teaching). The middle ground is a formal reckoning (*appropriata imputatio*). This reckoning would be empty if it took place only up in heaven in the tribunal of God and were manipulated, as it were, behind the back of the sinner. But the sinner is himself active in this matter of reckoning through the Holy Spirit working in him through the Word; he receives God's imputed verdict concerning him, a verdict in which the Holy Spirit attributes the whole transaction as applying to him. And so the sinner emerges from this transaction as one who has

18 cf. Baier, *Compendium*, de justificatione, par. 3. Dannhauer, *Hodosophia*, ed. 1713, p. 461.

19 *Die Disputation de iustificatione* (1536). WA 39.97–98.

20 cf. Barth, *Church Dogmatics*, IV, 1.95; Berkouwer, *Faith and Justification*, 87; Bultmann, *Theology of the NT*, I, 276.

21 *Ev.-Luth. Dogmatik*, Milwaukee, 1912, III, 345.

righteousness, not a righteousness achieved by his works, not a righteousness infused into him, but a righteousness spoken over him according to God's unfailing verdict.

Thus with the forensic justification, with the *justitia aliena*, with the strong emphasis on the validity and reality of the imputation we have the basic elements of Lutheran orthodoxy's doctrine of justification. And if the terminology has changed the main strands and emphasis of the Reformation teaching remains intact.

THE VICARIOUS ATONEMENT
IN JOHN QUENSTEDT

"The Vicarious Atonement in John Quenstedt" furthers Preus's analysis of this important latter Lutheran orthodox father. It was published in 1961 by *Concordia Theological Monthly*.

THE LAST DECADES HAVE WITNESSED some significant and provocative studies in the doctrine of the Atonement. Two of these studies particularly have stimulated interest by the way in which they have broken with the old Lutheran and Protestant treatment of the doctrine while attempting at the same time to be entirely Biblical in the approach and presentation of the doctrine. On the one hand, Gustaf Aulén classifies the post-Reformation teaching as only a slight and more logical modification of the doctrine of Anselm, a teaching dominated by the idea of satisfaction and the legal motif. In contrast to this, Aulén offers his well-known "classic idea" with its victory motif, and identifies this with Luther's teaching.[1] Barth, on the other hand, primarily in Vol. IV,1 of his *Church Dogmatics*, deals with the Atonement as a part of his discussion on justification and reconciliation. He feels that the forensic image so common in Scripture is the best point of departure in setting forth the doctrine of the Atonement and is to be preferred to the way in which Orthodoxy considered the matter, viz., under the locus on the sacerdotal office of Christ. Barth makes no sweeping criticism of the method and manner in which Orthodoxy treated this doctrine, although he cannot agree always with the conclusions of the older orthodox theologians. Barth, then, is much closer to the older doctrine than Aulén and seems to have read the Reformed and Lutheran dog-

---

1 G. Aulén, *Christus Victor* (New York, 1931), pp. 142ff. R. Prenter, *Skabelse og Genløsning* (København, 1955), p. 448, seems to follow Aulén in his judgment of orthodoxy.

maticians with more appreciation and understanding than Aulén—in fact, he often draws upon their arguments.

Because of the rather frequent reference to the old classical Lutheran doctrine of the Atonement and the rather scanty firsthand knowledge of this doctrine, and also because of the new approaches made to this doctrine in recent times, I have attempted here to clear the air, so to speak, to establish so far as possible in an article of this nature what Orthodoxy actually taught on this matter. It is my opinion that if we can overcome our antipathy to some of their scholastic terminology and the rather schematic order of their material, we shall discover that the old Lutheran theologians offer something which is remarkably well balanced and solidly Scriptural.

We might comment on Aulén's charge that Orthodoxy's doctrine of the atonement was one-sided. Quenstedt has discussed the object for which Christ's satisfaction was made under five points: (a) sin, (b) punishment for sin, (c) the curse of the Law, (d) the power of the devil, (e) death. All of these *obiecta* are somehow related to the idea of satisfaction according to this treatment, although in the last two cases the concept of satisfaction is not allowed to color or even enter into his exegeses so as to vitiate the thought and image of Scripture. The victory motif which Aulén finds in Scripture was not neglected or toned down by Orthodoxy, but was clearly set forth and given its place along with the other themes which Scripture uses in speaking of the work of Christ. On the other hand, it is clear that Quenstedt has offered far more than merely a logical modification of the legal satisfaction motif of Anselm, as Aulén charges. Barth[2] is more Biblical than Aulén when he admits that he prefers the forensic image in setting forth the doctrine of Christ's work but that the ransom picture or victory motif might also be used as the point of departure in treating Christ's work. However, the procedure of older Lutheran dogmatics would seem to be far preferable when they dealt with the work of Jesus Christ under the title *Munus Christi sacerdotale*, for the Bible points more often to this "cultic" picture in speaking of the work of Christ. Barth says he prefers his forensic point of departure to the cultic, because the latter is not so meaningful today. We would probably disagree with Barth's choice and say rather that it must be our purpose as theologians to make Christ's highpriestly office meaningful also today. But at the same time we will grant that the forensic figure would not be the most unfortunate starting point in dealing with this doctrine. At any rate we can learn one thing from studying Quenstedt: he draws in every Scripture image which will help him to set forth the doctrine of the vicarious atonement. His treatment is well bal-

---

2 *Church Dogmatics* (Edinburgh, 1956), IV, 1, pp. 273ff.

anced and not dominated by a legal motif or any other. It is Aulén's doctrine which is one-sided, with its exclusive emphasis on the victory theme.

This study of a typical Orthodox Lutheran discussion of the doctrine of the vicarious atonement will, I hope, serve to show us two things: first, how much we today owe to the orthodox Lutheran theologians for the theology which has been handed down to us, and second, how we can still learn from their careful, Scriptural treatment of all doctrine.

In this delineation I shall restrict myself to the presentation by John A. Quenstedt (1617–88). This, I believe, is fair and adequate inasmuch as Quenstedt was the Thomas Aquinas, so to speak, of Lutheran Orthodoxy, the last great representative. To anyone following his arrangement of material and noting his exegesis it will become evident that he was fair and meticulous in his work and drew from the best which his precursors had to offer. The strong exegetical basis for his entire treatment will be noticeable throughout. Quenstedt's systematic section on the Atonement actually presents nothing but exegesis of passages pertaining to the doctrine, arranged according to a quite skeletal scholastic outline.[3] The reader will notice, too, how very closely Quenstedt's terminology and understanding of this great doctrine approximate what has always been believed and taught concerning the vicarious atonement within conservative Lutheranism. This fact alone makes a study like the following relevant and useful today.

1. Like the other Lutheran and Reformed theologians Quenstedt offers his treatment of the vicarious atonement within his discussion of the priestly office of Christ. His thesis is simple and straight-forward:

> The priestly office is a work of the God-man; accordingly Christ by the eternal counsel of God and by His own voluntary decision placed Himself in time under God's Law and did so on our behalf and in our stead. And by fulfilling that Law perfectly and by suffering all punishment He presented an obedience to divine righteousness which was sufficient to the last ounce (*ex asse*) and also freed us from the wrath of God, the curse of the Law, from sin and all evil. This obedience He now offers God the Father, and by His intercession He obtains everything good and needful for us. (Thesis 14)

We see from this statement that the priestly office of Christ is divided into two parts: satisfaction and intercession. We shall review only Quenstedt's treatment of the former.

---

3 The present study is based entirely on Quenstedt's *Theologia didactico-polemica sive systema theologicum*, 1685, Part Three, Cap. III, Membrum II, "De officio Christi," Sec. 1, Th. 14 to 44.

Quenstedt begins his discussion by pointing out that the term *satisfactio* was not found in the Vulgate. However, the idea of satisfaction is expressed by many images of Scripture: (a) Restoration. Ps. 69:4: "Then I restored that which I took not away"; (b) λύτρον, Matt. 20:28; (c) ἀντίλυτρον, 1 Tim. 2:6; (d) Propitiation, 1 John 2:2; 4:10; (e) ἱλαστήριον, Rom. 3:24,25; (f) Reconciliation, Rom. 5:10; 2 Cor. 5:18ff.; (g) ἀπολύτρωσις, Eph. 1:7; Col. 1:14; (h) λύτρωσις, 1 Peter 1:18; (i) ἀγόρασις, 1 Cor. 6:20, "Ye are bought with a price"; (j) ἐξαγόρασις, Gal. 3:13. Also other terms are used in Scripture, such as oblation, expiation, sacrifice for sins, etc.

The satisfaction and the merit of Christ are not to be taken as equivalents. There are a number of differences in the two concepts.

a. Satisfaction compensates for a wrong (*iniuria*) against God, it makes expiation (*expiat*) for sin, it pays a debt and frees fully from eternal punishment. Merit, on the other hand, restores us into a state of divine favor, it gains for us a reward of grace (the grace of forgiven sins), it acquires justification and eternal life for sinners.

b. Satisfaction is a cause; merit an effect. Merit arises out of satisfaction. "Christ made satisfaction for our sins and for the punishment of sins, and thus He merited for us the grace of God, forgiveness of sins, and eternal life."

c. Satisfaction is something which has been rendered to the Triune God, not to us, although it was made *for us*. Christ, however, did not merit anything for the Triune God, but for us.

d. The humiliation of Christ, His obedience under the Law, His suffering and death, are both satisfaction and meritorious. The exaltation, resurrection, ascension, and session at the right hand of God are not works of satisfaction, but they are meritorious, thereby assuring our resurrection and reserving a place in heaven for us.

e. Satisfaction arose because a debt had to be paid (*satisfactio ex debito oritur*), but merit is not something owed, it is free. Quenstedt remarks that not all theologians observe these distinctions, but many speak of merit in a broad sense as embracing also the idea of satisfaction.

2. The One who made the satisfaction (*principium quod satisfactionis*) is Christ, the God-man. To illustrate this, Quenstedt considers two Scripture passages in great detail. (a) Is. 63:3: "I have trodden the winepress alone; and of the people there was none with Me." Here is a reference to the Messiah, who comes with red garments from Bozrah, who speaks righteousness and is mighty to save. This Savior treads the winepress alone. He conquers the enemies, Satan, death, and sin, treads them underfoot, and gains complete victory. But not without wounds. He suffers and dies to gain the victory. (b) 1 Tim. 2:5,6. Just as there is only one God among all

false gods, so there is only one Mediator. A mediator is one who intervenes or intercedes. He also may be one who placates another and brings peace where there was formerly wrath between two hostile parties. A μεσίτης is never one who merely reveals and interprets another's will (Socinus). Jesus is a Mediator of a new covenant by reason of the shedding of His blood in redemption. (Heb. 12:24)

This Mediator is described in the above passage (a) according to His personal majesty.

> He is called man, but not an ordinary man or merely a man. The Mediator is One who, although He was God, was made man that He might fulfill the office of a mediator. Therefore the term man in this passage is not a person in the abstract, or what would be the same thing, the human nature in the concrete, but it is the entire person in the concrete, although only one nature, namely, the human, is referred to. This is seen from the fact that (1) this man is immediately called Jesus Christ and this name points to the entire unity of the Person, and that (2) this man is the One who gave Himself a ransom for all, v. 6. Now this is no mere man, but θεάνθρωπος, the God-man, for no mere man was able to effect such a redemption (Ps. 49:7). Therefore this man is clearly a singular man, who in the unity of His person is God and the Lord God (2 Sam. 7:19) . . . who is over all, God blessed forever (Rom. 9:5). . . . The apostle calls our Mediator in this verse man and not God because (1) it was for the sake of the mediatorial office that He was made man, and (2) we then might come to this Mediator with greater confidence and flee to Him, as men to a man and brothers to a brother. (Thesis 2B, Obs. 3)

The Mediator is described in this passage (b) according to the dignity of His office. He is called Christ, the Anointed One, who according to His human nature was anointed with the infinite glory of the Holy Spirit. He is called Jesus, Savior, because that is the purpose of His office as Mediator, to save His people from their sins. (Matt. 1:21)

The satisfaction is accomplished by Christ with the participation of both the human and the divine nature, the divine as source and formally (*originaliter et formaliter*) and the human nature as a means (*organice*) by virtue of its personal union with the divine nature.

> Note: The suffering and death of only the flesh of Christ could not free us from sin, from the wrath of God and the curse of the Law, and from eternal perdition, nor could it render an adequate price for redeeming the human race. No, the satisfaction for the sin of the entire world, the propitiation of divine wrath, the bruising of the serpent's head, the performing of perfect righteousness, required a divine and infinite power. Therefore the divine nature fortified the suffering flesh

so that it did not sink under these sufferings, and it procured for these sufferings and death infinite effectiveness. (Thesis 29)

3. Quenstedt strongly insists that only the Triune God is the indirect object of the satisfaction. Against Him we have sinned (Ps. 51:4). Therefore the ransom and satisfaction must be made to Him.

> The One to whom the satisfaction was made (*objectum cui*) was exclusively the Triune God. The entire Trinity was offended with sin and angry with men; and because of the immutability of God's justice and the holiness of His nature and the truth of His threatenings, He could not remit sins without punishment (*impune*), nor can He receive men into grace without satisfaction. Therefore the human race was reconciled to the whole Trinity through Christ. And that old cuckoo-cry that no one can offer satisfaction to himself or mediate in respect to himself does not hold true. If the Father King is offended, the Son is offended, too; but nothing prevents the Son from procuring mercy for the one who is accused of the Father. Thus 2 Cor. 5:19 says: "God was in Christ, reconciling the world unto Himself," and in Rom. 5:10 we are said to be "reconciled to God through the death of His Son." (Thesis 30)

Quenstedt goes on to insist that there is nothing wrong according to 2 Cor. 5:19 with saying that Christ reconciled the world unto Himself, inasmuch as He is God, the subject of the action in the verse. Thus in this transaction God is the injured party and the party who is placating. He makes satisfaction to Himself as the injured party (*satisfecit sibi ipsi ut offenso*).

Quenstedt says that Rom. 5:10 teaches such a full reconciliation. Grotius had entertained the idea that the reconciliation was conditional, depending upon our accepting it all in faith. Quenstedt argues that our appropriating to ourselves God's deed is not the completion of the deed itself. The reconciliation through the death of the Son was accomplished *plene, imo plenissime.* "We were not redeemed or reconciled nor were our sins paid for in any way conditionally, but we were reconciled completely and perfectly and fully." This applies both to the actual carrying out of the reconciliation and to our appropriating it by faith. For faith is nothing else than accepting the finished reconciliation.

When we discuss reconciliation and satisfaction, we must bear in mind that God is a just Judge who demands satisfaction for every infraction of His Law. That God is a righteous God and deals with sin according to righteousness is brought out clearly in Rom. 3:25: "Whom God hath set forth to be a Propitiation through faith in His blood, to declare *His righteousness* for the remission of sins that are past." Here it is indicated that punishment for sin is necessary, either upon the guilty, namely, sinful man, or upon his surety (*vas*), Christ. "If God had been able to overlook man's transgression without satisfaction and without compromising His infinite righteousness, so great a sacrifice on the part of the only-begotten Son would not have been necessary. God, who is infinite, was offended by sin, and because sin is an offense and outrage and profaning of the most high God (I might call it deicide), it carries with it a kind of infinite wickedness . . . and deserves infinite punishment; and therefore it required the price of satisfaction which only Christ could pay." (Thesis 31)

Quenstedt insists against the Socinians that God must not be thought of merely as a private creditor (*creditor privatus*) but as a just Judge (*creditor publicus iudicarius*) who cannot let sin go unpunished without violating His own righteousness. According to 2 Tim. 2:13, God cannot deny Himself, that is, He cannot go back on His Word of promise or of threat. Sin is not something with which the one sinned against can do as he pleases, but sin is always in reference to God's righteousness, which is of His very essence, and God cannot connive against His own righteousness. Certain scholastics had said that God by an absolute decree of His power could remit sin without any satisfaction.[4] Quenstedt claims that it is wrong to speak of such absolute power in God, for it conflicts (a) with the very nature of God, who cannot be not angry against sin, (b) with the integrity of God, who told Adam that he would die if he ate from the tree of the knowledge of good and evil, (c) with the holiness of God, which is unchangeable and cannot remit any sin without punishment.

4. The real object for which (*objectum reale pro quo*) Christ made satisfaction is sin, all sin, original and actual, all sin which ever has or ever will be committed, even the sin against the Holy Ghost. This is shown in Is. 53:4ff. "Surely He hath borne our griefs and carried our sorrows. . . . But He was wounded for our transgressions, etc." (Cf. Matt. 8:17; Acts 8:32; 1 Peter 2:24, where the same fact is taught.) In the NT βαστάζειν expresses the same idea of Christ carrying our sin. The object of this bearing and carrying are griefs and sorrows, which are to be taken as disorders of the soul, spiritual griefs and sorrows, that is, sins which are the cause of all punishment and of all sorrow and grief. This is clear from the context (v. 6) and from parallel references such as 1 Peter 2:24: "His own self bare our sins in His own body. . . ." That Christ carried our sins means that indirectly He carried also the miseries and sicknesses of our bodies (*portando peccata Christus etiam morbos portaverit*); and thus we have healing and forgiveness. Commenting on Is. 53:8b: "For the transgression of My people was He stricken," Quenstedt says,

---

4 Thomas Aquinas, *Summa theologica*, Part III, qu. 46, art. 2.

Our sins deserve wounds, our transgressions bruises, our iniquities stripes. But we were unable by suffering these wounds and bruises and stripes to free ourselves from sins and transgressions and to heal ourselves from iniquities. In such a manner there could be no satisfaction made to divine righteousness so that we should be whole and well. Therefore by a judicial imputation the Lord made the sins of all fall upon the Messiah: like a storm they would carry Messiah away, like an army they would destroy Him (הִפְגִּיעַ, v. 6, means to meet, to run against, to make an impact upon someone, to wield a sword. See Judg. 8:21; 15:12). Christ voluntarily bore that load of sin, the wounds, the bruises, the stripes; and thus He made satisfaction to God for us. (Thesis 33)

This is just a portion of Quenstedt's long discussion of the important Is. 53 passage.

The second passage for consideration is Titus 2:14: "Who gave Himself for us, ἵνα λυτρώσηται ἡμᾶς ἀπὸ πάσης ἀνομίας." The δόσις points to Christ's giving Himself over to suffering and death, although He was delivered by other persons, viz., Judas (Matt. 26:15), the high priests (Matt. 27:2, 18), Satan (John 13:2), Pilate (Matt. 27:26), and also the Father (Rom. 8:32) out of His great love for mankind. These words "who gave Himself" (also Gal. 1:4; 2:20; Eph. 5:2) point to Christ's free and willing oblation unto the death of the cross, an oblation performed out of the most ardent love toward us. And so He gave willingly, not because He was forced; but He was moved only by His love for us, moved to give not gold or silver or animals, not another man or even all angels, but Himself (ἑαυτόν). Elsewhere He is said to give His flesh (John 6:51), His body (Luke 22:19), His blood (Luke 22:20), His life (Matt. 20:28). All this means that the whole Christ was given, not merely His body or merely His soul, but Himself, God and man.

Speaking next about the redemption which is expressed here, Quenstedt mentions that the redemption should be considered qualitatively and quantitatively. Taken *qualitatively*, Christ's redemption is a true and proper and satisfactory redemption and must not be regarded as something metaphorical (Socinus). When the apostle uses the term λυτροῦν, he is not signifying merely a liberation, but a real redemption and satisfaction, which was made with an adequate ransom (*interventu* ἰσορρόπου λύτρου καὶ ἀντιλύτρου), 1 Tim. 2:6. It is true that the term redemption can be taken broadly as a mere freeing without any price, but in the present context and in other similar contexts there can be no doubt as to its meaning (cf. Matt. 20:28; 1 Peter 1:19, where the price is mentioned). Taken *quantitatively*, the redemption of Christ may be considered in respect to the *sub-*

jects involved, namely, all sinners ("that He might redeem *us*"), or in respect to the *object* involved, namely, that from which all sinners are redeemed, i.e., "all iniquity." "All iniquity" means that there is no sin which is not covered by Christ's expiation.

The last passage to be discussed under the first *objectum reale pro quo satisfactum* is 1 John 1:7: "The blood of Jesus Christ, His Son, cleanseth us ἀπὸ πάσης ἁμαρτίας." It must first be noted that this blood is precious, because it is the blood of God's Son (τοῦ υἱοῦ, 1 Peter 1:19 and Acts 20:28). To Him nothing can be compared in heaven or earth; therefore the ransom which is His life has infinite value before God, and we have τὸν πλοῦτον τῆς χάριτος θεοῦ διὰ τοῦ αἵματος αὐτοῦ, and we have reconciliation as well through His blood (Eph. 1:8; Col. 1:20). Secondly, this verse indicates the efficacy of Christ's blood to cleanse us from sin. Here we learn that Christ did not shed His blood merely to declare and show that God would cleanse us from all our sins, but Christ's blood cleanses us really (ὄντως). The work of cleansing is attributed to His blood. "The blood of Christ all by itself (*immediate*) produces and brings about this effect, viz., καθαρισμόν, cleansing, propitiation from sins." The Son of God is said to have washed us from our sins in His own blood (Rev. 1:5). [Cf. also Heb. 1:3: "Christ purged our sins," where the same *objectum reale* of the atonement is pointed to]

The second *objectum reale pro quo* of the vicarious atonement is the punishment for sin, both temporal and eternal. Christ made satisfaction for all the punishment which men deserved on account of sin, and that by enduring these punishments Himself. Again Is. 53:5 is cited. The מוּסָר is the guilt and blame against which punishment is brought. The punishment which was essential for our peace and our good was endured by Him. The peace here means *bonum impunitatis, pacificatio*, reconciliation with God (Rom. 5:9ff.). "The punishment for our sins in Christ brought to us and acquired for us impunity, peace, and reconciliation with God."

More specifically the Scriptures speak first of God's wrath, as that for which atonement was made, for it is the wrath which brings the punishment which is the sinner's due. Rom. 5:9 makes it clear that the suffering and death of Christ are a ransom by which the wrath of God is appeased and by which we are reconciled to God. The fact that Paul says in the next verse that we shall be saved by Christ's life, i.e., His resurrection, should present no difficulty. "Salvation from wrath is attributed to the death of Christ *respectu acquisitionis*, it is referred to the resurrection and life of Christ *respectu manifestationis, applicationis, confirmationis et actualis a peccato absolutionis*" (Thesis 34, β, Obs.). The wrath is eschatological (σωθησόμεθα cf. 1 Thess. 1:10: "from the wrath to come"). Quenstedt quotes Augustine:

"God's wrath is not a disturbance (*perturbatio*) of His mind, but is His righteous decision to punish sin" (*De civitate Dei*, Book XV, c.25).

The next specific *objectum reale pro quo satisfactum* is the curse of the Law. According to Gal. 3:13 and its immediate context we learn that all men are under the Law and obligated to obey it. But because of the sin clinging to us we cannot do this. Therefore we are under the curse (v. 10). But Christ redeemed all who were under this curse (cf. 4:5). The evil from which Christ redeemed us the apostle calls κατάρα τοῦ νόμου. This is much more than only saying that we were redeemed from the Law. The curse of the Law is the sentence of the divine Law, the damning sentence which metes out punishment against sin. This punishment is not only temporal but eternal. It was under such a sentence that we placed ourselves by our violation of God's Law (v. 10). The means by which we were freed from this curse the apostle first mentions in a general way when he says ἐξηγόρασεν. The word means to buy back or redeem, and always denotes an acquisition which is bought with a price (2 Peter 2:1). The prefixed word (ἐξηγόρασεν), which Paul does not ordinarily use in similar contexts, is employed here to indicate the depth of misery from which Christ redeemed us and the firm and complete nature (*soliditas*) of His redemption (cf. Zech. 9:11). The apostle then proceeds to recount more explicitly the means by which we were redeemed from the curse. This he does with the words γεγόμενος ὑπὲρ ἡμῶν κατάρα. The intensity of the noun is brought out by the composite ἐπικατάρατος which immediately follows. He who is cursed is detestable, abominable, hateful, damnable, in the eyes of God. And Christ is not simply called cursed but a curse, which means an outcast (κάθαρμα), *fex*, *excrementum*, destruction, filth, offscouring (1 Cor. 4:13; Gal. 1:8). The noun is used for emphasis, as when we call an infamous person (*scelestus*) wickedness (*scelus*).[5] Christ was made a curse, the curse of all curses descended upon Him. This thought must not be glossed over; just as the Word was made (ἐγένετο) flesh and made (γενόμενον) of a woman, He was truly made (γενόμενος) a curse, and that according to "the judgment of God which is according to truth" (Rom. 2:2). Against all who would take away the force of this statement the words of Chrysostom apply (*Hom. 10 in Joh.*), "When Christ took on flesh for us, He took on the curse for us." The words of Augustine are also pertinent (*Con. Faustum*, 4), "He who denies that Christ was a curse denies also that He died." Here belongs also the reference to 2 Cor. 5:21, where Paul says that Christ became a great sinner. Thus Christ was covered and clothed, as it were,

---

5 Cf. Luther, WA, 40/1, 449: "Non solum igitur fuit Maledictus, sed factus est pro nobis Maledictum. Hoc vere est interpretari apostolice Scripturas. Nam homo sine Spiritu Sancto non potest ita loqui."

with the foulness of all sinners because the Lord laid the iniquity of us all upon Him (Is. 53:6), and consequently He was covered with the misery of divine wrath and curse and abomination against sin, and bore it away. (John 1:29)

The *pro nobis* depends upon Christ being made a curse. *Pro nobis* means not for our benefit but in our place.

> Therefore the curse which we brought down upon ourselves by our transgression of the Law Christ bore and sustained for us by taking our place. That is to say, He paid by His Passion and death all the penalties which were owed by those who transgressed the Law. God imputed our obligations to His Son as to our Surety and Bondsman. On the basis of the Law God required from Him, as the one standing surety for the accused, the due penalties of sin. The Son voluntarily put Himself at the disposal of God the Father Ps. 40:10,11; Heb. 10:7, 9) and in our stead and place made Himself a bondsman on behalf of sinful man and a debtor. He took our cause upon Himself, that is, He undertook to pay all the debts of the world and to expiate all its sins. Thus the curse of the Law was not directed against the one who deserved it, but by an imputation arising from His suretyship against the One who took up our cause, and He truly felt and experienced that divine curse. (Thesis 34, γ, Obs. 3)

Christ was not made a curse in only a verbal or symbolic manner like the beasts of the OT which were merely types, but by implication and direct association, by imputation and involvement (*coniectione imputatione et applicatione*). And Christ was not merely a curse according to our way of thinking, but He was a curse to God. Nor was there anything contingent or fortuitous about this occurrence, but it was according to the determinate counsel of God (Luke 22:22; Acts 2:23). Christ submitted Himself knowingly and willingly (John 13:1; 18:4; Heb. 10:7, 9; 9:14)

We can speak of still another specific *objectum reale pro quo* of Christ's atonement, namely, the power of the devil. Heb. 2:14,15 must here be considered. "Forasmuch then as the children are partakers of flesh and blood, He also Himself likewise took part of the same, that through death He might destroy him that had the power of death, that is, the devil, and deliver them who through fear of death were all their lifetime subject to bondage." Notice first that the power of death is attributed to the devil, not, however, as a lord, but as a lictor and hangman. It is God, the Giver of the Law, who has absolute power over death, but since the entrance of sin into the world He allows the devil to be His hangman. The κατάργησις does not mean an annihilation of the devil but a taking away of his power and tyranny. The κατάργησις will occur most completely when all things are put under Christ's feet (1 Cor. 15:23–28; Rev. 20:14). The means of this victory and destruction is again the death of Christ. Through death He destroys him who had power over death, and this occurs partly by the confusion of Satan, whose machinations fail and bring about his utter disgrace, and partly through the overthrow of his power in that Christ broke the bands of death and hell and opened for us a way of escape (Ps. 68:20), and partly finally by taking the devil captive, restraining his power and allowing him to harm no one belonging to Christ. Notice that the apostle in this passage does not say we are freed from death but from the fear of death. Although Christ has freed us from eternal death, which is the second death, and also from temporal death, which is the result of sin, so that death no more has any claim over us, still there is nothing more dreadful to a sinner than death. By fear of death the apostle means a bad conscience, which knows the just judgment of God and is disturbed by sin. By bondage he means the state of corruption; after the Fall and before regeneration all men are in such a state and are under the devil, they are unable not to sin and do evil and serve the devil. But from such servitude Christ freed us by His Passion and death, and when we become His we can bear not only the fear of temporal death but death itself, for He has suffered it in our place. The ἀπαλλάξη points significantly to the great reconciliation of the human race with God whereby the wrath of God and curse of the Law which we deserved for our sins was endured by another, Christ.

We may speak finally of death and hell as a specific *objectum reale pro quo* of the atonement. Death, both temporal and eternal, is the result of sin (Rom. 6:23). Hos. 13:14 and 1 Cor. 15:54 tells us Christ is the plague of death and the destruction of the grave; thus He ransoms and redeems us from these enemies. Through Christ the destruction of death is effected: it is called κατάποσις, a swallowing up. This victory over death Christ really accomplished by descending into hell and taking captivity captive, being gloriously triumphant over the devil, death, and hell.

5. The personal object of Christ's satisfaction is the entire sinful race (cf. Rom. 5:6; 1 Peter 3:18; 1 John 3:16, where the context indicates that the ὑπέρ means in the place of, denoting a substitution).

According to God's serious and sincere good pleasure, by which He desires all men to be saved, we must say that satisfaction was made for *all* men, not just apparently or according to a particular way of thinking, but really and truly. This important fact is brought out explicitly in many passages from Scripture. Is. 53:6: "All we like sheep have gone astray; we have turned everyone to his own way; and the Lord hath laid on Him the iniquity of us all." The hiphil of פָּגַע, which means to light upon, strike, encounter, denotes that sins have settled down upon the Messiah and like a torrent overwhelmed Him. The context shows that as the whole human race went astray, the sins of the entire race were laid upon the Messiah. Speaking to Matt. 20:28, Quenstedt makes note of the ἀντί, which would indicate that Christ was a victim in our place. The "many" is not to be taken in an exclusive sense for some, but extensively and universally for all (cf. this common Hebraism also in Dan. 12:2 and Rom. 5:19). Quenstedt comments next on Rom. 8:32: "God spared not His own Son, but delivered Him up for us all." God allows the torments and punishment to strike His Son and does not spare Him; He is tortured and crucified for us. But the apostle adds significantly "for us all." Here universal grace is set forth so that every sinner may have the promise of complete satisfaction for all his sins.

The same thought is expressed in 2 Cor. 5:14,15, where it is said in so many words that Christ died for all, meaning clearly that the death of Christ was effective and adequate as a ransom for all sinners. Quenstedt expends great pains showing how the words of this verse teach (1) that Christ's death was a true death; (2) that it was a vicarious death; (3) that it was universal in scope. The clause "then all were dead" will admit no limitation to the universal effect of Christ's death. In passages like this the *finis competens* of Christ's death must always be borne in mind. It is not an absolute death; it is always spoken of in reference to sin, the curse, the world. It is the world which has been reconciled to God, and the Word of reconciliation is to be brought to the whole world. Surely no one would seriously think of restricting the preaching of the Word to only some. The meaning of the verse then is quite simple. When Christ died for sin, it was according to God's reckoning as though the whole world died for sin.

Quenstedt has some interesting comments on Heb. 2:9: "That He [Jesus] by the grace of God should taste death for every man." What is implied when it is said that Christ tasted death? The term γεύεσθαι is employed with death in a number of other passages where the context points without doubt to physical death (Matt. 16:28; Mark 9:1). However, in John 8:52 the γεῦσις θανάτου must be understood as referring to eternal death, or hell. For here the words οὐ μὴ γεύσηται θανάτου εἰς τὸν αἰῶνα can only point to θάνατος αἰώνοις. This is the death which Christ, the Captain of our salvation, tasted: a death corporal and temporal, but spiritual and eternal as well. The death which He endured was, of course, not eternal by virtue of its duration, for that was accidental to eternal death. But in that Christ endured pains of soul and the horror of being forsaken by God, He suffered eternal death and the suffering of hell. A second point to be observed is that Jesus tasted death "for every man." Notice the use of ὑπὲρ παντός, *pro omni*, not ὑπὲρ πάντων, *pro omnibus*: Not just the human race as a whole has been benefited by the death of Christ, but He has tasted the pains of eternal death in the place of each and every sinner. Finally we are to notice that Christ tasted death for each and everyone according to the *grace* of God. Christ's death did not happen out of necessity or because we were deserving of anything from God, much less because there was any guilt associated with His life, but Christ tasted death χάριτι θεοῦ, because God is merciful toward us and wants His Son to die for us.

The ὑπέρ πάντων is brought out also in 1 Tim. 2:6, where Christ, the Mediator between God and men, is called a ransom (ἀντίλυτρον) for all. That the "all" does not mean only the elect is seen from v. 1 of the same chapter, where Paul urges prayers and intercessions to be made for all men (ὑπὲρ πάντων ἀνθρώπων), and again in 4:10, where this Mediator is said to be the "Savior of all men" (cf. also John 4:42; 1 John 4:14), and in the most immediate context of v. 4, which announces the will of God to save all men and to lead them to a knowledge of the truth.

That Christ's vicarious work extends to all the world is brought out again by John 1:29, where the term "Lamb of God" may be understood *analogically* as pointing back to the Passover victim spoken of in Ex. 12:3ff. and elsewhere. The Paschal Lamb was a type of Christ who was to be the Sacrifice for us (1 Cor. 5:7). But the term must also be taken *materially* as the true Lamb which all the Old Testament offerings only prefigured. Therefore the emphatic ὁ ἀμνός, contrasting this Lamb with all the Levitical lambs as the One who the prophets had predicted would come and wash away sin. This is no ordinary lamb, but is the Lamb *of God*, the One appointed by God Himself to be a victim. "Therefore He was the true Lamb of God, the heavenly Lamb, the Lamb who was Himself God, the Lamb who offered Himself to God that He might perfect the saints" (Rom. 3:25). The αἴρων denotes the act of carrying or bearing, the transferal of a burden and as well the bearing of a transferred burden. The burden which Christ carried is sin, and He bore this burden as One guilty of sin (Lev. 5:5), as One taking the burden away from another (Is. 38:17). The burden is the singular ἡ ἁμαρτία, which is the reading in the best ancient MSS. By ἡ ἁμαρτία is not to be understood only original sin (Bellarmine), but everything which can be called sin, all sin collectively. There are many other passages where the singular ἡ ἁμαρτία refers not to original sin, but to specific acts of sin (cf. John 8:46; 15:22, 24; Rom. 3:9, 20). Finally it must be noted in this passage that the term κόσμος means all men and cannot be narrowed to future generations (Socinians) or those who have been chosen for eternal life by some absolute decree (Calvinists).[6]

---

6 Cf. *Canons of the Synod of Dort*, II, viii: fuit enim hoc Dei Patris liberrimum consil-

The last passage taken up by Quenstedt to illustrate that Christ's vicarious atonement extends to the entire world is 1 John 2:1, 2: "And He is the Propitiation for our sins, and not for ours only, but also for the sins of the whole world." The "He," of course, is Christ θεάνθρωπος who in the unity of His natures became our ἱλασμός by suffering and dying and shedding His blood for us and thus destroying the works of the devil and bringing eternal righteousness to us. Of special importance in this verse is the οὐ μόνον, ἀλλά which denotes, according to Quenstedt, an αὔξησις, an intensifying of the meaning. By the οὐ περὶ τῶν ἡμετέρων δε μόνον the apostle is indicating all his readers who believe, all believers at that time, both Jews and Gentiles, for his epistle is catholic and addressed to all. If all believers of all times are included in the first part of the statement, then the contrasting καὶ περὶ ὅλου τοῦ κόσμου of the second half of the verse can only mean the entire human race.

> The apostle contrasts a part with the whole (ὅλος ὁ κόσμος), that is to say, he contrasts himself and other believers with the entire human race; he is not contrasting some believers with other believers, nor does he distinguish between believers in respect to time and place. By the words ὅλου τοῦ κόσμου are understood all men, even those who are lost. Thus the sense of the verse must be this: Christ is the ἱλασμός not only for the sins of believing Christians, but of each and every sinful man and thus also of the damned. For here we have not only the general term κόσμος, which quite often in the Sacred Scriptures embraces men of all ages (Rom. 3:6, 19; 5:12, etc.), but we have added another term of universal connotation ὅλου τοῦ κόσμου, "of the whole world." This is done so that we do not suppose that propitiation has been made only for some, but rather believe that propitiation has been made for all men in the world equally through Christ. (Thesis 36–II, β, Obs. 3)

The basis which establishes the vicarious satisfaction is the value (*pretium*) of the entire obedience of Christ. This obedience includes (a) Christ's perfect obedience of the Law, and (b) His suffering the punishment which was due transgressors. "By *doing* He made compensation for the guilt which man wrongfully incurred, and by *suffering* He bore the punishment which man rightfully was to suffer." Thus we commonly speak of active and passive obedience. Quenstedt proceeds to speak in a more detailed manner of this obedience and its twofold nature:

---

ium, et gratiosissima voluntas atque intentio, ut mortis pretiosissimae Filii sui vivifica et salvifica efficacia sese exereret in omnibus electis, ad eos solos fide iustificante donandos, et per eam ad salutem infallibiliter perducendos. (*Acta Synodi . . . Dodrechti habitae Anno MDCXVIII et MDCXIX* [Leyden: Isaac Elzevir, 1620], p. 251)

Christ made atonement for sinful man in a twofold manner: first, by performing a complete and perfect obedience of the Law in our place and in this way fulfilling the Law; second, by taking upon Himself the punishment and curse of the Law which we had merited by our disobedience and willingly suffering all this. The point is that man not only had to be delivered from the wrath of God, the righteous Judge, but he also had to stand before God with a righteousness which he could not acquire except by the obedience of the Law. Therefore Christ undertook both tasks. He not merely suffered for us, but He also fulfilled the Law in all things, to the end that His fulfilling of the Law and His obedience might be reckoned to us for righteousness. (Thesis 37, n. 1)

Quenstedt then points out that the distinction between active obedience and passive obedience (which he traces back to St. Bernard) is not the most fortunate one. For the passive obedience must not be thought of as excluding the active, but rather including it. In His deepest suffering Christ was active and willing.[7] All three passages chosen by Quenstedt to support his thesis that the basis of the vicarious satisfaction is the obedience of Christ refer to the so-called active obedience. In Quenstedt's polemical section these passages are taken up in proving that Christ perfectly fulfilled the Law in our stead.[8] Quenstedt no doubt feels that he has already discussed sufficiently the Scripture passages dealing with the suffering and death of Christ. The first passage for consideration is Ps. 40:6, where the Messiah speaks, "Thou hast opened Mine ears." This was the common way in which a Hebrew would indicate his willingness to obey the Lord (Ex. 21:6; Deut. 15:17). Thus when the Messiah speaks these words, the meaning is: "Thou, O God, hast brought Me, Thine only-begotten and beloved Son, into Thy continuous service. To this continuous obedience I give Myself as a faithful Servant." The opening of the Messiah's ears denotes a prompt, steadfast, and perfect obedience which the Son of God performed when He took upon Himself the form of a servant and became obedient unto death (Phil. 2:7). It must be noted that Hebrews, ch. 10, verse 5, follows the reading in the LXX in quoting this passage, "A body hast Thou prepared Me σῶμα δὲ κατηρτίσω μοι." There is no difference here between the meaning of David and the New Testament when, quoting the LXX, it substitutes "body" for "ears." The

---

7 Quenstedt's caution here reminds us of Gerhard's words (*Loci theologici* [Tubingae: Sumtibus I. G. Cottae, 1762], VII, 70a): "To separate the active and passive obedience of Christ is to upset and reverse the whole order of things and to substitute for the whole righteousness and obedience of Christ only a certain part of it."

8 *Systema*, Part Three, Cap. III, Membrum II, "De officio Christi," Sec. 2, Quaes. 3.

Hebrew כָּרָה means not only to dig or open but also to prepare by digging and opening and thus to give the means of hearing and obeying. The LXX and the New Testament merely substitute an antecedent action for a consequent one, or a means for an end. The result is that there is this extension of meaning: The Son is to be provided a body in order that His ears may be opened and He may obey the Father in accomplishing our redemption. "Hence the καταρτίζω corresponds beautifully to the verb כָּרָה. For all these things were accomplished at once: The flesh was united with the Logos; at the same time the flesh was enriched by the excellencies of the divine nature; and at the same time also the flesh was appointed to the priestly office." (Thesis 37, *ad* Ps. 40:7)

Citing next Matt. 5:17, Quenstedt remarks that the κατάλυσις, which is placed in opposition to the πλήρωσις, points to more than just a violation and transgression of the Law; it points to an abolishing of the Law. Contrariwise the πλήρωσις is more than a mere explaining of the Law; it is a perfect obedience and conformity of Christ's whole life and of all His actions.[9]

Citing finally Gal. 4:4, 5, Quenstedt points out how the purpose of Christ's being made under the Law was that (ἵνα) He might redeem us. The ἵνα clause shows conclusively that the basis of our redemption was Christ's obedience under the Law.

6. What is the nature of this satisfaction? What precisely takes place? A payment in kind and entirely adequate is made for all that we owed. Put slightly differently, Christ freely took upon Himself our whole debt; God in divine righteousness imputed this debt to Him, and He paid it fully: thus the Messiah says, "I restored that which I took not away" (Ps. 69:4). After a full exegesis of Ps. 69:4 Quenstedt proceeds to emphasize that Christ's payment was entirely in kind and entirely satisfactory. He says:

> This payment of another's debt which was freely undertaken by Christ and imputed to Him according to divine judgment was not sufficient just because God accepted it. God did not, out of liberality, accept something in this satisfaction which was not in itself sufficient. Neither did God by demanding rightfully the punishment due us, a punishment which was taken by our Bondsman (*Sponsor*), relax any of His justice. No, in the satisfaction Christ endured everything which the rigor of God's righteousness demanded, even to the degree that He experienced hellish punishments, although not in hell and not eternally. At the same time there is, of course, here a certain tempering of divine mercy and divine justice and a sort of softening of the Law in this, that

---

9 Cf. p. 405, 1715 ed.

the Son of God Himself took His stand as our Bondsman and Satisfier, that the satisfaction which He brought was accepted, that another Person was put in the place of those who were actually guilty; but this takes away nothing from the satisfaction itself. Hence the satisfaction of Christ is completely sufficient and final in itself by virtue of its own intrinsic, infinite value. This infinite value arises from two facts: 1. the Person making the satisfaction is infinite God, 2. the human nature by means of the personal union was made to share in the divine and infinite majesty, and therefore its suffering and death are regarded as having infinite value and worth as though belonging to the divine nature. (Thesis 39–40)

The last sentence of this statement is so important to a proper delineation of the doctrine of the atonement that Quenstedt feels constrained to repeat briefly what he has already said in great detail in his discussion of the personal union and the second genus of the communication of attributes. He confines himself to a study of one significant Scripture passage, Acts 20:28: Ὁ θεὸς τὴν ἐκκλησίαν περιποιήσατο διὰ τοῦ ἰδίου αἵματος. The subject in this verse, the *causa efficiens* περιποιήσεως *ecclesiae*, is God in the proper and absolute sense of the word, i.e., the one true and infinite God. That the subject is not God the Father (Socinians), but Christ or *Deus* ἔνσαρκος, Quenstedt attempts to prove in the following manner: (a) Scripture indicates that Christ possesses the church equally with the Father. For instance, 1 Cor. 1:2 speaks of "the church of God" as "those who are sanctified in Christ Jesus." Again in 1 Cor. 10:32 we meet the term "church of God," but again Christ is not excluded from the thought, for He is the "Lord" referred to in vv. 26 and 28 and clearly in v. 21 (cf. 1 Cor. 11:23, 32). (b) The reference to God's own blood indicates that Christ must be subject of the clause and that the τοῦ θεοῦ refers to Him. (c) Περιποίησις *ecclesiae* is never attributed in Scripture to the Father or the Holy Spirit but only to Christ (Eph. 1:14; 1 Thess. 5:9; 2 Thess. 2:14). (d) The God who has purchased the church with His own blood is the One who has instituted the ministry according to the context of the verse. This is Christ (Acts 20:24; 1 Cor. 3 :11). The conclusion can only be that Christ, the Son of God, sheds His blood (which of course is a property of His human nature), and that this is an act of God. The *mode* of this transaction of Christ is brought out by the περιποιεῖν, which in Scripture is used to express what takes place in bringing about our redemption (Eph. 1:14; 1 Thess. 5:9). We have here a redemptive transaction (*negotio redemptionis*) which does not imply that something is gotten without a price being paid, but rather that a possession is acquired by the correct payment of a correct price (*interveniente vera veri pretii solutione*), that is, we become

Christ's own by the sufficient doing and suffering of Christ (*satisfactionis et satispassionis Christi negotium*). The περιποίησις is accomplished with God's own blood; therefore it is not a simple acquisition, but an adequate acquisition (*satisfactoria acquisitio*). The object of this περιποίησις is the church, the called of God, whom Paul commends to the care of the bishops and ministers, among whom grievous wolves will enter in, and out of whom false teachers shall arise. The context indicates that Paul refers to the church here not as the elect, but as the called, as the visible body which contains hypocrites along with the believers. The means of the περιποίησις is God's blood. It is called God's "own blood" not because it is natural to the Son of God, but because it is His personal blood.

7. On the part of God there are two purposes for the vicarious atonement. First, His divine justice must be satisfied, for God is not willing to remit sins without satisfaction being made. Quenstedt insists that this contention is not his personal conjecture, but is based solidly on what Paul says in Rom. 3:24–26. The δωρεάν here does not rule out a price paid (cf. Matt. 10:8; 2 Cor. 11:7), but human work-righteousness and merit. The *causa finalis* of Christ's work here is ἔνδειξις τῆς δικαιοσύνης αὐτοῦ (v. 25). The δικαιοσύνη in this verse is to be taken as *iustitia* διανεμητική *et* ἀνταποδοτική, a righteousness which rewards or requites, not viewed according to the rigor of God's justice only, but as an evangelical, equitable righteousness (ἐπιείκεια *evangelica*). This righteousness is a modulation of righteousness and mercy. Thus God punishes the sins of others in His Son, who was made a bondsman for sinners.

> The ἔνδειξις of God's righteousness consists in this, that the sins of the entire world were heaped upon Christ by a fair and equitable transferal, and these sins were punished in Him, although He was in Himself free of all sin. Paul points to this purpose [of the satisfaction] when he says in v. 26, "that He might be just," that is, that God might be recognized to be just in punishing with all severity the sins of the human race in His Son, the Mediator, and in not remitting sins except by means of and because of the bloody redemption of Christ and through faith in Him. (Thesis 41, *ad.* Rom. 3:24–26, Obs.)

The second purpose of the vicarious atonement on God's part is to show forth the mercy which He has toward our fallen race. And how more clearly could He show His love for us than by sending His own Son to be our Substitute (Rom. 5:8; John 3:16; 15:13; Eph. 5:25; 1 John 3:16)? Commenting on the meaning of the ἀγάπη in these verses, Quenstedt has these touching words to say:

> This is the love of God: rather than banish men eternally from heaven, He removed Himself from heaven, clothed Himself with flesh, became

a Creature of a creature, enclosed Himself in the womb of the virgin, was wrapped in rags, laid in hay, and housed in a barn. Nor does His love stop at this point; but after a life spent in poverty and adversities this love drove Christ to the ground on Olivet, bound Him in chains, delivered Him to jailers, cut Him with the lash, crowned Him with thorns, fastened Him with nails to the cross, and gave Him to drink the cup of bitterness. And finally this love compelled Him to die, to die for adversaries and enemies (Rom. 5:6). Continuously and in these sundry ways Jesus, who thirsted so greatly for our salvation, declared His love and mercy toward the human race. (Thesis 41, *ad*. Rom. 5:8, Obs. 1)

The purpose of the vicarious atonement so far as we are concerned (*ex parte nostri*) is that we might have the perfect righteousness of Christ and be saved eternally. Here the first passage to be considered is Dan. 9:24: "Seventy weeks are determined upon thy people and upon thy holy city, to finish the transgression, and to make an end of sins, and to make reconciliation for iniquity, and to bring in everlasting righteousness, and to seal up the vision and prophecy, and to anoint the Most Holy." The angel is commemorating for Daniel the results and fruits of the vicarious suffering and death of the Messiah. The *first* result is the restraining of transgression, which in Hebrew denotes a malicious and persistent rebellion against the holy God. Significantly the verb used here means to subdue, hold back, restrain. Thus this restraining of transgression is like the imprisoning and subduing of a savage and unmanageable beast. This has been accomplished by the Messiah, lest any further trouble come upon our poor human race. Luther has correctly rendered the passage: *der Suende wird gewehret werden*. The *second* result is the sealing up of sins. Here the Hebrew word חַטָּאות denotes every aberration from the standard of the Law, whether voluntary or involuntary, whether a sin of omission or commission. There is a variant reading of the verb in this strophe. The LXX and Luther seem to have followed a reading which would denote a sealing up of sin, thus a removal of sin from God's sight by an act of closing it off. The Vulgate and Aquila must have read וּלְהָתֵם, for they render the Hebrew by *finem accipiet* and τοῦ τελειῶσαι τὴν ἁμαρτίαν respectively. In this case the sense would be that an end is made of sins—not that they are no more, but that they are not imputed to those who embrace the merits of Christ. The *third* result is reconciliation, or the expiation of iniquity. In this verse עָוֹן means the offscouring of the sins of the whole human race, the results of sin. לְכַפֵּר, which means to propitiate sacrificially, points to the erasing and wiping out of our iniquity. In the Old Testament the blood of the sacrificial beast (which was a type) propitiated for sin, and sin no longer remained in God's judgment. The sacrificial animal was looked upon as the one to which sin and guilt attached. In the same manner the Messiah makes a propitiation or ἱλασμός; within 70 weeks He makes a propitiation by offering Himself as a victim (Eph. 5:2). The *fourth* result, according to this verse, is the bringing or restoring of everlasting righteousness (cf. Jer. 23:5, 6; 33:15, 16, where the Messiah is called "a righteous Branch" and "the Lord, our Righteousness"). Through Adam the original righteousness of man was lost (Eph. 4:24). The "everlasting righteousness" (*iustitia seculorum*) in the text is that original, primeval righteousness. Now it is promised that this righteousness shall be restored. The Messiah will come with His perfect active and passive obedience, which will be imputed to believers. The Messiah will atone for sin, suffer our punishment, and render perfect obedience to the Law, not for His own sake, but for others (cf. v. 26). Thus it is not the righteousness of our works that is spoken of here; such a righteousness is only momentary and transitory and does not avail before God. It is rather צֶדֶק עֹלָמִים, not restricted to a certain time; it is the righteousness of faith (Rom. 4:11), a righteousness of infinite worth. The righteousness is called eternal because God from eternity decreed that this righteousness would avail before Him and be imputed to faith. It is called eternal righteousness also because of the Person who acquired it, a Person who is eternal and therefore performed in time an eternal and infinite righteousness. Finally it is called eternal because the fruits of this righteousness remain to all eternity.

The second passage which brings out the results of Christ's atonement *ex parte nostri* is 2 Cor. 5:21. Quenstedt is most thorough in dealing with this *sedes doctrinae*. The subject of the verse is ὁ μὴ γνοὺς ἁμαρτίαν, viz., Christ (cf. v. 20). When Christ is said to know no sin, this is no reference to His divine omniscience (cf. 1 John 3:20), or to some sort of *negatio notitiae* on his part, but the reference is to His deeds (like the τὸ μὴ ποιῆσαι ἁμαρτίαν in 1 Peter 2:22 and Is. 53:9). Christ did no sin and was removed from any inclination toward and possibility of sin. In Him was only simple holiness and righteousness. The apostle speaks of the holiness and sinlessness of Christ according to His human nature to bring out the fact that according to that nature Christ was made the subject of sin by imputation and was made a victim for sin. The explanation for the sinlessness of Christ is the personal union which we observe mentioned in v. 19, "God was in Christ, reconciling the world unto Himself." This "being in Christ" is not of the same kind as when God is said to be present in believers; rather it is the fullness of the Godhead dwelling in Christ (Col. 2:9); it is the divine nature and infinite essence of the Logos united with the flesh in the person of Christ. Thus in this union the human nature cannot be touched by sin.

Three things are predicated in this verse: (1) Christ is made to be sin by God, (2) He is made to be sin for us, (3) He is made to be sin that we might be made the righteousness of God. The term "sin" has several significations: it may denote the results or punishments for sin (Gen. 19:15), or it may denote the victim or sacrifice for sin (Hos. 4:8; Lev. 4:3; Ps. 40:6). Both of these meanings must be understood in the present context. Some (Socinians) have said that the verse means only that Christ was found among sinners, as Isaiah says, "He was numbered with the transgressors." But the term ποιεῖν ἁμαρτίαν is never found with such a meaning in Scripture. And the verse clearly says that Christ was sin according to the reckoning of God. "Hence Christ will be that very thing which God makes Him to be, that is to say, He will be a true sinner by a true and most real imputation. Nay, He will be the greatest of all sinners under the sun, as the abstract noun used here wishes to emphasize." The abstract is often used for the concrete or the substantive for the adjective, and this for the sake of emphasis (Gen. 3:6; 12:2, etc.). Thus when God made Christ sin, the meaning is that He made Him a sinner, the greatest of all sinners. The verb ποιεῖν is used to denote a divine imputation (cf. Rom. 2:25, 26). The making is an imputation and does not imply that there was any sin actually dwelling inherently in Christ. The ὑπὲρ ἡμῶν expresses substitution. "It is clear that Christ was made to be a sinner by imputation that He might be a substitute and representative in the place of our human race, although in His person He was and would always be utterly holy." Finally this text says that Christ was made sin that we might become the righteousness of God. The δικαιοσύνη θεοῦ is not the original or essential righteousness of God. It is indeed a righteousness which is foreign to us (*ex parte nostra aliena*), not inherent, but imputed to us by a merciful God. It is opposed to any righteousness which we work out for ourselves (cf. Rom. 10:3 and Phil. 3:9). The ἐν αὐτῷ tells us the nature of this righteousness. It is the righteousness of Christ acquired in His life and death, a righteousness which becomes ours through faith.

> Here we have a most precious exchange taking place: Christ takes to Himself our sin that He might give to us His righteousness. He who in Himself is completely holy and inherently righteous has been made sin by the imputation of our sins. In like manner we who in ourselves are sinners and inherently unrighteous are made to be the righteousness of God, that is, we are made perfectly righteous before God by the imputation of Christ's righteousness. (Thesis 42, β, Obs. 2)

The third passage chosen by Quenstedt to express the fruits of Christ's satisfaction is Heb. 9:11, 12. Here an eternal redemption is spoken of, eternal in the absolute sense. This redemption acquired by Christ is eternal in God's just reckoning because it was considered by the Father from eternity and into eternity and because it is eternally valid in that it frees us from eternal death and acquires for us an eternal inheritance. It is said that Christ by His own blood "found" this eternal redemption for us. This redemption was something no one else could "find." That Christ found this redemption means that He alone is its Author. And He found it only with much care and labor. The εὐράμενος expresses not only the idea that Christ laboriously worked out our redemption but also a judicial thought (cf. the use of the verb in Gal. 2:17; 2 Cor. 5:3; Acts 13:28). Thus the forensic idea is coupled with the image of redemption.

Another Bible passage bringing out the fruits of the vicarious satisfaction is Heb. 5:8, 9: "Though He were a Son, yet learned He obedience by the things which He suffered; and being made perfect, He became the Author of eternal salvation unto all them that obey Him." The learning which is here spoken of does not refer to a gradual comprehending of teaching and facts (doctrinae perceptio) but to a knowledge which is acquired by experience (experimentalis notitia). By experience Christ understood (cognovit) and became well acquainted with the difficulty of obeying God, the difficulty of suffering the crucifixion and actually dying the shameful death of the cross. He endured His Passion out of obedience, and therefore that suffering pressed Him all the more. The obedience is to be understood in the broad sense as having its beginning with the κένωσις and the λῆμψις μορφὴν δούλου and as being accomplished in all the deeds and in all the sufferings of Christ until the last moment of His exinanition. The τελείωσις points to the perfect rendering of Christ's priestly work. A perfect sacrifice has been offered by this Priest. A perfect absolution has been acquired for all people. He is therefore said to have been made the cause (αἴτιος) of an eternal salvation to all who obey Him. Christ is called a cause of an eternal salvation by virtue of His execution and fulfillment of a duty given Him in the eternal counsel of the Godhead (Rom. 16:25; Eph. 3:9; Col. 1:26; 2 Tim. 1:9). The force of the αἴτιος must not be minimized (cf. Heb. 2:10). Christ is not merely a means (causa media) whereby we are saved; He is the Source (causa principalis) of our salvation; not merely the minister but also the Author and Lord of our salvation; He has merited salvation, and He gives it us. "Therefore the fruit of Christ's suffering and obedience is our eternal salvation, for by His obedience unto the death of the cross He not only merited eternal salvation for us but also imparts it to believers." (Thesis 42, δ, Obs. 3)

8. The vicarious atonement begins at the moment of Christ's exinanition and terminates with His death. Every act of Christ from the moment of His conception to His death was substitutionary. That He was in the

womb nine months, that He was born in poverty, that He endured throughout His life misery, hunger, thirst, cold, etc.—all this He endured for our sakes and in our place.

9. Quenstedt concludes his discussion of the vicarious atonement with a final definition of satisfaction:

> Satisfaction is an act of the priestly office of Christ, the God-man. From an eternal decree of the Triune God and for the sake of His great mercy Christ gladly and willingly substituted Himself as the Surety and Bondsman for the entire human race, which had been cast into unspeakable misery through sin. By taking upon Himself each and every sin of the whole world, by His most perfect obedience, and by His suffering of the punishments which men had merited He satisfied the Holy Trinity, who had been grievously offended, and that through the whole time of His exinanition on earth and especially in His last agony. By thus making satisfaction He procured and merited for each and every man remission of all sins, exemption from all punishments of sin, grace and peace with God, eternal righteousness and salvation. (Thesis 44)

The purpose of this article has been to review the doctrine of the vicarious atonement as formulated in Lutheran Orthodoxy. The study has shown us not only that the Lutheran theologians of this era have left us a mass of useful terminology in this area but it has also demonstrated that they present a well-balanced and most timely Scriptural account of the whole doctrine.

The Doctrine of Justification in the Theology of Classical Lutheran Orthodoxy

> "The Doctrine of Justification in the Theology of Classical Lutheran Orthodoxy" is a brief but systematic synthesis of the thinking of the Lutheran fathers on the central article of faith. Citing Martin Chemnitz, Balthasar Mentzer, Abraham Calov, John Quenstedt, Johann Gerhard, Sebastian Schmidt, Jesper Brochmand, Martin Luther, and others, Preus presents the consistent orthodox Lutheran view and in the process provides a handy outline of the church's doctrine. It was published by *The Spingfielder* in 1965. (Permission has been granted for reproduction in this collection.)

THE PURPOSE OF THIS ARTICLE is not to present the classical Lutheran doctrine of justification *in toto*. Even to summarize what such theological giants as Chemnitz, Hutter, Brochmand, Gerhard and Quenstedt have said on the central theme of the Gospel would be quite impossible in a brief article. During the period of orthodoxy which prevailed for nearly a century and a half (ca. 1580–1715) no other article of faith was given such thorough treatment as the locus on justification. Not only did dogmaticians like Chemnitz and Gerhard and Calov devote hundreds of pages in their dogmatics to the doctrine, but immense monographs were written on the theme (H. Hoepfner) and vast commentaries were written primarily to present the article of justification in all its depth and breadth (Gerhard, Seb. Schmidt, Calov, Balduin, Brochmand).

The aim of this paper is rather threefold: (1) to trace some of the more significant emphases in the orthodox Lutheran doctrine of justification, (2) to compare these emphases with Luther's doctrine, and (3) to examine whether the post-Reformation presentation of the doctrine is relevant in the light of contemporary issues. These three purposes shall be carried out concurrently as we consider what I believe to be the three main features of the doctrine of justification as taught by the orthodox Lutheran theologians of the sixteenth and seventeenth centuries.

I. THE CENTRALITY OF JUSTIFICATION

No other article of faith is developed by orthodox Lutheran theology with such conscious dependence upon Luther as the article on justification. One can read pages in the works of the orthodox Lutherans on the doctrine of God or Christology without finding a reference to Luther. On the Sacraments and the doctrine of the Church more dependence upon Luther is noticeable. The doctrine of Justification, however, is often little more than a paraphrase of what Luther had said. Indeed, a major criticism of the dogmatics from Chemnitz to Hollaz might center in the almost total lack of originality in developing the doctrine of justification—that is, if we considered any advance from the presentation of Luther necessary. Perhaps the most notable contribution which begins with Chemnitz is the systemization which takes shape; and by the time of Gerhard and Quenstedt we observe the doctrine being presented according to a neat outline: viz., the meaning of justification, the subject of justification (man), the author of justification (God), the meritorious cause (Christ's work), the means, the *organon leptikon*, the nature of justification, etc. But there is nothing new in all this. Another new feature is the increased use of scholastic terminology which we today would consider of doubtful value and which we have long since abandoned. Such terminology was a sort of theological short hand in the seventeenth century (although it seldom lent itself to brevity), a technical language which was thoroughly known and used by Roman Catholic, Reformed and Lutheran theologians alike. Scholastic terminology served as a medium of scholarly communication in those days, like the Latin language, and the Lutherans were compelled to employ it in the interest of interconfessional dialogue, just as we are forced to use a good deal of Kantian and Existentialist jargon today. In respect to the doctrine of justification, a minimum of scholastic terminology was used by Lutheran theologians, adhering very closely to Luther's and Melanchthon's terminology, especially to the forensic imagery. The reason for this was that as Chemnitz and the later dogmaticians rejected the medieval doctrine of justification, they were compelled to abandon as well the scholastic terminology which conveyed this doctrine.

Following Luther, Lutheran orthodoxy makes the article of justification the *articulus stantis et cadentis ecclesiae*. In this they are not merely repeating a cliche. The insistence upon the centrality of justification does not result from a mere adherence to party spirit or an inability to see beyond the polemics of the day. It was the earnest conviction of Lutheran theology that justification was a summation of the result of Christ's work, a paraphrase of the Gospel itself. It is highly significant that Chemnitz begins his treatment of the locus on justification with a thorough discussion of Law and Gospel and of the grace of God.[1] And Gerhard subsumes his entire lengthy treatment of the work of Christ under the locus on justification. For justification is meaningless without an understanding of the distinction between Law and Gospel; and justification is impossible without its basis in the obedience of Christ. The point is that justification is not considered to be a narrow Pauline or "Lutheran" formulation, but it is a doctrine embracing the entire Gospel, a summation of the entire doctrine of Christ's work, His obedience under the Law, His suffering for our sins, His resurrection for our justification and His lordship over His Church. This is why the article of justification assumes such immense significance in Lutheran theology, why nothing pertaining to this article must by yielded "even if heaven and earth and all things should sink into ruin." "Everything," says Calov, "which we teach, witness and urge against pope, devil and the whole world in this life is centered and set forth in this one article."[2] Calov is only echoing what Luther and Chemnitz said before Him. We recall the statement of Luther's:

> This doctrine [of justification] can never be urged and taught enough. If this doctrine is overthrown or disappears, then all knowledge of the truth is lost at the same time. If this doctrine flourishes, then all good things flourish, religion, true worship, the glory of God and the right knowledge of all conditions of life and of all things.[3]

Chemnitz goes into even greater detail to express his conviction that justification is the central, focal point of the Gospel and of all theology. He says,

> This teaching is the most important in our Christian doctrine. For anxious and frightened minds which struggle under sin and the wrath of God seek this one gate through which they might have a God who is pacified and propitiated.

---

1 *Loci Theologici*. 1653 ed. II, 200ff.

2 *Synopsis Controversiarum*. Wittebergae, 1653. p. 18. Cf. Smalkald Articles II, I, 5.6

3 Er. Lat. 21,12.

In times of temptation and trouble one can only lean on this, that God who condemns sin will nevertheless receive the poor sinner in grace. There is nothing left the poor sinner to depend on.[4] Chemnitz is not indulging in rhetoric, but speaking in all seriousness. To him all theology is practical, and the heart of all Christian theology is the word concerning our justification before God:

> This locus contains the sum of the Gospel. For it indicates the benefit which we derive from Christ, and offers immovable consolation to pious souls; it teaches which are the proper ways of worshipping God, what it means truly to call upon Him; and it sets the Church of God apart from other peoples, Jews, Mohammedans, and Pelagians, that is, from all who imagine that a man is righteous by the Law or by outward discipline and who bid us doubt concerning the remission of sins.[5]

Not only are pious souls comforted, but the Gospel and all theology is preserved when the one article of justification is kept pure. We notice the sense of urgency and the optimism also in another of his statements:

> This article is in a sense the stronghold and the high fortress of all the doctrine and of the entire Christian religion; if it is obscured or adulterated or set aside, the purity of doctrine in other articles of faith cannot possibly be maintained. but if this article is kept pure, all idolatry, superstitions, and whatever corruptions there are in other articles of faith tumble down of their own weight.[6]

From the above it is clear that to Lutheran orthodoxy, as to Luther himself, justification is not merely "*an* image present in the earliest Christian tradition," one image among others "used to set forth the significance of God's deed in Christ." But justification is God's inspired account of the result of the saving act of Christ; it is a description of what really takes place when a sinner comes to faith in Christ. It is more than a mere image or metaphor which may be discarded if modern man finds it irrelevant. But as a matter of fact our justification before God is never irrelevant; we have God's Word for this.

But did not Lutheran orthodoxy, like Luther, with the emphasis upon the justification theme in Scripture, see "the message of the Bible in unitary and almost monolithic terms," as the study document prepared for the LWF assembly in Helsinki implies?[7] I think it would be difficult to find

---

4 *Examen Concilii Tridentini*, Berolini, 1861. p. 146ff.

5 *Loci Theologici*, II, 215.

6 *Ibid*. II, 200).

7 *Christ Yesterday Today Forever*, par. 4.

one motif in Scripture dealing with the work of Christ (reconciliation, redemption, forgiveness, propitiation, victory, etc.) which is not given thorough attention in the Lutheran dogmatics of the sixteenth and seventeenth centuries. The orthodox theologians recognized that these themes are all interpretations of Christ's one saving work. And they included all these themes under the concept of justification in their discussions of the doctrine. Like Scripture and the Lutheran Confessions, they used such terms as "justification," "forgiveness" and "reconciliation" promiscuously and interchangeably. Thus, when they spoke of justification as the *articulus stantis et cadentis ecclesiae*, they had in mind justification in the wider sense including both its basis (Christ's work) and its effects (*unio mystica*, sonship, peace of conscience, sanctification and eternal life). They were, of course, aware that the term "justification" was not even found in many books of the New Testament and that the Gospel could be proclaimed without any allusion to the term. Indeed, they never "considered the doctrine of justification by faith" a fundamental article of faith.[8] The centrality of justification in the theology of Lutheran orthodoxy is not an example of "the way controversy shapes and warps theological thinking." For classical Lutheran theology the centrality of justification means the centrality of the Gospel, the centrality of Christ crucified in the theology and the proclamation of the Church.

II. FORENSIC JUSTIFICATION AND THE *Justitia Aliena*

The results of theological controversy are both good and bad. Sometimes it warps theological thinking and drives one into untenable positions. At other times it forces the theologian to clarify his thinking and to search the Scriptures anew. The latter was the case as a new generation of Lutherans, beginning with Chemnitz, sought to defend Luther's doctrine of justification and to reply to the charges and condemnations of the Council of Trent and its apologists (Andrada and Hosius) and a throng of later able controversialists such as Bellarmine, Adam Tanner, Jacob Gretzer and others.

According to the Lutheran theologians the entire controversy with the Church of Rome hinged on one crucial issue, viz., the nature of justification. What does it mean to stand justified before God? A typical definition of justification was offered by B. Mentzer, and we might examine his words carefully.

---

8 Baier, *Compendium Theologiae Positivae*, prol. I,33. Hollaz, *Examen Theologiam Acroamaticum*. Prol. II, q. 19–24.

Justification is an act of God the Father, Son and Holy Spirit, an act which forgives the sinner all his sins, imputes to him the righteousness of Christ and receives him into everlasting life. It is an act of pure grace, love and mercy, performed because of the most holy obedience which our Mediator Christ rendered to the entire divine Law and because of the full satisfaction He made. The sinner is justified who through the ministry of the Gospel truly believes that Christ is the Redeemer of the whole world, and he is justified by grace without his own work or merits.[9]

Apart from the emphasis upon the divine monergism of grace, we notice the forensic imagery which dominates the description of justification. Justification is an act of judgment of God which entails a verdict of acquittal and an imputation of Christ's obedience to God's Law. About this time of Mentzer and Gerhard justification came to be commonly defined in Lutheran circles as embracing formally (1) the forgiveness or non-imputation of sins and (2) the imputation and gift of Christ's righteousness (obedience). The forensic picture is portrayed even more graphically as Mentzer goes on to speak of the basis of our justification in Christ:

The basis which merits our justification is Jesus Christ the God-man who in both of His natures is the one Mediator and Redeemer of the entire human race. Although He was Lord over the Law, for our sake He was made under the Law to redeem those who were under the Law, that we might receive the adoption of children (Gal. 4:4.5). He not only observed the whole divine Law, but fulfilled it completely and exactly (Matt. 5:17.18). Thus He is called the end (telos) and the perfection of the Law (Rom. 10:4). But He also sustained the punishment which we deserved by our sins, He suffered and died in our place, as the whole Gospel history abundantly testifies. This entire obedience of His, both in what He did and what He suffered (which is commonly termed active and passive obedience), is called the righteousness of Christ, i.e. the righteousness which avails before God, and the righteousness of the Gospel, i.e. the righteousness which is revealed in the Gospel, and the righteousness of faith, i.e. the righteousness which is apprehended by faith and counted for righteousness to us who believe.[10]

Again we see how the legal and nomistic nature of Christ's work of redemption (His obedience, His being punished by the Law, etc.) informs the article of justification. We can easily understand how Chemnitz and Gerhard could consider the work of Christ under the locus on justification:

9 Mentzer, B. *Exegesis Augustanae Confessionis.* (*Opera Latina. Francofurti*, 1669. I,60).
10 *Ibid.*

Christ is the heart and center of the doctrine of justification, just as He is the heart of the Gospel.

The emphasis upon the forensic nature of justification springs not merely from a loyalty to Luther, who unabatedly stressed the doctrine of imputed righteousness. The Lutheran dogmaticians were fully persuaded that they were presenting the doctrine of Scripture. Schrenk in Kittel's Woerterbuch has made no more intensive a study of the term *dikaioō* and its cognates than did Chemnitz, for instance, in his *Loci Theologici* and his *Examen Concilii Tridentini*. And the two come to the same conclusion: the entire New Testament is haunted by the forensic image. The term *dikaioō* is never used in the New Testament to denote a qualitative change in man, but as a judicial act of God. This is shown from the fact that the term is so often found in a judicial setting, as in Rom. 3, 5 and 8, and is shown from neutral evidence (Lk. 7:29; 10:29; 16:15; 7:35; 1 Tim. 3:16). That forgiveness of sins is used interchangeably with justification indicates to Chemnitz that forgiveness too is a forensic concept. The forensic nature of justification is brought out unmistakably in Rom. 4 where righteousness is said to be imputed without works (v. 8), and faith, not works, is reckoned for righteousness (v. 5). Justification is often contrasted to the forensic term "condemnation" in Scripture (Rom. 5:18; 8:33.34; John 5:24). And Chemnitz points out that not only the *dikaioi katastathēsontai hoi polloi* of Rom. 5:19 is forensic phraseology, but even the terminology of binding and loosing sin is judicial terminology (John 20:23). The forensic picture is found, actually, throughout the Bible (Gen. 44:16 [Cf. LXX]; 2 Sam. 15:4; Isa. 43:9; Ps. 51:4; Deut. 25:1; Prov. 17:15; Isa. 5:23; Matt. 12:37; Ps. 19:9; 143:2; Dan. 8:14; Job 13:18; 34:5; 33:9–12,32; 32:2).

The conclusion to which such evidence leads is that in justification God reckons the ungodly to be righteous—and this is done forensically, legally, not arbitrarily, capriciously or without a cost, as Luther would say.[11] In other words, God is just when He justified the sinner (Rom. 3:26). We might quote Chemnitz at length on this important point:

> The forensic term indicates that the justification of the sinner is not something trifling or perfunctory; but the whole man stands in the

---

11 *WA* 103, 161–2: "I have often said before that faith in God is not enough; but there must also be a cost. And what is the cost? For the Jews and Turks believe too, but without means or cost. The Gospel shows us what the cost is. For the Holy Spirit teaches there that we do not have the Father without means and we cannot go to the Father without means. Here Christ teaches us that we are not lost, but have eternal life, that is, that God loved us so much that He willed to pay the cost of thrusting His own dear Son into our misery, hell and death and to have Him drink that up. That is the way we are saved." Cf. Chemnitz, *Loci Theologici*, II, 234 who is alluding to Luther.

presence of God's judgment, and he is examined according to his nature and his works—and that by the rule of divine Law. However, after sin entered the world, man in this life does not truly and completely conform to the Law of God. Thus nothing can be found in man, either in his nature or his works, which he can offer so that he might be justified before God. Rather the Law pronounces the sentence of condemnation upon him, a sentence written with the finger of God. Now God does not justify the ungodly through some error, like a judge who passes a verdict when he has not examined or acquainted himself sufficiently with a case. Nor does God justify the ungodly carelessly, as though He were not really disturbed over the transgression of His Law. Nor does He justify in an unfair manner, as though He approved of injustice and connived and colluded with the ungodly. God Himself would adjudge such a justification to be an abomination (Ex. 23:1; Isa. 5:23; Prov. 17:15). No, God cannot take back His decision of condemnation which is revealed in the Law unless He has been given satisfaction (Matt. 5:18). If God is to justify, justice and satisfaction are required. Luther correctly said, God remits no sin unless satisfaction has been rendered for it to the Law. . . . And so because God does not justify out of fickleness or carelessness or mistakenness or injustice and because nothing can be found in man by which He can be justified by God—and yet the righteousness of the Law must be fulfilled in the one to be justified (Rom. 8:4)—it is necessary that a foreign righteousness intervene. This foreign righteousness is such that the payment of guilt and the complete obedience of the Law satisfied divine wrath. And the result is that there can be a propitiation for the sins of the whole world. To this righteousness the sinner, terrified and condemned by the voice of the Law, flees with true faith. He desires, implores and seizes this righteousness. To this righteousness he surrenders himself. This righteousness he sets against the judgment of God and the accusation of the Law. And by virtue of this righteousness and its being imputed to him he is justified, that is, absolved from the sweeping sentence of condemnation, and he receives the decree of life eternal.[12]

What a beautiful and comforting statement this is. Here again we notice how important the vicarious atonement of Christ is to the Lutheran doctrine of justification. Christ's work is not merely a remote meritorious cause which makes justification a possibility, as in Roman theology,[13] but a part of the very form of justification. Christ's obedience of life and death,

---

12 *Ibid*. Cf. also *Examen Concilii Tridentini*, p. 160.

13 Trent. Sess. 6, C.7. Especially Canon 10: "Si quis dixerit, homines sine Christi justitia, per quam nobis meruit, justificari, aut per eam ipsam formaliter justos esse: anathema sit."

His righteousness which alone avails before God, becomes mine, is imputed and transferred to me. This is the heart of the doctrine of justification, the heart and core of the Gospel.

It was upon the idea of imputation that Rome's chief criticism of the Lutheran doctrine of justification was centered. A justification by imputation, according to Roman theology, was merely relational and not ontological. And a relation without an ontological foundation was a fiction and a fantasy. There must be a basis for justification in us, or there can be no righteous imputation. Chemnitz replies that God does not wish to justify anyone unjustly or without an adequate basis. Satisfaction must be made for sins. It is just that the foundation for our justification is not in us believers, but in Christ the Mediator, who obeyed the Law of God and carried away our sins. "Thus, we have a true verdict," says Chemnitz, "and its foundation is in the obedience and redemption of Christ." There is nothing fictitious about the forgiveness of sins or the imputation of Christ's righteousness in classical Lutheran theology. In justification our sins "which are in us and not in Christ" are actually transferred to Christ according to God's decree and determination, and Christ's righteousness is actually transferred to us (*justitia Christi, quae est in Christo et non in nobis, Dei decreto et aestimatione transfertur ad nos.*).[14] Justification means that "he who is justified was not previously righteous, but becomes [*fieri*] righteous."[15] Justification does not happen in another life, but now; it happens once and for all here and in this life (*hic et in hac vita*). We are justified by faith which we have now. The publican went to his house justified. Justification never takes place apart from men in the counsels of God's heaven.[16]

The reality and the greatness of our justification, of the forgiveness of sins and the imputation of Christ's righteousness to us, cannot be over emphasized. Speaking against the accusation that the Lutheran doctrine makes justification a legal fiction, Quenstedt says:

> The imputation consists in a real reckoning. According to the judgment of God the sinner who believes in Christ is absolved of sins and the righteousness of Christ is truly reckoned to him. True, this reckoning does not result in the righteousness of Christ existing inherently in the believer; but the imputation is not, nevertheless, thereby fictitious and imaginary, a mere opinion of a just person, without any actual effect, as the papists maliciously report us as teaching. No, this *imputatio* or imputation is earnest and real. It has its gracious founda-

---

14 Quenstedt, *Systema*. P. III, C.7, P.1, Th. 13 (III, 522).

15 Calov, *Socinismus Profligatus*, p. 735.

16 *Loc. cit.*, p. 743.

tion in Christ and its termination in us [*ad nos*]. It consists in a gracious determination of God and in a real conferring and transferring of Christ's righteousness to the believer. And so when one believes, he is by this imputation made and accounted righteous in the judgment of God's mind. And this is a most real judgment of God which from the throne of His grace extends over the sinner who from the Gospel believes in Christ.[17]

With these words Quenstedt shows himself a true disciple of Luther who staked everything on the truth and validity of God's verdict over the lost sinner who believes, the truth and reality of God's imputation. "This imputation," Luther said, "is not a thing of no consequence, but is greater than the whole world, yea, than all the holy angels. Reason cannot see all this, for reason disregards the Word of God; but we (I say) thank God that we have such a Savior who is able to pass us by and reckon our sin as nothing."[18]

In my opinion the most disappointing feature of the LWF study document on justification is the absence of all reference to the forensic nature of justification and to its basis in the *Christus pro nobis*, to the *justitia aliena* and the *justitia imputata*, all of which was so central and crucial to Luther and the Lutheran Confessions and classical Lutheran orthodoxy. The doctrine of forensic justification is more than a convenient safeguard against Romanism with its doctrine of work righteousness and uncertainty; it is the account of how God actually deals with the lost sinner who, crushed by the Law and despairing of himself, turns to Jesus, the friend and Savior of sinners. The Church cannot afford to ignore this great fact today any more than in Luther's day.

III. Justification by Faith

In the matter of justification by faith Lutheran orthodoxy again makes a concerted effort to be faithful to the legacy of Luther. We can and need not summarize all that was said on this crucial issue. There are, however, I believe, in connection with the doctrine of justification by faith a number of points which are given great emphasis by all the orthodox Lutherans. To mention and discuss briefly these points may serve to give a good resumè of their position and concerns.

---

17 *Systema*, P. III, C. 7, P. 1, Th. 19 (III, 525).

18 *Die Disputation de Justificatione* (1536). *WA* 39, 97–98. Elert (*The Structure of Lutheranism*, Saint Louis, 1962, p. 74ff.) shows that the imputation and "juridical" character of justification were fundamental for Luther as for Paul. The same must be said of Lutheran orthodoxy.

A. THE ORDER OF JUSTIFICATION

The order (*ordo*) which God uses in preparing the sinner and bringing him to forgiveness and justification is set forth in very clear and simple terms. It is structured on the Biblical idea of repentance. According to Chemnitz[19] there must first be contrition; that is to say, before there can be justification one must come to a real knowledge of his sin and must experience terrors of conscience when he knows God's wrath against sin. This point is stressed by all the orthodox Lutherans as it was by Luther and Melanchthon. And it is the *contritio passiva*, emphasized by Luther and the confessions, that they are speaking of, i.e. flight from God, "terrors in the conscience aroused by the knowledge of sin."[20] But then "to these terrors," Chemnitz says, "must be added faith. With its knowledge and trust in the promised mercy of God faith takes courage because of God's Son and gives comfort to the soul. Otherwise we become overwhelmed with despair and fall into eternal ruin. But faith approaches God; faith asks, desires, seeks, seizes and receives the forgiveness of sins. In such a manner, set forth by the Word of God, our Lord prepares the way for us so that in Him, through Him, and because of Him we come to faith and gain justification." We see how simple this *ordo* is. It is constructed according to the preaching of Law and Gospel and the effects of Law and Gospel. Chemnitz emphasizes this simple, Biblical *ordo* in contrast to the Roman doctrine of *meritum congrui* by which the sinner actually merits God's grace and forgiveness[21] and *gratia gratis data* which had the function merely of inciting the free will of man who then by his own natural powers disposes himself toward justification. All this meant that faith was merely the preparation for justification (or sanctification). Faith does not apprehend justification; it opens the way for hope and charity which are works necessary before justification can be achieved. Chemnitz insists that only the Biblical *ordo* gives God all glory and offers the sinner lasting comfort and peace of conscience.

The order of justification (Law and Gospel, contrition and faith) which Chemnitz outlines is most important to Lutheran theology and scrupulously observed. Faith, says Hans Poulsen Resen,[22] is a persuasion of a

---

19 *Examen*, p. 178.

20 Mentzer, *Op. cit.*, I, 195. Cf. *WA* 39/1, 103.

21 Cf. Bonaventura, *Libri Senteniarum*, I, 41, 1,1: "Est meritum congrui, digni et condigni. Meritum congrui est, quando peccator facit quod in se est et pro se. Meritum digni, quando iustus facit pro alie. Meritum condigni, quando iustus operatur pro se ipso, quia ad hoc ordinatur gratia ex condigno."

22 *De Sancta Fide*, Hafniae, 1614. pp. 1–4.

very singular kind, a spiritual confidence, a confidence in eternal life. Such faith is born out of extreme need, and can only flower in one who has felt his sin. "Where there is no contrition there can be only a feigned and painted faith." This is why it is so important, Resen says, to preach Law before Gospel, sin and wrath before faith. For faith is simply believing that our sins are remitted for Christ's sake, and then peace and comfort and joy follow. "But such joy and comfort will not be felt where there is no contrition and terror." It is because faith is what it is, that pastors must be so extremely conscientious in preaching both Law and Gospel. Sinners first "must be provoked to fear;" they must be confronted "with the overwhelming wrath of God against sin" and be shown "that no one could make atonement for sins except Christ alone." And "if Christ has to suffer so for our sins, how much more will we suffer, if we despise this wrath of God and do not repent of our sins (Lk. 23:31)?" But then the Gospel enters in and without delay proclaims that our life need not close with death and terror. God does not desire our death, but offers life. "For His anger endureth but a moment; in His favour is life" (Ps. 30:5; Ex. 18:23). No matter how involved and unsatisfactory the *ordines salutis* of later orthodoxy became, this simple *ordo* in justification is faithfully followed.

B. THE NATURE OF FAITH (*fides justificans*)

In defining the faith by which the sinner is justified, Lutheran dogmatics seems carefully stereotyped, wishing to say neither too much nor too little. Against Roman theology it is maintained that faith is not a bare knowledge of facts, a mere assent to doctrine, a mere belief that certain things are true. But neither is faith only an opinion or feeling. Rather it is something that involves the whole man, the sinner crushed by God's Law, and all his faculties. May I offer three descriptions of faith given by three orthodox Lutherans far removed from each other in time and place, and then comment briefly? First, Martin Chemnitz:

> In the matter of justification faith must be understood not merely as knowledge and a general acceptance that the promise of the Gospel is true, but faith embraces also activities of the heart and will. That is to say, there is a desire and trust by which sinners in their wrestlings with sin and with the wrath of God apply to themselves the promise of grace. Hence each believer includes himself in these general promises, and arouses himself to say without hesitation that the promise of the Gospel is effectual also in respect to him. And thus he re-receives comfort and life in times of temptation.[23]

---

23 *Loci Theologici*, II, 251.

Second, Jesper Brochmand:

> Justifying faith is true knowledge and firm assent to the divine Word. It is first and foremost the heart's unhesitating confidence that in all necessities, even when the entire soul is quaking because of sin, the poor sinner can conclude with all certainty that God wishes to forgive sins for the sake of His Son Jesus, not just the sins of others, but his own sins, even though he is the greatest of sinners, and that God reckons to him Christ's righteousness and gives him eternal life.[24]

Third, Abraham Calov:

> Justifying faith is our confidence of divine mercy in Christ, it is trust in Jesus, assurance that He has paid for our sins, restored us to righteousness and gained eternal salvation for us; and it is therefore confidence that for Christ's sake God forgives us our sins and in His grace wishes to rescue us for an inheritance of eternal life.[25]

From these three statements we notice that it is the troubled, desperate sinner who believes. We observe also the emphasis upon *fides specialis* in all three statements; faith is first of all my personal trust in Jesus Christ. No crisis theologian today could state the case more emphatically. We see furthermore that faith is essentially trust and confidence and that it is linked with the forgiveness of sins offered in the Gospel. But above all we notice that the subject of faith (man) is barely alluded to; it is the object of saving faith which is portrayed very clearly in every description. Faith looks away from self to the treasure God offers in Jesus Christ. Faith is "coming to undisturbed rest and taking one's refuge in God's promises."[26] Lutheran theology speaks indiscriminately of forgiveness, the Gospel, the promises, Christ, God's grace, the mercy of Christ, Christ's work as the object of faith. But there is really only one object of faith; faith clings to Christ the Redeemer who is the heart of the Gospel and the manifestation of God's mercy. True, justifying faith includes the so-called *fides generalis* in all God has revealed; but this is only because everything revealed in Scripture leads to the doctrine of the forgiveness of sins for Christ's sake, whether Scripture speaks of the history of God's people, of sin, or the life of obedience. When the papists bring up such passages as Heb. 11 to show that the whole *corpus doctrinae* is the object of faith, Chemnitz replies that here the apostle is speaking of the activity of faith after justification, viz., that faith is patient and obedient under crosses and offences. But the chief question

---

24 *Definitiones Articulorum Fidei*. Hafniae, 1662. A7.

25 *Apodixis Articulorum Fidei*. Luneburgi, 1684. p. 300.

26 Calov, *Ibid*.

which I as a sinner must have answered is always whether God is at peace with me, whether He is reconciled and propitiated, a question which must be answered before there can be any activity of faith, and a question which is answered only in the promises of the Gospel.

One more point might be noted relative to the orthodox Lutheran doctrine of faith. Faith is in the unseen, the unempirical, the absurd—viz., in forgiveness, grace and eternal life. May I merely cite one statement of Brochmand's to bring out this point:

> Those deep mysteries which cannot be grasped by our senses or reason and which are considered to be utter foolishness by the carnal man, those deep mysteries faith makes certain and definite and worthy of our acceptance. By the Word and Spirit of God and by faith our minds and hearts are fully persuaded that those things are completely true which our senses and reason think should be rejected as unlikely or quite impossible. Thus it is that faith convinces the mind and heart to assent unquestioningly to those things which are unseen. . . . And so life is promiscd to us, but wc are dead; we are certain of a blessed resurrection although our bodies are subject to decay; . . . we are proclaimed blessed by the Word, and yet all the time we are hemmed in by all sorts of evils; God's present help is promised us in all adversities, and yet we seem to wait this divine succor in vain. Thus it is that faith is truly the evidence of things unseen.[27]

Our faith cannot be proved or demonstrated in any ordinary way. It has its own proof, the *testimonium Spiritus Sancti internum*, the demonstration of the Spirit and of power.

C. JUSTIFICATION *per Fidem*

In speaking of faith's place in justification, orthodox Lutheranism leaned heavily upon the contributions of Luther and Chemnitz and is quite unoriginal. Chemnitz points out that faith does not justify because it is an assent to something, or because it is an act of man, but by virtue of the fact that it grasps, desires, and accepts "in the promise Christ with all His merits, and in Christ also the mercy of God who forgives sins."[28] Justifying faith is receptivity, an *actio passiva*, a *lēpsis Christi* (*lambanein*, John 1:12; Rom. 5:17; Gal. 3:14; *katalambanein*, John 1:5; *paralambanein*, John 1:11; *dechesthai*, Luke 8:13; Acts 8:14; *apodechesthai*, Acts 2:41; 1 Tim. 1:15). And so it is *by* faith (*pistei*, Acts 26:18; *ek pisteōs*, Gal. 3:7, 8, 9, 11, 12; *dia tēs pisteōs*, Rom. 2:30, 31; *meta pisteōs*, 1 Tim. 1:14; *epi tē pistei*,

---

27 *Commentarius in Epistolam ad Hebraeos*. Hafniae, 1706. p. 489.
28 Cf. *Formula of Concord*, SD, III, 10.

Phil. 3:9) that we are justified. Good works, acts of love do not receive anything. Faith is the only means suitable to receive the justifying object, Christ. In the very nature of the case justification is by faith alone, without works. Quenstedt says:

> On our part it is this faith alone which justifies us and effects (*influit*) our justification. Whatever merely embraces apprehends to itself the promises of grace, the forgiveness of sins and the merit of Christ does so without any admixture of works. And only that on the part of man which enters into the picture when we consider God justifying him can be said to justify. Thus we are said to be justified by faith exclusively without the deeds of the Law (Rom. 3:28; Eph. 2:8,9). True, faith is never alone, never all by itself and isolated from good works, and yet faith alone apprehends the merit of Christ, and we are justified by means of faith alone.[29]

The Lutheran dogmaticians are most careful to maintain the instrumentality of faith in justification and that faith justifies only by virtue of its object. Faith does not justify in so far as it is an acceptance and reception (*quatenus est apprehensio*), but "the whole justifying power of faith depends on the thing apprehended."[30] Only when this point is kept clear will the sinner ever be certain of his own forgiveness and salvation.

The Lutheran emphasis upon faith as certainty wrought by the Holy Spirit and upon justification by faith *propter Christum* is to assure every believer in Christ that he can and ought to be sure of his salvation. Here we see the comforting and practical consequences of our justification before God. Lutheran orthodoxy upholds at great length one of the great issues of the Reformation: that every believer in Christ can be certain with

---

29 *Systema*, P. III, C.8, S.1, Th. 11 (III, 519).

30 *Ibid.*, "When the hand of a starving man seizes bread which is offered to it, it is not this taking of the bread which satisfied the man, for he could seize a piece of mud or a stone or something else which could not satisfy him, but his being satisfied depends on the object which he takes to himself and on his eating it, i.e. it depends upon the bread. When the lips of a thirsty man drink water which has been drawn with a bucket from some well, it is not the drinking as such that quenches his thirst, for you can also draw sand or blood with a bucket. No, if his thirst is to be satisfied, the drink which he consumes must have the power to quench thirst. Thus he who hungers and thirsts after righteousness receives it through faith, as the begging hand which receives the bread coming down from heaven (John 6:50,51) and as the vessel of the thirsting soul draws the water springing up into everlasting life (John 4:14); but it is not this receiving and drinking as such which drives away the spiritual hunger and quenches the thirst. Man does not possess anything of such a nature as can accomplish this, such as his own merits, his own pretended autonomy, satisfactions which are the inventions of the Synagogue of Rome. No, the whole strength of man's receiving depends on the thing received through faith, the redemption and the blood of Jesus Christ." Cf. *Formula of Concord*, T.D. III, 13ff.

an infallible and divine certainty of God's grace and forgiveness and eternal life. It is always with the discussion of justification, and rightly so, that this comfort is stressed.[31]

D. THE ACTIVITY OF FAITH (FAITH AND GOOD WORKS)

The most common argument of Roman theologians against the Lutheran doctrine of justification was that it separated faith and good works, justification and sanctification. The charge then followed that Lutheran theology did not sufficiently emphasize the importance and necessity of good works. From the time of Chemnitz Lutheran theologians make every effort to show that such a charge is utterly unfounded. Chemnitz insists that it never occurred to the Lutherans to separate faith and good works. He says:

> The Lutheran Church has always taught that renewal must and does follow reconciliation, and in such a manner that the Holy Spirit comes with the remission of sins, and He begins renewal in us. Therefore the Holy Spirit initiates sanctification and renewal in those who have been reconciled because of Christ the Mediator . . . Thus in no sense do we teach that justifying faith is all alone, that is, that it is a mere persuasion which is without repentance and with no good works springing from it. Such faith without works is barren and dead. We insist that it is not true and living faith at all which does not work by love (Gal. 5:6).[32]

Rome's charge is childish. Because faith and good works are present at the same time does not imply that both faith and good works justify. We have ears and eyes at the same time, yet we do not see with both ears and eyes. The conclusion therefore must be: "True faith apprehends Christ; at the same time true faith is not without works (Jas. 2) and works through love (Gal. 5)."

The Lutherans during the period of orthodoxy, unlike Luther, are by no means embarrassed by the book of James. Rather they accept its canonicity unquestioningly and use it in enunciating their doctrine of justification. One of the greatest commentaries written during the period was Jesper Brochmand's work on James. One of Brochmand's purposes in writing this commentary was to demonstrate that Lutheranism takes James seriously on every point. According to Brochmand, James, unlike Paul, is not seeking to show how a man is justified before God; he rather wishes to explain how a believer "gives evi-

---

31 Chemnitz, *Examen*, p. 189. Quenstedt, *Systema* (III, 526); Calov, *Apodixis Articulorum Fidei*, p. 302ff.

32 *Examen*, 188.

dence to his fellow man that his professed faith is neither fiction nor sham, but real and living faith."[33] And the only conclusion one can come to as one reads James is as follows: "It is absolutely vain to profess faith if it is devoid of good works." Faith and good works are inextricably bound together, like fire and light. It is true, Brochmand says, "that we exclude works as a cause of salvation, but we require them as definite testimonies to the presence of faith and as the results of salvation. For there is no true and living faith which is not active through love (Gal. 5:6) and which is not productive of good works (Matt. 7:17–18; Jas. 2:14–15ff). He who says he believes in Christ who died is a liar, if by the power of Christ's death he does not daily die to sin; and he who claims to believe in the risen Christ deceives himself, if he does not by the power of the risen Christ advance daily in newness of life. This is specifically taught by Paul in Rom. 6:1ff. Therefore our adversaries are making sport in a very serious matter and oppressing our churches with a false accusation when they say that we urge faith in Christ in such a way that we turn men away from good works and from the earnest desire for a holy life. For just as we urge this saying to our churches (Jn. 6:40): 'This is the Father's will who sent me, that every one who believes in me may have eternal life,' we also commend the statement of Paul (1 Th. 4:3) and zealously impress it upon our hearers, 'This is the will of God, even your sanctification.' Thus we extol faith in Christ, but in such a way that we establish the great value and place of good works." Sincere statements such as that of Brochmand can be found throughout all the writings of the orthodox Lutherans.[34]

Time does not permit us to pursue this matter further. Suffice it to say that the Lutherans following the Formula of Concord felt constrained for many good reasons to stress the necessity and importance of good works, the Christian life and sanctification. On this particular point there is a greater balance in the later Lutheran theology than one finds in Luther.

---

33 *In Canonicam et Catholicam Jacobi Epistolam Commentarius.* Hafniae, 1640. p. 153.

34 Cf. e.g. Calov. *Historia Syncretistica, d. i. Kirchlich. Bedenken Uber den Kirchen-Frieden.* Wittebergae, 1685. p. 407: "We confess that true faith by which we are justified cannot exist without love and other good works. And we therefore deny that true justifying faith can in fact be separated from love and other virtues." *Apodixis Articulorum Fidei*, p. 310: "Justifying faith is not without good works, and on the other hand good works are never independent of justifying faith. . . . There can be no faith without its fruits." Kromayer, J. *Theologia Positivo-Polemica*, Lipsiae, 1711, II, 281: "Sola fides justificat, sed solitaria non existit."

Conclusion

The doctrine of justification as it is presented in orthodox Lutheran theology is perhaps the most impressive, thorough, balanced and evangelical section in all of Lutheran dogmatics. With the emphasis upon forensic justification, the *justitia aliena*, Christ as the object of faith and the *sola fide*, we have a doctrine which is not only faithful to the heritage of Luther and the Lutheran confessions, but central to evangelical Christianity and of abiding comfort to poor sinners.

The LWF study document has asked whether this doctrine as formulated by classical Lutheranism is relevant to modern man? This is a highly personal question which one can hardly answer for another. To one who has been justified by faith in Christ, who has experienced God's irrefutable verdict of acquittal, justification is the most relevant thing in all the world, and to such a person the old Lutheran doctrine will mean very much. To the materialist, the secularist, the humanist, the communist today, as for the practical atheist of Ps. 14 or the humanist and philosophers of bygone days, the idea of justification before God will represent merely the religious reflections of man in ancient or feudal times with no significance for our modern age. But certainly one thing is obvious: no Biblical theme or Lutheran teaching is better calculated to be understood in our twentieth century when courts, laws, justice, injustice, verdicts, punishment and retribution are the stock vocabulary of all men. And if it seems that the world no longer listens to the message of forgiveness, have we really any alternative to following our Lord's great commission and preaching the Gospel of forgiveness to every creature? And certainly we who are evangelical Lutherans ought to be assured that, however vast the changes in our modern world view and in the Zeitgeist of twentieth century man, there will always be conscience stricken sinners who feel the wrath of God; and for them a divine verdict of acquittal will be of ultimate and eternal relevance.

PERENNIAL PROBLEMS IN THE DOCTRINE OF JUSTIFICATION

> "Perennial Problems in the Doctrine of Justification"
> is an apologetic for the doctrine of justification
> against chronic and current assaults identified by
> Preus. This helpful piece demonstrates that even
> and especially the article of justification requires
> constant defense against both the attacks of the
> Church of Rome and, surprisingly, some ostensibly
> Lutheran detractors. This article was published in
> 1981 by *Concordia Theological Quarterly*. (Permis-
> sion has been granted for reproduction in this col-
> lection.)

THERE ARE, OF COURSE, NO PROBLEMS in the doctrine of justification, no problems at all. The doctrine presents God's revealed answer to all the major problems of sinful man. Does God exist? What is He like? Does He love me? What must I do to be saved? Can sinful man ever stand before a holy and righteous God? These and all the other nagging questions of fallen man are answered truly and clearly and decisively by the revealed doctrine of justification by grace for Christ's sake through faith.

And so in this essay I address myself not to any problems in the doctrine of justification itself, but to some of the great problems we have made for ourselves in the church, problems which have perennially in the church tended to obscure that brilliant light of justification by grace, to mitigate the doctrine, to deny it, to corrupt it, to ignore it, or to relegate it to the vast limbo of meaninglessness.

What are some of these perennial problems with which, it seems, we evangelical Christians and Lutherans must constantly contend as we seek to confess and teach the Gospel of justification? What are some of the major assaults within the church against this article on which the church stands or falls? I will address myself to five.

1. *The first assault against the article of justification by faith is to define justification as something other than a divine forensic act of acquittal.* Let us repair to our Confessions for our definition. Apology IV (305) has this comment on Romans 5:1: "In this passage 'justify' is used in a judicial way to mean 'to absolve a guilty man and pronounce him righteous,' and to do so on account of someone else's righteousness, namely, Christ's, which is communicated to us through faith" (cf. 252).[1]

It is true that such statements are not definitions as such. They are passing statements touching either the meaning of *dikaioo* as Scripture uses it or the nature of justification (what happens when a person is justified). But these statements, along with every article on justification in our Confessions, indicate that the Lutheran Reformers had a very clear idea of what it meant to be justified and that they held firmly that their entire doctrine was dependent upon and centered in the fact that justification was simply a divine, gracious, forensic act of acquittal and a corresponding imputation of Christ's righteousness (the obedience of His "doing and suffering," SD, III, 15). If this understanding of the meaning of justification, including and emphasizing as it did so consistently the imputation of Christ's righteousness, the *justitia aliena* which was *extra nos* in every sense, was held, then all problems connected with the doctrine would disappear. For the correct understanding of what justification is would exclude as incompatible all aberrant notions concerning infused grace, *fides formata*, human merit, and the like; and would solicit, as the Gospel always does, the response, the only possible response, to a verdict (or promise), the response of *sola fides*.

It is instructive to note that, as time went on, the dispute between the later Lutherans and the great Roman Catholic anti-Lutheran polemicists such as Bellermine, Stapleton, Gretzer and others centered more and more upon the meaning of justification, on what happens when a person is justified.[2] Elert[3] is correct both historically and theologically when he notes

---

1 SD III, 9: "Concerning the righteousness of faith before God we believe, teach, and confess unanimously, in accord with the summary formulation of our Christian faith and confession described above, that a poor sinner is *justified before God (that is, he is absolved and declared utterly free from all his sins, and from the verdict of well deserved damnation,* and is adopted as a child of God and an heir of eternal life) without any merit or worthiness on our part, and without any preceding, present, or subsequent works, but sheer grace, solely through the merit of the total *obedience,* the bitter passion, the death, and the resurrection of Christ, our Lord, whose *obedience is reckoned to us as righteousness*" (cf. 4, 17).

2 The most extensive review of the debate is in John Gerhard's, *Loci Theologici* (Tuebingen, 1766), VII, 257ff., where he polemicizes against Andradius, Bellarmine, and others who taught that justification was both the imputed righteousness and the inherent righteousness of the Christian's renewal. See also Chemnitz, *op. cit.,* 168ff.

that from Luther through Chemnitz and Gerhard the fundamental issue with Roman theology was concerning the imputation of Christ's righteousness to the sinner in his justification before God.

We need not here rehearse the Roman Catholic doctrine of justification with which Luther and the Reformers contended and with which we still contend as Lutherans.[4] I might just mention, however, that Roman Catholic theologians have always been willing to grant that justification is in a sense a forensic act of God, although only partially so. After all, God does and will at the day of judgment, render a forensic verdict concerning every person who has ever lived, whether he be righteous or not, or how righteous he is. But this is no concession at all to the Lutheran understanding, for in classic medieval and post-Reformation Catholic theology God's judgment, or reckoning, over every man is analytical. God judges a person to be righteous because he is in himself and inherently righteous, and that because of what he is and what he has done. Under no circumstances can the foreign righteousness of Christ which He wrought independently of us and is utterly *extra nos* be imputed to a believer so as to constitute his righteousness as he stands before God. The Council of Trent makes the position very clear in Canon 10 of the sixth session, "If anyone should say that a man is justified either without the righteousness of Christ whereby He has gained merit for us or that through this merit we become righteous formally, let him be anathema."[5] Trent affirmed that the merits of Christ's atonement were the basis (*causa meritoria*) of our becoming righteous before God and that they are actually communicated (*communicantur*) to us, but piecemeal only and as love is infused, never by a gracious divine reckoning. But it is the second condemnation of the canon which so utterly devastates the evangelical doctrine. For here the doctrine that the merits of Christ, His righteousness, become mine, and that my righteousness before God in its very nature (*forma*) is all that He has done for me by His living and suffering, is condemned. And this was the heart of Luther's evangelical understanding of justification.

To this day the position of Rome has not changed and the doctrine of Trent prevails, in spite of all the changes which have taken place in the Roman Catholic Church. In dialogues with Roman Catholics and in the writings of some we do, indeed, note an openness to the forensic justifica-

---

3 *The Structure of Lutheranism*, tr. Walter A. Hanson (St. Louis: Concordia Publishing House, 1962), p. 109.

4 Ad. Tanquerey, *Brevior Synopsis Theologiae Dogmaticae* (Paris: Typis Societas Sancti Joannis Evang. Desclie, 1946), p. 498, *passim*. Ludwig Ott, *Fundamentals of Catholic Dogma*, tr. Patrick Lunch (St. Louis: Herder, 1954).

5 See Martin Chemnitz, *Examen Concilii Tridentini* (Berlin, 1861), p. 146.

tion and the comfort it offers as it opens up the entire Scriptures and focuses attention on the saving work of Christ; but nothing substantive can be seen. The Lutheran-Roman Catholic dialogues in this country have not even dealt with the subject. And in Europe, where the subject has been broached rather seriously,[6] representatives on the Roman Catholic side have not been particularly representative, and the discussions have been devoted mainly to probings and explorations into the possibility of amalgamating the Roman Catholic and evangelical doctrines or of the Roman Catholic Church accepting Article IV of the Augustana in the light of a Roman Catholic understanding of it.

But the attempt to merge and synthesize the two understandings of justification is an impossible undertaking, as well as an affront to the evangelical doctrine, and every such undertaking, whether by Lutheran or Roman Catholic has failed.[7] For the *justitia aliena*, which is imputed to me and which alone constitutes my righteousness before God, is exclusive and absolutely rules out anything in me (love, works, qualities, virtues— yes, even faith) which would prompt God to adjudge me righteous. And God's forensic justification which takes place in His tribunal (SD III, 32) and therefore absolutely outside (*pure extrinsica*) of man (*circa et extra hominem*)[8] absolutely excludes the doctrine that justification is as a whole or in any part a process taking place in man whereby he becomes progressively more righteous.

2. *The second assault against the article of justification by faith is to separate God's act of justifying the sinner through faith from its basis in Christ's atonement.* The doctrine of justification is threatened when it is not based upon and taught in connection with the universal redemption and legal propitiation wrought by Christ (Apol. IV, 40, 46, 53, 230–1, 244, 269, 291, 299,

---

6 George Forell and James F. McCue, editors, *Confessing the Faith* (Minneapolis: Augsburg, 1981). Joseph Burgess, ed., *The Role of the Augsburg Confession: Catholic and Lutheran Views* (Philadelphia: Fortress Press, 1981).

7 Hans Kung, *Justification, the Doctrine of Karl Barth and a Catholic Reflection*, tr. by Thomas Collins, Edmond E. Tolk , and David Granskou (New York: Thomas Nelson and Sons, 1964). See particularly Karl Barth's letter to the author, pp. xix–xxii. See also Robert Scharlemann, *Thomas Aquinas and John Gerhard* (New Haven: Yale University Press, 1964).

8 When the Lutheran Fathers insistently spoke of justification taking place *in foro Dei* or *coram tribunali judicis supremi* (cf. John Quenstedt, *Systema* [Leipzig, 1702], P.III, C.8, S.1, Th.16 [II, 754]; *ibid.* S.2, Q.6, Ekth.6 [II, 789]; *passim.*), they did so not to establish a locus for justification in heaven and not on earth, but to retain the forensic image against the idea of an *actus medicinalis* or *physicus* which can only be a gradual process in man whereby he becomes more and more just. Cf. Luther WA 56, 158.

308, 382, 387; XXI, 28; XII, 87, 108; XXIV, 19, 23, 38, 58; AC XXI, 2.).
Again let me cite the Confessions (SD III, 14–15):

> Therefore the righteousness which by grace is reckoned to faith or to
> the believers is the obedience, the passion, and the resurrection of
> Christ when he satisfied the law for us and paid for our sin . . . His obe-
> dience consists not only in his suffering and dying, but also in his spon-
> taneous subjection to the law in our stead and his keeping the law in so
> perfect a fashion that, reckoning it to us as righteousness, God forgives
> us our sins, accounts us holy and righteous, and saves us forever on
> account of this entire obedience which, by doing and suffering, in life
> and death, Christ rendered for us to his heavenly father.

In this statement we note the close connection between the righteousness
of faith, our justification, and the vicarious atonement of Christ. They
entail each other. There can be no imputation of Christ's righteousness
with which I can stand before God, if Christ did not by His atonement
acquire such a righteousness. The purpose of Christ's vicarious work of
obedience is that it might be imputed to me and all sinners. Therefore, to
deny the vicarious atonement or to separate it from my personal justification threatens or vitiates the doctrine of justification by faith entirely.

This was done already in the Middle Ages when Abelard denied the
vicarious atonement, but also by the nominalists who taught that justification was indeed a forensic act of God, but made it dependent upon His will
rather than the atonement and righteousness of Christ. But the same tendency to separate God's justification of the individual sinner from its basis
in Christ's atoning work really pervades all Roman Catholic theology, with
a few exceptions, to this very day. Luther rails incisively against this Christ-
less soteriology:

> There are some within the new high schools who say that forgiveness
> of sins and justification of grace depend entirely upon the divine impu-
> tation, that is, on God's reckoning; and that it is enough that God
> imputes or does not impute sins to a person, for in that manner he is
> either justified or not justified of his sins, as Psalm 32 and Romans
> speak, "Blessed is the man to whom the Lord will not impute sin." If
> this were true, then the entire New Testament would be nothing and
> useless. Then Christ worked foolishly and unnecessarily when He suf-
> fered for sin. Then God Himself in all this carried out a mock battle
> and a tricky game [Kauckelspiell]. For He was able to forgive and not
> reckon sins without the suffering of Christ. And therefore a faith other
> than faith in Christ could bring righteousness and salvation, namely, a
> faith which would rely on such gracious mercy of God which makes
> one free of sin. Against this miserable and shocking opinion and error
> the holy apostles have had the custom always to refer to faith in Jesus

Christ and to speak of Christ so often, that it is a wonder that there is anyone to whom such a cause is not known. Thus these learned men in the high schools know no longer what Christ is or why He is necessary, or what the Gospel and the New Testament means. They make Christ only a new Moses, a teacher, who gives them new laws and commandments by which man is to become pious and live.[9]

Listen to Luther again as he hammers home his crucial point:

I have often said before that faith in God is not enough; but there must also be a cost. And what is the cost? For the Jews and Turks believe too, but without means or cost. The Gospel shows us what the cost is. For the Holy Spirit teaches there that we do not have the Father without means and we cannot go to the Father without means. Here Christ teaches us that we are not lost, but have eternal life, that is, that God loved us so much that He was willing to pay the cost of thrusting His own dear Son into our misery, hell and death and having Him drink that up. That is the way we are saved.[10]

Such statements of Luther's could be greatly multiplied. What Christ the Redeemer did then is mine now. Everything He did as Savior and Substitute for me and the whole human race I claim as my own.

Bear in mind that Luther is not reproaching merely the gross denial of the atonement by a few remote scholastic theologians, but his own contemporaries who held to the vicarious atonement in all its Anselmic purity, but did not relate it to personal justification. And we need not look just to Unitarianism or Rome to find this tendency today; it is right within the bosom of Lutheranism wherever pastors think they are preaching the Gospel when they expound the great themes of regeneration, faith, peace with God, yes, even forgiveness of sins, and neglect to mention the work of Christ, His once-and-for-all active and passive obedience, and to proclaim that that and that alone is not only the basis, but the very essence of our righteousness before God and our eternal salvation.

And so it is, strictly speaking, not talk about forgiveness, or talk about faith, or even talk about justification by faith which is the Gospel, but the work and righteousness of Christ (Apol. IV, 43) which we apprehend by faith, as our Confessions assert again and again (SD III, 13, 25, 30, 38, 41, 42, 43; Apol. XXVIII, 3, 19, 30, 34; X, 7; XII, 42, 61, 65, 116; XIII, 19–20; IV, 45, 43, 50, 48, 56, 55, 304, 264, 267, 272, 291, 292, 217, 270, 299, 338, 386).

---

9 WA 10/1, 469.
10 WA 10/3, 161–2.

In the seventeenth century the Lutheran doctrine of justification which represented the greatest breakthrough of the Gospel since apostolic times was condemned by the Roman Catholic theology for three reasons: (1) because it ruled out every human being's righteousness and good works as a factor in justification, (2) because it gave no place to sanctification or renewal in justification, and (3) because it taught that God works all holiness and righteousness in us through Christ.[11] True, it was granted by Thomas Stapleton that "Christ's actual righteousness (His atoning work) merits righteousness for us, that is, not only the remission of sins, but also the communication of grace by which, when it is given us, we are truly justified."[12] But that we are justified *formaliter* through the imputation of Christ's righteousness is categorically rejected. "Christ justifies us intrinsically by dwelling in us, not extrinsically through an imputed righteousness." Stapleton's final sally against the Lutheran doctrine reveals only his utter ignorance of what the issue is. "If Christ's righteousness is our righteousness formally, it then follows not merely that all our virtues and excellencies are in fact virtues of Christ's righteousness and that we are justified through all these, but it also follows that we cannot be reckoned righteous by any other virtue and no other virtue is able to have any bearing on our imputed righteousness." Exactly so. This is precisely what the Lutherans taught.

In the nineteenth century the greatest Jesuit controversialist of the era, Perrone, argued in exactly the same fashion.[13] Commenting on Romans 4:5, he says, "God accepts our faith gratuitously, and this faith as an actual disposition of ours he imputes for righteousness in view of the merit of Christ. However, He does not impute the formal righteousness of Christ to us, so that by this we are counted just."[14] Again the same blind refusal to see anything but a remote connection between Christ's atoning work and man's present justification before God, the same pathetic refusal to see that Christ's obedience constitutes our righteousness before God and our salvation.

At the same time in Germany, a converted Jew, Philippi, was teaching in Germany, upholding the centrality of the atonement for the doctrine of justification which had meant so much to Luther. With power and pathos

---

11 Thomas Stapleton, *Opera* (Paris, 1620), II, 215ff.

12 *Ibid.* 221.

13 *Praelectiones Theologicae*, 27 ed. (Regensberg: 1856), II, 235.

14 Later he says, commenting on Rom. 5:19, "Per unius obedientiam justi constituentur multi *meritorie*, C. *formaliter*, N."

he gave the final answer to the piddling and shallow theological produc-
tions of his day by Roman Catholics and liberal Protestants:

> He who takes away from me the atoning blood of the Son of God, paid
> as a ransom to the wrath of God, who takes away the satisfaction of our
> Lord and Savior Jesus Christ, vicariously given to the penal justice of
> God, who thereby takes away justification or forgiveness of sins only by
> faith in the merits of this my Surety and Mediator, who takes away the
> imputation of the righteousness of Jesus Christ, takes away Christian-
> ity altogether, so far as I am concerned. I might then just as well have
> adhered to the religion of my ancestors, the seed of Abraham after the
> flesh.[15]

The denial or diminution of the vicarious atonement is *eo ipso* a denial of
the evangelical doctrine of justification.

3. *The doctrine of justification by faith is threatened or vitiated when any
deviation whatsoever from the evangelical, confessional (and biblical) structure,
conceptualization,* Vorbild *(pattern), or* hypotyposis[16] *of the doctrine is insinu-
ated, defended, or taught.* What is this evangelical, apostolic "pattern of
sound words" as it applies to the doctrine of justification? Let us once
again repair to our Confessions for an answer (SD III, 4, 25):

> The righteousness of faith is forgiveness of sins, reconciliation with
> God, and the fact that we are adopted as God's children solely on
> account of the obedience of Christ, which, through faith alone, is reck-
> oned by pure grace to all true believers as righteousness, and that they
> are absolved from all their unrighteousness because of this obedience.

> The only essential and necessary elements of justification are the grace
> of God, the merit of Christ, and faith which accepts these in the
> promise of the Gospel, whereby the righteousness of Christ is reck-
> oned to us and by which we obtain the forgiveness of sins, reconcilia-
> tion with God, adoption, and the inheritance of eternal life.

(See also SD III, 9; Apol. IV, 214, 217; XII, 72, 76). On the basis of these
two pre-eminent statements, which draw upon Apology IV and summarize
it, we can quite easily offer a Lutheran model for the doctrine of justification by faith.

---

15 Quoted in Albrecht Ritschl, *The Doctrine of Justification and Reconciliation* (Clifton,
  N.J.: Reference Book Publishers, 1966), I, 551.
16 *Begriff und Form; forma et quasi typus* (SD Rule and Norm, 1). *Summa und Vorbild der
  Lehre; compendiaria hypotyposi seu forma sanae doctrinae* (SD Rule and Norm, 9),
  Form der Lehre; compendiaria hypotuposi sanae doctrinae. Begriff, Vorbild, form and
  hypotyposis (2 Tim. 1:13) might best be rendered by "pattern" or "model." The reference is not to the exact wording of the doctrine, which is always drawn from the
  words of Scripture, but to the proper conceptualization of it, based on Scripture.

God counts the sinner righteous (i.e., forgives him and imputes Christ's righteousness to him), by (a) grace (not works), (b) for Christ's sake, (c) through faith (in the Gospel). Any deviation from this model buries Christ, burdens consciences, and takes away from the comfort of the Gospel, as Melanchthon says throughout Apology IV—any deviation at all from any aspect of the pattern. For the article of justification according to the above model is the chief article of Christian doctrine (Apol. IV, 2; SA II, II, 1–3), which is an organic whole, like a human body, so that a distortion or unsoundness of any part affects the whole body.[17]

Likening this simple model to a skeleton, let me add some flesh and blood to the body by explaining terms and mentioning implications and connections within the model and as it relates to all of Christian doctrine and practice. Justification is clearly a forensic act, but so also are the less obviously soteriological terms so often used interchangeably with justification or as part of its definition, such as forgiveness, reconciliation, propitiation,—yes, even redemption.[18] This is clear in our Confessions from the passages cited above and many others. The forensic theme is the dominant soteriological theme which undergirds all others; this was one of the reasons Melanchthon and Luther viewed justification as the "chief article."

Grace, according to our model, is the free and active motivating power of God which has mercy and saves man, always without works, for man is totally sinful (AC II; FC I, II) and unable to contribute anything to his salvation. Grace is always in Christ; the two are inseparable. Does God out of grace send Christ to take my sin and be my Savior? Or does Christ by His perfect obedience and His propitiatory sacrifice make God gracious toward me? Both. In the evangelical Lutheran model of justification it is both. Elert says perceptively, "God lets Christ bear the curse because He loves me, and He loves me by letting Him feel and bear the wrath provoked by me."[19]

---

17 How this happens is demonstrated throughout Article IV and SA II. See Robert Preus, *The Theology of Post-Reformation Lutheranism* (St. Louis: Concordia Publishing House, 1970), I, 138–9, for a discussion of Luther's and others' view of Christian doctrine as *una copulativa*. See also Francis Pieper, *Christian Dogmatics* (St. Louis: Concordia Publishing House, 1950), I, 91.

18 See Sebastian Schmidt, *Commentarius in epistolam D. Pauli ad Romanos* (Hamburg, 1704), pp. 254ff., for an excellent commentary on Rom. 3:23–26 which illustrates this point well.

19 It is interesting that as much as our Confessions speak of the universal grace and love of God—and the later dogmaticians emphasize this theme even more because of the Calvinistic menace—they stress with equal emphasis Christ as "propitiator," as the one who placates God's wrath against us and makes God gracious and disposed to justify us. This is clearly the basic model for Christ's work in the Apology (see above, p. 4). This was also a common theme of Luther (WA 10/3, 136–7):

In our model we note that the forensic nature of justification and the *sola gratia* are linked together. There can be only one explanation for God behaving in a fashion contrary to an earthly judge who condemns the guilty and acquits the innocent, whose verdict is always analytical—only one reason for God absolving the sinner and imputing to him the righteousness of Christ. The reason is His grace.

But our discussion of the model has now brought us into the middle of a consideration of the work of Christ and the *propter Christum* (for every aspect of the model entails every other aspect). And as we speak of Christ and His work "for us," we find ourselves in the midst of a consideration of faith which alone can apprehend His work.

Faith's role in justification and its relation to its object are affirmed throughout the Apology. We receive forgiveness of sins for Christ's sake through faith (XXVII, 13). What is more certain than this, that men obtain (*consequuntur*) the forgiveness of sins by faith (*fide*) for Christ's sake (*propter Christum*) (XXVII, 19; cf. 30; XXVIII, 7)? The Gospel promises the gracious remission of sins, and this promised mercy in Christ is apprehended through faith (XXVII, 34, 54).

On the basis of these assertions we can make several comments. The *propter Christum* is exclusive in that it is the *only* basis for God's verdict of justification; and human works are explicitly ruled out of consideration by the *propter Christum*. "We must hold to the doctrine that we obtain the forgiveness of sins by faith (*fide*) on account of Christ (*propter Christum*), not because of our works, either preceding or following (*non propter nostra opera praecedentia aut consequentia*) (XII, 116). But the work of Christ referred to in the phrase *propter Christum* is also the object of faith. Of course, the object of faith can be conceptualized differently as the mercy of God, the Gospel, or forgiveness, and we may observe this phenomenon

---

"To believe in the resurrection of Christ is nothing else than to believe that we have a Propitiator before God, and that Christ makes God into a kind and merciful Father. From birth and from his own reason man has nothing but sin and corruption by which he deserves God's wrath. For God is an everlasting righteousness and brightness who by His nature hates sin. Therefore men and God are always enemies and cannot be friends and agree. For this reason Christ became man and took our sin on Himself and the Father's wrath, and drowned them both in Himself that He might reconcile us to the Father . . . Whatever we receive from God must be got and secured through this Christ who has made Him a gracious Father for us. Christ is our support and our protection under which we hide like little chicks under the wings of the hen. Only through Him may we pray to God and be heard. Only through Him do we receive favor and grace from the Father. For He has made satisfaction for our sins and turned an angry judge into a kind and merciful God."

throughout the Confessions. But all these exist only by virtue of Christ's redemptive work and His righteousness.

Finally, we must comment briefly about faith in our model. First, and most importantly, it must be considered in the article of justification as pure receptivity. Melanchthon made this point crystal clear in the statements cited above when he consistently used verbs for receptivity (*consequor, apprehendo, accipio*) in describing the place of faith in what our later Lutheran theologians called God's *modus justificationis*.[20] But does not Melanchthon also call justifying faith trust (Apol. IV, 48, German text; 337)? Yes, but trust very definitely in that it receives the promises or its appropriate object. And faith as receptivity has the element of trust in it (Apol. IV, 48, 227). Years later, in defending the confessional understanding of justifying faith Quenstedt calls it a *fiducialis apprehensio*.[21]

The Lutheran doctrine of justifying faith was rejected by Trent (Session VI, Canon 12). Chemnitz replied that the Lutherans in no way denied a *fides generalis* which believes all the articles of faith; such belief is presupposed by the believer in Christ; but in no sense does it enter into the article of justification. And the Formula of Concord scores of times makes the object of faith a teaching in its constant use of the introductory formula, "We believe, teach, and confess." But such an explanation in no sense satisfied the Roman theologians. Bellarmine calls Melanchthon's understanding of justifying faith (personal trust in God's mercy) "the seed of every heresy of our time."[22] This is a significant statement and, unless it represents merely another case of Bellarminian bombast, quite perceptive in a sense. Like the scholastics, Bellarmine held that faith justified in a meritorious sense, as "faith formed by love"; and if the Lutheran understanding of faith's merely instrumental and receptive role in justification is correct, the entire Roman Catholic dogmatic structure (whether pertaining to justification, penance, sacraments, or whatever) breaks down.

At least a century was spent by the greatest Lutheran theologians of the age, attempting to defend and clarify the Lutheran position, so crucial to the understanding of justification and communicating the Christian message. Their adversaries were the Romanists who denied that justifying faith was trust and receptivity, but taught that justifying faith was an act of man which could be considered a good work (formed by love); its object was the entire Christian dogma (*fides dogmatica*, Bellarmine). The Arminians too

---

20 See Sebastian Schmidt, *ibid.*, p. 190ff. Cf. Chemnitz, *op. cit.*, p. 146ff.

21 *Systema*, P.III, C.9, S.1, Th.6, Nota 2 (II, 836).

22 Robert Bellarmine, *De controversiis adversus hujus temporis haereticos* (Paris, 1583), cap.IV de justificatione (III, 722).

opposed the Lutheran doctrine by making faith (which they granted was trust) a work (*actus*) of man. Like the Romanists they had a synergistic notion of how man came to faith. And, of course, there were the Socinians, who held to an acceptilation theory of the atonement and viewed faith (not in Christ's righteousness but in God's mercy apart from Christ's atonement) as a meritorious work of man. These deviations from the evangelical model of justification are in force today, although in somewhat less gross form. And we have all encountered them.

The Lutherans of the post-Reformation period and up to the present time have countered these aberrations in three ways. First, following Article II of the Formula of Concord, they show that man's receiving the grace of God in faith is itself a gift of grace, and that the absolution that forgives works the very faith to receive the forgiveness (Apol. XII, 39, *passim*.).[23] Secondly, they point out continually that faith's role in justification is purely instrumental, that faith is an *organon leptikon*, like the empty hand of a beggar receiving a gift,[24] that it alone (*sola fide*) is the appropriate vehicle to receive reconciliation, forgiveness, Christ and His merits (SD III, 30–38; Apol. IV, 163; AC XX, 28). Thirdly, they show that justification is *per fidem*, not *propter fidem*, by pointing out that faith justifies by virtue of its object, as Melanchthon used to say (Apol. IV, 56, 338, 227; SD III, 13), and that this is really only a different way of saying, "We are accounted righteous before God for Christ's sake through faith" (Apol. IV, 214).[25]

---

23 Jacob Heerbrand, *Disputatio de gratia* (Tuebingen, 1572), p. 15. "Faith is not a human persuasion, which some falsely ascribe to us, a persuasion which would in any case fail. No, it is a work of God and gift of the Holy Spirit in us. We are not justified by faith insofar as it is a quality in us, as once again the enemies of God's grace, the neo-Pelagians, falsely accuse us of teaching that the ungodly are justified when they have a certain idea (or rather dream) that they are righteous. No, we are justified by faith insofar as it apprehends Christ who was made righteousness for us by God, sanctification and redemption, and insofar as faith applies Christ's merit to itself." Cf. also Jacob Andreae, *Disputatio de evangelio* (Tuebingen, 1572), p. 3.

24 Quenstedt, *Systema*, P.III, C.8, S.2, Q.6 *Bebaiosis* 1 (II, 791): "To accept, to apprehend, or rather to receive something, these on the part of the one who receives are purely instrumental actions." Quenstedt goes on to list, all the biblical terms for faith which denote receptivity, and he traces Paul's consistent use of the instrumental genitive or dative when speaking of justification by faith. George Calanus (*Fasciculus dissertationum theologicarum pio libro concordiae* [Abo, 1660] p. clv) has a very extended, typical discussion of this kind, but really such is standard for all Lutheran teachers from the time of the Formula of Concord. See also Olav Odhelius, *Disputationum homologeticarum in Augustanam Confessionem primasexta* (Uppsala, 1653), p. 227: "Now since there is no other medium in man through which righteousness and salvation are apprehended except faith, there is every reason in the world to say that we are justified by faith alone."

25 Odhelius, *ibid.*, p. 226: "This faith does not justify absolutely as a quality in us, nor by its own power as our action, nor by any capacity it has to choose; but only

And so we see that Lutherans with a good deal of consistency have conscientiously adhered to the biblical and confessional form of sound words in respect to justification—God justifies the sinner by grace for Christ's sake through faith. But we can observe through the study of history and our own times that the assaults against this pattern, along with their disastrous consequences, never cease.

---

organically and relatively insofar as it has to do with its object, God in Christ, and as it embraces the grace of God and the atonement of Christ." Cf. Quenstedt, *Systema*, P.III, C.8, S.2, Q.6, Ek.9 (II, 789) and Obj. dialusis 1 (II, 793). Probably the most adamant debate between Roman Catholics and Arminians, on the one hand, and Lutherans, on the other, centered in just this issue, whether faith justified by virtue of its object only or whether there is some aspect to his faith which prompts God to look favorably upon the believer. The debate centered upon the right understanding of Rom. 4:5 ("His faith is counted for righteousness.") as the crucial passage in determining how faith justifies (Quenstedt, *ibid.*, P.III, C.8, S.1, Th.13, Nota 2 [II, 749]). The Arminian Episcopius maintained that faith in us as such is counted by God for righteousness, not the object of faith, according to Paul. Bellarmine held that the apostle in this context had *fides formata* in mind. And the great Catholic exegete, Estius, held that the faith Paul referred to was *fides ut opus spectata*. Quenstedt's response is entirely faithful to the Lutheran model of justification by faith and clarifies the issue as it was, and is, debated. He says, "In this passage faith does not denote merely an instrument which apprehends something, nor does it merely denote metonymically the thing that is imputed, namely, the righteousness of Christ; but here faith must be viewed symplectically and according to its intimate connection with its object as a complex term signifying the righteousness of Christ insofar as it is embraced and received by true faith. In this verse faith is not to be taken as pointing to its activity, but as pointing to its relationship with its object, that is, it is not to be understood as some work of ours, for here expressly and also in other passages faith is opposed to good works. Neither can faith be understood here in some qualitative sense as a quality or virtue, as if in the judgment of God it is thought to be in and through itself so great that God pronounced sinful man to be righteous on account of it. No, faith must be taken here in a *relative* sense insofar as it looks to Christ, who is our righteousness before God and apprehends His merits, or as it is faith in His blood (Rom. 3:25). Nor is this faith righteousness itself as Bellarmine dreams, but it is imputed *for righteousness*, that is to say, faith, or one's trusting *apodoche*, is accepting and receiving Christ and His righteousness as one's own. This faith presupposes an explicit knowledge of its object who justifies us and an assent on our part which is not just general but personal. It is this faith which is imputed to us for righteousness. Or, to say the same thing, God who pronounces forgiveness from the tribunal of His grace reckons the righteousness of Christ apprehended by true faith to the one who believes as his very own righteousness, just as though the believer himself had established his own righteousness as availing before God. And so the imputation of the righteousness of Christ and the imputation of faith for righteousness are one and the same. For faith is envisaged as justifying not by its own dignity, but by the dignity of its object, not by reason of itself, its own virtue or action or because it is our believing, but by reason of its object, that is, Christ whom it apprehends. In this sense faith is imputed by God's reckoning to us for righteousness, that is, reckoned as our own righteousness and obedience as though we had done it ourselves."

4. *The fourth assault against the doctrine of justification is to deny its reality, or, what is the same thing, to define it merely formally.* Let me again introduce the discussion of this point with citations from the Apology (IV, 72, 78, 117):

> And "to be justified" means to make unrighteous men righteous (*ex iniustis iustos effici*) or to regenerate them, as well as to be pronounced or accounted righteous. For Scripture speaks both ways. Therefore we want to show first that faith alone makes (*efficiat*) a righteous man out of an unrighteous one, that is, that it receives the forgiveness of sins.

> Therefore we are justified by faith alone (*sola fide*), justification being understood as making (*effici*) an unrighteous man righteous or regenerating him.

> What we have shown thus far, on the basis of the Scriptures and arguments derived from the Scriptures, was to make clear that by faith alone we receive the forgiveness of sins for Christ's sake, and by faith alone are justified, that is, out of unrighteous we are made (*efficiamur*) righteous men and are regenerated.

Now what are we to make of these passages which seem to be defining justification in non-forensic terms? The answer is not that Melanchthon is sloppy at this point, for on just this issue he would be meticulously careful. Nor in this discussion in 1531 can it be conjectured that he is acting politically and softpedaling an issue lest he antagonize the Romanists. The fundamental issue in the controversy was whether justification was a forensic act, and Melanchthon has made his position crystal clear (IV, 252, 305, *passim*) throughout the Apology. No, Melanchthon is deliberately using realistic terminology as he defines justification, terminology which could well have been used by his opponents; but he does so not to goad them, but to make clear that man is really made righteous—he becomes righteous when God justifies and imputes Christ's righteousness to him. The term *efficio* consistently used by Melanchthon in the above contexts unquestionably has a forensic connotation. Melanchthon is saying, prior to the Osiandrian error, prior to Trent and its caricature of the Lutheran doctrine of justification as a kind of pious fiction, that the sinner's justification before God is no fiction, but a real gracious reckoning by God whereby man actually becomes righteous,[26] but by imputation. This is

---

26 That Melanchthon, and Luther who used much bolder terms (*justitia infusa* [WA II, 145ff.]), employed such concrete, realistic terms did not seem to impress the Roman theologians at all. They still in Trent and after Chemnitz's *Examen Concilii Tridentini* represented the Lutheran idea of justification as merely putative and therefore unreal. The final answer to this caricature which should have clarified the Lutheran position completely and concluded the matter, but did not, is given by Quenstedt. It is worth citing a few of his statements. Concerning the reality of the

wholly in accord with Melanchthon's "realist ontology" (making no reference to scholastic or to post-Idealistic realism), which means that reality underlies theological assertions about God (*wahrhaftiglich ist Gott*, AC I, 2), sin (*vere peccatum*, AC II, 2), Christ (*vere Deus, vere homo, vere resurrexit*, AC III, 2,4,), and Christ's body and blood in the communion (*vere adsint*, AC X, 1). One cannot overemphasize the importance of this ontology to Luther and Melanchthon; without it all Christianity has no substance, but is a great fiction.

At this elemental point Lutheran theologians since the eighteenth century have attacked the evangelical doctrine of justification. The great Liberal theologian, Albrecht Ritschl, did so in the nineteenth century when he distinguished between religious judgments of value (*Werturteil*) and judgments of being (*Seinurteil*) and when he denied the vicarious atonement,[27] for obviously if there is no real satisfaction made for sins and no real righteousness to be imputed, there can be no justification at all in the realistic Lutheran sense. In our day we see the same rejection of the reality of

---

imputation of Christ's righteousness he says (*Systema*, P.III, C.8, P.2, Q.5, Observ. 12 [II, 777]), "The righteousness of Christ is not our formal righteousness nor a righteousness that inheres in us subjectively, but is our real (*realis*) and sufficient righteousness by imputation. We do not through this righteousness become righteous by a righteousness inhering in us, but through the imputation of this righteousness we are formally justified in such a way that without it there is not substance to our righteousness before God. From this fact that the righteousness of God is extrinsic to us we conclude that it does not dwell in us formally and intrinsically. And yet it does not follow therefore that righteousness cannot be reckoned to us extrinsically and objectively. For certainly our sins were extrinsic to Christ, and yet they could be imputed for punishment and guilt to Him and be reckoned to Him." (Cf. *ibid*. Observ. 10, 10). Quenstedt insists that the righteousness imputed to us is real and that we are really righteous by it being imputed to us (*Systema*, P.III, C.8, S.2, Obj. dial. 1 [II, 783]): "We must distinguish between a mere putative righteousness which denies the reality of the righteousness and the imputed righteousness which can be reckoned to others. The righteousness of Christ which has been reckoned to us is in itself neither putative nor fictitious, but absolutely real, corresponding exactly to God's mind and will expressed in the Law, nor as a reckoning is it a mere act of imputing something, but it is an absolutely real judgment of God which is rendered from the throne of grace through the Gospel in respect to the sinner who believes in Christ." Quenstedt is so bent on maintaining the reality of our justification, that, like Melanchthon, he includes this matter in his very definition of justification (*Systema*, P.III. C.8, S.1, Th.3, Nota [II, 738]): "The word 'justify' in the Scriptures never signifies to infuse a quality of righteousness into someone, but denotes nothing else than to account a person righteous judically, or to make one righteous (*justum facere*) by an act totally extrinsic to man, an act extrinsically designating its own subject." Even in his definition of justification as a forensic act he speaks of God *making* the sinner righteous. Why? To nail down the reality of the divine action and the effect upon man, that he *is* righteous.

27 *The Doctrine of Justification and Reconciliation* (Clifton, N.J.: Reference Book Publishers, 1966), I, 9; III, 474.

justification by Rudolf Bultmann as outlined in his notorious programatic essay[28] espousing the radical demythologization of the New Testament theology. Again we can only conclude that, if the vicarious atonement is a myth, then any real transferral or imputation of the results of the atonement in a divine forensic act of justification is impossible. Paul Tillich too affirms an ontology of his own[29] in which *ex hypothesi* the reality of a divine verdict of acquittal is both impossible and unnecessary.

Is any such fundamental assault being waged against the doctrine of justification in Lutheran circles today? I think so. This is, in effect, what Robert Jenson is doing in his recent popular book, *Lutheranism*, written in collaboration with Erik W. Gritsch.[30] To Jenson justification is not a "content item" of the Gospel, along with other content items (p. 43). Dogma, which (I take it) teaches what justification is, is "not a particular proposed content of the church's proclamation, along with other contents. It is rather a metalinguistic stipulation of what *kind* of talking—about whatever contents—can properly be the proclamation and word of the church." Thus, one "does gospel." Jenson rejects the "whole Western ontological tradition," which, as far as I can see, boils down to a repudiation of the view that reality is made up of "substances" with "attributes" (p. 65). "This ontology is inconsistent with the gospel as understood by the Reformers," Jenson confidently asserts. In the place of this outmoded ontology, Jenson substitutes what I would call his own ontology of "communication." He says that a person has his identity by communication (p. 66); thus justification is not a real, divine forensic act ("Lutherans created the doctrine of justification 'in the heavenly court,' " p. 67) whereby I become forgiven and really righteous before God, but a (divine) "communication" which makes me what I am and becomes the "locus" for "God's reality" for me. What reality means in this context is anyone's guess, but probably it has nothing to do with God's existence, but refers to His gracious presence, or to my existential awareness of that presence which is "real" only in communication. So much for Jenson's position.

Now, if asked, I suppose Jenson would reply that in some sense our justification by God is real, real in communication and dependent upon the absolutely "unconditional promise" (which he never defines—at least, not in Western ontological terms so that the rest of us can understand him). But does my justification rest upon reality, the reality of the *propter Chris-*

---

28 "New Testament Mythology," in *Kerygma and Myth*, ed. Hans Werner Bartsch, tr. Reginald H. Fuller (New York: The Macmillan Company, 1953), pp. 1–44.

29 *Dynamics of Faith* (New York: Harper and Row, 1957).

30 Eric W. Gritsch and Robert W. Jenson, *Lutheranism* (Philadelphia: Fortress Press, 1976), pp. 42–44, 64–67, 101–109.

tum, which is *extra et ante fidem* or any "communication"? And is the verdict of justification itself real, declared *coram tribunali divino*, and not merely real in "communication"? Jenson's reply to these questions, although never explicitly given, is clearly "no."

Now I would be the last to accuse Prof. Jenson of building his entire theology of justification upon some quasi-idealistic philosophy, or upon an ontology of relationship or process which makes cognitive theological assertions unnecessary. But he is certainly applying his orthodox and tradition terminology (e.g., "unconditional promise," faith as "hearing," etc.) to an entirely different *Vorbild*, or pattern, than that of the Lutheran Confessions, something like putting new wine into old bottles. After all, the old *Vorbild*, or doctrinal model, affirmed that the subject of theology, the living God and His actions, was ontologically antecedent to any conceptualization of Him, or pattern of theology. In fact, any pattern of theology must conform to what God is like in Himself and to what He has done according to His own revelation of Himself. According to this classic Christian model, God is real, the creator and sustainer of all that exists; He is really Triune (an immanent, not just an economic Trinity); the first Adam really fell and his sin was really imputed to the whole human race; the Son of God really became incarnate; He really suffered and died and rose again; the atonement is real; heaven is real; hell is real; forgiveness and justification are real, not just metaphors for something else. Unless all this is included in our theological *Vorbild*, there is nothing left of our Christianity and our Gospel, except words, empty words, impotent words, words without referents and without meaning, like tinsel on a discarded Christmas tree, or bridgework on a corpse.

Again let me say I am not accusing Prof. Jenson of attempting a brilliant and sinister *coup de grace* whereby he has deftly and unobtrusively laid to rest outmoded thought-forms and ontologies and offered a whole new *Vorbild* for theologizing, and thus negated the Lutheran doctrine of justification by negating its reality. I am not quite sure I understand him well enough to say that. Perhaps no one does. Perhaps no one can. I am simply suspicious of theologians—not of philosophers or scientists, who have their own stock in trade—but of theologians, whose only source of theology is allegedly the divinely revealed Scriptures, who make light of ontology, especially when it happens to be the ontology of Western (and Eastern) Christianity and of the Lutheran Confessions.

5. *The fifth assault against the evangelical doctrine of justification by faith is to make faith a condition for justification.* The Formula emphatically excludes such a view (SD III, 43; cf. SD III, 13; Apol. IV, 5y, 338):

Faith justifies solely for this reason and on this account, that as a means and instrument it embraces God's grace and the merit of Christ in the promise of the Gospel.

I could have discussed the aberration of conditioning justification on faith under thesis 3, but I think it deserves special attention because it has been such an insidious and persistent force in the church since the Reformation, also among Lutherans. Crassly, of course, historic Roman and Arminian theology made faith as a work and virtue of man a condition for fellowship with God and for salvation. But in a more subtle form the tendency to condition justification on faith is found in every form of synergism and pietism and religious emotionalism, in ideologies which stress inwardness and subjectivity, in Christian Existentialism and Crisis Theology (Emil Brunner), all protestations of adherence to the *sola gratia* notwithstanding. We find the tendency wherever there is a preoccupation with faith as such or an inordinate interest in the phenomenology of faith, rather than in the object of faith, Christ and His atoning work, and in the Gospel. For my faith is not the Gospel or the content of the Gospel, but rather embraces and applies the Gospel. Faith is never directed toward itself. Soren Kierkegaard made faith a condition for justification, not by teaching such an aberration—he was too good a theologian for that—but by an emphasis, by stressing always the *fides heroica*, the *fides activa* in the Christian life, in answer to the question "How can I become a Christian?" rather than stressing the *fides passiva* which does nothing, but is pure receptivity.

This tendency to make justification dependent upon faith has a long and sorry history in the Lutheran church, which in its Confessions hints at no such thing. The tendency has its origin in synergism (Calixtus, Musaeus) and pietism (Baier, Hollaz). To be sure the monergism of divine grace was consistently affirmed by these theologians along with the conditionality of faith, but the result was confusion and their theology became synergistic all the same. The position taken by Baier is particularly offensive.[31] He asserts, "Now also faith in Christ is rightly considered to be a cause of salvation." How is this to be understood? Baier explains that he is not speaking of faith as an *actus* or quality in man, but only as directed toward Christ. Nor is he implying that faith is any kind of efficient or formal cause. "But its causality," he says, "consists in this, that it presents to God the merit of Christ as something which has been apprehended by man, and in this way faith moves God to grant out of grace salvation to

---

31 John William Baier, *Compendium Theologiae Positivae*, ed. C. F. W. Walther (St. Louis: Concordia Publishing House, 1879), I, 41.

that man. And so faith is rightly referred to as a moving cause, because it moves God, not by its own merit, but by the dignity of the merit of Christ. Thus in distinction from the merit of Christ, faith can be called a *causa impulsiva minus principalis* of salvation." Baier thinks he has safeguarded himself by his reference to the object of faith. And, of course, we must realize that his use of the term cause (*causa*) is not freighted with our present day understanding, but meant only "factor," or "role." But, nevertheless, his misleading, ill-conceived notion of faith as a moving cause of salvation cannot fail to detract from the objective *causa meritoria* of justification, namely, the obedience of Christ, which, along with the grace of God, later called the *causa impulsiva externa* of justification,[32] was the only basis or cause mentioned by Melanchthon in the Apology. Baier's view cannot fail, therefore, to lead to synergism and all kinds of subjectivistic aberrations, which we see later in Hollaz and the pietists.[33] Can you imagine Luther speaking in such a cold way? Listen to him as he speaks of faith's role in a person's salvation:

> Faith holds out the hand and the sack and just lets the good be done to it. For as God is the giver who bestows such things in His love, we are the receivers who receive the gift through faith which does nothing. For it is not our doing and cannot be merited by our work. It has already been granted and given. You need only open your mouth, or rather, your heart, and keep still and let yourself be filled.[34]

---

32 Quenstedt, *Systema*, P.III, C.8, S.1, Ekthesis 7 (II, 741).

33 What Baier does here is really a far cry from Quenstedt's procedure, which was also unwise, in making faith a *causa media*, or organic cause, of justification, and attempted to clarify faith's instrumental role in an individual's justification as an *organon leptikon* (*ibid*. Th. 10, Nota 1 and 2 [II, 742–3]). And Quenstedt (Th. 11) safeguards himself from such consequences being drawn from his calling faith a cause of justification by saying, "The causality of faith in the act of justification is nothing other than organic in that it justifies simply by apprehending the merits of Christ. The reason for its causality, its justifying role, has to do with faith not it itself and insofar as it is an apprehension of something and thus our act which has some kind of dignity, small or great, either in itself and by its own nature, or because it is highly pleasing and acceptable to God. No, the reason for the causality of faith consists only in the justifying object which is apprehended." The error of Baier can be traced back beyond Quenstedt to Gerhard, who in his long and excellent study on justification by faith has a section entitled "On the effect of faith which is justification" (*de effectu fidei qui est justificatio*). The actual discussion is inoffensive and never insinuates that faith is a moving cause of justification. But the seed was sown. There are troubles in the causal method brought into Lutheran dogmatics by Gerhard. C. F. W. Walther (*The Proper Distinction between Law and Gospel*, tr. W. H. T. Dau [St. Louis: Concordia Publishing House, 1929], p. 274) calls it a "dangerous method." In this case it certainly caused a lot of trouble and paved the way for synergism. And synergism, regardless of one's good intentions, is still synergism.

34 WA/2 XI, 1104.

Baier's view of faith as a moving cause of justification is really quite inconceivable and self-contradictory. To revert to the well worn Lutheran analogy, how could the empty hand of the beggar, viewed as that which receives a priceless gift, move the benefactor to bestow the gift?

But what about the biblical language which often says that if one believes, God will save, or justify, him (e.g. Rom. 10:9; 4:24). It is, of course, an undeniable fact that Scripture speaks in such a way, as our pietistic and synergistic friends never cease to remind us. How do we reply to this? We must affirm emphatically that, when the Scriptures or our Confessions speak in such a fashion, they are speaking of faith as an ordinate condition, which is really no condition at all in the usual sense. Commenting on Romans 3:22, Sebastian Schmidt concedes that faith may be called a condition, but only in the sense of a *mode* according to which God Himself saves and justifies us, namely, through faith.[35] Gerhard offers us more aid as we combat the synergists and pietists on this sensitive issue: "The term 'if' is either etiological or syllogistic; that is, it designates either cause or consequence. In the preaching of the Law, 'if you do this, you shall live,' the term is etiological, inasmuch as obedience is the cause on account of which eternal life is given to those who obey the Law. But in the Gospel promises, 'if you believe, you will be saved,' the term 'if' is syllogistic, inasmuch as it relates to the mode whereby God applies the divine promises, and this is through faith alone."[36]

It is difficult to understand how one can make faith a condition of justification (in the causal sense), without teaching that justification is *propter fidem* or at least *post fidem*, rather than *per fidem*. But where do the Scriptures or our Confessions ever say that faith creates, causes, occasions, precedes or conditions God's gracious justification? Faith does not create as it receives; it receives what is already a reality. It is, in fact, the word of forgiveness, already acquired and objectively offered and imparted, that creates faith. Melanchthon (Apol. XII, 42) says, "Faith is conceived and confirmed through absolution, through the hearing of the Gospel."

The danger and the tragedy of making faith a condition for justification is that one begins to look for assurance of salvation and grace, not in the objective atonement and righteousness of Christ, but in the quality or strength of one's faith, as if justifying faith is something other than pure trust and receptivity. C. F. W. Walther has a most enlightening and helpful

---

35 *Op. cit.*, p. 326. Earlier he says (p. 254), "The apostle has pointed out the true mode of justification in Rom. 3:21-2, not through the Law or our own righteousness, but through the righteousness of God appropriated by faith. This universal mode of justification is for all men, provided that (*modo*) they believe."

36 *Loci Theologici*, VII, 117.

chapter on the danger of making faith a condition for justification.[37] Walther points out that to make justification depend upon faith ultimately robs a poor sinner of comfort, for then his faith becomes, not a result of the Gospel's powerful working, but a part of the Gospel itself. Walther shows how foolish it is to go this route by means of many telling examples. Let me use one of my own. Let us say that you and I are engaging in a Kennedy evangelism program and we are admitted to the home of an old unchurched man who, as far as we know, is unconverted. I witness to him, telling him of the boundless grace of God toward all sinners, grace which sent His own Son into the flesh to be our Savior and Substitute, grace which sent Him to the cross to pay for the sins of us all, grace to forgive us totally and save us forever. The man responds with utter joy. "What a wonderful message," he says, "what a wonderful, comforting message for a poor old sinner." But you interject, "Wait a minute, sir, you have to believe this message! Everything my friend here has said is of no value to you unless you believe it." How do you react to this little scenario? Do you think your interjection helped the old man? Is not what you did rather foolish and dangerous? It is like taking in a beautiful sunset on my front porch and being told that somehow my appreciation of it conditioned it, like the *esse est percipi* of the subjective Idealists. But we Lutherans, following Apology IV, the most magnificent treatise ever written on the subject of justification by faith, are realists, and our faith rests on the realities of the Gospel of justification.

---

37 *Op cit.*, chapter 25.

LUTHER AND THE DOCTRINE OF JUSTIFICATION

> "Luther and the Doctrine of Justification" is primarily a study in the practical value of justification. It presents the doctrine, then occupies itself with a presentation of how the reformer applied the comfort and assurance of the article on justification to the sinner and to the theological task. It was published by *Concordia Theological Quarterly* in 1984. (Permission has been granted for reproduction in this collection.)

IN THIS ARTICLE I WILL ADDRESS myself to the centrality of the doctrine of justification in Luther's theology and how it worked its way out in Luther's hermeneutics and theological enterprise as a whole.

I.

Stress has always been placed by Lutheran theologians and historians on the importance of the doctrine of justification for Luther in his search for a gracious God and in his theological writings. May I merely cite a small representative number of statements from Luther on the *centrality*, *importance*, and *usefulness* of the article of justification.

> If we lose the doctrine of justification, we lose simply everything. Hence the most necessary and important thing is that we teach and repeat this doctrine daily, as Moses says about his Law (Deut. 6:7). For it cannot be grasped or held enough or too much. In fact, though we may urge and inculcate it vigorously, no one grasps it perfectly or believes it with all his heart. So frail is our flesh and so disobedient to our spirit![1]

---

1 *Luther's Works* (American Edition), 26, 26; cf. *LW* 26, 116, 126.

Again Luther says,

> This is the true meaning [*vera ratio*] of Christianity, that we are justified by faith in Christ, not by the works of the Law.[2]

> This is the highest article of our faith, and if one should abandon it as the Jews do or pervert it like the papists, the church cannot stand nor can God maintain His glory, which consists in this, that He might be merciful and that He desires to pardon sins for His Son's sake and to save.[3]

> If this doctrine of justification is lost, the whole Christian doctrine is lost.[4]

> This doctrine can never be urged and taught enough. If this doctrine is overthrown or disappears, then all knowledge of the truth is lost at the same time. If this doctrine flourishes, then all good things flourish, religion, true worship, the glory of God, and the right knowledge of all conditions of life and of all things.[5]

For Luther we see that the article of justification is indeed the article upon which the church stands and falls, so far as its doctrine is concerned. Luther puts the matter even more emphatically when he says,

> There is one article and one basic principle in theology, and he who does not hold to this article and this basic truth, to wit, true faith and trust in Christ, is not a theologian. All other articles flow into and out of this one, and without it the other articles are nothing. The devil has tried from the beginning to nullify this article and to establish his own wisdom in its place. The disturbed, the afflicted, the troubled, and the tempted relish this article; they are the ones who understand the Gospel.[6]

The article of justification, or, as Luther often puts it, faith in Christ, is at the center of all Christian doctrine and is the heart of the Gospel itself. But the article of justification, or the forgiveness of sins through faith in Christ, is for Luther not merely the center of theology; it is the very heart of the content of Christian faith:

---

2 *LW* 26, 136.

3 Erlangen Ausgabe, Opera Latina, 10, 137.

4 Erl. Lat. 21, 20.

5 Erl. Lat. 21, 12; cf. WA 30/2, 651.

6 Weimar Ausgabe, *Tischreden*, No. 1583.

> In my heart one article alone rules supreme, that of faith in Christ, by whom, through whom, and in whom all my theological thinking flows back and forth day and night. And still I find that I have grasped this so high and broad and deep a wisdom only in a weak and poor and fragmentary manner.[7]

Luther maintains, "It is above all for this doctrine, on which we insist so diligently, that we bear the hate and persecution of Satan and of the world. For Satan feels the power and results of this doctrine."[8] Luther is not only insistent but at times downright arrogant as he maintains the centrality and rectitude of his doctrine of justification, or Christian righteousness:

> Thus I do not listen to anything at all that is contrary to my doctrine; for I am certain and persuaded through the Spirit of Christ that my doctrine of Christian righteousness is the true and certain one.[9]

And he had better be certain of his position at this point, for whoever loses this article of justification loses Christ, no matter how great his sanctity may be.[10]

It is in his *Lectures on Galatians* that Luther's views on the centrality and supreme importance of the article of justification are most prominent and articulate. Significantly, even in the early pages of this great commentary and even before he gets to Paul's discussion on justification, he speaks at length about the article and its significance, and positions it, as it were, vis-a-vis the Law and legalism (including Judaism, papism, fanaticism, etc.), the Gospel (which is the revelation of God's love in Christ and Christ's redemptive work), false doctrine (which always stems from a misunderstanding or rejection or ignoring of justification), the interpretation of the Bible, Christian instruction, confession of the faith, *Seelsorge*, and any other concerns. Luther sees the book of Galatians as a Pauline commentary on the doctrine of justification. And he emphasizes repeatedly that justification is based upon God's grace in Christ and upon Christ's redemption. This is a matter of crucial importance for Luther.[11]

---

7 Erl. Lat. 21, 3.

8 *LW* 26, 285; cf. *LW*, 24, 319.

9 *LW* 26, 198.

10 *LW* 26, 395. "Whoever falls from the doctrine of justification is ignorant of God and is an idolater. Therefore it is all the same whether he then returns to the Law or to the worship of idols; it is all the same whether he is called a monk or a Turk or a Jew or an Anabaptist. For once this doctrine is undermined, nothing more remains but sheer error, hypocrisy, wickedness, and idolatry, regardless of how great the sanctity that appears on the outside."

11 *LW* 26, 54. "It seems to be a trivial matter to teach the Law and affirm works, but this does more damage than human reason can imagine. Not only does it mar and

II.

What precisely dues Luther mean and include when he speaks about the article of justification?[12] When he extols the article and speaks of its supreme value for the Christian and its usefulness for the Christian theologian, he does not have in mind a narrow formulation requiring the term "justify" and embracing exclusively its sense in Romans 3:28 or Galatians 2:16, apart from their broader context. We must bear in mind that Luther in his Small Catechism never even uses the word "justify." Nor may we conclude that Luther has in mind merely a kind of theological shorthand resume of the Holy Spirit's work in bringing the individual to faith in Christ and forgiving him, as is expressed in the Third Article. No, for Luther the article of justification is grounded not in what the Spirit does as He brings a person to faith, but in the redemption and righteousness of Christ. Christ and His work are for Luther the substructure of the sinner's justification.[13] We have justification and the forgiveness of sins only through Christ's death and resurrection.[14] Almost as often as Luther says that the sinner's justification is through faith in Christ he says simply that it takes place *sola Christi justitia*,[15] or "by grace through Christ."[16] Any discussion of justification by faith in Christ will automatically introduce us to the work of Christ's atonement, or rather Christ's work of perfect obedience as a prerequisite to the preaching of justification.[17] And so, if one would speak of justification before God, one must approach the matter from the vantage point of the Gospel which deals with the person of Christ and His work as the mediator who brings righteousness and reconciliation and salvation to lost sinners.[18]

To Luther the article of justification enhances the work of Christ,[19] points to it, and emphasizes it as the basis of our justification. How often does Luther in a hundred different ways say that if justification is not by grace through faith in Christ, then Christ died in vain![20] For Luther the

---

obscure the knowledge of grace, but it also removes Christ and all His blessings, and it completely overthrows the Gospel, as Paul says in this passage."

12 Terms which Luther uses in this respect are *articulus*, *doctrina*, and occasionally *locus* (theme).

13 *LW* 26, 396.

14 *LW* 26, 224.

15 *LW* 26, 40; cf. 247.

16 *LW* 26, 99.

17 *LW* 26, 33, 35, 38.

18 *LW* 26, 30.

19 *LW* 26, 179.

work of Christ is not only the basis for God's justifying us and the meritorious cause of our justification, but actually constitutes our righteousness
before God, as Luther emphatically puts it in his "Disputation on Justification" of 1536.[21]

Actually, Luther says precisely the same things about the "article concerning Christ" (*Artikel von Christo*), or the article concerning our knowledge of Christ (*Artikel von Erkenntnis Christi*), and extols this article in his
Sermons on the Gospel of St. John as he does the article of justification in his
Lectures on Galatians and elsewhere. One can only conclude that for Luther
the two articles involve each other and are really one article, or that the
article concerning a person's justification through faith is based upon the
article of Christ's redemption. This fact is made emphatically clear in the
Smalcald Articles (II, II, I) where Luther makes the office and work of
Jesus Christ, or our redemption, the "first and chief article" of the Christian faith. After quoting four pertinent Bible passages dealing with Christ's
redemption and atonement, he then proceeds to say, "Inasmuch as this
must be believed and cannot be obtained or apprehended by any work, law,
or merit, it is clear and certain that such faith alone justifies us, as St. Paul
says in Romans 3, 'For we hold that a man is justified by faith apart from
the works of the Law' (Romans 3:28), and again, 'That [God] Himself is
righteous and that He justifies him who has faith in Jesus' (Romans 3:26)."
When Luther continues by saying that "Nothing in this article can be
given up or compromised," and cites Acts 4:12 and Isaiah 53:5, I assume
that he is speaking of the article of redemption, but redemption as it is to
be appropriated through faith.

III.

What specifically is the value and use of the article of Christ, or the article
of justification? From the statements cited above and many others in which
Luther extols the doctrine, I think we can come to four very definite conclusions.

1. First and foremost, the doctrine gives abundant comfort to the pen-
itent sinner, the comfort of the very Gospel itself. For the doctrine of
Christ and of justification *is* the Gospel. In the article of justification,
Luther says, is assurance and peace.[22] If one loses justification, he loses the
Gospel itself.[23] Faith in Christ alone gives comfort. "We must turn our

---

20 *LW* 26, 17, 19, 26, 27, 28, 32, 182, 440.
21 WA 39, 97–98.
22 *LW* 26, 27.
23 *LW* 26, 26.

eyes completely to that bronze serpent, Christ nailed to the cross (John 3:14). With our gaze fastened firmly to Him we must declare with assurance that He is our righteousness and life and care nothing about the threats and terrors of the Law, sin, death, wrath, and the judgment of God. For Christ on whom our gaze is fixed, in whom we exist, and who also lives in us, is the Victor and Lord over the Law, sin, death, and every evil. In Him a sure comfort has been set forth for us, and victory has been granted."[24] At this point Luther is often wont to contrast the works of the Law which thunders against our sin and the Gospel of Christ which gives joy and peace to the believer.[25] For the Gospel, the doctrine of Christ, tells us of the "price," or "cost," that God would pay to deliver us from our sins.

It is chiefly in Luther's comments on the death and redemption of Christ, which constitute the sinner's righteousness before God, that he emphasizes the consolation to be found in this doctrine. Commenting on John 16:10, where Christ tells His disciples that the Holy Spirit will convince the world of righteousness because He goes to the Father, that is, carries out His work of redemption, Luther says, "There is no other consolation than Christ's going to the Father. This is our chief possession and inheritance, our ultimate trust and eternal righteousness."[26] This knowledge of Christ, "that He became a curse for us and set us free from the curse of the Law," offers the believer the most "delightful comfort."[27] And so it "is our highest comfort, to clothe and wrap Christ this way in my sins, your sins, and the sins of the entire world, and in this way to behold Him bearing all our sins."[28] The doctrine of Christ and His redemption "is the most joyous of all doctrines and the one that contains the most comfort. It teaches that we have the indescribable and inestimable mercy and love of God."[29] Of course, the inestimable comfort to be derived from the doctrine of Christ is possessed only by one who believes in Him, by the Christian. And so Luther defines the Christian as follows: "A Christian is not someone who has no sin or feels no sin; he is someone to whom, because of his faith in Christ (*propter fidem*), God does not impute his sins. This doctrine brings firm consolation to troubled consciences amid genuine terrors. It is not in vain, therefore, that so often and so diligently we

---

24 *LW* 26, 166.

25 *LW* 26, 175; cf. WA 28, 271; *Tischreden* 1, 2457b.

26 *LW* 24, 349. The entire discussion (pp. 345–349) stresses the comfort to be found in the "doctrine of Christ."

27 *LW* 26, 278.

28 *LW* 26, 279.

29 *LW* 26, 280.

inculcate the doctrine of the forgiveness of sins and of the imputation of righteousness for Christ's sake, as well as the doctrine that a Christian does not have anything to do with the Law and sin, especially in a time of temptation . . . . Therefore when the Law accuses and sin troubles, he looks to Christ; and when he has taken hold of Him by faith, he has present with him the Victor over the Law, sin, death, and the devil—the Victor whose rule over all these prevents them from harming him."[30]

2. Only the doctrine of justification according to Luther could give certainty to the believer. "Whoever does not know the doctrine of justification takes away Christ the Propitiator [*propitiatorem*]."[31] One who attempts to make atonement for himself apart from Christ the Mediator can only fall into utter despair.[32] Luther gives this advice:

> Therefore if sin makes you anxious, and if death terrifies you, just think that this is an empty spectre and an illusion of the devil—which is what it surely is. For in fact there is no sin any longer, no curse, no death, and no devil, because Christ has conquered and abolished these things. Accordingly, *the victory of Christ is utterly certain*; the defects lie not in the fact itself, *which is completely true*, but in our incredulity. It is difficult for reason to believe such inestimable blessings. In addition, the devil and the sectarians—the former with his flaming darts (Eph. 6:16), the latter with their perverse and wicked doctrine—are bent on this one thing: to obscure this doctrine and take it away from us. It is above all for this doctrine, on which we insist so diligently, that we bear the hate and persecution of Satan and of the world. For Satan feels the power and results of this doctrine.[33]

In this significant statement Luther makes it clear that it is the doctrine of Christ's victory that gives certainty, and that faith clings to this doctrine, or to the content of it; namely, Christ's redemption. Of course, no one "has" certainty who does not hold with "a firm faith" to this doctrine. But it is clear that for Luther the believer's certainty is based on the objective righteousness of Christ and His work of redemption, not on his own faith in Christ. For it is the righteousness of Christ which the Christian receives through faith. For Luther certainty is an element of faith which clings to Christ and His redemption. And in this sense the Christian's certainty is a certainty of faith.[34]

---

30 *LW* 26, 133. I have no explanation for the use of *propter fidem* here except that Luther is not speaking of justification here, which is always *per fidem*. Luther uses the phrase *per fidem* in the immediate context.

31 *LW* 26, 28.

32 *LW* 26, 29.

33 *LW* 26, 284–285.

3. The article of justification is a bulwark against heresy and the sects. This is a strong emphasis of Luther's which crops up in many of his writings but again most often in his Galatians commentary:

> Therefore I say (as I have often said) that there is no power and remedy against the sects except this one article of Christian righteousness. If you lose this it is impossible to avoid other errors or the sects. We see this today in the fanatics, the Anabaptists, the Sacramentarians, who having set aside this doctrine never stop doing away with other doctrines, erring and seducing others. And there is no doubt that they will raise up more sects and invent new works. But what are all these things, even though they seem fine and very holy, compared with the death and the blood of the Son of God who gave Himself for me?[35]

Luther is very emphatic in this matter. He points out "that throughout history we find that all heresy and error have arisen where this doctrine has disappeared,"[36] or where people become smug about the way of salvation and think they know everything. On the other hand, he points out that history teaches us that when the article concerning Christ has been set forth as the chief article and has been understood correctly, as in the case of certain of the fathers, the other articles of faith were retained as well. Among the papists and the sects of his day he sees clear examples of other articles of the faith being attacked when the chief article concerning Christ is ignored or distorted.

On the other hand, the Christian cannot smugly assume that he can remain perfectly orthodox in all the articles of faith simply by giving formal adherence to the doctrine of justification. For the matter of justification is a "slippery thing"—not because of itself, for in itself the doctrine is "absolutely sure and certain." But it is slippery in respect to us. How often, in tribulations, will even the best theologian slip away from the "firm footing" afforded by this doctrine into doubt, false doctrine, and, very commonly, misapplication of Law and Gospel. And thus everything is ruined and one forgets justification, grace, Christ, and the Gospel. The Christian and the Christian theologian must be very aware of how easily this doctrine can slip away and how, as a result, the other articles of faith are lost as well as Christ and the Gospel.[37]

---

34 *LW* 26, 172. In such a sense Luther speaks of a "certain faith": "Here you have the true meaning of justification described, together with an example of the certainty of faith (*exemplum certitudinis fidei*). 'I live by faith in the Son of God, who loved me and gave Himself for me'—anyone who could say these words with Paul in a certain and constant faith (*certa et constanti fide*) would be truly blessed."

35 WA 41/1, 296.

36 *LW* 24, 320.

4. The doctrine of justification is a fundamental principle for the Christian in applying and integrating Law and Gospel and the entire Christian doctrine. When Luther says that justification by faith, or the doctrine of Christ, is the chief doctrine, he means very definitely that no teaching drawn from reason or even from the Bible itself (such as the accusations of the Law) can be used against it. He says, "Therefore any doctrine at all that does not teach as mine does, that all men are sinners and are justified solely by faith in Christ, must be false, uncertain, evil, blasphemous, accursed, and demonic, and so are those who either teach or accept such a doctrine."[38] In his *Smalcald Articles* (II, II, 1–4) Luther scrupulously applies this principle against the various legalistic aberrations and false practices of the papacy. In no way is he hereby placing the article of justification in opposition to other clear articles of faith, but only to false papistic interpretations of Scripture and practices which undermine the Gospel. And so the theology and practice of the papacy are in this sense subjected to the scrutiny of the Gospel of justification. Luther does not shrink from affirming that an understanding of and adherence to the article concerning Christ will enable the theologian to keep all the articles pure, as we have mentioned above.[39]

Why is this so? I am not sure that one can answer this question completely, but certainly one reason is that the doctrine of justification is for Luther the "principal doctrine of Christianity" (*praecipuus articulus christianae doctrinae*).[40] "And what is all creation in comparison with the doctrine of justification?" But the doctrine of justification is not only the *articulus praecipuus*, but is at the very center of all Christian theology to Luther. "The other articles are rather far from us and do not enter into our experience; nor do they touch us . . . but the article on the forgiveness of sins comes into continual experience with us, and in daily exercise, and it touches you and me without ceasing. Of the other articles we speak as of something strange to us (e.g., creation, Jesus as the Son of God). What is it to me that God created heaven and earth if I do not believe in the forgiveness of sins? . . . It is because of this article that all others touch us."[41] What good does it do a Jew to believe that there is one God who is Creator, even to believe all the articles and accept all of Scripture, but deny Christ?

---

37 WA 40/1, 128–129; cf. *LW* 26, 10; 63, 232.
38 *LW* 26, 59.
39 See Footnote 36.
40 *LW* 26, 106.
41 WA 28, 271ff.

To Luther all doctrine—with the doctrine of Christ at its center—is like a golden ring,[42] like a ring without the tiniest crack, or it would not be perfect. There is an organic relationship that all the articles of faith have with each other. Obviously, then, the very heart of Christian theology will have a bearing on all the articles of faith. Thus, the chief article of justification helps the theologian to coordinate and understand and, most important of all, apply the other articles of faith. It affords the theologian a kind of posture, orientation, vantage point for applying the articles of faith, and particularly for dividing Law and Gospel. For, as we have seen, it is primarily the misapplication of the Law which distorts the doctrine of justification and the Gospel and thus the whole Christian faith.

Is the article of justification a hermeneutical principle which transcends or opposes sound grammatical and historical exegesis? I am sure that no Luther scholar would venture to accuse Luther of exalting the doctrine of justification to such a sovereign role. But may the doctrine be used as a hermeneutical principle alongside of Scripture, not only to clarify texts which are obscure, but even to mitigate the *sensus literalis* of texts which seem to conflict with the chief article?

Only in a restricted or indirect sense can the article of justification be called a hermeneutical rule for Luther. The many statements of Luther's that we have cited would rather indicate that it is a very important *theological tool* for *applying* and *relating* the articles of faith, not primarily a *norm* for *interpreting* the Scriptures. In no case does Luther use the article of justification or of Christ to mitigate what he finds to be the intended sense of a Scripture passage. What we find him doing again and again in his lectures on *Galatians* and throughout his writings is to set passages of Scripture dealing with the chief article of redemption or justification against passages teaching the Law, or to distinguish between Law and Gospel. He seems always to do so on the basis of sound exegesis of the passages under consideration. In every case the text itself determines its own meaning, not another text affirming the Gospel of justification or redemption. And so Law and Gospel (as the Gospel is expressed in the article of justification) stand against each other as two contrary teachings. But just as the Romanists ought not use Law passages to mitigate the *sensus literalis* of passages affirming justification by grace, so passages affirming justification and the redemptive work of Christ may not be employed to change or negate the meaning of passages affirming the Law. The chief article of the Gospel indeed transcends and negates the claims and accusations of the Law, but it does not and cannot alter the *meaning* of Scripture passages teaching the

---

42 *LW* 27, 38.

Law. Thus, the chief article exercises a mighty *theological* function, but not a direct hermeneutical one.

Even the proper distinction between Law and Gospel (justification) is, strictly speaking, not a hermeneutical principle, but a theological one. That is to say, the distinction does not ordinarily determine what passages *mean* in given cases, but rather it aids us in appropriating and applying the Scriptures:

> Such a proper distinction between the function of the Law and that of the Gospel keeps all genuine theology in its correct use. It establishes us believers in a position as judges over all styles of life and over all the laws and dogmas of men. Finally it provides us with a faculty for testing all the spirits (1 John 4:1). By contrast, the papists have completely intermingled and confused the doctrine of the Law and that of the Gospel, they have been unable to teach anything certain either about faith or about works or about styles of life or about judging the spirits. The same thing is happening to the sectarians today.[43]

Notice that in this passage Luther says the same of the function of the proper distinction between Law and Gospel that he said so often concerning the function of the article of Christ and of justification. We might conclude that the theological function of the article of justification is an aspect of properly dividing Law and Gospel in the total activity of the theologian.

If what I have said is a correct understanding of Luther, then we can conclude two things. *First*, there is no conflict for Luther between the article of justification and its authoritative role in the theological enterprise and the authority of Scripture and its role as the *principium cognoscendi*, which also is the basis for the pure doctrine of justification.

There are two passages in Luther which have been used by Luther scholars to indicate that he indeed made the article of justification a hermeneutical norm over Scripture itself. The first is in his *Preface to the Epistle to James* of 1545,[44] in which Luther makes the true test for the apostolicity and so canonicity of the New Testament antilegomena whether they "deal with Christ" or not. The second is a passage from his *Lectures on Galatians*[45] where, speaking metaphorically, Luther opposes Christ the "Lord" and "Author" and "King" of Scripture, that is, the Gospel of justification, against the "Servant," that is, "Scripture," or

---

43 *LW* 26, 331.

44 *LW* 35, 395–396.

45 For a thorough discussion of this interpretation of Luther's words see Gerhard Maier, *The End of the Historical-Critical Method*, translated by Edwin W. Leverenz and Rudolph F. Norden (St. Louis: Concordia Publishing House, 1977).

"passages in Scripture about works." In neither case does Luther intimate that he is opposing the article of Christ to the Scriptures as such or that he is making the article of Christ an authority above the Scripture or any of its verses, or that he is affirming a "norm within the norm of Scripture."[46] In the passage dealing with the canonicity of James Luther is simply applying the necessary principle of Christocentricity which he affirms in the very context of his statement to argue that the Book of James does not

---

46 *LW* 26, 295: "Therefore one should simply reply to them as follows: 'Here is Christ, and over there are the statements of Scripture about works. But Christ is Lord over Scripture and over all works. He is the Lord of heaven, earth, the Sabbath, the temple, righteousness, life, sin, death, and absolutely everything. Paul, His apostle, proclaims that He became sin and a curse for me. Therefore I hear that I could not be liberated from my sin, death, and curse through any other means than through His death and His blood. Therefore I conclude with all certainty and assurance that not my works but Christ had to conquer my sin, death, and curse. Even on natural grounds reason is obliged to agree and to say that Christ is not my work, that His blood and His death are not a cowl or a tonsure or a fast or a vow, and that in granting me His victory He was not a Carthusian. Therefore if he Himself is the price of my redemption, if He Himself became sin and a curse in order to justify and bless me, I am not put off at all by passages of Scripture, even if you were to produce six hundred in support of the righteousness of works and against the righteousness of faith, and if you were to scream that Scripture contradicts itself. I have the Author and the Lord of Scripture, and I want to stand on His side rather than believe you. Nevertheless, it is impossible for Scripture to contradict itself except at the hands of senseless and stubborn hypocrites; at the hands of those who are godly and understanding it gives testimony to its Lord. Therefore see to it how you can reconcile Scripture, which, as you say, contradicts itself. I for my part shall stay with the Author of Scripture,' " (Compare *LW* 37, 50, where Luther accuses Oecolampadius of opposing Scripture against Scripture as he argued from a number of Bible passages against the real presence of Christ's body and blood in the Lord's Supper.) Theologians of various persuasions have interpreted this comment of Luther as making justification a category of hermeneutics, a kind of "norm within the norm." See Gerhard Goelge, "Die Rechtfertigungslehre als hermeneutische Kategorie," *Theologische Literaturzeitung*, 89:3 (March 1963), pp. 162–175; Emil Brunner, *Revelation and Reason*, tr. by Olive Wyon (Philadelphia: The Westminster Press, 1946), p. 12 *infra*; Hermann Sasse, *Sacra Scriptura* (Erlangen: Verlag der Ev.-Luth. Mission, 1981), p. 310, *passim*. Sasse clearly makes the doctrine of justification the analogy of faith for Luther and represents Luther as making this article a *norma* "over the *norma normans* of Scripture," and only with this idea in mind can the Lutheran accept the Formula of Concord statement that the Holy Scripture "remains the only judge, rule, and norm according to which as the only touchstone all doctrine should be and must be understood and judged as good and evil, right or wrong" (FC, Ep., Rule and Norm, 2). Ironically, Sasse, Goelge, Emil Brunner, and the many others who have misinterpreted Luther on the basis of the aforementioned passage to be saying that the authority of Christ, or the doctrine of justification, can set aside the force of Scripture passages or at least is a category of hermeneutics or is a "norm within the norm" have missed a Luther statement in which he, carried away as he often is by the inestimable value of the article of Christ and the crucial function it exercises in the activity of the theologian and in the life of the church, actually praises the fathers for basing all their teach-

qualify for canonicity according to this criterion. He is not attempting to use the article of justification either to interpret James against himself or to mitigate the intention of James' discussion of the doctrine of justification. In the second passage (in his *Lectures on Galatians*) Luther is not only speaking metaphorically in the sense mentioned above, but he also takes occasion to stress the authority of Scripture as such (against the papists who stress only Law passages) to establish doctrine and to insist in the strongest terms that Scripture does not contradict itself, as the papists intimated when they pitted Law passages of Scripture against the chief article of the Christian faith.[47]

Secondly, there is no real conflict between God's Law and the Gospel of justification *as such*, although the two chief themes (*praecipui loci*) found throughout Scripture *appear* as contraries; and the differences between the two teachings must always be held in strict tension, even though the Scriptures thereby may appear to teach contrary doctrines. For instance, Luther often makes statements like the following, "A Christian is righteous and beloved by God [according to the teaching of the Gospel of justification], and yet he is a sinner at the same time [according to the teaching of the Law in Scripture]."[48] It is for Luther basic to the believing exegete, as he reads the Scriptures and listens to God speak to him there, that he hold to the Word of God no matter how inconsistent and absurd it may

---

ings on the central article of redemption. Commenting on John 16:3, Luther says, "If one abides by this article [of Christ] diligently and earnestly, it has the grace to keep one from falling into heresy and from working against Christ or His Christendom. For the Holy Spirit is surely inherent in it, and through it illumines the heart and keeps it in the right and certain understanding, with the result that it can differentiate and judge all other doctrines clearly and definitely, and can resolutely preserve and defend them. This we see in the old Fathers. When they retained this article of faith *and based their doctrines on it, or derived them from it*, they preserved purity of doctrine in every detail; but when they departed from it and no longer centered their arguments in it, they want astray and stumbled with a vengeance as happened at times to the oldest Tertullian and Cyprian. And this is basically the failing not only of the papists but of our schismatic spirits, who rant against baptism and other doctrines. They have already surrendered this article of faith and have paid no attention to it. Instead they have put forth other matters. In this way they have lost a proper comprehension of all doctrines, with the result that they cannot teach anything about them that is right and can no longer preserve any doctrine as unquestionable" (*LW* 24, 320). One can only conclude that Luther is obviously overstating himself here. Shortly before he had said, "Although other doctrines are also based on Scripture [just as is the chief doctrine of Christ]—for example, Christ's birth from a pure virgin—it does not stress them so much as it does this one" (p. 319).

47 *LW* 26, 235; cf. *LW* 26, 282; WA 56, 269–71, 347; 40/1, 368; 4, 320; 46, 342; Erl. Lat. 19, 43.

48 *LW* 26, 235; cf. 232.

seem. Commenting on Galatians 3:6, Luther says, "For faith speaks as follows: 'I believe Thee, God, when Thou dost speak.' But what does God say? Things that are impossible, untrue, foolish, weak, absurd, abominable, heretical, and diabolical, if you consult reason."[49] To Luther, quite obviously, not only do the Law and the Gospel seem to contradict each other, but the articles of faith in general (such as the real presence of Christ's body and blood in the Lord's Supper, baptismal regeneration, the virgin birth, the resurrection, and the ascension) all go against the grain and seem to be foolish and wrong. The faith which Luther speaks of as believing in the Gospel promise (*fides specialis*) involves also a *fides generalis* which believes all the articles of faith subsumed under the general categories of Law and Gospel, no matter how absurd they may seem or how contradictory to each other they may seem at times.

Thus, the Christian and the believing exegete must simply hold to all the articles of faith in all their apparent inconsistency. But the Christian who understands the article of justification is enabled to transcend paradoxes in the articles of faith, including the apparent opposition between Law and Gospel. "Who will reconcile those utterly conflicting statements (*illa summe pugnantia*), that the sin in us is not sin, that he who was damnable will not be damned, that he who is rejected will not be rejected, that he who is worthy of wrath and eternal death will not receive these punishments? Only through the Mediator between God and man, Jesus Christ (I Tim. 2:5)."[50] In fact, when one understands the doctrine of justification, one finds that there is no real contradiction between Law and Gospel at all, but that the two teachings are in complete agreement (*consentientes*). But "to a man who is ignorant of the doctrine of faith, these statements seem to be utterly contradictory."[51]

For Luther, therefore, there is no opposition whatsoever between the doctrine of justification as an integrating principle of theology and the *sola Scriptura* principle, that is, that all our theology is drawn from Scripture and that Scripture alone is the judge of teachers and teachings in the church. The more I read Luther, the more clear it becomes to me that as he extols the doctrine of justification, he extols also the formal principle of our theology, and vice versa.[52] In that very passage where he says that Christ is the Lord and King of Scripture, he strongly warns against con-

---

49 *LW* 26, 227.

50 *LW* 26, 235.

51 *LW* 26, 252.

52 *LW* 26, 98, 104. "I am making such a point of all this to keep anyone from supposing that the doctrine of faith is an easy matter. It is indeed easy to talk about, but it

cluding that Scripture contains any contradictions whatsoever.[53] To believe in Christ and the forgiveness of sins is to believe in His Word. If one has Christ, one has His Word. If one loves Him, one loves His Word. The Word of Scripture was so precious to Luther because Christ and the forgiveness of sins, which are central to Scripture, were so precious to him.[54]

---

is hard to grasp; and it is easily obscured and lost. Therefore let us with all diligence and humility devote ourselves to the study of Sacred Scripture and to serious prayer, lest we lose the truth of the Gospel."

53 WA 40/1, 458–459.

54 *LW* 24, 317.

CLERGY MENTAL HEALTH AND THE DOCTRINE OF JUSTIFICATION

> "Clergy Mental Health and the Doctrine of Justification" is perhaps Preus's most practical work. It briefly defines clergy burnout, then applies the central article to this one painful human problem. Helpful and even devotional at times, it shows that both Lutheran theology and Lutheran theologians can be quite pastoral. It was published in 1984 by *Concordia Theological Quarterly*. (Permission has been granted for reproduction in this collection.)

THE PURPOSE OF THIS STUDY is to find and describe the connection between clergy stress and burnout and the doctrine of justification, often called in Lutheran circles the chief doctrine ("praecipuus locus," Apology of the Augsburg Confession, IV, 5) of our religion. It will address these questions:

- Does the gospel of justification help pastors to cope with the tensions of their office?
- Does it alleviate clergy stress?
- Does it mitigate burnout and help the pastor to transcend the causes of it?

I am using the term "gospel" as the "doctrine of the gospel"; that is, as the cognitive and true message of God's grace and forgiveness of the sinner for Christ's sake. I am using the term "justification" as I believe St. Paul and our Lutheran confessions employ it—as an event; a real, divine action; a verdict of acquittal which has happened and is happening vis-a-vis the world of concrete sinners. The terms "stress," "burnout" and "mental health" are meant here as they are uniformly described and defined by the many psychologists and clergy who have studied the subject.

Burnout is found most often among those in helping or people-related professions, among those who bear heavy responsibilities—therefore often among pastors. The causes cited for burnout are role overload, role confusion, inability to shed continual responsibility and inability to get time off. Christian psychologists, pastors and therapists suggest that burnout can be headed off or overcome by prayer, Scripture reading, physical therapy and exercise, spiritual development, free time and having a support system.

Charles Rassieur in "Stress Management for Ministers" suggests that "the issue" for the church as it copes with pastoral burnout is how to keep it at a manageable level so that the pastor does not conclude that the only viable option is to leave the ministry.[1] If he is correct, the issue of this paper might be this: What role does theology or the gospel—more specifically, the fact of the sinner's justification before God—play in a pastor's reaction to stress and incipient burnout? Does it help the pastor to handle stress, and if so, how?

Rassieur offers some statistics to show that ministers, despite periods of career-related stress, generally do not leave their calling due to burnout or nervous exhaustion as do other professionals. But his statistics do not tell us whether more pastors leave the ministry today than in former years due to inability to cope with stress, nor do they inform us about Lutherans. I suspect that many more Lutheran pastors are quitting their ministries today than sixty or even thirty years ago, due in large part to the inability to cope with stress. Figures on this subject would be most helpful.

Even if few pastors are leaving the professional ministry, how many pastors just "cave in," as one old Norwegian Lutheran pastor used to put it, for lack of another job or profession to enter? Lutheran Church—Missouri Synod statistics, and no doubt those of other church bodies, indicate that thousands of our congregations do not gain members throughout a given year. Certainly that does not mean merely that there is no mission work to be done or that thousands of pastors (and congregations) are just lazy. It could indicate that many pastors have just "gone to seed," in the words of that same Norwegian pastor, in that they just endure the ministry. A valid relationship between the purely secular concept of burnout and the theological concept of justification can be found in an almost parenthetical

---

1 Charles L. Rassieur, *Stress Management for Ministers* (Philadelphia: The Westminster Press, 1982), p. 20.

statement in Cary Cherniss' "Staff Burnout": "When a worker burns out, what was once a 'calling' becomes merely a job."[2]

As Christians we believe that the gospel of justification impacts the total life of the Christian, including bodily and mental functions. As Christians we would agree with stress analysts on the basis of Scripture and experience that stress in itself is neutral and may be either beneficial or detrimental to one's physical, mental and spiritual health. Pressure, along with prayer and Scripture study, makes on a theologian and therefore can be a blessing to a pastor. Just as, according to a secular understanding, two people in the same job or profession respond in utterly different ways—one experiencing frustration, discouragement and demoralization (symptoms of burnout), the other enthusiasm for work, fulfillment and happiness—so two pastors under stress, believing the gospel and trying to apply it to themselves and their flocks, may well react in totally different ways. We cannot guarantee that a Christian pastor will attain a higher degree of mental health under extreme stress than a social worker or some similarly highly motivated person in a helping profession.

Clergy burnout's symptoms include not only fatigue, tension and exhaustion but also anxiety, worry, insecurity and even guilt. Therefore the biblical doctrine of justification by faith and of the monergism of grace bears directly on the matter, for it is calculated to remove anxiety, worry, insecurity and guilt. Burnout can be construed as indicative of failure, lack of vocation and even the breakdown of faith in God's providence and of communion with Him as well as with the staff structure within which the pastor labors. Here too the doctrine of free justification for Christ's sake alone can be applied to help immeasurably the victim of burnout.

Perhaps the gospel of justification has not been comforting, therapeutic or encouraging to the pastor under stress because it is misunderstood, distorted or manipulated. I believe this must be the case. So I propose to review justification in its broad scope with the hope that it might be better understood and applied to the broad subject of clergy mental health.

THE CENTRALITY OF JUSTIFICATION

Following Martin Luther the church of the Augsburg Confession has consistently treated its article on justification as the "articulus stantis et cadentis ecclesiae" (article on which the church stands and falls). This phrase is not a hermeneutical cipher but a principle of theology and religion which affects and permeates the life of the church and the faith and life of the

---

2 Cary Cherniss, *Staff Burnout* (Beverly Hills: Sage Publications, 1980), p. 25.

Christian. Luther says: "This is the highest article of our faith, and if one should abandon it as the Jews do or pervert it like the Papists, the church cannot stand nor can God maintain His glory which consists in this, that He might be merciful and that He desires to pardon sins for His Son's sake and to save."[3] Again he says: "This doctrine can never be urged and taught enough. If this doctrine is overthrown or disappears, then all knowledge of the truth is lost at the same time. If this doctrine flourishes, then all good things flourish—religion, true worship, the glory of God and the right understanding of all conditions of life and of all things."[4]

This article alone makes one wise for salvation, forgives and comforts sinners and affords them the spiritual equipment to endure, although imperfectly, crosses—such as stress—of God's sending. Luther asserts that ". . . he who does not hold to this article and this basic truth, to wit, true faith and trust in Christ, is no theologian. All the other articles flow into and out of this one, and without it the others are nothing. . . . Those who are disturbed and afflicted, those who are troubled and tempted relish this article; they are the ones who understand the gospel."[5]

When Luther speaks of the justification article, he is referring not primarily to a doctrine but to a real, objective event, a divine action which we experience and which controls dynamically the life of a Christian. In this the article is like no other article of faith or divine work. "The other articles are rather far from us and do not enter into our experience; nor do they touch us. . . ," Luther observes. "But the article on the forgiveness of sins comes into continual experience with us, and in daily exercise, and it touches you and me without ceasing."[6]

One's justification for Christ's sake, the fact of one's righteousness before God, often becomes obscured and slips away in times of tension and stress, temptation and testing. In his commentary on Galatians Luther speaks with great sensitivity on this point: ". . . the question of justification is an elusive thing—not in itself, for in itself it is firm and sure, but so far as we are concerned. I myself have had considerable experience of this, for I know how I sometimes struggle in the hours of darkness. . . . But when in a struggle we should use the Gospel, which is the Word of grace, consolation and life, there the Law, the Word of wrath, sadness and death, precedes the Gospel and begins to raise a tumult. The terrors it arouses in the conscience are no smaller than was the tremendous and horrible spectacle

---

3 *Luther's Works*, Erlangen edition, 10, p. 137.

4 *Ibid.*, 21, p. 12

5 *Luther's Works*, Weimar edition, Table Talk, no. 1583.

6 *Ibid.*, 28, pp. 271–272.

on Mount Sinai (Exodus 19:18)."[7] This central article which alone offers consolation (Apology IV, 5) therefore must be well taught and understood. It must be seen and applied in the context of a right understanding of sin and grace.

PRESUPPOSITIONS OF JUSTIFICATION:
SIN AND GUILT, DIVINE WRATH AND GRACE

God's justification of the sinner is a response to two realities: on the one hand, human sin and guilt before God and God's wrath against the sinner; on the other hand, God's grace by which He justifies the ungodly. It is highly significant that throughout the Lutheran Confessions sin is portrayed as what humanity is rather than what it does. Original sin, the corruption of human nature, is the source of all evil affections and actions. This "Erbsuende" or inherited corruption is not a mere term, weakness, lack or doctrine. It is "vere peccatum" (Augsburg Confession, II, 2), as our Augustana puts it, an actual "morbus" (vice) which is an active force and power toward evil.

Philip Melanchthon says: "Original sin is a sort of living power ['vivax quaedam energia'], in no way and at no time bringing forth any other fruit than vice . . . but the most noble affections few people feel. True, there are those who live honorable lives outwardly . . . But such persons have no reason to glory, for their souls are subject to the most base and miserable affections while they are not even aware of it."[8]

This sin brings damnation to everyone who is not regenerated through the means of grace (AC II, 2). Hardly a mention is made of actual sins as our confessions relentlessly describe man's terrible predicament, his status before God: he is guilty. What people are renders them guilty before God more than what they do, proceeding from what they are (Mark 7:21). "As the proverb of the ancients says, 'Out of the wicked comes forth wickedness . . .' " (1 Samuel 24:13). The exemplary prayer of the publican asks God to be propitiated to him, "the sinner." He repents of what he is by nature. He confesses not his actual sins but his sin or condition.

If sin is a reality which must be repented of, so guilt is a reality. It is not a subjective reality—merely an experience, a feeling of guilt or estrangement. Scripture seems never to speak of guilt as a subjective emotion or affection resulting from sin or anything else. The terms for guilt always

---

7 *Luther's Works*, American edition, 26, pp. 63–64.

8 *Loci Communes* (*Melanchthons Werke*, herausgegeben von Hans Engelland [Guttersloh: Bertelsmann Verlag] II, 1) p. 21.

refer to the fact that the sinner or offender is under judgment (Romans 3:19; Matthew 26:66), even though the sinner may feel no repentance nor even awareness of his or her status (Leviticus 5:17).

God's wrath and grace are the presuppositions for any presentation of the sinner's justification. As Rudolph Bultmann points out, in Paul's theology they are not emotions of God primarily but actions of God's truthfulness and justice.[9] Therefore to be justified and to stand in a state of grace (Romans 5:1–2) means not that God is not angry with sin and the sinner nor that there is no divine judgment but that we have been rescued from His wrath (Romans 5:9). God's grace is the grace of the living God who acts, gave His son (Romans 3:24) and justifies sinners. God works and gives and determines the life of the individual believer (1 Corinthians 15:10; 2 Corinthians 12:9). Grace and power are linked in Scripture. In Lutheran theology God's wrath and His grace that removes His wrath (law and gospel) must be preached and applied to both Christian and unbeliever alike and certainly also to the stress-ridden pastor. These two themes which pervade the entire Scriptures must be portrayed and applied not as mere ideas, gimmicks or metaphors for something else, but as realities which, if they do not always affect the greatly troubled pastor, are the only real spiritual therapeutics he has.

The Basis of Justification

The basis of the sinner's justification is Christ's righteousness, the obedience of His doing and suffering, as our Formula of Concord puts it (Solid Declaration III, 30, 58). Luther emphasized the reality of Christ's atoning work as he continually counseled people who were depressed, fearful, discouraged and ready to quit the ministry. This is what must be done for those who, because they make too little of the sin that has caused their depression, fear and discouragement, cannot apply the gospel of justification to themselves.

To stress his point, Luther makes seemingly outrageous statements at times. But in effect these statements are profoundly comforting. To the troubled Melanchthon he said: "If you are a preacher of God's grace, then preach not an invented but a real grace. If it be real grace, then you dare not bring up any invented sin. God does not justify imaginary sinners. Be a sinner and sin boldly [pecca fortiter], but believe more boldly and rejoice in Christ, the Victor over sin, death and the world. We must sin as long as we are here; life is no house of righteousness. It is enough to confess the

---

9 Rudolph Bultmann, *Theology of the New Testament*, trans. Cedrick Grobel (London: SCM Press, 1952), p. 288–289.

Lamb who carries the sin of the world. From Him no sin can separate us, even if we whored and murdered a thousand times a day. Do you think the redemption and price is so small which such a Lamb paid for our sins? Pray boldly for you are a bold sinner."[10] Luther never tired of preaching the cost of our redemption: the innocent life and death of God's own Son.

THE NATURE OF JUSTIFICATION

What does it mean to be justified? According to the Formula of Concord, the word "justify" means "to declare righteous and free from sins and from eternal punishment of these sins on account of the righteousness of Christ which God reckons to faith" (Philippians 3:9; FC SD III, 17; cf. Apology IV, 305). I believe pastors under severe stress can be benefited greatly by recognizing this objective, forensic, "extra nos" nature of their personal justification. They need to know that justification before God, strictly speaking, is not a subjective experience any more than my acquittal of a charge for speeding, although concomitant with God's gracious verdict of forgiveness are regeneration and the gift of faith (Apology XIV, 72; FC SD III, 19).

The troubled sinner who perceives the objective and forensic nature of justification will not look inwardly to feelings, experiences or quality of faith to gain assurance that he or she is right with God. Rather, such a person looks to Christ crucified and risen "for our justification" (Romans 4:25) and to the Word which proclaims and confers this justification. Of course, justified sinners feel joy and at peace with God, but these emotions are the results, not the criteria, of their justification, God's acceptance of them for Christ's sake.

THE NATURE AND FUNCTION OF FAITH
IN JUSTIFICATION

What is the nature of justifying faith ("fides justificans" or "fides specialis") in Christ in contrast to "fides generalis," or faith in doctrine? We all know the pat answer: faith is trust. But what is trust? This question may be answered best by a study of the Hebrew word *batach*, the term in the Old Testament which most nearly approximates the *pistis* of Paul and John when they speak of justification or salvation through faith. The term means to lean on another (Proverbs 3:5), to prostrate one's self and fall on one's face in utter dependence upon another, to trust another for everything. The object of our trust is always the Lord throughout the Old Tes-

---

10 *Luther's Works*, Weimar edition, Briefe 2, p. 372.

tament, no one and nothing else. In the New Testament the object of our trust is the same: Christ the Lord and His Word of gospel and pardon (John 1:11–19; Luke 8:13; Acts 8:14; 2:41; 1 Timothy 1:14).

In the Apology of the Augsburg Confession Melanchthon beautifully portrays the nature of this trust as it pertains to the sinner's justification. He describes this "justifying faith" as confidence or trust in Christ's promises of mercy ("fiducia promissae misericordiae propter Christum," Apology IV, 79). In essence, the faith through which we are justified is receptivity, whether it be called trust or knowledge of Christ. As Theodore Mueller says in a very perceptive article,[11] faith is not an action verb but a stative verb. The faith through which we are justified is not to be considered "the act of faith,"[12] but an "actio passiva" or, better, an *organon leptikon*—that is, a receiving instrument.

Pastors who suffer stress and affliction, like any Christian in similar circumstances, may be tempted to look to their faith as a reason for self-esteem and assurance rather than to the only object of faith, Christ and His pardoning Word. They conclude that failure and inability to cope are due to weak faith or the lack of faith altogether. They are viewing faith as their act rather than as their reception of God's mercy.

Mental and Spiritual Health

Pastoral burnout or nervous exhaustion is not necessarily a sign of weak faith, works righteousness, spiritual malaise or a particular guilt. Poor mental health does not necessarily denote poor spiritual health. Too many factors pertain to both to allow for any sure correlation.

Luther had periods of deep depression owing largely but not entirely to physical ailments. He was often given to anger and impatience, the inability or unwillingness to cope and to suffer adversities and afflictions and wrongs with calmness and love and without complaint. But he understood what it meant to be right with God. Certainly no legalist, he had experienced the forgiveness of sins. So too had the Apostle Paul, with all his failures and complaining—or rather boasting—of his infirmities, persecutions and frustrations (Romans 7; 2 Corinthians 11:18ff.; 7:5). Pastors who become dependent or aggressive in response to stress are not necessarily so because they are living with a guilt template over their lives. It is perfectly possible for pastors who know they are forgiven, are certain of

---

11 Theodore Mueller, "Repentance and Faith: Who Does the Turning?" *Concordia Theological Monthly*, 44, numbers 1–2, January–April 1981, p. 29.

12 Collin Brown, ed., *The New International Dictionary of New Testament Theology* (Grand Rapids: Zonderan Publishing Company, 1978), I, p. 358.

their salvation and live in the grace of God to suffer burnout and mental exhaustion.

Perhaps an old theologian who knew nothing of psychology or mental health in the modern sense has something helpful to say at this point. C. F. W. Walther offers as his seventeenth thesis in his well-known book, *The Proper Distinction between Law and Gospel*, the following: "The Word of God is not rightly divided when a description is given of faith, both as regards its strength and the consciousness and productiveness of it, that does not fit all believers at all times."[13] Pastors like any Christian may in their own minds be under-achieving, guilt-ridden, uncertain even of their salvation, lazy, despondent and unhappy—and still be believers.

Walther was speaking to young pastors about their preaching, warning them not to paint a false picture of a Christian lest Christians confused and weak in faith conclude that they are not under grace—a terrible tragedy. But I think that today his principle might apply well to pastors or counselors treating victims of nervous exhaustion. They must be cautious in drawing conclusions concerning another's spiritual life in Christ and the inability to cope with the stress and strains of a calling.

While justification before God surely has a profound effect of eternal significance upon a life, nevertheless it cannot be said to be a prevention or cure for nervous exhaustion in any given case. In many cases justification before God, properly applied, will prevent burnout or alleviate it. There is no iron curtain separating the realms of nature and grace, the psychosomatic and the spiritual. But if we pastors are to "use" the gospel of justification at all in reference to mental health, we ought to do so pastorally, not as the medical doctor or psychologist might treat a patient.

In speaking about the psychological and physical effects of the gospel, we must be very cautious as we try to judge empirically what it does or does not do. Even as we trust in providence without seeing its ways, we believe firmly in the gospel's power to heal. We see its effects, but we dare not dogmatize about these effects in given cases.

JUSTIFICATION, ELECTION, AND PROVIDENCE

One pericope from Scripture has been brought to bear on the subject of mental health remarkably often: Romans 8:28–39. It brings together three great theological themes: justification, which Paul has been speaking of throughout the preceding chapters; election, which he introduces with this verse; and providence, which he so beautifully illustrates throughout

---

13 C. F. W. Walther, *The Proper Distinction Between Law and Gospel*, trans. W. H. T. Dau (Saint Louis: Concordia Publishing House, 1929), p. 308.

and especially in verse 32. God's providence serves His grace. His kingdom of power is in the service of His kingdom of grace. Those who are made elect by God likely will suffer stress and strain and cross and affliction in this life, but all of these ultimately are blessings in God's gracious economy. The justified sinner is reminded that Christ's atonement has removed totally and forever the guilt and punishment and burden of sin; that the sins of the flesh, which still remain, are continually forgiven for Christ's sake; but that sickness and pain, the results of sin, are nevertheless the predicted and expected portion of every child of God. Among these chastenings God sends His chosen people may be nervous breakdown and clergy burnout.

If the justification of the sinner is not a prevention or cure for pastoral burnout or mental breakdown, what is its purpose? First, the sinner is justified in order to be saved eternally and to live forever with God, to praise Him in this life and in the life to come. Paul and all of Scripture continually link justification and the forgiveness of sins, together with all the soteriological themes such as redemption and reconciliation, with eternal life, an eschatological reality.

Secondly, God justifies the sinner in order to sanctify him or her (1 Peter 2:9), in order that the justified sinner might love and serve God and neighbor. Melanchthon puts this matter eloquently in the Apology: "We are justified for this very purpose, that, being righteous, we might begin to do good works and obey God's Law. For this purpose we are reborn and receive the Holy Spirit, that this new life might have new works and new impulses, the fear and love of God, hatred of lust, etc." (Apology IV, 348–349).

But what of those pastors who feel unable to cope even in the light of or because of what Melanchthon has said? What of those who see themselves as failures, suffer guilt and have a low self-esteem? They should give heed to Melanchthon's assertion that all the works of a Christian are pleasing to God even though in themselves they are quite neutral and seemingly unimportant. "The incipient keeping of the Law does not please God for its own sake but for the sake of faith in Christ," he says (Apology IV, 166; cf. 177, 172). If this is true, then surely we should be able to carry out our calling with great joy, even with all the tensions and failures, knowing that however things turn out God is using us, and we are the apple of His eye. My self-esteem is in Christ, not in myself. In Christ all my works and activities are pleasing to God.

Can and ought a pastor view mental breakdown or nervous exhaustion as a chastening from a loving God calculated only to bless and bring the pastor (and the congregation) closer to Him? The answer must be a resounding "yes." Yes, if the pastor believes in a loving God who sent His Son to be our Savior. Yes, if the pastor believes in a faithful God who has promised again and again, "I will never leave you." Yes, if the pastor believes in an almighty and providential God who through His Apostle Paul has assured us, "He who did not spare His own Son but gave Him up for us all, will He not also give us all things with Him?" (Romans 8:32). Yes, even if the pastor has difficulty believing all these things or in confusion rejects them for a time. This is not a theology of failure but a theology of victory in failure. God's divine calling and providence allows us to believe and practice this theology of the cross.

Objective Justification

"Objective Justification" is a brief explanation and application of the doctrine of objective justification to a particular controversy in the church. It was written in response to accusations against a professor at Concordia Theological Seminary whom Preus defended politically but with whom he disagreed theologically. This article shows Preus dealing forthrightly with theological conflict especially as it relates to the central article.

THE DOCTRINE OF OBJECTIVE JUSTIFICATION is a lovely teaching drawn from Scripture which tells us that God who has loved us so much that He gave His only Son to be our Savior has for the sake of Christ's substitutionary atonement declared the entire world of sinners for whom Christ died to be righteous (Romans 5:17–19).

Objective justification which is God's verdict of acquittal over the whole world is not identical with the atonement, it is not another way of expressing the fact that Christ has redeemed the world. Rather it is based upon the substitutionary work of Christ, or better, it is a part of the atonement itself. It is God's response to all that Christ died to save us, God's verdict that Christ's work is finished, that He has been indeed reconciled, propitiated; His anger has been stilled and He is at peace with the world, and therefore He has declared the entire world in Christ to be righteous.

The Scriptural Support

According to all of Scripture Christ made a full atonement for the sins of all mankind. Atonement (at-one-ment) means reconciliation. If God was not reconciled by the saving work of Christ, if His wrath against sin was not appeased by Christ's sacrifice, if God did not respond to the perfect obedience and suffering and death of His Son for the sins of the world by forgiveness, by declaring the sinful world to be righteous in Christ—if all this were not so, if something remains to be done by us or through us or in us, then there is no finished atonement. But Christ said, "It is finished." And God raised Him from the dead and justified Him, pronounced Him, the sin bearer, righteous (I Timothy 3:16) and thus in Him pronounced the entire world of sinners righteous (Romans 4:25).

All this is put beautifully by an old Lutheran theologian of our church, "We are redeemed from the guilt of sin; the wrath of God is appeased; all creation is again under the bright rays of mercy, as in the beginning; yea, in Christ we were justified before we were even born. For do not the Scriptures say: 'God was in Christ reconciling the world unto Himself, not imputing their trespasses unto them?' This is not the justification which we receive by faith, but the one which took place before all faith . . . . That is the great absolution which took place in the resurrection of Christ. It was the Father, for our sake, who condemned His dear Son as the greatest of all sinners by causing Him to suffer the greatest punishment of the transgressors, even so did He publicly absolve Him from the sins of the world when He raised Him up from the dead." (Edward Preuss, *The Justification of a Sinner Before God*, pp. 14–15)

OBJECTIVE JUSTIFICATION AND JUSTIFICATION BY FAITH

The doctrine of objective justification does not imply that there is no hell, that God's threats throughout Scripture to punish sins are empty, or that all unbelievers will not be condemned to eternal death on the day of Christ's second coming. And very definitely the doctrine of objective, or general, justification does not, threaten the doctrine of justification through faith in Christ. Rather it is the very basis of that Reformation doctrine, a part of it. For it is the very pardon which God has declared over the whole world of sinners that the individual sinner embraces in faith and thus is justified personally. Christ's atonement, His propitiation of God and God's forgiveness are the true and only object of faith. Here is what George Stoeckhardt, perhaps the greatest of all Lutheran biblical expositors in our country, says, "Genuine Lutheran theology counts the doctrine of general [objective] justification among the statements and treasures of its faith. Lutherans teach and confess that through Christ's death the entire world of sinners was justified and that through Christ's resurrection the justification of the sinful world was festively proclaimed. This doctrine of general justification is the guarantee and warranty that the central article of justification by faith is being kept pure. Whoever holds firmly that God was reconciled to the world in Christ, and that to sinners in general their sin was forgiven, to him the justification which comes from faith remains a pure act of the grace of God. Whoever denies general justification is justly under suspicion that he is mixing his own work and merit into the grace of God."

THE REALITY OF OBJECTIVE JUSTIFICATION

Objective justification is not a mere metaphor, a figurative way of expressing the fact that Christ died for all and paid for the sins of all. Objective justification has happened, it is the actual acquittal of the entire world of sinners for Christ's sake. Neither does the doctrine of objective justification refer to the mere possibility of the individual's justification through faith, to a mere potentiality which faith completes when one believes in Christ. Justification is no more a mere potentiality or possibility than Christ's atonement. The doctrine of objective justification points to the real justification of all sinners for the sake of Christ's atoning work *before* we come to faith in Christ. Nor is objective justification *merely* a "Lutheran term" to denote that justification is available to all as a recent *Lutheran Witness* article puts it—although it is certainly true that forgiveness is available to all. Nor is objective justification a Missouri Synod construct, a *theologoumenon* (a theological peculiarity), devised cleverly to ward off synergism (that man cooperates in his conversion) and Calvinistic double predestination, as Dr. Robert Schultz puts it in *Missouri in Perspective* (February 23, 1981, p. 5)—although the doctrine does indeed serve to stave off these two aberrations. No, objective justification is a clear teaching of Scripture, it is an article of faith which no Lutheran has any right to deny or pervert any more than the article of the Trinity or of the vicarious atonement.

THE CENTRALITY AND COMFORT OF THE DOCTRINE

Objective justification is not a peripheral article of faith which one may choose to ignore because of more important things. It is the very central article of the Gospel which we preach. Listen to Dr. C. F. W. Walther, the first president and great leader of our synod, speak about this glorious doctrine in one of his magnificent Easter sermons: "When Christ suffered and died, He was judged by God, and He was condemned to death in our place. But when God in the resurrection awakened Him again, who was it then that was acquitted by God in Christ's person? Christ did not need acquittal for Himself, for no one can accuse Him of a single sin. Who therefore was it that was justified in Him? Who was declared pure and innocent in Him? We were, we humans. It was the whole world. When

God spoke to Christ, 'You shall live,' that applied to us. His life is our life. His acquittal, our acquittal, His justification, our justification . . . . Who can ever fully express the great comfort which lies in Christ's resurrection? It is God's own absolution spoken to all men, to all sinners, in a word, to all the world, and sealed in the most glorious way. There the eternal love of God is revealed in all its riches, in its overflowing fullness and in its highest brilliance. For there we hear that it was not enough for God simply to send His own Son into the world and let Him become a man for us, not enough even for Him to give and offer His only Son unto death for us. No, when His Son had accomplished all that He had to do and suffer in order to earn and acquire grace and life and blessedness for us, then God, in His burning love to speak to us sinners, could not wait until we would come to Him and request His grace in Christ, but no sooner had His Son fulfilled everything than He immediately hastened to confer to men the grace which had been acquired through the resurrection of His Son, to declare openly, really and solemnly to all men that they were acquitted of all their sins, and to declare before heaven and earth that they are redeemed, reconciled, pure, innocent and righteous in Christ."

THE ISSUE AT OUR SEMINARY

Many of our readers know that our seminary, and one professor in particular, has been recently criticized for undermining this comforting and clear teaching of objective justification. The criticism and garbled accounts of the situation have become so widespread lately that I must now comment on the matter in this issue of the *Newsletter*.

For over 15 years now Professor Walter A. Maier, Jr., has been teaching a course in the book of Romans, and, although he states he has always presented the doctrine of objective justification as taught in our synod (e.g. in the *Brief Statement*), he has taught in class that some of the key passages used in our church to support the doctrine actually do not speak to the subject at all. As a result some within the seminary community and some outside concluded that Dr. Maier did not in fact believe, teach, and confess the article of objective justification. A few—very few—complaints were brought against Dr. Maier and against the seminary for letting this go on.

The president of our synod, who has the responsibility for supervising doctrine in the synod, contacted me and asked me to try to settle the issue and to persuade Dr. Maier to teach an interpretation of the pertinent passages (Romans 4:25; Romans 5:16–19; II Corinthians 5:19) compatible with that which the great teachers of our church in the past (C. F. W. Walther, Francis Pieper, Theodore Engelder, George Stoeckhardt, Martin

Franzmann, William Beck and others) publicly taught. Meetings and discussions immediately took place between Dr. Maier and myself. Later on the matter was considered in faculty meetings, in department meetings, and in special committees appointed to discuss and hopefully to settle the issue. During these meetings, which were always most cordial, Dr. Maier has remained unpersuaded that his interpretation of the pertinent passages is faulty. At the same time he has consistently assured all that he has always taught the doctrine of objective justification as understood in the Missouri Synod. He has, however, referred to other biblical evidence for the doctrine.

In the meantime the president of the synod, growing anxious for a clear solution to the problem, wrote to the entire church body a letter cautioning congregations not to nominate Dr. Maier for president of the synod until the issue was cleared up to his satisfaction.

Now the issue became political, and protests and criticisms against the president of the synod for his action and also against Dr. Maier's teaching began to multiply all over the synod. People naturally began to take sides, not always so much on the doctrinal issue which was not always understood and is still being discussed at our seminary, but for ecclesiastical and personal reasons. We now know that the warning of our synodical president against Dr. Maier not only failed to dissuade congregations from nominating Dr. Maier for the presidency of our synod (as Fourth Vice-President Dr. Robert Sauer had forewarned when attempting to persuade the synodical president not to send his letter), but possibly gained more nominations for Dr. Maier. Dr. Maier is now one of the five men nominated for the presidency of our synod.

On January 30, 1981, the Board of Control met with Dr. Maier and three representatives of the synodical praesidium (which had severely criticized Dr. Maier's doctrinal stance). We heard from two members of the praesidium and then from Dr. Maier and two faculty members whom he had requested to accompany him. The results of this meeting, many of us believed, represented a real breakthrough in understanding, and the Board exonerated Dr. Maier of any false doctrine. It was my belief that the representatives of the praesidium present were also satisfied and happy with the report. In the discussions of this meeting Dr. Maier expressed many genuine concerns related to the doctrine of objective justification, e.g., that no one is saved eternally who is not justified by faith, that God is even now angry with those who reject Christ and do not repent, and that objective justification ought to be preached and taught in such a way that the biblical doctrine of justification by faith is always prominent. The report, in the form of a news release, is found on page 4 of the *Newsletter*, and I urge the reader to read it because *The Reporter*, *The Lutheran Witness*, and most of the newspapers over the country which reported on the matter did not reproduce the report in its entirety. At the same meeting the Board of Control strongly expressed its disapproval of some of the actions of our synodical president in the matter.

Meanwhile the administration of the seminary, with the concurrence of the Board of Control, determined that it would be best for the seminary and for Dr. Maier if he not teach the course in Romans during the next academic year. At first I tried to keep this matter private, but later I decided to make a public report of the fact. My reason for this was three-fold. First, Dr. Maier was reported in news media all over the country as stating that he had not changed his position on the doctrine of objective justification, suggesting to many that three years of discussions with him had been quite fruitless and that he still did not wholeheartedly believe in objective justification. Second, several people sympathetic to Dr. Maier had threatened to withhold funds from the seminary and had even reported our action to the accrediting association of our seminary, The Association of Theological Schools; it was obvious to me that they would make the matter of Dr. Maier's courses public whenever it served their purposes. Third, the president of the synod was preparing a release revealing the fact that Dr. Maier would not be teaching Romans during the next academic year. I thought it would be preferable that the president of the seminary make this fact known rather than those who have no business making such an announcement and who might make the announcement in a way detrimental to either Dr. Maier or the seminary.

This is where the matter now stands. The Board of Control has stated its confidence in the doctrine of Dr. Maier. Dr. Maier is presently teaching Romans, will teach the course this summer, but is slated to teach courses other than Romans next year. The faculty will continue to discuss and try to achieve total agreement in the interpretation of those passages of Scripture which teach objective justification.

A PLEA FOR CONCERN AND UNDERSTANDING

Through this entire uncomfortable time the Board of Control and the administration of the seminary have found themselves in an understandably awkward position. We are pledged to remain faithful to the doctrinal position of our church, a position which we believe with all our hearts, and we will not deviate from this obligation one iota. We are at the same time pledged to defend a professor and colleague if he falls under unjust attack or abuse. I think we were able to maintain this delicate balance while the present issue was pending, until the political issue was injected. Now we find ourselves uncomfortably between two rather large conflicting elements in our synod, both friends of our seminary; those who believe that the president of the synod, whether they agree with his actions or not, had legitimate concerns about the doctrinal position of Dr. Maier, and those who believe that Dr. Maier has been wronged by the president of the synod and that the seminary could have done more to defend and protect him. How can we respond to this divisive situation in the middle of which we find ourselves? We can only say that we regret deeply the anxiety and consternation which good friends of our seminary have experienced because of the episodes I have just recounted. May I ask these friends to bear with us and put the best construction on how we have acted in these circumstances. If you question Dr Maier's teaching on justification, please read and believe the report on page 4 and trust the honesty and sincerity of those including Dr. Maier, who had a part in releasing it. If you believe that Dr. Maier has been wronged by various parties during the last three years which have been trying to him, please believe that our Board of Control and all here at Concordia agree with you; but God, who saved this lost world and forgave the sins of mankind before anyone ever asked Him, commands us also to forgive those who wrong us. And please do not try to defend Dr. Maier by denying the public teaching of the Lutheran Church. God's forgiveness shines bright and clear above all the pettiness and weakness and wrongs and controversy that have transpired in connection with our dear colleague Dr. Maier, and it *will* cover the sins of us all. Lent teaches us this, and Easter confirms it.

For those who wish to read more on Objective Justification, see the following articles:

H. J. Bouman, "Conference Paper on Romans 4:5" *Concordia Theological Monthly (CTM)*, Vol. 18, 1947, pp. 338–347.

Theodore Engelder, "Objective Justification," *CTM*, Vol. 4, 1933, pp. 507–516, 564–577, 664–675.

Theodore Engelder, "Walther, a Christian Theologian," *CTM*, Vol. 7, 1936, pp. 801–815.

Martin H. Franzmann, "Reconciliation and Justification," *CTM*, Vol. 21, 1950, pp. 81–93.

E. W. A. Koehler, "Objective Justification," *CTM*, Vol. 16, 1945, pp. 217–235.

Miscellanea, "God Purposes to Justify Those That Have Come to Faith," *CTM*, Vol. 14, 1943, pp. 787–791.

George Stoeckhardt, "General Justification," *Concordia Theological Quarterly*, April, 1978, pp. 139–144.

LAW AND GOSPEL IN EARLY LUTHERAN DOGMATICS

FROM MELANCHTHON TO THE FORMULA OF CONCORD

> "Law and Gospel in Early Lutheran Dogmatics: From Melanchthon to the Formula of Concord" is, as the title suggests, a rather thorough discussion of the distinction between Law and Gospel found in those contemporaries of Luther who were ultimately key figures in the development of the Formula of Concord. This paper was delivered at the sixth annual Free Conference of the Association of Confessional Lutherans held in Chicago, Illinois, in the spring of 1995, only six months before the untimely death of Robert Preus. (Permission has been granted for reproduction in this collection.)

Blessed are the dead which die in the Lord from henceforth: Yea, saith the Spirit, that they may rest from their labors, and their works do follow them.

INTRODUCTION

The topic of Law and Gospel forms the basis and framework of the first works in dogmatic, or what was later called systematic, theology written by Luther and Melanchthon. Already in his 1521 *Loci Communes* Melanchthon discusses the topic thoroughly, and his original exposition of the topic becomes a pattern for subsequent dogmatic studies and books for the next two hundred years. The Augsburg Confession, which (like all the Lutheran Confessions) is a project in dogmatic theology, is structured according to the framework of Law and Gospel, Article IV on justification constituting the middle and high point in a classic delineation of the chief articles of faith. The Apology of the Augsburg Confession is structured according to the same pattern, the subject of Law and Gospel and the proper distinction between these two topics (*loci*) being brought pointedly into the discussion of the crucial articles of justification and repentance. In fact, Melanchthon makes it clear that justification and repentance can only be presented and understood within the context of Law and Gospel. We see Luther following the same procedure implicitly in the Large and Small Catechisms, and expressly in the Smalcald Articles. In Part II of the Smalcald Articles he subjects all doctrine and practice to the scrutiny of the Gospel of redemption and justification (Christ and faith) as the *Hauptartikel* of the entire Christian body of doctrine.[1] In Part III, he organizes his discussion of the articles of faith according to a pattern similar to Melanchthon's arrangement in the Augsburg Confession. We see the same procedure in the Formula of Concord which, however, addresses only the controverted issues of the day. The arrangement of the articles addressed is essentially according to the outline of the Augsburg Confession. The distinction between Law and Gospel is explicitly treated in Article V and underlies and permeates the exposition of the other articles.[2]

We can only conclude that the topic of Law and Gospel plays a paramount role in the rationale and production of the Lutheran symbols as well as of the many and often massive dogmatics books of the sixteenth and seventeenth centuries which were written in conscious conformity with these symbols. One can also not fail to note that the practical teaching and preaching of Law and Gospel was a primal factor in the life of the church during those two centuries as the Gospel was preached and the Sacraments administered.

Such is not the case in respect to the Reformed Confessions. These symbols display no conscious attempt to follow any theological hermeneutic based upon the proper distinction of Law and Gospel. True, the earlier Calvinistic Confessions (The First Helvetic Confession of 1536 and the Heidelberg Catechism of 1563) generally follow Melanchthon's outline in his *Loci Communes* or the Augsburg Confession. But that is all. And the Westminster Confession of Faith written in the next century (1644) significantly departs from Melanchthon's outline in a number of ways, not

---

1 See Robert Preus, "How Is the Lutheran Church to Interpret and Use the Old and New Testaments?" *Lutheran Synod Quarterly*, 13, 4 (December 1973).

2 See Robert Preus, "The Hermeneutics of the Formula of Concord," in *No Other Gospel*, ed. Arnold J. Koelpin (Milwaukee: Northwestern Publishing House, 1980), 328–332.

only by ignoring the topic of Law and Gospel, but notably by introducing the topic of predestination to "everlasting life" and "eternal death" immediately after the article on the Trinity before any of the other themes pertaining to Law and Gospel are presented.[3]

PHILIP MELANCHTHON

There is no Lutheran book in systematic theology which does not treat the subject of Law and Gospel, but the subject is treated at various points and in various ways in the many dogmatics books published during the sixteenth and seventeenth centuries and thereafter. In his *Loci Communes* of 1521[4] Melanchthon treats the topic early on after his discussion of free will and sin. He makes no direct reference at this point to the relationship between Law and Gospel or even to the Gospel. In his treatment of sin he mentions only in passing that sin is against divine Law. Sin—he is speaking of original sin—is defined as an "innate propensity", an impulse (*impetus*), and active power (*energia*) propagated from Adam upon all mankind and drawing all into sins.[5] Scripture does not distinguish between original and actual sin, but calls both the propensity, the vice (*vitium*, "flesh" in Scripture), and the overt activity sin. Original sin is an activity, an "active depraved desire." This means that fallen man is without the Holy Spirit, without heavenly light or life, loving only himself, seeking only his own desires and despising God.

LAW AND SIN

To Melanchthon the topics of Law and sin entail each other. He chooses to discuss Law in the context of sin, not vice versa, although of

---

3 Hermann Sasse, in *Here We Stand*, [tr. Theodore G. Tappert (New York: Harper & Brothers, 1938), 137ff.] comments on the far reaching significance of what he believes is the Calvinistic replacement of the *articulus stantis et cadentis ecclesiae*, namely the article of justification by grace, with the doctrine of predestination as taught by the Westminster Confession and Calvin himself. This Calvinistic replacement amounts to a different way of speaking about God, Sasse avers, and it substitutes Luther's frightful *Deus absconditus*, the God "who makes us responsible for demands which we cannot fulfill, who asks us questions we cannot answer, who created us for good and yet leaves us no other choice than to do evil" (Werner Elert), the God of predestination and "pitiless sovereignty"—substitutes this God for Luther's *Deus revelatus*, the God of love who steps out of profound darkness and becomes incarnate, our brother, whose name is Christ, "of Sabaoth Lord, and there's none other God." To Sasse Calvinism at this crucial point has substituted Law for Gospel as the dominant principle to organize the articles of faith into a dogmatics book or a confession of faith.

4 *Melanchthons Werke*, 2 (Guetersloh: C. Bertelsmann Verlag, 1952), 1–163.

5 Ibid., 17.

necessity the power of sin is discerned only when the Law reveals it.[6] Why? Because every preachment of sin is a preachment of Law, and every pronouncement of Law is a pronouncement against sin; for the precepts of the Law cannot be obeyed. Fallen man without the Spirit can do nothing but sin (*non posse nisi peccare*). Thus, the Law shows that fallen man is a sinner and that God, the giver of the Law, is angry with him. Melanchthon's treatment of sin becomes a proclamation of Law before he even treats the topic of Law.

As he proceeds to treat the locus on Law in the broad sense Melanchthon says at the outset, "The locus on laws will more clearly show the power and behavior of sin, for the Law provides the knowledge of sin."

Formally the Law is a determination, or judgment (*sententia*) whereby good things or actions are enjoined and evil things or actions prohibited. Some laws are natural, some divine. Natural laws are drawn up by reasoning. God has also placed in man an innate conscience to confirm that certain actions are good or bad. Melanchthon concedes that no one has successfully drawn up a consistent content for all natural law, although he can accept what the lawyers refer to as natural law. Romans 1 and 2 teach that natural law is a legitimate category.

NATURAL LAW AND DIVINE LAW

Melanchthon affirms four principles of natural law.[7] 1) God should be worshiped. Melanchthon can assert no more than just this generality, since who God is and how He is to be worshiped is known only by divine revelation. 2) We are born into and we live in a definite public society in which no one should be injured, but rather all should be helped and served. 3) Within human society all things should be used for the common good. If injury must take place, the smallest number of people should be injured, and this by the removal of those who disturb the public peace and the punishment of the same by magistrates authorized to do so. 4) Possessions (*res*) should be shared for the sake of the public peace. In reference to other matters pertaining to social life some can arrange to support others in need. These principles are quite general, but they can be applied to all kinds of specific situations such as marriage, redress, ingratitude, hospitality and the perpetuation of wealth. But Melanchthon can be specific at times, even when Scripture is silent. For instance, he says, "What is more alien to natural law than the servitude of slaves?"

---

6 Ibid., 30.
7 Ibid., 44.

Melanchthon defines divine Law as that which has been ordained by God in Scripture. There are three orders of divine Laws: moral, judicial and ceremonial. Moral Law is summed up in the Ten Commandments. The first table of moral Law, which enjoins all people to fear, love and trust in God above all things, cannot be known by the light of reason, by a contemplation of nature or the orders of creation, nor by conscience, but only by divine revelation. The second table of moral Law corresponds to natural law which heathen sages and philosophers have in part and imprecisely figured out. True, we must submit to civil magistrates according to natural law; however, in so doing we not only obey natural law, but also the Fourth Commandment of the moral Law, which perfectly agrees with and perfectly interprets natural law at this point.

The agreement between natural law and moral Law in reference to human social behavior is fundamental to the practical preaching of the Law. Natural law is able to convict man of his sin just as effectively as the second table of the moral Law for they are identical; they are both God's Law. Because fallen man, blinded by sin, perverts and obscures natural law, God throughout the Old Testament era repeatedly propounded His Law to His people, and this Law has been handed down to our day. So the many injunctions and explications of the Law throughout Scripture clarify natural law.[8]

Among the Jews in the Old Testament God commanded civil and ceremonial laws through Moses, and in this sense added to natural law.[9] But such laws do not apply to us today. Today the papists invent new laws, called counsels or exhortations, which are above God's moral Law and natural law, and which, they say, man is free to obey or not. Actually, these counsels (loving our enemies, resisting evil, abstaining from suing in civil court, etc.) are no more than God's Law of love, which applies to everyone. By teaching that such "counsels" may or may not be obeyed the papists are denying the force of God's moral Law and blunting the preachment of the Law. By teaching that such "counsels" can be obeyed the papists are denying the concupiscence of original sin and blunting the preachment of the Law. The papists also urge vows of obedience and poverty and the like, teaching that they are laws of perfection, higher than God's moral Law. But these laws are nothing at all and foster only Pharisaism.

---

8 Ibid., 67.

9 See Luther on the scope of Mosaic law in "Against the Heavenly Prophets," [*Luther's Works*, 40 (Philadelphia: Fortress Press, 1958), 97ff.] where Luther affirms the disobedience to civil law, murder, theft, etc., are forbidden not merely because they are contrary to the Decalog given to Moses, but because they violate natural law, which God has written into the heart of man in creation.

The Gospel

On the heels of his comprehensive discussion of Laws, Melanchthon follows with an equally extensive treatment of the locus on the Gospel. As the Law pertains to sin, the Gospel pertains to grace.[10] And "as the nature (*ratio*) of sin is not understood except from the prescription of the Law, so the power of grace is not recognized except from the report (*descriptione*) of the Gospel." Then, before defining materially what the Gospel is, Melanchthon states the hermeneutical principle which later introduced and gave form to his classic discussion of justification in the Apology of the Augsburg Confession (Ap. IV, 5ff.):

> In Scripture as a whole there are two parts, the Law and the Gospel. The Law shows us our sin, the Gospel God's grace. The Law points to the sickness, the Gospel to the remedy. The Law is the minister of death, to use Paul's words; the Gospel the minister of life and peace. "The strength of sin is the Law" [1 Cor. 15:56], the Gospel is the power of salvation to all who believe.

Melanchthon is speaking of Law and Gospel functionally in terms of the power of both and of their goals and effects. He proceeds to point out that both the words of the Law and the promises of the Gospel are scattered throughout Scripture, and, against any chiliastic or dispensational notions of his day, he adds that there are no successive periods of Law and Gospel (judgment and grace) in history.

Excursus: The Gospel Hermeneutic, Law and Gospel

We must pause at this point to address briefly Melanchthon's hermeneutical principle just cited. When he asserts that the teaching of the Law and Gospel pervade the entire Scriptures, he is not speaking of Scripture distributively, as if every passage or pericope or chapter or even book of the Bible necessarily contains assertions of either Law or Gospel. Such an understanding would be nonsense. Rather, he is speaking of the Scriptures collectively, of the Scriptures as a whole.[11] He is simply saying that throughout the Scriptures the themes (*loci*) of Law and Gospel recur. And in his statement in the Apology he adds that to recognize these themes and to distinguish (*distribui*) between them is necessary for the correct understanding and application of the doctrine of justification, which is the

---

10 *Melanchthons Werke*, 66ff.

11

chief article, or topic, of the Gospel. When Melanchthon says that the whole of Scripture "ought (*debet*) to be divided" into Law and Gospel, he is not saying that Scripture divides itself into Law and Gospel, but that the Christian reader of Scripture ought to distinguish between the Law and the Gospel. By so doing the theologian will view all of Scripture from a proper perspective. The distinction between Law and Gospel constitutes a posture, as well as a dogmatic viewpoint from which the theologian and exegete interprets and applies the Scriptures. But never does Melanchthon intimate that distinguishing between Law and Gospel is a hermeneutical cipher or a substitute for grammatical exegesis.

In his *Loci Theologici* Chemnitz treats the theme of Law and Gospel within his lengthy discussion of justification, just as Melanchthon did in the Apology. As far as I can determine all the later Lutheran dogmaticians accept and apply Melanchthon's hermeneutical principle.

Melanchthon then defines the Gospel. It "is not the Law," but the promise of divine grace and mercy, the promise of forgiveness and God's love "through Christ" (See Ap. IV, 5). All the promises of the Gospel, starting with the "first Gospel" of Gen. 3:15, reveal Christ and "must be referred to Him." In fact, the promises can be understood only as they refer to Christ. The promises of Christ are nothing else than the Gospel, and the Gospel is nothing else than the promises of Christ. What was promised in the Old Testament the New Testament proclaims to be revealed and fulfilled in Christ (Rom. 1:1–2).

Melanchthon belabors with much evidence and exegesis the fact that Law and Gospel, sin and grace, are clearly included and proclaimed in both Old and New Testaments. He does so to rebut the common notion among the papists that Christ was a second Moses, who brought to the world a new and better Law than Moses, a Law called the Gospel. Such a notion betrays an utter confusion of Law and Gospel and turns the Gospel into Law. Melanchthon's presentation of what the Gospel is constitutes a necessary polemic against a legalistic understanding of Christ's saving mission and work.

His presentation also establishes another hermeneutical principle, inextricably related to the dividing of Law and Gospel as a canon of exegesis, namely the Christocentricity of Scripture. This second principle was also followed by Chemnitz and all subsequent Lutheran dogmaticians for two centuries and became fundamental in their production of Christian dogmatics and their presentation of the articles of faith.

In his delineation of the Gospel, Melanchthon at several points refers to the relationship between Law and Gospel and the proper distinction between the two. Law and Gospel must be distinguished, but they belong together. "Grace cannot be preached without the Law."[12] For the Law by revealing our sin and God's wrath and fury against sinners (Ps. 92:2ff: Isa. 11:13; Ps. 75:9) shows us our need of a Savior. "For without the Law sin cannot be understood, and unless we perceive our sin, we will not understand the power and fullness of grace. Therefore Law and Gospel ought to be preached at the same time, and both sin and grace ought to be made known."

THE POWER OF THE LAW AND THE POWER OF THE GOSPEL

Melanchthon dwells at some length on the power, or work, of Law and Gospel as they are preached and taught. The power of the Law is to show sinful man his sinful nature and works, his total corruption and willful rebellion against God, to show him that its demands are impossible to obey and that he is a hypocrite for presuming that he can do so, to terrify and confound him because of his sin, to condemn him and mortify him, to show him God's wrath against sin and sinners. This is the power and "first work" (*primum opus*) of the Law, or rather of God powerfully working through the Law, to reveal our sin and all its features and horrible consequences.

The power of the Gospel is to console and encourage by the promise of divine grace and mercy those who have been terrified and condemned by the Law. From beginning to end the Scriptures offer examples of those with afflicted consciences being brought to faith by the promise of the grace in Christ, and then being resuscitated and revived by faith. Examples of this are Adam and Eve, David, Peter, and all those who came to Jesus for help and salvation. From these examples one learns the power of the Law and the power of the Gospel.

> The Law terrifies; the Gospel comforts. The Law is the voice of wrath and death; the Gospel is the voice of peace and life . . . And he who is encouraged by the voice of the Gospel and believes God's promise, that person is already [*iam*] justified. Christians know full well how great joy and gladness this comfort [of the Gospel] affords (Exod. 19–20; 2 Cor. 3:13ff; Matt. 17:4; John 3:14ff.).

To Melanchthon the power of both Law and Gospel are in their "voice," their word of condemnation and of forgiveness.

---

12 *Melanchthons Werke*, 71.

Melanchthon's discussion on the power of Law and Gospel introduces explicitly his fundamental concern about the proper distinction between Law and Gospel, a concern which is definitely apparent throughout the remainder of his *Loci Communes*. And this discussion of Law and Gospel leads directly into a lengthy discourse on the subject of justification, which is the chief topic (*praecipuus locus*) of Christian doctrine (Ap. IV, 2). To Melanchthon an understanding of the proper distinction between Law and Gospel is a hermeneutical necessity for the correct teaching on justification and all the articles of faith. He measures all theology according to the criterion of the right understanding of Law and Gospel and then organizes all Christian doctrine around the central article of justification. His very opening words in his lengthy section on justification in the *Loci Communes* weld together three closely correlated theological themes that entail each other: Law and Gospel, justification, and repentance.

> We are justified, [he says], when, having been put to death by the Law, we are restored to life by the word of grace that is promised in Christ, or in the Gospel which remits our sins and to which we cling in faith, not doubting that Christ's righteousness is our righteousness and that Christ's satisfaction is our means of atonement and His resurrection our resurrection. Put briefly, we are justified when we have no doubts that our sins are forgiven and that God already loves us and is compassionate toward us.[13]

Clearly, Melanchthon here is not defining what justification is, but is describing what happens when a sinner is justified through faith in Christ and how justification, or, more precisely, our acquisition of justification, takes place in the context of the works of Law and Gospel.

It might be helpful at this point to mention that both Luther and Melanchthon in their prolific discussions on justification spoke of God's declaration of justification from two different biblical perspectives, or approaches. The two perspectives, or biblical paradigms, complemented each other and are both absolutely necessary if one is to teach the Gospel of justification correctly. The two paradigms, or contexts, are usually found together in the biblical presentation of justification. First, the grace of God and Christ's work are mentioned in the context of the biblical portrayal of the justification of the sinner as the basis of God's verdict of justification. Second, the biblical account almost always links faith to justification: faith is man's response to the Gospel of justification, the vehicle, or means (*organon leptikon*), which receives God's verdict. What is significant in this regard is the fact that neither Luther nor Melanchthon

---

13 Ibid., 88.

formulated or employed any distinction between a) justification as it was acquired by Christ's work of redemption and based upon Christ's obedience and b) justification as it is received by faith in Christ and His work. The two motifs are simply lumped together in both their positive and their polemical presentations of justification.[14] It remained for later generations of Lutheran dogmaticians to articulate sharply the conceptual distinction between the *cause* of salvation and justification (which is the grace of God and the merits of Christ) and the *means* through which the sinner receives the benefits of Christ's work and is justified (which is faith). This distinction led to the later distinction between Christ's acquiring salvation for the entire race of sinners and the individual sinner's appropriation of Christ's merit, and later still to the distinction between objective and subjective justification.[15]

The Gospel and Christian Dogmatics

In the Augsburg Confession Melanchthon clusters all the articles of the faith around Article IV on justification and arranges them as either antecedent or consequent to it. This procedure becomes clearer in the Apology of the Augsburg Confession and in the later editions of his *Loci Communes*. There Melanchthon incorporates an explanation of the differences between Law and Gospel within his treatment of justification and demonstrates that the article of justification cannot be rightly taught apart from a correct understanding of the different works of Law and Gospel.[16] For

> this locus [on grace and justification] contains the sum and substance of the Gospel. It shows us the special blessings we have in Christ [*benefi-*

---

14 As late as the Formula of Concord (SD III, 25) there seems to be no distinction made between the two motifs in the discussion of justification. The statement is simply made, "The only essential and necessary elements of justification are the grace of God, the merit of Christ, and faith which accepts these in the promise of the Gospel, whereby the righteousness of Christ is reckoned to us and by which we obtain the forgiveness of sins, reconciliation with God, adoption, and the inheritance of eternal life." Cf. SD III, 9 and Ap. IV, 214, 217; XII, 72, 76. In these and countless other statements in the Confessions, Luther and all the Lutherans through the time of the Formula of Concord clearly state the role of the biblical *sola gratia, propter Christum,* and *sola fide* in the justification of the sinner and in the presentation of the doctrine of justification.

15 See Kurt Marquart, "Justification, Objective and Subjective: A Translation of a Doctrinal Essay Read at the First Convention of the Synodical Conference in 1872" (Fort Wayne, Concordia Theological Seminary Press, n.d.). The essay contains copious citations from the seventeenth century Lutheran theologians.

16 See especially Ap. IV, but also Philip Melanchthon, *Loci Communes,* 1543 edition, tr. J. A. O. Preus (St. Louis: Concordia Publishing House, 1992), 81ff. Throughout

cium Christi proprium], it offers a firm comfort to pious minds, it teaches the true worship of God, true invocation, and it especially distinguishes the church of God from other people.[17]

In his 1543 edition of the *Loci Communes*[18] and again in his 1559 *Loci Prae-cipui Theologici*,[19] Melanchthon adds a new dimension to his definition of the Gospel. It has three distinctive benefits (*beneficia propria*), or parts (*membra*). He says 1) that our sins are remitted freely for Christ's sake, 2) that we are freely declared righteous, that is, reconciled to God and accepted by Him, and 3) we become heirs of eternal life. The remainder of Melanchthon's discussion of Law and Gospel deals with these three components, or effects, of the Gospel. And then Melanchthon launches immediately into his discourse on justification by faith. The discussion, as in the first edition of his *Loci Communes*, centers upon the meaning of grace and faith and the role of faith in the sinner's justification. It comes far short of his classic discussion in Apology IV with its strong emphasis on Christ the Propitiator as the basis of our justification and the object of justifying faith. But again this treatment adds something to what he had said in Apology IV, namely, a brief definition of what justification is. "Justification means the remission of sins and reconciliation, or the acceptance of a person into eternal life."[20] What is remarkable about this definition of justification is that it parallels Melanchthon's description of the benefits and

the locus on justification Melanchthon weaves the theme of Law and Gospel into his portrayal of the doctrine. As the later editions of the *Loci Communes* address the topics of Law and Gospel, little of substance is added to what was said in the 1521 edition. However, Melanchthon becomes more articulate as he rewrites his dogmatics book. In his final 1559 edition he links the work of Christ more directly and emphatically to the content of the Gospel (see *Melanchthons Werke*, vol. 2, 344ff.). The promises of the Gospel are gratuitous and unconditioned just because they are based upon the work of Christ the propitiator. If there is to be a promise of pardon, reconciliation, and justification, a sacrifice must be made for us. Only when based upon such a foundation do the promises of the Gospel become certain. "Therefore Christ was given for us and made an offering for us, in order that, on account of Him, we might with certainty have a status which pleases God" (*Melanchthons Werke*, 345). In the Apology of the Augsburg Confession, where Melanchthon subsumes the discussion of Law and Gospel under the locus on justification, he bases the justification of the sinner before God solely on the work of Christ, the "Mediator and Propitiator" (Ap., IV, 42, 46, 53, 81, 82, 211, 212, 213, 221, 230, 238, 246, 387; XII, 76; XXIV, 57). This is what it means to be justified by grace.

17 Melanchthon, *Loci Communes* (1543), 85.
18 Ibid., 82.
19 *Melanchthons Werke*, II, 346.
20 *Loci Communes* (1543), 86; *Loci Praecipui Theologici* (1559), in *Melanchthons Werke*, II, 385.

effects of the Gospel. To Melanchthon the Gospel is in its essence the doctrine of justification, understood in its broad sense.

JACOB HEERBRAND

After Melanchthon, the most significant Lutheran book in dogmatics to be written before the appearance of the Formula of Concord and Chemnitz' *Loci Theologici* was the *Compendium Theologiae* of Jacob Heerbrand, first published in 1573 in Tuebingen.[21] Like Chemnitz, Heerbrand was a student of Melanchthon and patterned his *Compendium* after Melanchthon's order and rationale. But he does not parrot Melanchthon. When he discusses Law and Gospel he correlates the two topics much more closely than Melanchthon did, and addresses many new questions related to the subject. All in all, his treatment is quite innovative.

NATURAL LAW AND DIVINE LAW

Like Melanchthon, Heerbrand begins by defining God's Law and distinguishing between divine and natural law. He then launches out anew, listing the three kinds of Mosaic law: moral (which is either judicial or forensic), political (*Weltlich Recht*) and ceremonial, encompassing biblically supported church law and church order (*Kirchenrecht oder Kirchenordnungen*) in Heerbrand's day. God is the author of moral Law, which has been given by God that man might know His will and conform to it by love (1 Tim. 1:5). In effect, the Law not only shows man God's will, but reveals man's inability to obey it, as well as God's judgment upon all who disobey His commandments. Accordingly, the Law, which acts as a school master and shows man his sin and God's wrath and judgment against sin, tacitly, as it were, drives us to seek Christ as our Mediator, whom the ceremonies and sacrifices of the Old Testament Law foreshadowed.

THE LAW AND JUSTIFICATION,
UNDER THE LAW AND FREE FROM THE LAW

Heerbrand's brief allusion to the work of the Law immediately leads to the critical question of justification.[22] Can sinful man be justified before God by obedience to the Law? "Absolutely not" (Rom. 8:7; 3:20; Gal. 2:16; Acts 15). Why? "Because no one can perfectly satisfy the Law of God" (Gen. 6:5; 8:21; Ps. 14:1; Rom. 3:19–20). The papists deny this, according to Heerbrand, and claim that man by his own powers can love

---

21 See Jacob Heerbrand, *Compendium Theologiae* (Wittenberg: 1582), 332ff.
22 Ibid., 350ff.

God above all things and his neighbor as himself. They claim the Law can be satisfied by performing the "substance" of the act commanded. They even claim that man can do more than the Law requires and thus perform works of supererogation.

Here Heerbrand enters into debate with the Roman Catholics, a practice that by then had become an integral component of Lutheran dogmatics. If we cannot satisfy the demands of the Law, then God is unjust to demand impossible things of us, the papists argued. Why would God issue commands which are impossible to obey? Heerbrand replies to these arguments by referring to the three "effects", or uses, of the Law: 1) to restrain gross sins and preserve order within the political realm, even among the regenerate, 2) to show men their sin and God's wrath against sin, and thus to prepare men to receive the Gospel of Christ, and 3) to teach Christians what worship and works are pleasing to God, namely those which are done out of gratitude and faith in Christ. We observe that Heerbrand at this point has advanced beyond Melanchthon's treatment of the Law by repairing to the threefold use of the Law in his refutation of the Roman error, a category later introduced by the Formula of Concord (cf. Ep. VI, 1) and accepted and employed by all Lutheran dogmaticians thereafter.

The obverse of the Roman Catholic view, that the Christian was obligated to obey the Law and could actually do so, was the opinion of the Antinomians (John Agricola, et al.), already in Luther's day, that Christians, renewed by the Spirit, no longer needed the preachment or direction of the Law. The Antinomians, Heerbrand insisted, denied not only the third, but also the second use of the Law.

Heerbrand responds that insofar as all Christians still labor with the flesh they are never completely renewed in this life; they need the prodding of the Law, which, together with crosses and afflictions of God's sending, mortifies the Old Adam. This "ministry" of the Law, worked by the Holy Spirit, is the first part of repentance which marks the life of a Christian. Unless this work of the Law takes place and the Christian is cast down and condemned by his sin, the Gospel, whose ministry is to work faith and salvation, will not take effect. There is a sense, however, in which the Law has been abrogated:

> Christians through Christ and on account of Him are free from the condemnation and guilt exacted by the Law (Rom. 8). "You are not under the Law, but under grace" [Rom. 6:14]. In like manner, "There is no condemnation to those who are in Christ" [Rom. 8:1]. And again, "Christ has redeemed us from the curse of the Law, being made a curse for us" [Gal. 3:13]. Furthermore, Christ has abrogated the vexation and weariness involved in the highest obedience to the Law. And

so, even if we feel in our members the Law being resisted, still the Law of God delights us according to the inner man.[23]

Heerbrand presses the point that Christians are never free to disobey the Law, but are always under obligation to obey it:

> Because the decalog is the immutable and eternal will of God and is an explication of the law of nature, therefore all men are obligated to obey it. Christ said, "Not one dot or iota will pass from the Law until all things are fulfilled" [Matt. 5:18].

But by the same token,

> The decalog has been abrogated by Christ for Christians, and Christians are free from it in respect to its accusations and condemnations. Christians are not condemned even if they cannot satisfy the Law perfectly. You see, Christ took that intolerable yoke of the Law from our shoulders when He made satisfaction to the Law in our place. He did this by doing and suffering all things which the Law required. In this way the Law is established by Christ when He fulfills it for our sake. Furthermore, the Law is also fulfilled in us by faith through imputation, and it is fulfilled in us incipiently in this life, and it is fulfilled in us perfectly in the future life. But it is not abrogated in respect to our obedience, for Christians are always obligated to observe it in that respect. We are not debtors to the flesh. For if we live by the flesh we shall die.

It is clear from the course of Heerbrand's discussion that a Lutheran dogmatician cannot present the doctrine of the Law without reference to the Gospel. Law and Gospel differ from each other in respect to their content and their effects, but they are correlative to each other and entail each other, and neither can be understood or applied correctly apart from the other. An error in teaching the Law will inevitably result in a false doctrine of the Gospel, and vice versa. Rome erred in contending that a Christian could obey the Law. Antinomianism erred in contending that a Christian did not need the Law. Both obscured and distorted the Gospel.

Heerbrand goes on. What does it mean to be under the Law? It means to be under its curse. But we who believe in Christ and belong to Him are not under the Law, but under grace. That means that the Law by its own authority (*sui jure*) cannot condemn us, even though we cannot obey it. "For we have a God who has been propitiated and pacified by Christ and for the sake of Christ who fulfilled the Law for us. Hence, we are certainly not under the Law. Nevertheless, we live in the Law and delight in it". Again we note how Heerbrand observes the organic connection between

---

23 Ibid., 359.

Law and Gospel and is constrained to describe the Christian's relationship to the Law in the light of his relationship to Christ and the Gospel.

He follows the same practice as he addresses the question how the Law is fulfilled. It is fulfilled in two ways, he says. First, by imputation. Christ obeyed and fulfilled the Law in our place, and His perfect obedience is imputed to us who believe in him, just as if we had made satisfaction to the Law ourselves. The Apostle Paul expounds this when he says that Christ is the end of the Law unto righteousness to all who believe (Rom. 10:4).[24] Second, the Law is obeyed incipiently. This happens when God for Christ's sake accepts the incipient obedience of His children as a perfect obedience. "For the perfection of His Son covers our imperfection." In both kinds of obedience the Law is fulfilled by grace, in the one case by imputation of Christ's righteousness to the believer, in the other by the indwelling of the Spirit helping the believer.

There is nothing new in what Heerbrand has said. Melanchthon discussed all these points in his brilliant discourse on justification by faith in the Apology to the Augsburg Confession. What is new is that Heerbrand incorporates these Gospel motifs as a necessary element in his treatment of the locus on the Law, something Melanchthon had not done at this early point in his *Loci Communes*, although he and Luther had advocated such a general procedure.[25] Neither is there anything new in Heerbrand's using both the papists and Antinomians as foils in his treatment of the Law and other theological loci. This was the common procedure among the post Reformation dogmaticians. What is new is the way in which Heerbrand sets the locus on the Law and the other loci within the context of the doctrine of Christ and His work.

And so, Heerbrand concludes against the Antinomians that the Law must be taught and preached in the church, for only then will repentance be preached in the church.

CEREMONIAL LAW AND CHRIST'S WORK

As Heerbrand addresses the subject of ceremonial law, he again applies the Lutheran hermeneutic of viewing all articles of faith under the aspect of Christ's saving work. With the advent of Christ and His perfect

---

24 Ibid., 362. Here Heerbrand cites St. Augustine's well known statement [*Retractationes*, I, 19, 3, in *Patrologiae*, Series Latina, ed. J. P. Migne, 32 (Paris: Migne, 1844–1891), 615] cited by Melanchthon (Ap. IV, 172), "All the commandments of God are kept when what is not kept is forgiven."

25 See Ap. IV, 2 (German text), where Melanchthon subjects Scripture, and therefore also all Christian doctrine, to the scrutiny of the Gospel of justification. See also footnote 1.

redemption through His sacrificial oblation the entire Law was fulfilled and the ceremonial law repealed. No longer are the children of God required to observe the Old Testament ceremonial "laws," which in their most important aspect were promissory and therefore not Law at all, but Gospel. The Levitical sin offerings adumbrated Christ's atoning death and applied the benefits of His work retroactively to the Israelites. Christ by His death established a kingdom and a New Testament, which rendered all the Old Testament ceremonial laws obsolete and ineffectual.

CIVIL LAW

Like the Old Testament ceremonial law, the Mosaic civil law pertained only to the Israelites and does not apply to Christians today. However, as the Israelites were required to obey the civil laws of Moses, so Christians today are obliged to obey civil law. The Gospel today does not abolish or abrogate civil law and civil government when these laws "agree with the natural law and reason," but the Christian is to honor government and its laws (Matt. 18:15ff.). Meanwhile the Gospel brings about a spiritual and inner righteousness, the righteousness of faith. Heerbrand points out that when a sinner is justified, he is acquitted of infractions not only against ceremonial (church) law and civil (forensic) law, but also and especially of moral Law and the decalog. Only this Law reveals the enormity of our sin and our deep concupiscence (Rom. 7).

THE GOSPEL

Heerbrand then turns to the topic of the Gospel and discusses it briefly. His discussion is brief because he has already addressed the subject repeatedly and because the entire remainder of his *Compendium* deals largely with Gospel themes (e.g. the rule of Christ, faith, justification, election, church and ministry, the sacraments, *etc.*). He has already spoken many words about what the Gospel is and its power, but now he offers a pithy definition of the Christian Gospel:

> It is a doctrine and promise from heaven, revealed from the heart (*sinu*) of God the Father by His Son. It sets forth the gracious mercy of God, the forgiveness of sins, liberation from the tyranny of Satan, hell and eternal death. It proclaims righteousness, confers the gift of the Holy Spirit. The Gospel is freely promised and offered to all to be received in faith by those who truly believe in Christ. It is offered and given through Christ and for His sake.

Having defined the Gospel in terms of its nature (promise) and the content of its promises (forgiveness, the gift of the Spirit, eternal life), Heerbrand proceeds to address the critical subject of the *causae evangelii*. Heerbrand now employs a scholastic presentation of the basis, rationale, nature, content and effects (goal) of the Gospel, an approach to these important aspects of the doctrine that was first emulated only two generations later by John Gerhard and then by all the subsequent Lutheran dogmaticians.[26] The basis of the Gospel, the *causa efficiens et principalis*, is the Son of God, who being in the bosom of the Father, has "described" (*enarravit*) God to us through the Gospel (John 1:18). That which prompted God to give us the Gospel (the *causa impulsiva interna*) is the Father's immeasurable love and mercy. "The Father, who fashioned man in His own image, is unwilling that mankind perish in sins." It was the terrible plight of sinful man, the misery and damnation of the human race on account of sin, that as an external cause (*objectum externum*) prompted the Father and the Son to reveal the Gospel to lost mankind. The instrumental cause, the medium through which the Gospel is declared, are the preachers of the Gospel (*ministri Evangelii*) "who, having received this doctrine from God through the Holy Spirit, propagate it." Such ministers are the patriarchs, prophets, and apostles, and their true successors today.

The Gospel and Justification

As his exposition of the Law was directed consistently at the correlation between Law and Gospel, so Heerbrand's briefer development of the doctrine of the Gospel is focused at the relationship between Gospel and Law. This theological bent is clearly noticeable as Heerbrand addresses the promises of the Law and of the Gospel. Both Law and Gospel promise eternal life, but there is a world of difference between the promises of the Law and those of the Gospel. The promises of the Law are conditioned upon our perfect obedience to it. The promises of the Gospel are unconditional. This is a very important issue to Heerbrand. He is well aware of the conditional construction of the grammar in Rom. 10:9 and elsewhere in Scripture which says if one believes the Gospel, one will be saved. And the Gospel in the nature of the case requires, or solicits, faith. But, strictly speaking, faith is not a condition, nor is it required by the Gospel "as a condition". Heerbrand explains:

> Justification is not promised or offered because (*propter*) of our faith's dignity or value or insofar as faith is a work, for faith is imperfect. Faith is rather, in a sense, a means (*modus*), a blessing which has been bestowed upon one and has been given by Christ and for His sake. In

---

26 Chemnitz, Hutter and even Brockmand, who often imitated Heerbrand, stick with the Melanchthonian pattern, which refrained from the use of scholastic terminology. But they all presented the same substantive material, as did Heerbrand, and, as a matter of fact, in much greater detail.

this sense it is an instrument, like one's hand, receiving Christ and His benefits offered in the Gospel and applying these benefits to oneself. When a beggar stretches forth his hands to receive alms and receives them with his hands, we do not call his hands a condition by which he accepts the alms, but rather a means and instrument whereby he receives the alms.

Heerbrand has said nothing in this succinct statement that had not already been said repeatedly and in far greater detail by Luther and Melanchthon and later in the Formula of Concord (FC SD, III, 13. cf. III, 38, 43). What is new is that he makes the statement in his delineation of the Gospel. He cannot speak of the Gospel without speaking also of how it is received and applied, without pointing to its material content, without referring to the doctrine of justification. To him the doctrine of the Gospel is the doctrine of justification. And faith is the *organon leptikon* of the Gospel, just as [it] is the means and instrument that receives the righteousness of Christ and God's verdict of justification (cf. FC SD III, 34). This simple pattern of doctrine is central to Christian dogmatics.

To Heerbrand, justification by grace and salvation in Christ are correlative. To be saved is to be justified. This fact is brought out as he focuses his attention on the explicit promises of the Gospel: the promises center in forgiveness (justification) in this life and in salvation and eternal life in the future. Again he anticipates the Formula of Concord (FC SD, V, 1ff; cf. Ap. IV, 5ff; 53, 57) in stressing the fact that the Gospel promises are the same for all sinners in all times, for God's people in the Old Testament as well as in the New (Acts 10:43).

> Therefore it is a horrendous error when the scholastics taught that the patriarchs were justified and saved by observing natural law, the Jews by complying with Mosaic law, and Christians by obeying a new and evangelical law. For no new law is propounded in the New Testament. Rather the Law in the Old Testament which was distorted by the Pharisees was explained in the New Testament. Nor are men justified before God by the observance of any law, deserving of the name.

And so the "doctrine of the Gospel" and faith in the Gospel were the same in the Old Testament as in the New. The difference is only in reference to time. The Old Testament believers trusted in the promises of a Messiah to come, the New Testament believers in a "more clear and distinct doctrine" of a Savior who has come.

The promises of the Gospel are universal (Ezek. 18:23; Matt. 11:28; John 3:16; Rom. 10:12; 11:32; 1 Tim. 2:4). How often do the Scriptures tell us that the Gospel is offered to "all." We see again how Heerbrand adjusts his presentation to the Formula of Concord and its concerns (SD XI, 15–23), in this case against Calvinism.

THE DIFFERENCES (*Distinctiones*) BETWEEN LAW AND GOSPEL

The distinction and division (*discrimen*) of Law and Gospel was emphasized anew by Luther, according to Heerbrand. The two teachings must be diligently distinguished, lest "a confusion of all theology" ensue, and the central doctrine of justification be obscured and lost, and sinners be led to despair. What are the differences between Law and Gospel, which it is so crucial to discern?

First, the Law is known by nature, for the moral Law of Moses is no different from the law of nature. Since the Fall of our first parents, the Law has been obscured and distorted, but it has not been completely extinguished. The Gospel, on the other hand, is a mystery, it is wisdom hidden from our age, a wisdom God has predestined from eternity to reveal to us for our glory (1 Cor. 2:7). The message of Christ crucified is foolishness to the Jews and a stumbling block to the Gentiles (1 Cor. 1:23).

Second, the content of the Law differs radically from the content of the Gospel. The Law teaches and tenders precepts, and demands that we obey them, that we do this and omit doing that. The Law accuses and condemns all who do not obey it and conform to it perfectly. "The Gospel on the other hand, is the promise of the forgiveness of sins and of eternal life to be given us for Christ's sake. It offers and gives everything freely to all, who believe it."

Third, Law and Gospel differ in respect to the nature of their promises. The Law promises eternal life and good things in this life. But its promises are conditioned on our perfect inward and outward obedience to its precepts and fulfillment of it. The only promise given those who disobey is God's curse (Gal. 3:10; Luke 10:28). The Gospel's promises, however, are both free and universal. They are offered always for the sake of the "obedience and merit" of Christ "who gave himself a ransom for our sins." The Gospel promises issue alone from the goodness and mercy of God and offer us forgiveness of sins, righteousness, and eternal life (John 3:16; Rom. 1:16; 3:24).

Fourth, the Law and the Gospel differ in respect to their consequences. The Law reveals our sin and our inability to comply with its demands. It proclaims the wrath of God and His punishment upon all who do not perfectly obey Him, but never provides man with the power to keep the Law. The Gospel confers remission of sin and eternal life through faith in Christ. Through it the Holy Spirit ministers, comforting consciences terrified by the voice of the Law. The Gospel "displays" Christ the Mediator (John 1:29; Matt. 11:28).

Fifth, Law and Gospel differ in respect to those to whom they are to be preached. The Law is to be preached to secure and impenitent sinners, Epicureans and hypocrites, showing them the corruption, enormity, and shamefulness of their sin. The Gospel is to be brought to terrified sinners, who have felt the wrath of God, come to their senses, and acknowledged their lost condition. Such poor sinners are no more to be frightened by the Law, but "encouraged and comforted by the sweet promises of the Gospel concerning Christ"; and this in order that weak and broken reeds do not be dismayed and lose hope (Is. 42:1–8; 61:1–3).

Sixth, the distinction between Law and Gospel must be diligently observed in presenting the doctrine of justification. In this article, Law and Gospel oppose each other. The "doctrine of the Gospel" justifies sinners, not the voice of the Law. We are justified by faith in the Gospel, not by the Law. We receive the Holy Spirit by the hearing of faith, not by the deeds of the Law.

It is to be expected that Heerbrand's locus on Law and Gospel will differ from Melanchthon's in many ways, even though he patterns his treatment after that of his teacher. Although Luther and Melanchthon had been gone only a generation, a tremendous amount of debate and study had been expended during that short time by the second generation confessional Lutherans as they sought to present their Reformation theology. This was particularly the case as they addressed the subjects of Law and Gospel and the relationship and distinction between the two. Thus, we find some significant innovations in the presentation by the students of Luther and Melanchthon. And the innovations are all propitious. Heerbrand introduces a summary of the similarities and of the radical differences between Law and Gospel, which became standard in all later Lutheran dogmatics. He brings the doctrine of justification and the obedience of Christ into his treatment of Law as well as his exposition of Gospel. He stresses the crucial fact that the promises of the Gospel are not conditional, contingent on man's response. And we notice throughout Heerbrand's discussion the close nomistic and forensic correlation between Law and Gospel more distinctly enunciated than in Melanchthon's *Loci Communes*. Like all who wrote in the time of the Formula of Concord, he introduced the subject of the threefold use of the Law into the discussion, a notion which proved to be helpful in combating the errors of Romanism and Antinomianism. What Melanchthon had initiated by structuring dogmatics according to the pattern of Law and Gospel was faithfully continued and improved by Heerbrand and the succeeding Lutheran dogmaticians.

MARTIN CHEMNITZ AND THE FORMULA OF CONCORD

As we trace the development of Lutheran dogmatics in the sixteenth century we cannot fail to perceive that the *Loci Theologici* of Martin Chemnitz
was the most excellent and enduring contribution in that emerging field of
theological endeavor. At the same time that Jacob Heerbrand was publishing his brief and pithy compendium, Chemnitz was hard at work producing his monumental and definitive dogmatics work, which, more than any
other contribution he made, gained for him the title "The Second Martin."[27] Both Heerbrand's and Chemnitz' books, so different from each
other in format, became the two most popular and influential dogmatics
books of the late sixteenth century. Until the appearance of Calov's massive
Systema Locorum Theologicorum[28] and the introduction of the analytical
method of doing systematic theology, Chemnitz' *Loci Theologici* reigned as
the dominant paradigm for all Lutheran involvement in writing dogmatics
books. Leonard Huffer, Jesper Brockmand, and John Gerhard, just to
mention the most celebrated dogmaticians to write according to the synthetic method, all follow rather closely Chemnitz' general outline and pattern of words, also in their treatment of Law and Gospel. But the Formula
of Concord, especially in Article V, exerted a far greater influence on subsequent dogmatics as the later dogmaticians treated the topic of Law and
Gospel. So we turn to Chemnitz' chief contribution to the subject in the
Formula of Concord.

Article V of the Formula of Concord, of which Chemnitz was the chief
author, exerted a greater influence on the course of the discussions of Law
and Gospel in Lutheran dogmatics than any other theological work. It
was the Formula of Concord which secured the subject of the distinction
between Law and Gospel as a locus in all subsequent Lutheran dogmatics.
All dogmatics works after the Formula of Concord incorporated the motifs
which are found in the Formula. For the next century and a half, the Formula became a norm and pattern for later treatments of the themes pertaining to Law and Gospel.

Unlike Chemnitz' *Loci Theologici*, which was first published three years
later, Article V of the Formula of Concord is written within a confined theological situation. As a result, the confessional exposition of the distinction
between Law and Gospel focused on the controversies of the day and was

27 This judgment is well established by J. A. O. Preus in his excellent book on Chemnitz, *The Second Martin, The Life and Theology of Martin Chemnitz* (St. Louis: Concordia Publishing House, 1994).
28 Abraham Calov, *Systema Locorum Theologicorum* (Wittenberg: 1655–77).

more narrow in scope than the larger dogmatic treatises, which encompassed the whole biblical teaching on the subjects of Law and Gospel.

The Formula of Concord stresses at the outset the importance of the distinction (*Unterschied, discrimen*) between Law and Gospel. The distinction is a "brilliant light" in dividing the Word of God, the Scriptures (SD V, 1; Ep. V, 2; cf. 2 Cor. 3:7–9; 2 Tim. 2:15). To distinguish between Law and Gospel in Scripture is a hermeneutical task essential for the correct interpretation and application of Scripture, and therefore also for the confession of the church. To understand and correctly expound the Scriptures one must recognize what in Scripture is Law and what is Gospel. In doing so the interpreter imposes nothing upon the Scriptures, but discerns and applies what is already there. For therein are recorded two proclamations that have been set forth in the church of God from the beginning of the world (SD V, 23). And to the end of the world the two teachings (*beide Lehren, duo doctrinae Christianae capita*) must be urged constantly and diligently in the church, but always properly distinguished from each other. Only then will the Law serve to convict the sinner of his sin and the Gospel minister to comfort, strengthen, and forgive him (SD V, 24; Ep. V, 3–4).

Actually, the distinction between Law and Gospel in FC V is as much practical advice as a statement of faith, as much a norm for applying the Scriptures as for interpreting them, as much a guide for doing dogmatics as for doing exegesis. And so the Formula states a number of important observations which enable the Christian to divide Law and Gospel:

1. In Scripture and ecclesiastical usage the terms "Gospel" and "repentance" are used in a narrow and in a broad sense (SD V, 3–9; Ep. V, 6). Sometimes the term "Gospel" refers to the good news in Christ in contrast to the Law; sometimes it refers to the whole body of doctrine. Sometimes the term "repentance" refers to contrition and sorrow over sin only; sometimes it refers to contrition and faith in Christ.

2. The Gospel is never a proclamation of God's wrath, but only of His grace and forgiveness (SD V, 12; Ep. V, 9–10). If the passion and death of Christ are preached in such a way as to condemn the sinner and portray God's anger against sin, then this is not the pronouncement of Gospel, but of Law.[29]

---

29 The Formula cites Luther at this point: "In fact, where is there a more earnest and terrible revelation and preaching of God's wrath over sin than the passion and death of Christ, his own Son? But as long as all this proclaims the wrath of God and terrifies man, it is not yet the Gospel nor Christ's own proclamation [*eigene Predigt*], but it is Moses and the law pronounced upon the impenitent. For the Gospel and

3. If only the Law were preached, people would be led into despair or presumptuous pride (SD V, 10).

4. The Holy Spirit's alien work (*opus alienum*) through the "ministry" of the Law is to convict the sinner of sin and preach God's wrath. The Spirit's appropriate work (*opus proprium*) through the ministry of the Gospel is to comfort and to preach grace to poor sinners (SD V, 11–12; cf. Ap. XII, 49–53).

5. Only the Law reproves unbelief, although the Gospel sheds light on this matter (SD V, 19 *passim*).

6. Law and Gospel are taught throughout Scripture, the Old Testament as well as the New, and the content of both teachings is the same in both testaments (SD V, 23; cf. Ap. IV, 5–6; XII, 53–54).

7. Law and Gospel differ in several ways.

a. As to their functions: The Law condemns; the Gospel raises up and comforts.

b. As to their objects: The Law is preached to impenitent and hardened sinners; the Gospel is preached to penitent and frightened sinners.

c. As to their goals: The Law is preached to drive the sinner to despair; the Gospel to comfort and bring forgiveness.

d. As to their didactic function: The Law is a "divine doctrine" that teaches the "righteous and immutable will of God" and teaches that man's nature, thoughts, words, and deeds are corrupt (SD V, 17); the Gospel teaches the grace of God, that He forgives sinners for Christ's sake (SD V, 21).

Every point included in the Formula of Concord was discussed in all dogmatics books from that time on, and a greater awareness and occupation with the distinction between Law and Gospel became common.[30] The

---

Christ are not ordained and given us to terrify or to condemn us, but to comfort and lift upright those who are terrified and disconsolate." WA, 15:228.

30 This is especially the case in the many works in symbolics that were written after 1580. Such books comprised either historical studies on the Lutheran symbols or doctrinal commentaries on them, or both. The most notable of such studies are the following: Nikolaus Selnecker, *Erinnerung vom Concordienbuch* (Leipzig, 1581); Nikolaus Selnecker, *Erklaerung etlicher streitiger Artikel aus der Concordienformel* (Leipzig, 1582); Leonard Hutter, *Augustanae Confessionis Analysis Methodica* (Wittenberg, 1602); Leonard Hutter, *Libri Christianae Concordiae: Symboli Ecclesiarum Nuvissimo hoc Tempore, Longe Augustissimi; Explicatio Plana & Perspicua* (Wittenberg, 1609); Leonard Hutter, *Concordia Concors, de Origine et Progressu Formulae Concordiae Ecclesiarum Confessionis Augustanae* (Wittenberg, 1614); John Kromayer, *Epitome Christiane Concordiae* (Leipzig, 1620); John Benedict Carpzov, *Isagoge in Libros Ecclesiarum Lutheranarum Symbolicos* (Leipzig, 1665); Sebastian Schmidt, *Articulorum Formulae Concordiae Repetitio* (Strasbourg, 1696).

Formula of Concord, Article V (and VI) influenced and standardized the systematic and exegetical theology of the next century. One might almost say that all Lutheran dogmatics published after 1580 consisted mainly of footnotes to Melanchthon's *Loci Communes*, Heerbrand's *Compendium*, and the Formula of Concord. It can safely be said that faithfulness to the doctrinal pattern of Article V on Law and Gospel helped more than any other single factor to keep the later dogmaticians committed to all the articles addressed in the Formula of Concord and unite the Lutheran Church doctrinally. For all the articles of faith were correlated to the distinction between these two contrary words of God.[31]

---

31 This fact is brought out in Abraham Calov's *Consensus Repetitus Fidei Vere Lutheranae* (Wittenberg, 1666), which the author intended to be a formal confession of faith to settle certain controversies raging between confessional Lutherans and Lutheran Syncretists (Georg Calixt, John Latermann, Christian Dreier, et al.). In this confession Calov follows the outline of the Augsburg Confession (the entire Book of Concord had not been accepted in Helmstedt, where many of the Syncretists were located). However, as he discusses AC V ["The Office of the Ministry"], he devotes himself only to a presentation of the theology of FC V on the subject "The Word of God: Law and Gospel," a locus not explicitly dealt with in the Augsburg Confession. He says,

> We confess and teach that there is a difference between God's Word of Law and His Word of Gospel. This difference must be guarded and maintained with careful diligence lest the two teachings be confused or the Gospel be changed into Law. Should that happen, the merits of Christ would be obscured and the sweetest comfort of the Gospel would be snatched away from those whose consciences are disturbed. This comfort is in the Gospel of Christ when it is faithfully preached. By this Gospel sinners sustain themselves when they are in the most intense temptations before the terrors of the Law. Strictly speaking, the Law is a doctrine, divinely revealed, which teaches what is right and acceptable to God. It also opposes whatever is sin and contrary to God's will. The Gospel, on the other hand, must be treasured as a doctrine which teaches what a man, who cannot satisfy the Law and is therefore damned by it, should believe. He should believe this, that Jesus Christ has taken all sins upon Himself and made satisfaction for them. He has forgiven sinners, established His righteousness before God and has procured eternal life for sinners not by any intervention of theirs, but by his merits alone (Jer. 31:31–34; Heb. 10:8–13; 2 Cor. 3:9; Gal. 3:11–12).

Calov then proceeds to reject just one antithesis, the error of Conrad Hornejus and Georg Calixt. Hornejus taught that both Gospel and Law were premised on conditions. The Law required the "condition" of good works. The Gospel, in addition to bestowing grace and forgiveness, "sets forth" a "condition" with which man must comply, namely the "new life." To Calov such a conditional Gospel made the Gospel into Law, which was the most perilous confusion of Law and Gospel one could make. This deep concern of Calov, which echoes Heerbrand's position (cf. *Compendium*, 379), was shared by all the later dogmaticians and discussed at length. Johann Andreas Quenstedt, *Theologia Didactico-Polemica sive Systema Theologiae* (Wittenberg, 1685, P. III, C. 2, S. 2, q. 2, 64ff.) devotes attention to the question,

"Whether the Promises of the Gospel are Conditional". Responding at length in the negative, he contends that the Gospel is conditioned only by the grace of God in Christ, not by anything in respect to us—not even faith. He says, "We state that faith is required, but as an organ of apprehending [the Gospel] and a medium of divine arrangement (*taxis*) rather than as a condition." Faith does not condition the Gospel, but receives it. The truth, efficacy, and message of the Gospel obtain, whether it is believed or not. This crucial point was simply misunderstood or denied by Papists, Arminians, Socinians and "Novatians" (Lutheran Syncretists), according to Quenstedt.

The Significance of Luther's Term *Pure Passive*

As Quoted in Article II of the Formula of Concord

> "The Significance of Luther's Term *Pure Passive* as Quoted in Article II of the Formula of Concord" is Preus's first published scholarly article. It furthers the monergistic theme confessed in his 1947 letter to the Evangelical Lutheran Church and offers a cogent statement, applicable even in the twenty-first century, of the importance of Lutheran doctrine and Lutheran terminology in presenting the articles of justification by faith and the new birth. It was published by *Concordia Theological Monthly* in 1958.

THE LUTHERAN DOCTRINE OF CONVERSION, standing as it does between Calvinism and synergism, is always a difficult position to maintain and defend; for it is built on a paradox, a paradox of exclusive divine action and complete human participation. Faith is at the same time passive and active: passive in that man, blind and dead spiritually, in coming to faith only suffers God to work this change in his heart, active in that man himself believes and is in no way coerced in this nor divested of any of his faculties. This position is stated by the Formula of Concord:

> It is nevertheless true that a man before his conversion is still a rational creature that has an intellect and will, although not an intellect in divine things, or a will to will something good and salutary. Yet he can do absolutely nothing toward his conversion (as has been said above), and in this case he is much worse than a stone or a log, because he resists the Word and the will of God, until God raises him from the death of sin, enlightens him and renews him. And although God does not force a person to be converted (for those who always resist the

Holy Ghost and who continually put themselves into opposition to the truth even after they have recognized it, as Stephen says of the hardened Jews, Acts 7 [51], are not going to be converted), yet God the Lord draws the person whom He wills to convert and draws him such a way that a darkened intellect becomes an enlightened intellect, and a perverse will becomes an obedient will. And this Scripture calls creating a new heart.[1]

It is significant in this regard that the first two heresies to be condemned by the Epitome of Article II of the Formula of Concord are deterministic Stoicism (and Manichaeism), which would have all things happen by necessity, even robbery and murder, and Pelagianism, which denies the necessity of grace. All other errors come under the heading of one or the other of these heresies, However, not determinism but synergism has since the Reformation been the bane of this Lutheran doctrine. Striving to find some place for human responsibility in conversion, the synergist brings against every statement which speaks of the passivity of faith the charge of irresistible grace, compulsion, Calvinism, Manichaeism. This is of course unfair and is to misunderstand completely the paradoxical nature of the Lutheran doctrine. It is also a denial of the Scripture principle and a rationalizing, just as clearly as Calvinism is.

The term *pure passive*, applied to the will of man in conversion, occurs three times in the Formula of Concord.[2] The cognate expression *capacitas passiva* occurs in the Latin version;[3] its omission from the German original occasioned a good deal of criticism. Again it is said that the intellect and heart and will of man are only *subiectum patiens* and *subiectum convertendum* in conversion, that God does the converting and that man only suffers conversion.[4] All these expressions are taken from the writings and teachings of Luther and by their inclusion in the Formula of Concord achieve symbolical status.

The idea of the passivity of faith, taken from the church fathers and the medieval scholastics, is not very often voiced by Luther, but it is intrinsic in all his writings on free will; and when he does speak of this passivity, it is in strong terms. Luther speaks of a capacity inhering in the natural man, but it is only a passive capacity, meaning that man is able to be converted, as distinguished from animals and inanimate things. "When the fathers defend free will, they mean that it is capable of being free, that it can be

---

1 F[ormula of] C[oncord,] S[olid] D[eclaration,] II 59, 60.

2 FC Ep II 18; SD II 73, 89.

3 FC SD II 73.

4 FC SD II 89, 90.

turned to good by the grace of God and be made truly free, to which end it was created."[5] Again Luther states his position even more clearly in a parallel utterance from *De servo arbitrio* (1525): "If we call the power of free will that by which man is capable of being caught by the Holy Spirit and touched by God's grace, as one created unto eternal life or eternal death, that is perfect all right; for this power, or aptitude, or as the sophists call it, disposition-quality and passive aptitude, I, too, confess. And who does not know that this is not in trees or animals? For heaven, and they say, is not made for geese."[6] These statements should be sufficient to show what Luther is driving at in speaking of capacity or the power of free will in the natural man and that it is far from his mind to imply that God deals with man as with a brute or an inanimate thing. That Luther employs the term *passivity* only for the purpose of ruling out all synergism to is clearly shown by another statement: "We conclude that the free will is purely passive (*esse mere passivum*) in every act in which it is said to will something; and the sophists prattle in vain about the distinction that an entire good act is from God (*totum a deo*) but not from God entirely (*totaliter*). For what is entire from God is also entirely from God, because the will is seized and borne and moved only by grace; and this movement of the will, bringing its influence upon the members and powers of either mind or body, this and nothing else is its activity; just as the movement of a saw sawing wood is a merely passive movement of the saw by the one sawing, for the saw does not co-operate in this moving in any way, but it moves on the wood by being moved and not by itself moving. And this sawing is said to be the saw's work along with the one who saws, although it merely undergoes the movement."[7] That this passivity is only spiritual and obtains only in the spiritual realm is also clearly taught in Caspar Cruciger's (1544) edition of Luther's lectures on Genesis: "In a certain sense we have free will in those things, which are beneath us. By divine mandate we have been made lords

---

5 *Contra malignum Ioannis Eccii indicium defensio* (1519), Article IX (W II 647, 28–31). Luther quotes exclusively from St. Augustine in this article.

6 W XVIII 636, 16–22, See also John Andrew Quenstedt, *Theologia didactico-polemica, sive systema theologicum*, Pars secunda, caput III (*De libero arbitrio hominis post lapsum*), sectio II, quaescio II, observatio VII (Leipzig: Thomas Fritzsch, 1715), I, 1099: "If by free will one understands a capacity or passive potentiality that the mind and will of man can be converted through the ordinary grace of God, then we grant that in this stoat free will has not been destroyed. For in man there is given a certain capacity by which he cannot indeed convert himself but can be converted by God, provided he uses the divinely appointed means."

7 Cf. *Resolutionus Lutherianae super propositionibus suis Lipsiae disputatis* (1519). W II 421, 7–15. See also Franz Herman Reinhold von Frank, *Die Theologie der Concordienformal*, I (Erlangen: Theodor Blaesing, 1858), 141.

over the fish of the sea, the birds of the heavens, and the beasts of the field. These we kill when it pleases us. We enjoy the food and other advantages which they supply. But in those things that pertain to God, which are above us, man has no free will, but he is truly like clay in the hand of the potter, being in a position of mere potentiality which is not active but only passive. For in such matters we do not choose, we do not do anything, but we are chosen, we are prepared, we are reborn, we are received, as Isaiah says [64:8]: 'Thou art the power and we Thy clay.' "[8] One more statement of Luther might be quoted. Commenting on John 1:12, which Erasmus had used in defense of free will, he says in *De servo arbitrio*: "John is not speaking of any work of man, either great or small, but he speaks of that renewal or change of the old man, who is a child of the devil, into the new man, who is the child of God. Here man behaves in a purely passive way (*mare passive sese babet*), as they say, nor does he do anything, but is wholly acted upon."[9]

In all these statements Luther's meaning is clear, and it would be unfair to press his words beyond the point of comparison. His adversaries, however, chose to misunderstand him. The expression *pure passive* as Luther used it was attacked first by John Eck as early as 1525,[10] and finally in unmistakable terms by the Council of Trent, which said: "If any should say that man's free will, moved and aroused by God, by assenting to God's action and call, does not cooperate toward disposing and preparing itself to obtain the grace of justification, that it cannot resist if it wishes, but like some inanimate thing does nothing and is merely passive, let him be damned."[11] It is apparent that Luther has been grossly and purposely misunderstood and his teaching misrepresented.

This being the case, it became a matter of confession to defend not only Luther's doctrine but also his very terminology. To change terminol-

---

8 W XLII 64, 28–36.

9 W XVIII 697, 25–28.

10 *Enchiridion locorum communium advarsus Lutherum et alios bostes ecclesiae* (Landshut: 1525) caput 31. Melanchthon also seemed to misunderstand the point that the *pure passive* wished to bring out; and consequently we find him attacking a sort of Manichean caricature of Luther's doctrine, e.g., *CR* 21, 658–659: "Praeterea si nihil agit liberum arbitium, interea, donec sensero fieri illam regenerationern, de qua dicitis, indulgebo diffidentiae et aliis vitiosis affectibus. Haec Manichaes imaginatio horribile mendacium est, et ab hoc errore mentes abducendae sunt et docendae agere aiiquid liberurn arbitrium." *CR* 23, 280: "Sed excruciat mentes haec quaestio, Cum sine Spiritu sancto nulla virtus inchoetur, aut placeat, otiosine expectabimus consolationem, donec rapi nos novis motibus sentiemus, sicut Enthusiastae et Manichaei imaginati sunt?"

11 Sess. VI, can. 4.

ogy would have implied a yielding to the attacks of the adversaries. A clear explanation of the usage of the expression and defense of the same was therefore offered in the Formula of Concord: "When Lather says that man relates himself to his conversion in a purely passive way, that is, he does nothing but only suffers God to work in him, he does not mean that conversion, is brought about without the preaching and hearing of God's word, nor does he wish it to be understood that in conversion no new movements within us are evoked by the Holy Spirit and no new spiritual changes are begun in us. But he means this, that man of himself and of his own natural powers cannot do anything or help in any way toward his conversion and that conversion is not only in part but entirely an operation, gift, and work of the Holy Spirit alone who works it and brings it about by his power and might through the word in the intellect, will, and heart of man, *tamquam in subiecto patiente*, that is, where man does and works nothing but only suffers. But it does not occur in the same way as a statue is chiseled from a stone or a seal impressed on wax, which knows nothing about it and neither feels nor wants it. But it takes place in the manner and way that we have set forth and explained briefly above."[12] Even more in detail Chemnitz interprets the expression of Luther and the Formula in his *Examen Concilii Tridentini*. He says: "They [the Romanists] get very excited over the fact that Luther has said that in regeneration, renewal, or conversion man behaves in a merely passive way. If one were not acquainted with the terminology of the scholastic writers, one might understandably be offended at this expression, as if it were meant that the Holy Spirit works conversion in such a way that absolutely no new emotion is experienced by the will which is being renewed, and that the will is entirety inactive and idle and simply overcome and driven by brute force. But such a thought never occurred to Luther. However, there is no doubt that the theologians who were consulted in the Council of Trent, indoctrinated as they were and accustomed to the manner of speaking which the scholastic writers employed, knew very well what was meant by behaving in a purely passive way (but they could not conceal their desire of caviling), especially since they felt the term could be not wrongly applied to men when it concerned the natural powers of free will, if not entirely, then in part, in renewal, or conversion. Now this was the argument set forth by the scholastics: A subject in assuming some form, quality, condition, action, or what have you, insofar as it receives, behaves passively. True, there are some subjects which, besides being passive in receiving, have in themselves a certain activity which they bring to bear and with which they

---

12 FC SD II 89; cf. 80.

co-operate, so that form, quality, action, or condition are brought about in the subject. Such a subject does not behave in a purely passive way in producing a form, but partly passively and partly actively. But there are certain subjects which have no power in themselves to produce a form, they merely receive a form. These are said to behave in a purely passive manner. Such manner of speaking of the scholastics, at one time much used and well known in the schools, Luther accommodated to his doctrine of free will. Now insofar as the mind and will are the subject in which the Holy Spirit works conversion or renewal, this subject behaves in a purely passive manner, according to the phrase of the scholastics. But this is the question: Whether the mind and will, corrupt from birth through sin, has any activity, any power, or efficacy which it exerts and by which it co-operates with the Holy Spirit in engendering conversion, pious thoughts, good intentions, desires, endeavors, struggles, etc., in spiritual movements and actions; in other words, whether the unregenerate will in spiritual conversion behaves partly actively and partly passively (as the scholastics put it). Now, because Scripture records that this power in spiritual matters has been lost through sin, so that the will can do nothing of itself; and because Augustine also does not wish to call grace through which God works in us to will a co-operating grace, Luther therefore employed this term of the scholastics in such a way explained his thoughts that man behaves in a purely passive manner. But he never caught that conversion happens without the inflection of the mind and the agreement of the will. He wished to say only this, that God draws by their wills those whom he converts."[13] So important was the proper understanding and defense of this point that Chemnitz chose in his *Loci theologici* to discuss the entire matter of synergism under the question whether the will is purely passive in conversion, for everything revolved around this point.[14] The term *pure passive* to Chemnitz applied only in the case of man's spiritual powers, in a contributory sense, not in a psychological sense. This had to be explained again and again by him and the other orthodox Lutherans. A synergist is blind to the difference between Manichaeism and monergism, between coercion and a gracious drawing of man's will by God, blind to the fact that it is the will of man that is acted upon in conversion. Therefore the synergist insists that the monergistic doctrine violates the personality and will of

---

13 Martin Chemnitz, *Examen Concilii Tridentini*, Prima pars, locus VII (*De libero arbirio*), sectio V, par. 8, ed. Eduard Preuss (Berlin: Gustav Schlawitz, 1861), p. 144. Chemnitz was closely followed by Leonhard Hütter, *Loci communes theologici* (Wittenberg: Ionnes Matthaei, 1619), 283.

14 Martin Chemnitz, *Loci theologici*, ed. Polycarp Leyser (Frankfurt am Main: Heirs of Dr. Tobia Mevius and Filert Schumacker, 1653), I, 183–186.

man and that God forces man to become a Christian against his will. This was precisely the position the Jesuit Robert Bellarmine took. Even the crystal clear explanation of Chemnitz could not satisfy him, and he violently attacked Chemnitz' presentation of the matter.[15] So again the Lutheran position was patiently and clearly defined, this time by John Gerhard: "Luther did not teach that conversion is brought about without the reflection of the mind and agreement of the will, but he denied that the will concurs with these activities of its own natural powers; that is to say, he denied that in the mind and will there remained any working power which could reach out when grace was offered and for that reason co-operate with the Holy Spirit. And the analogy of the clay in the hand of a potter— which he uses—must not be pressed beyond its point of application."[16]

But the doctrine of the passivity of the will in conversion was not settled even in the Lutheran Church by Chemnitz and the Formula of Concord. Synergism cropped up again within the Church of the Augsburg Confession, this time in the school of the "syncretists" of the 17th century, e.g., Lattermann, Dreier, Calixt.[17] Again the *pure passive* was attacked and on the same old psychological, rationalistic grounds. In answering these objections the later orthodox dogmaticians did not go beyond Chemnitz. No more really could be said. But again they admirably upheld the old Lutheran position, as may be illustrated from the following quotation from Quenstedt: "It is one thing to concur in one's conversion contributively, actively, and as an efficient cause of the same, another thing to be receptive in conversion, passive, and the subject to be converted. Not the former but the latter we hold in respect to the unregenerate man. For the unregenerate man, because of the corruption of his nature, has no activity,

---

15 Robert Bellarmine, *De gratia et libero arbitrio*, VI, cap. 9, in *Disputestiones de controversies Christianea fidei adversus huius temporis bearaticos* (Venice: 1596), IV, Part three.

16 John Gerhard, *Loci theologici*, locus XII, caput VI, section VI, par. 81, ed. Johann Friedrich Cotta, V (Tübingen: Johann Georg Cotta, 1766), 172.

17 Johann Lat(t)ermann (1620–1662), educated at Helmstedt, Königsberg and Rostock; in 1647 professor extraordinarius of theology at Königsberg, in 1649 second court preacher at Rostock, in 1652 general superintendent at Halberstadt; died while serving as a military chaplain; author, among other works, of *De gratia et libero arbirio*; opponent of Abraham Calov and Celestine Myslenta.—Christian Dreier (Dreyer) (1610–1688), educated at Jena, Wittenberg, Rostock, Copenhagen, and Königsberg, where he became professor extraordinarius of theology in 1644, ordinarius in 1652, and primarius in 1657; partisan of Michael Behm and his colleague Latermann versus Calov and Myslenta. —George Calixt (Kallison) (1586–1656), educated at Helmstedt, Jena, Giessen, Tübingen, and Heidelberg; in 1614 professor of theology at Helmstedt, in 1625 senior of the theological faculty, and in 1636 absentee abbot of Königslutter Abbey, in addition to his professorship; prolific and influential author.

power, or faculty which he can direct toward his conversion and by which he can co-operate with the Holy Spirit in his conversion.

"We note that man does not concur in his convention by doing but by receiving. Still he is not converted without means but mediately, through Word and Sacraments, not violently but by persuasion, not by force but by being instructed, not by divine inspiration but by hearing, not through any physical necessity, but through the free use of means.

"We must distinguish between an active and a passive capacity. We deny that man can co-operate in conversion and with the grace of God by his own natural and active strength or by his own efficacious ability, aptitude, or capacity. But we do maintain that in man there is a passive capacity which cannot be ascribed to a stone or block; for the unregenerate man is endowed with a mind and a will, and thus in man is to be found a subject already existing in whom enlightenment and conversion by the power of the divine Spirit can be brought about, whereas in a stone or block there is neither mind nor will and hence no subject which can be any way be capable of enlightenment or conversion."[18] If Quenstedt and the other later orthodox teachers said nothing which was not already stated by Luther and the Formula, they served one important purpose by their definitive discussion of the Lutheran position regarding the *pure passive*: They established the term as something so sacrosanct to orthodox Lutheranism that it was no longer openly rejected.

But the indirect attacks by modern enemies of this doctrine are really just as aggressive and ingenious as the older frontal attacks. If, for instance, this passivity, this refraining from willful resistance (considered as something residing in some men or given to some men), this "suffering" what God works in man, is made to account even to some small degree for man's conversion, then clearly the *pure passive* has been abandoned. Then man is somehow conceived of as acting in that he "suffers," and passivity becomes activity, even though it is obviously impossible in a contributory sense to be simultaneously active and passive with reference to the same process. As Sebastian Schmidt put it, "How can it be said that one behaves himself actively when he does not in any manner aid the Holy Spirit who works in him, but must be overcome by Him?"[19] Precisely here, in the passivity of man in his conversion, is the crux of the continuing controversy between synergism and monergism, and all the Lutheran teachers from

---

18 Quenstedt, op. cit., Pars tertia, caput VII (*De conversione*), sectio I, quaestio II, observationes XX I, II, VII, Vol. II, 727–728.

19 Sebastian Schmidt, *Articalorum Formulae Concordiae repetitio, Disputatio IV in Formulam Concordiae de libero arbitrio posteriov*, par. 38 (Strasbourg: Josiah Stardelius, 1696), 128.

Chemnitz to Quenstedt were correct in emphasizing this point. As long as theologians refuse to accept the paradox of exclusive divine action and at the same time full human experience in conversion, the issue will not die. But as long as the monergist retains the *pure passive* in the sense in which Luther first used it and the Formula of Concord adopts it, he knows he is on solid ground.

THE CHURCH:
HER CONFESSIONS
AND FELLOWSHIP

The church's theology, to Robert Preus, is of little use if it is not publicly taught and confessed. Confession occurs not only through the spontaneous statements of Christians but also especially through formal symbols of the church that are universally recognized as biblical. The Lutheran Confessions contained in the 1580 *Book of Concord* are such symbols and are worthy of both subscription and analysis if the church is to be united in her confession of Christ.

My Confession

"My Confession" is a brief letter from Preus to the Council of the Evangelical Lutheran Church on the eve of his erstwhile ordination in 1947. It states his reasons for leaving the ELC and provides an insight into the character of Robert Preus, who saw fit to confess his faith, though the confession might have negative consequences.

DEAR SIRS:

I, Robert Preus, was born on October 16, 1924, at St. Paul, Minnesota, of Mr. and Mrs. J. A. O. Preus, now of Chicago, Illinois, and I was baptized into the Christian faith by my uncle, the Rev. J. C. K. Preus. I attended Sunday school and church services and was confirmed in Redeemer Lutheran Church of Highland Park, Illinois, the Rev. W. F. Suhr being pastor. In 1941 I matriculated at Luther College, Decorah, Iowa. During my stay there, I decided by the grace of God to enter the holy ministry. In 1944 I began my theological education at Luther Theological Seminary. After a year and a half, I was assigned to a year's period of internship but am now back at the seminary, scheduled to graduate in the spring of this year.

I wish at this time to confess my personal faith in the triune God and in Jesus Christ as my only Savior from sin, death, hell, and Satan. I, a corrupt, miserable, contemptible, and helpless sinner, claim no responsibility whatever as over against the faith which I confess, but I believe with all my heart that it is solely a work and gift of the Holy Spirit in me. At Luther Theological Seminary I have been taught that this, my conviction on the important doctrine of conversion, is not in accordance with the teaching of the Holy Scriptures but is sectarian and that, in a sense, my salvation—and indeed that of every other person on earth, whether unregenerate or regenerate—depends on me in that I am responsible as over against the acceptance or the rejection of grace. I have been taught that the unregenerate man under the influence of the Holy Spirit has a free will either to accept or reject Christ. I have often been told in class that faith is not a gift or work of the Holy Spirit in me, and the whole class has been challenged to find a single Bible passage which teaches otherwise (Com. Eph. 2:8–9: Phil. 1:29; Formula of Concord, II, 40). It also has been stubbornly maintained that the unregenerate man is not spiritually dead, dead in his sins, but is only asleep (Com. Eph. 2:1, 5; Col. 2:13; Formula of Concord, II, 11). It has also been publicly stated to the whole senior class that this teaching—that man is responsible for the acceptance or rejection of grace—is the official position of the Evangelical Lutheran Church since the Church Council of the Evangelical Lutheran Church had, in stating that all official teaching must be in accordance with the Madison Agreement, received that this doctrine must be taught. This petition has been maintained although—and I have personally investigated this matter and have been told by the secretary of the Church Council that it is true—no recorded—and therefore no official—action had been taken by the Church Council on this question. After consulting the proper authorities on this matter, I found that this false teaching—that man is responsible for the acceptance or rejection of grace—was not only tolerated but also defended, and I was also given no indication that anything would be done to rectify this deplorable situation. Therefore knowing, after personal consultation with all parties concerned, that heresy is being taught, tolerated, and defended at Luther Theological Seminary, the theological heart of the Evangelical Lutheran Church, and seeing that there is no possible means of removing this offence, I hereby bring to the attention of the venerable Church Council of the Evangelical Lutheran Church the fact that, for conscience sake, I cannot present myself as a candidate for ordination in the Evangelical Lutheran Church of America. I make this decision only after prayerful and sincere study of God's Word, and it is with sorrow and regret that I terminate fellowship with the Evangelical Lutheran Church.

Understand that this action is a protest against the condition at Lutheran Theological Seminary. Please also believe that I will always be praying for your synod and especially for the theological faculty, and should these offences be removed, I will be the first to extend the hand of true Christian fellowship.

I will gladly place myself at the disposal of any of you who would like to discuss this matter with me personally, either at the time of the colloquium or at some other time.

Soli Deo Gloria
Robert Preus

CONFESSIONAL SUBSCRIPTION

> "Confessional Subscription" is a 1970 piece that appeared in *Evangelical Directions for the Lutheran Church*, edited by Erich Kiehl and Waldo Werning. This article is a primer on the meaning of confessional subscription, how it is misrepresented, and why it is important evangelically. This important article was first presented at a 1970 Free Lutheran Congress in Chicago. (Permission has been granted for reproduction in this collection.)

WHAT IS A LUTHERAN? What is the nature of subscription to the Lutheran Confessions? These two questions which are often considered together and which are as inseparably related as Siamese twins have become increasingly important in our day when Lutheranism is fighting for its identity and life. Today most of the Lutheran pastors and teachers throughout the world subscribe, at least *pro forma*, all the confessions of the Evangelical Lutheran church: the ancient catholic creeds and the great Lutheran confessions of the 16th century, i.e. the Augsburg Confession, the Apology of the Augsburg Confession, Luther's two catechisms, the Smalcald Articles and the Formula of Concord. What does such subscription mean? Is such subscription any longer possible in our day of academic freedom and vaunted autonomy, ecumenism and dialogue? Many today think that subscription to any creed or confession is no longer viable and can represent only an impossible legalistic yoke upon an evangelical Christian or pastor. This is the conviction not only of Baptists and other traditionally non-credal denominations, but also of such renowned and conservative theologians as Karl Barth who holds that any human formulation of doctrine (as a creed or confession must be) is only a quest, an approximation, and therefore relative.[1]

---

1 Karl Barth, *Church Dogmatics* (Edinburgh: T. & T. Clark, 1936–69), I,1,9ff. The

Are such objections valid? Is the Lutheran church able to justify confessional subscription today? And is she able to explain and agree on precisely what is meant by such subscription?

Today questions concerning the nature and spirit and extent of confessional subscription have become a vexing problem, an enigma or even an embarrassment to many Lutherans.

There was no difficulty in answering such questions in 1530, however, when the great *Magna Charta* of the Lutheran Church, the Augsburg Confession, was presented by the Lutheran princes to Emperor Charles V, or again in 1580 when thousands of Lutheran pastors accepted and subscribed the Book of Concord.[2]

From the time of John Philip Spener in the late 17th century disagreement and debate among Lutherans concerning confessional subscription began to develop, and these problems centered largely in the extent of that subscription. The question was: ought one to subscribe the confessions *quia* (because) they agreed with Scripture, or only *quatenus* (in so far as) they agreed with Scripture. This latter *quatenus* mode of subscription meant that one subscribed the confessions with reservations; the act was therefore a contradiction in terms and no real subscription at all. As John Conrad Dannhauer said, one could subscribe the Koran in so far as it agreed with Scripture.

Questions still arise regarding the extent of confessional subscription, and one occasionally hears theologians asking whether we are bound to the belief in the perpetual virginity of Mary or to the judgment that the papacy is the Antichrist or to the number of sacraments listed in our symbols, etc. Often this sort of picayunish discussion and complaint is quite beside the point and represents only a subterfuge which serves to hide deeper mis-

---

same position seems to be taken by responsible Lutherans. Cf. the position paper, "Doctrinal Concerns", issued by the Church council of the ALC at Winnepeg, Manitoba, June 23–29 where par.c reads, "His [the believer's] best efforts to formulate a theology in terms of propositions and statements will fall short. To assume that the church can arrive at human concepts or expressions that are in every respect correct is as much a symptom of pride as to assume that the church or its members can achieve sinlessness in their daily life." Commenting on this statement, Hermann Sasse says, "What nonsense! . . . True Lutheranism has never and can never accede to that. The moment it does it has lost its sound confessional character and its certainty of the Gospel." See Waldo Werning, "Issues in Deciding the Lutheran Church—Missouri Synod American Lutheran Church Fellowship Matter" (Milwaukee: no publisher, no date), p.10.

2 Even in the early days of our Missouri Synod most Lutherans seemed able to comprehend the meaning of an unconditional subscription to the Lutheran symbols and were prepared to make this pledge, or not to. See C. F. W. Walther, "Why Should our Pastors, Teachers and Professors Subscribe Unconditionally to the Symbolical Writings of our Church?" Trans. by Alex Guebert, CTM, XVIII,4 (April, 1947).

givings concerning the theology of the confessions. Today, I am convinced, the confessional problem among Lutherans does not lie primarily in the extent of confessional subscription, or even in the theology of the confessions. After all, the Lutheran symbols can be used as a waxen nose (just like Scripture) and turned to suit the fancy of liberal theologians who find themselves in territorial churches or synods which still give some sort of formal status to the symbols. No, the problem facing us today, as Peter Brunner implies,[3] is whether a person can be loyal to any confession or creed at all, whether theologians who have abandoned the authority of holy Scripture can have confessions any longer, whether modern latitudinarianism and indifferentism so rampant in practically all synods and church bodies today is at all compatible with confessionalism. In short, the issue is with the very nature of confessionalism, with the spirit of confessional subscription, with the very possibility of subscription at all.

I. The True Nature
of Confessional Subscription Misrepresented

Today the *quia—quatenus* distinction is no longer in vogue. The mere *quatenus* subscription has been so thoroughly discredited that no Lutheran theologian, at least in our country, wishes to identify with it. Does this mean that a straightforward unconditional (*quia*) subscription is now acceptable to all Lutherans in our country? By no means.[4] There are current in the Lutheran church today many utterly inadequate approaches to

---

3 Peter Brunner, "Commitment to the Lutheran Confession—What Does It Mean Today?" *The Springfielder*, XXXIII,3 (Dec. 1969), pp.4–14.

4 Ironically theologians whose acceptance of the confessions is clearly conditional offer the most disparate opinions of the old distinction. Theodore Tappert holds that one can and ought to subscribe the confessions both *quia* and *quatenus* and holds that the confessions themselves assert this, a position which seems very like nonsense, and certainly contrary to the original sense of the distinction. See Theodore Tappert, "The Significance of Confessional Subscription" in *Essays on the Lutheran Confessions Basic to Lutheran Cooperation*, published by the Lutheran Church—Missouri Synod and the National Lutheran Council (New York, 1961), p.30. Compare this with the position of Carl Braaten who finds fault with both the *quia* and *quatenus* formula for subscription. See Carl Braaten, "The Crisis of Confessionalism" in *Dialog*, I,1 (Winter, 1962), p.46 *passim*. The *quia* formula, he avers, "can make it appear as if the confessions close off the circuit between ourselves and the Scriptures, as if the confessions exempt us from continually examining the Scriptures with modern tools to gain new light on our situation." There is no evidence for such a declamation, and so Braaten offers none. But he betrays his loose stance toward the confessions when he says, "It [the *quia* formula] suggests that we believe in the inerrancy of our confessions and therefore that we aprioristically preclude the possibility of correcting them."

the Lutheran confessions and to confessional subscription. And there are many Lutheran theologians who relativize the confessions and subscribe to them only with various sorts of qualifications. I shall now list four of these inadequate modern approaches which seem to be quite common.[5]

1. *The first inadequate approach to the Lutheran confessions today is to relativize them historically.* This is an old ruse, already called attention to by Dr. Walther.[6] Briefly put, this attitude toward the confessions argues that the Lutheran symbols, like every writing (including the Bible) are historically conditioned. They were indeed good and adequate confessions for their day. But we are living in a different age. And therefore these ancient writings cannot speak as directly to us as to their own day. And we cannot subscribe them in the same sense as the original subscribers. If we had been living at the time of the Reformation, however, we would have identified wholeheartedly with them. This seems to be the kind of qualified subscription that Theodore Tappert advocates when he says,[7] "When subscribing the confessions *today*, Lutherans assert that, in view of the issues which were *then* at stake and the alternatives which were *then* offered, the confessors were right." There is good reason for Carl Braaten to comment,[8] "This is merely a new declension of the old *quatenus* formula." And as we might expect Tappert's historically relativized subscription enables him to quarrel with the doctrine of the confessions, e.g. on the necessity of baptism and on the third use of the Law as a norm for Christian life.

---

5 Actually there is general disagreement, if not veritable confusion, among those Lutherans today who cannot accept the confessions unconditionally. This sad fact was brought out with force and pathos by the disparate reactions to Horace Hummel's recent sane attempt to recall Lutheran pastors to what they should all have confidently and intelligently affirmed at their ordination. See *Lutheran Forum*, Oct. 1969. Also Dec. 1969; Feb. 1970 and Mar. 1970.

6 *Op. cit.*, "Again some say: the Symbols must be understood in their historical setting. This is correct, for the historical background sheds the necessary light on the 'manner in which men understood and interpreted Scripture at the time when certain articles were in controversy in the church and the contrary doctrines were rejected and condemned.' But the statement is false if it is employed to create the impression that the doctrinal articles contained in the symbols are not eternal truths, but applicable only for certain times and conditions and therefore subject to revision and even rejection."

7 *Op. cit.*, p.29. A more radical example of this same approach, and showing none of the appreciation of the confessions evinced by Tappert, is shown by non-theologian, Rachel Wahlberg, who frankly feels that the confessions are out of date, although she offers nothing constructive for updating them, but only criticizes them. See Rachel Wahlberg, "Let's Update the Confessions", *Lutheran Forum*, Feb. 1970, p.10.

8 *Op. cit.*, 41.

2. *The second inadequate approach to the Lutheran confessions today is to relativize them reductionistically.* This approach reduces the role of the confessions to a function, namely as evangelical witness. This is the simplistic and arbitrary position of Carl Braaten.[9] Gratuitously assuming that the Confessions provide no formula of subscription for succeeding Lutherans, Braaten claims that we are free today to work out our own approach toward the confessions. He then polemicizes without abandon against any unconditional subscription to the confessions as such. This he calls "symbolatry" (a word not coined by him), "doctrinal legalism", "confessional totalitarianism", "repristination", "a kind of doctrinal methodism". Again the ruse, this time pompous, declamatory and misleading, to bully and intimidate anyone who would subscribe without reservation the doctrinal content of our confessions. And what does Braaten offer as the only legitimate attitude toward the confessions? "Constructive confessional Lutheranism" is the term he employs, which means that we accept the confessions as an example of evangelical witness which were formulated in a "special kairos" for the crisis of their day.

Now, certainly our confessions are such a witness, but they claim to be much more than that, namely true, ecumenical, permanently valid expositions and formulations of biblical truth, which claim the acceptance of every pastor who desires the name Lutheran and evangelical.

A similar type of reductionism may be found in the recent document "A Call to Openness and Trust" issued by certain persons within the Missouri Synod. The statement is there made: "We *identify* too with the historic confessions of the Lutheran Church, understood, as all such statements must be, in the historical setting and terms of their time. We see these confessional statements as *setting forth a life of Christian freedom in the Gospel.*" And that is all that is said! Again the confessions serve as a mere example for us today. Interestingly, this statement too feels free to break with the confessions on their insistence upon a definite doctrine of the presence of Christ's body and blood in the Lord's Supper.

3. *The third inadequate approach to the Lutheran confessions today is to ignore or avoid the issue of subscription.*

A true Lutheran does not need to protest and avow continuously his loyalty to the Lutheran confessions. His ministry and teaching and personal confession will be a witness to his commitment to our confessions. However, there are times and circumstances when one must clearly ennunciate his position toward the creeds and confessions of the church. To be silent would constitute a denial of meaningful commitment. Such is the

---

9 *Ibid.*

case with two "Position Papers" on the subject "The Status of the Nicene Creed as Dogma of the Church", delivered by Warren Quanbeck and George Lindbeck in consultation with several Lutheran and Roman Catholic theologians.[10] Not one word in either paper on the status of the Nicene Creed as Dogma of the church. The only statement pertaining to the subject mustered by Quanbeck, after all kinds of qualification, is the following: "Our confession of the Nicene Creed is our recognition that *given the fourth century situation* we stand with Athanasius against Arius on Trinitarian and Christological issues." Simply to take sides like this is a subscription to nothing. Meanwhile Lindbeck's presentation pedantically questions the Creed in a variety of ways, thus avoiding the subject of the status of the Creed in the church or our posture toward it today. How ironic to hear the Roman Catholic counterpart in the discussions, John Courtney Murray, addressing himself to the same subject and speaking unequivocally of "the immutability of the Nicene dogma", insisting that it will ever remain true and relevant to affirm that Christ, the Son, is consubstantial with the Father and that the Creed will always be relevant and "intelligible *suo modo* as a formula of faith."[11] Here is one speaking in the spirit of credal subscription.

4. *The fourth inadequate approach to the Lutheran confessions today is bombastically to reject subscription.* This approach resembles the relativizing principle ennunciated above (point 2) but is overt and frank. For instance, Richard Neuhaus writes,[12] "A theologian worth his stipend can hardly be constrained, either in methodology or conclusions, by the statements of theologians of the 16th century." (One might ask whether he would include theologians of the first century such as Paul or John or Jesus!) Then follows the bombast which serves to sweeten the fare, like canned gravy over rancid beef, and thus palliate a simple rejection of confessional subscription. "Theology must argue rather than assert," Neuhaus asserts, "convince rather than coerce, persuade rather than appeal to authority." Again he magniloquently and irrelevantly asserts that confessions are not like "traffic cops directing theology's course"; they are "not binding as a form of canonical law", etc. In the end, after the reader is sufficiently embarrassed over even the semblance of confessional subscription, the

---

10 *The Status of the Nicene Creed as Dogma of the Church.* Theological Consultation between Representatives of the U.S.A. National Committee of the Lutheran World Federation and the Bishops' Commission for Ecumenical Affairs held July 6–7, 1965, in Baltimore, Maryland.

11 *Ibid.*, p.21.

12 *Lutheran Forum*, April, 1969. p.15. Cf. also Ernst Werner, "The Confessional Problem", *The Lutheran Quarterly*, XI,3 (Aug.1959), pp.179–191.

bombast subsides and the concluding statement sounds almost magnanimous toward the confessions, although it turns out to be only a variation of the principle of relativizing the confessions historically (point 1).[13]

II. THE NATURE OF CONFESSIONAL SUBSCRIPTION ACCORDING TO THE CONFESSIONS

The modern approaches toward our confessions which I have just briefly described have one thing in common apart from their weakening or virtual rejection of confessional subscription: they all (except perhaps for point 1) obscure or confuse or complicate the notion of confessional subscription. There is, however, nothing obscure or confused or even complex about the concept of confessional subscription. This is the reason why the notion is not discussed at length but only touched upon by our confessions themselves. The creeds do not bother to explain what is meant and involved by the formula "I believe". Nor do our Reformation confessions go into any disquisition on the meaning and implications of the formula, *"Ecclesiae magno consensu apud nos docent"* (Our churches teach with great unanimity), or, "We believe, teach and confess." Why not? Because the notion of confession, subscription to confessions, commitment to the Gospel and all its articles and to a definite doctrinal position was clear and clearly understood by all.

In our day too there has been little discussion on the meaning and nature of confessional subscription for the simple reason that there does not need to be. When orthodox Lutherans have written on the subject it has been usually to clear up misunderstandings and aberrations introduced by those who wish to make only some sort of conditional subscription to the confessions (Walther) or to recall Lutheran pastors to their ordination vow and to rally behind the confessions (Hummel) or to emphasize certain aspects of confessional subscription such as its relation to the *sola scriptura* principle (Brunner).

---

13 "Within such historical realities, confessional statements continue to make a contribution to the living tradition of the Church." Perhaps it is fair to say that this position toward the confessions is the dialectical one that a person must break with them and even deny them to be truly faithful to them, analogous, I suppose, to the view that one must commit acts of civil disobedience and disloyalty to country in order to uphold the spirit of its constitution. If such a position seems illogical to us, we must not discard it as merely the gut reaction of an abnormally activistic but uncritical theologian. The position, I think, would be compatible with various existentialist theologies, process theologies and marxist theologies of our day, if not with the static rules of rational thought. For this reason we must take such a position seriously (even if nonsensical) as typical of the subjectivistic madness of our *Zeitgeist*.

What then is the nature of confessional subscription?

Confessional subscription is a solemn act of confessing in which I willingly (AC, Conclusion: FC SD XII,40) and in the fear of God (FC Epit. XII,13; SD Source and Norm,20) confess my faith and declare to the world what is my belief, teaching and confession. This I do by pledging myself with my whole heart (*bekennen wir uns; amplectimur; toto pectore amplectimur*; FC SD Rule and Norm, 4–7) to certain definite, formulated confessions. I do this in complete assurance that these confessions are true and are correct expositions of Scripture (*aus und mach Gottes Wort; weil sie aus Gottes Wort genommen und darin fest und wohl gegründet ist*; ibid. 5,10). These symbolical writings become for me permanent confessions and patterns of doctrine (*Begriff und Form; forma et typus. ibid.* 1; *einhellige, gewisse, allgemeine Form der Lehre*; ibid.10) according to which I judge all other writings and teachers (*wofern sie dem jetzt gemeldeten Vorbild der Lehre gemäzz. ibid.* 10).

Confessional subscription is not some sort of individualistic, autonomous act. It is not identical with what Jesus calls for when He tells me to confess Him before men (Matt.10:32; Rom.10:9; 1 Pet. 3:15; 1 John 4:2), although it includes that. It is a responsible *public* act of confession, done in fellowship and union with the Christian church and indicating that I share unconditionally the "unanimous and correct understanding" of the church which has steadfastly remained in the pure doctrine (*ibid.* 13). The confessions do not belong to me, but to the church as the unanimously approved pattern of doctrine (*ibid.*1). They are above me or any individual (*ibid.*10). As Schlink says,[14] the consensus, so often mentioned in the confessions and so important to them, "makes plain that the confession is not the doctrine of an individual but of the church."[15]

It is essential that we base our notion of the nature and extent of confessional subscription on what the confessions themselves say or infer about such subscription. It should go without saying that we must either subscribe the confessions in the spirit and sense in which they were originally intended to be subscribed, or not at all.

---

14 Edmund Schlink, *The Theology of the Lutheran Confessions*. Trans. by Paul F. Koehneke and Herbert J. A. Bouman (Philadelphia: Muhlenberg Press, 1961), p.19.

15 Because the confessions are above the individual the Lutheran church in the past has periodically examined and investigated its teachers and pastors. In the light of what the confessions are and claim to be, such action is the right and duty of the church. To complain that such action or investigation is tyrannical or legalistic or to label such investigations as "inquisitions" as those do who do not like to be examined doctrinally only reveals that such objectors do not understand the ecumenical nature of our confessions. See Preface to the Book of Concord, Tappert, p.14.

A few statements from our confessions will bear this out. In speaking of the entire Book of Concord the Formula of Concord says the following (FC SD, Rule and Norm, 10):

Our intention was only to have a single, universally accepted certain, and common form of doctrine which all our Evangelical churches subscribe [*bekennen; agnoscant et amplectantur*] and from which and according to which, because it is drawn from the Word of God, all other writings are to be approved and accepted, judged and regulated. Cf. par.13.

Concerning the Augsburg Confession and its permanent validity in the church the following is said (FC SD Introduction, 5):

Similarly we are determined by the grace of the Almighty to abide until our end by this repeatedly cited Christian Confession as it was delivered to Emperor Charles in 1530. And we do not intend, either in this or in subsequent doctrinal statements, to depart from the afore-mentioned Confession or to set up a different and new confession.

Possibly the strongest statement pertaining to confessional subscription is found in the Preface to the Christian Book of Concord (Trig.p.23). Having pledged themselves to the earlier symbols the confessors say:

Therefore we also have determined not to depart even a finger's breadth either from the subjects themselves nor from the phrases which are found in them, but, the Spirit of God aiding us, to persevere constantly, with the greatest harmony, in this godly agreement, and we intend to examine all controversies according to this true norm and declaration of pure doctrine.

On the basis of such statements which tell us as much about the spirit of confessional subscription as the nature and extent of it Walther offers the following splendid summary of the nature of confessional subscription,[16]

---

16 *Op. cit.*, cf. the similar statement by John Benedict Carpzov, *Isagoge in Libros Ecclesiarum Lutheranarum Symbolicos.* Leipzig, 1965. p.6: "Therefore he who binds himself to profess and defend the symbolical books, if he desires to do so seriously, cannot commit himself or subscribe to these books with any mental reservations or under the condition that they agree with Scripture and the ancient church. For the question is not concerning the truth or falsity of the dogmas contained in the symbolical books—these dogmas are presupposed by the one who subscribes and binds himself to these books—no, the question is concerning a person's professing and defending this doctrine in that church to which he pledges his support. Anyone who sincerely subscribes the symbolical books obligates himself to just such a profession. But he who doubts the doctrine contained in the symbolical books, and either does not allow himself to be correctly informed or attacks the doctrine and contradicts the language and matter of speaking, such a person transgresses the limitations which have been symbols he has subscribed.

An unconditional subscription is the solemn declaration which the individual who wants to serve the church makes under oath 1) that he accepts the *doctrinal content* of our symbolical books, because he recognizes the fact that it is in full agreement with Scripture and does not militate against Scripture in any point, whether that point be of major or minor importance; 2) that he therefore heartily believes in this divine truth and is determined to preach this doctrine, whatever the form may be in which it occurs, whether the subject be dealt with *ex professo* or only incidentally. An unconditional subscription refers to the whole content of the symbols and does not allow the subscriber to make any mental reservation in any point. Nor will he exclude such doctrines as are discussed incidentally in support of other doctrines, because the fact that they are so stamps them as irrevocable articles of faith and demands their joyful acceptance by everyone who subscribes the symbols.

Notice that Walther's description, like the confessions themselves, (Tr. Conclusion; FC SD Rule and Norm, 10ff; FC SD Introduction,3), makes the object of our subscription the *doctrinal content* of the confessions. That is what we pledge ourselves to, and that is all. To my knowledge no Lutheran ever required any more. Walther makes this clear, and so do the Lutheran Fathers before him.[17] It should be unnecessary therefore constantly to repeat this obvious fact,[18] unless theologians are deliberately beclouding the issue. We do not pledge ourselves and subscribe to the Latin or German grammar of the confessions, or to the logic or illustrations used there, or to what they might say about historical or scientific matters, or liturgical usages of vestments, or the numbering of the sacraments, or to the mode of baptism (which seemed to be immersion. See SC IV, 11. Latin: *quid autem significat ista in aquam immersio?*), or to non-doctrinal "pious" phraseology like the *"semper virgo"* which we find in Selnecker's translation of the Smalcald Articles.[19]

We are bound however to the *exegesis* of the Confessions. This assertion requires just a bit of explanation. Obviously, as Walther points out, we

---

17 Cf. *ibid. passim.* Also Abraham Calov, *Criticus Sacer vel Commentarius Apodicticoelenchticus super Augustanam Confessionem.* Leipzig, 1646. Cf. also competent Lutherans today, i.e. Arthur Carl Piepkorn, "Suggested Principles for a Hermeneutics of the Lutheran Symbols", CTM, XXIX,1 (Jan.1958), pp.5,14ff. Herbert Bouman, "Thoughts on the Significance of Confessional Subscription", in *Essays on the Lutheran Confessions Basic to Lutheran Cooperation*, p. 35ff.

18 See Hummel, *op. cit.*

19 Selnecker translated freely the words *von der reinen, heiligen Jungfrau Maria* with *ex Maria pura, sancta, semper virgine.* The *"semper virgo"* is a phrase used with great regularity by Selnecker as he spoke of the Virgin Mary.

are not bound to every choice of passages our confessions make in supporting their doctrine, or to every precise detail in their exegesis of Scripture passages. But we cannot reject the exegetical conclusions (many of which are only implicit in our creeds and symbols) of our confessions without rejection of the confessions themselves as being statements of doctrine *drawn from the Scriptures*. It is clear that a rejection one by one of the passages used to support Lutheran doctrine or a rejection of the exegetical methodology of our confessions is tantamount to a repudiation of the confessions themselves. It is not correct to say that it is un-Lutheran to require agreement in exegetical conclusions. Consensus, for instance, on the real presence of Christ's body and blood in the Sacrament of the Altar is contingent upon agreement on the exegetical conclusions drawn from the words of institution (FC VII). And the same could be said for any number of articles of faith which the confessions defend exegetically.

III. ADJUNCTS TO CONFESSIONAL SUBSCRIPTION (THE SPIRIT OF CONFESSIONAL SUBSCRIPTION)

Confessional subscription can be truly appreciated and understood not simply by knowing what it is, but by understanding what is involved and implied by it. Therefore we must mention two important adjuncts of confessional subscription.

A. CONFESSIONAL SUBSCRIPTION AND THE GOSPEL

Confessional subscription is an act motivated and determined by the Gospel. A Lutheran's attitude toward the confessions will indicate his attitude toward the Gospel itself.

1. Our Lutheran confessions are truly Gospel centered and were written for the sake of the Gospel.[20] The Gospel of Christ is the central theme (*praecipuus locus doctrinae Christianae; doctrina praecipua de fide; fundamentum; der erste und Hauptartikel.* SA II,1ff. also Intro.). The very structure of certain confessions such as the Augsburg Confession, the Apology of the Augsburg Confession, and the Smalcald Articles is centered around the article of the Gospel, and when secondary topics and abuses are discussed, such as the mass, the invocation of the saints, chapters and monasteries,

---

20 Preface to the Book of Concord, Tappert, p.13. See Herbert Bouman, *op. cit.*, p.41. Cf. also Walter Bouman, "The Gospel and the Smalcald Articles", CTM XL,6–7, pp.405–414, where the author shows the evangelical character and structure of the Smalcald Articles. Cf. also Robert Preus, "The Confessions and the Mission of the Church", Essay delivered at the 1970 meeting of the overseas representatives of churches in fellowship with the Lutheran Church—Missouri Synod, p.10 *passim*.

they are always related to the chief article of the Gospel which pertains to our knowledge of Christ (SA II,II,III). The two great discussions of the Apology which center in the doctrine of justification and repentance reveal the total Gospel concern and orientation of that great confession. Even the Formula of Concord which was written to settle controversies which had entered the Lutheran church deals with these problems and settles them from a definite Gospel perspective. For instance, the Flacian error concerning original sin is shown to conflict with the several articles of the Gospel (redemption, sanctification, resurrection, FC SD I,43–47).

Our confessions were written to preserve the Gospel. This is why Melanchthon in the Apology condemns so strongly the work righteousness of the papists; for such a doctrine "buries Christ", "obscures" and "abolishes" the glory of Christ and the knowledge of the Gospel (Apol. II,44; IV,204,213; XI,9,77). And why is the Gospel so important to Melanchthon, Luther and the other writers of our confessions? Not only because their personal salvation is involved, but because of their evangelical concern for lost sinners and their spiritual welfare, because of their loving concern over tender and terrified consciences, their concern over confused Christians (Apol. IV,301,321; XI,10; XII,28; XIV,4–5; SA Preface, 3,10; SC Preface,2,4,6), yes, concern for the eternal salvation of these people (FC Epit. Rule and Norm,5; SD, Rule and Norm, 8; XI,96; Apol IV,332. German, Bek.223).

It is this cause and concern with which a Lutheran pastor identifies when he wholeheartedly and joyfully subscribes and commits himself to the Lutheran symbols. The doctrinal content of the Lutheran symbols which he subscribes is the Gospel and all its articles.

2. The Gospel is doctrine. Subscription to the Lutheran Confessions, motivated and determined by the doctrine to the Gospel, involves total commitment to this doctrine. And this doctrine of the Gospel is a definite, authoritative, cognitive message and proclamation (FC Epit. V,5–7,9; SD, V,20 passim.).[21] No wonder our confessions take doctrine so seriously and

---

21 See Robert Preus, *ibid.* p.11: "We must bear in mind that the Gospel as understood by our Confessions is more than a mere divine dynamic. It is a cognitive, dianoetic message, a doctrine. The entire IVth article of the Apology of the Augsburg Confession struggles to articulate this Gospel of justification. True, the Gospel is no mere theoretical statement, but it is a true cognitive doctrine, nevertheless. Thus our Confessions speak of the *ministerium docendi evangelii* (AC V,1). The church whose burden is to preach the Gospel is a *teaching* church: *Ecclesiae magno consensu apud nos docent* (AC I,1). The church *teaches* the Gospel of Christ (Ap.IV, 400). The marks of the church are *the pure doctrine of the Gospel* (*pura evangelii doctrina*) and administration of the Sacraments (Ap. VI,5). And so the church is called the pillar of truth (1 Tim.3:15) because it retains the "pure Gospel" (Ap. VII,20). Without the true doctrine (*die reine Lehre*) concerning Christ and the righteousness of faith

insist that they believe, teach and confess the pure doctrine (FC SD Introduction,3). The salvation of souls is at stake. "These important matters
also concern ordinary people and laymen who for their eternal salvation
must as Christians know the difference between true and false doctrine. . ."
(FC SD Rule and Norm,8; cf. Epit. Rule and Norm,5). No wonder they
insist on condemning false doctrine with countless antitheses and condemnations wherever it crops up. Again the Gospel is at stake. "In order to
preserve the pure doctrine and to maintain a thorough, lasting, and God-
pleasing concord within the church, it is essential not only to present the
true and wholesome doctrine correctly, but also to accuse the adversaries
who teach otherwise (1 Tim. 3:9; Tit. 1:9; 2 Tim. 2:24; 3:16)" (FC SD
Rule and Norm,14).[22] No wonder the framers of our confessions, convinced that their doctrine is true and based upon the Word of God (FC SD
Rule and Norm 2,4,5,16), determine, as they put it, "by God's grace to
remain steadfastly in our commitment to this confession until we die" (FC
SD XII,6). Just listen to the spirit of doctrinal certainty, based upon Scripture and wrought by the Spirit of God, which breathes forth from their
confession,

> We have no intention (since we have no authority to do so) to yield
> anything of the eternal and unchangeable truth of God for the sake of

---

there can be no church at all (Ap. IV,377 German). Doctrine is stressed all through
the Confessions; and the church of the Lutheran Confession with its burden to
proclaim Christ's Gospel believes, teaches (*lehren*), and confesses the true doctrine
(*Lehre*). In fact the Gospel *is* doctrine (Ap. XII,10); the *doctrina evangelii* is the *doctrina apostolorum* (Ap. VI,38). In fact the [one] who teaches opinions contrary to the
Gospel teaches contrary to the truth of the church (Ap. IV,400)."

The modern tendency to place pure doctrine in opposition to the Gospel (See
Martin Kretzmann, "What on Earth Does the Gospel Change?" in *Lutheran World*,
XVI,4 (Oct. 1969), pp.311,313,315,316,321) is utterly un-Lutheran and contrary to
our confessions.

22 See the statement of the Gnesio-Lutherans in the *Protestatio Wimariensium* of
Sept.20, 1557 (*CR* IX,286) as they defend the Gospel motivation for their use of
antitheses: "Now if anybody should say that we are hereby seeking to exalt our
name and not what serves the glory of God and the common good of the church,
then we confess before God the Lord who also sees and judges the innermost
thoughts of all men that from the beginning to the present hour we have sought by
our condemnation of all corrupt teachings and now seek nothing else than the
preservation of the pure teaching of the Gospel and the separation of the true
church from all other rabble and sects." Hans-Werner Gensichen correctly says
that, as a matter of principle in any confession, "The antithesis exists in fact only for
sake of the thesis and must be used in its service." See Hans-Werner Gensichen, *We
Condemn, How Luther and the 16th Century Lutheranism Condemned False Doctrine*.
Trans. but Herbert J. A. Bouman (St. Louis: Concordia Publishing House, 1967),
p.209. So it is with out Lutheran confessions, as Gensichen points out abundantly.

temporal peace, tranquility, and outward harmony. Nor would such peace and harmony last, because it would be contrary to the truth and actually intended for its suppression. Still less by far are we minded to whitewash or cover up any falsification of true doctrine or any publicly condemned errors. We have a sincere delight in and deep love for true harmony and are cordially inclined and determined on our part to do everything in our power to further the same. We desire such harmony as will not violate God's honor, that will not detract anything from the divine truth of the holy Gospel, that will not give place to the smallest error but will lead the poor sinner to true and sincere repentance, raise him up through faith, strengthen him in his new obedience, and thus justify and save him for ever through the sole merit of Christ. (FC SD XI,95–96).

Listen again to the certainty, this time uttered with eschatological assurance, with which they make their confession also for their posterity:

Therefore, in the presence of God and of all Christendom among both our contemporaries and our posterity, we wish to have testified that the present explanation of all the foregoing controverted articles here explained, and none other, is our teaching, belief, and confession in which by God's grace we shall appear with intrepid hearts before the judgment seat of Jesus Christ and for which we shall give an account. Nor shall we speak or write anything, privately or publicly, contrary to this confession, but we intend through God's grace to abide by it. (FC SD XII,40.)

Here we see the glad, free, confident spirit of an unconditioned subscription to the Lutheran confessions.

The pastor who pooh-poohs purity of doctrine, who squirms when false doctrine and teachers are condemned, who cannot be certain of his own doctrinal position cannot subscribe the Lutheran confessions and forfeits all right to the name Lutheran.

The notion has been expressed for various reasons by theologians ever since the Reformation that subscription, total, unconditional and unqualified subscription, to the Lutheran confessions is legalistic, a violation of Christian freedom, etc.[23] Opposition has centered especially against the condemnation of false doctrine so common in our confessions. Such a reaction not only manifests an ignorance of the spirit of confessionalism which puts the truth of the Gospel above every other consideration, but is

---

23 This common slur against genuine confessionalism is not confined to our indifferentistic age (See the statements of Braaten and Neuhaus above), but was common also among the Calvinists and humanistically orientated Lutherans, like John Sturm, in the 16th century. See Gensichen for an excellent and full treatment of

itself a kind of insidious crypto-legalism, a pressure (using such pious phrases as "law of love", "freedom of faith", "tolerance" etc.) exerted to divert one from making total commitment to an articulated Gospel, a definite doctrinal position. Paul was an obedient servant of Christ who loved his Lord, but he also emphasized the great importance of pure doctrine (2 Tim. 1:13–14 [cf. FC SD Rule and Norm,9] 1 Tim. 4:16; Tit. 22). And he did not hesitate to condemn false teachers (2 Tim. 1:20; Rom. 16:16; Gal. l:8), even by name (1 Tim. 1:20; 2 Tim. 2:17). Was Paul a legalist? Not at all, he was positively and totally evangelical, motivated wholly by the Gospel. And so is the church and the individual who like Paul, the slave of Christ, determines to subscribe a body of doctrine, a "pattern of sound words" (2 Tim. 1:13), which both articulates the Gospel and is formulated and professed for the sake of the Gospel. No, the fact is that it is not only un-Lutheran but unevangelical *not* to subscribe the Lutheran confessions.[24] Confessionalism springs from a love of Christ, a love toward lost sinners, and a loyalty to the Gospel. As Peter Brunner says,[25] "It is not a matter of vindicating the Lutheran Confessions of the 16th century at all costs in the present ecumenical discussion, but it is a matter of vindicating the apostolic Gospel given to us in the Scriptures."

---

this entire matter. The Calvinists, who were really just as dogmatic as the Lutherans except in their confessions which did not usually contain condemnations, attacked the Lutheran confessional principle for political and psychological reasons. Sturm tried to rise above all "parties". It is primarily against the condemnations that the Calvinists railed, and, as Gensichen points out, they exploited the "law of love" in their polemics.

Today one of the tragedies of Lutheranism is its inability to understand the evangelical concern behind condemnations and the necessity of these antitheses to safeguard and clarify the true doctrine of the Gospel. For instance, the LWF at its recent meeting at Evian, France actually proposes, through its joint committee, the elimination of all doctrinal condemnations of the past as obsolete in the light of recent theological development. See NEWS BUREAU release 70–84, LCUSA, Erik W. Modean, ed. July 29, 1970. p.12. This is in the interest of fellowship with the Reformed. Thus we observe the tragic demise of all true confessionalism in large sectors of Lutheranism.

24 The Reformed in the 16th century argued that the Lutheran unconditional subscription to the confessions violated a Christian's freedom. Leonhard Hutter (*Libri Christianae Concordiae*. Wittenberg, 1608. p.34) astutely answers this objection: "In this way [the Reformed] show very clearly that they are not yet certain of the truth of their own doctrine and confession." And he accuses the adversaries of trying to impose their own uncertainty and indifferentism upon those who are able confidently to confess their faith. At the risk of poisoning the wells I would suggest that those who constantly harp and warn about a legalistic subscription to the confessions today are possibly revealing only the tentative nature of their own theology.

25 *Ibid.*, p.12.

To force legalistically, to pressure, to bribe or wheedle anyone into subscribing the Lutheran symbols has never been advocated or even suggested in the Lutheran Church.[26] Coersion would indeed have been legalistic and would constitute a denial of our confessions and what they are, namely symbols around which Christians rally willingly and joyfully and in all Christian freedom.[27]

B. CONFESSIONAL SUBSCRIPTION AND THE *Sola Scriptura*

The Gospel to which our symbols commit themselves and out of which they speak is the Gospel of Scripture. By relating oneself by unconditional subscription to the Lutheran Confessions one *ipso facto* relates oneself not only to the Gospel, but also to the Scriptures of which the confessions claim to be an exposition. "All talk of commitment to confession is senseless when Holy Scriptures have been lost as the concrete judge over all proclamation."[28] It is significant that the Introduction to the Book of Concord and particularly the FC Rule and Norm which speak of the authority of the confessions are the very sections which affirm and delineate the authority and infallibility of Scripture as the only source and norm for judging all doctrine and teachers. The unconditional subscription to the confessions, far from closing off Scripture to the theologian, as Braaten

---

26 *Concordia Triglotta*, F. Bente, Historical Introductions, p.248.

27 Cf. the excellent statement by F. E. Mayer, *The Religious Bodies of America* (St. Louis: Concordia Publishing House, 1945), p.138ff. "The Lutherans consider the confessions not only a doctrinal standard; they are more than a body of truth; they become a public confession, a confessional act. They are, in the *first place*, the believer's joyful response to God's gracious offer in the Gospel. The Lutheran confessions are kerygmatic and prayable, i.e. they belong in the pulpit and the pew. They are a doxology. In the *second place* the confessions establish the consensus with the fathers and with their own contemporaries. The act of confessing places the present church in the continuity of faith and is a public testimony that she shares the conflicts and the conquests of the faithful of all ages. And *finally* Lutherans believe that loyalty to the confessions is a precious heritage which each generation must recapture for itself and transmit to its descendants. Lutherans believe that divine truth is absolute, has not changed since Apostolic times, will not change during future generations in accord with Jesus' saying that His words shall never pass away. The Lutheran confessional principle is expressed in the slogan:
God's Word and Luther's doctrine pure
Shall to eternity endure.

28 Brunner, *op. cit.*, 4, cf. also p.5: "The Lutheran Confession commits congregations, their shepherds and teachers exclusively to the apostolic Gospel. Therefore the Lutheran Confession contains no truths that rest in or consist of themselves, but all valid expositions it sets forth receive their validity solely from the apostolic Gospel . . . By committing the church exclusively to the apostolic Gospel, the Lutheran confession frees the church from the binding power of all teachings not based on God's Word." Brunner's entire article is to show the inextricable relation between confessional subscription and the *sola Scriptura*.

suggests,[29] actually places the Lutheran pastor in the only correct relation to the divine Word, under its authority. The authority of the confessions as a definite form and pattern of doctrine (*Vorbild der Lehre, Form der Lehre,* FC SD Rule and Norm, 10) is the authority of writings which are drawn from the Scriptures (*aus Gottes Wort genommen*) and present the doctrine of Scripture correctly.[30]

What are the implications of this fact for our day? One implication is surely that confessional Lutheranism today must stand squarely upon the *sola scriptura* principle *as it is understood and employed in the confessions themselves.* Any diminution of the apostolic source of our doctrine, of biblical authority, will undermine or vitiate entirely our confessional subscription. As Peter Brunner puts it,[31] "If the New Testament no longer harmonizes, if in the canonical writings of the New Testament a consensus is no longer heard regarding the Gospel that is to be proclaimed, then a confessional commitment has become fundamentally impossible." Our confessions speak repeatedly of the apostolic Scriptures and identify the doctrine of the Gospel (*doctrina evangelii*) with the doctrine of the apostles (*doctrina apostolorum*).

It is clear what Brunner is disturbed about. He is frightened over the distructive results of the so-called modern historico-critical method of approaching Scripture, a method which undermines the apostolic and divine origin of the New Testament witness by cutting it off from direct line with the divine, historical Christ, and then by a naturalistic and pagan understanding of the historical process, reducing that witness to a mere *Gemeindetheologie* or pious self-understanding of early Christians. There are many Lutherans today who, unlike Brunner, do not understand that there is a war on, quiet and largely unnoticed, but deadly serious. They sit at the sidelines and wonder, or they uncritically judge that this method can somehow be employed with Lutheran presuppositions. They do not realize or will not admit that the method has its own built-in presuppositions (as every method must have) regarding history and scripture and these rule out the *sola Scriptura* of our Lutheran confessions. It is high time that we who wish to be and remain confessional and evangelical Lutherans recognize that the evangelical *sola Scriptura* of our confessions (as well as

---

29 *Ibid.,* 47.

30 Hutter, *op. cit.,* p.15: "It is easy to decide concerning the authority of these [symbolical] books. Although they can by no means be made equal with the canonical Scriptures, nevertheless because [*quatenus*] they agree with the Sacred Scriptures they deserve our faithful acceptance and they deserve that degree of authority which symbolical books can and ought to have."

31 *Op. cit.,* p.7.

many articles of faith drawn from the practice of this principle) is incompatible with the historico-critical method of approaching the divine Word of Scripture. If we cannot face up to this crisis which is the great crisis facing Lutheranism today, we will lose our identity, true Lutheranism will pass away, we "will deny the Spirit of God, who now, today, here, in our historical situation, demands loyalty to the apostolic Gospel together with its actualizing interpretation" (Brunner). And Christianity will be poorer for all that (We have an ecumenical obligation!).

But we must not fail. Too much is at stake. And by God's grace we will not fail. God will see to that. We too will stand, like those confessors before us, "with intrepid hearts before the judgment seat of Jesus Christ . . . and we shall give account." (FC SD XII,40). And then in that great day we will know all the glory of confessing Christ.

The Confessions and the Mission of the Church

With Special Emphasis upon the Ecumenical Movement

"The Confessions and the Mission of the Church" is a clear demonstration of the inherent mission attitude in the Lutheran Confessions and in one of their prime twentieth-century advocates, Robert Preus. Vital to aggressive mission work is an appreciation of the unique contribution the Lutheran Confessions have made to the endeavor, which this article reveals. The article was published in *The Springfielder* in 1975. (Permission has been granted for reproduction in this collection.)

Introduction

What is the mission of the church according to the Lutheran Confessions? One is surprised to find that this question, when phrased in this particular manner, is not answered in our Confessions. Nor do our Confessions even speak of mission work in the sense usually understood by that term.[1] Since our Confessions do not speak of a single or multiple

---

1 In a definitive article, "What the Symbols Have to Say about the Church," *CTM*, XXVI, 10 (Oct. 1955), p. 72ff., Arthur Carl Piepkorn points out that many of the categories of which we have learned to think of in reference to the church and its work are not to be found in our Confessions, e.g., the church visible and invisible, the *Kirche-Ortsgemeinde* antithesis, the church militant and the church triumphant. So it is with the term "mission in the church." Martin Kretzmann in a provocative article, "What on Earth Does the Gospel Change?" *Lutheran World*, XVI, 4 (Oct.

"mission" of the church we must direct a slightly different question to our Confessions. We therefore query: What is the church and how does it function according to our Symbols? What has it been commissioned to do? What is its activity? It is in this sense that we shall use the word "mission."

The idea may strike us that our Confessions cannot really answer our modern question concerning "mission," certainly not for missionaries in the many fields today, and not for a church which senses its mission to the "whole man" in our modern sense (whatever that may mean).[2] Here certainly the Confessions are conditioned to a day of absolute monarchy and semi-feudal society. What could the Confessions, written under somewhat Erastian conditions, say to us in a democratic society today? This query could, of course, be dismissed by replying that our Symbols, which see themselves as the exposition of Scripture, *must* be relevant wherever they speak, *if* they reflect a Biblical theology—unless we wish to imply that the Scriptures themselves, because of radical changes in society and *Zeitgeist* during the last two millennia, have nothing much to offer by way of definite and formative direction and prescription for the work and activity of the church today. In such a case we should be compelled to content ourselves with a radical "translation" (in the method of the New Hermeneutic) of the Biblical commissions, injunctions, commands, *paraklesis*, etc. But I should prefer to take the query seriously as sincere and pertinent. In this case, one's own predilections and assumptions concerning the mission of the church will tend to answer the question of the relevance of the Confessions on this point. For instance, one who believes that the church's priority or even secondary mission is to act out some sort of "social gospel" today will have trouble "translating" the New Testament into meaningful counsel and will find little or nothing of value in our Confessions.

With this frank introduction we now ask the question: How do our Confessions understand the mission, or work, of the church? This question can be answered under two inclusive headings: A) the church is a

---

1969), p. 307ff., maintains that the terms "mission" and "missionary" in their modern sense are not always used in the New Testament sense with its emphasis upon the church as having its origin in Christ. If this is the case, then we need not be too squeamish about using the term "mission" in a broader sense than is usually envisaged today.

2 See *The Mission Affirmations*, adopted at the 46th Convention of the Lutheran Church—Missouri Synod, June, 1965 (St. Louis: Concordia Publishing House, 1965). Affirmation V speaks of the church as Christ's mission to the "whole man," but it is not always clear whether the expression means the whole man, body and soul, or merely the body, and whether it refers to the whole man now (does salvation pertain to the body now?) or in eternity.

proclaiming church, and B) the church is a serving church. By subsuming everything under these two rubrics we find that our Confessions say a great deal about the church's mission. In fact, the entire Reformation is an answer to this question: What is the church supposed to be doing?

A. The Church Is a Proclaiming Church

This fact is seen in the very nature of our Symbols as proclamation, confession. How typical of our Confessions are introductory formulae such as the following, "Our churches teach with great unanimity (*Ecclesiae magno consensu apud nos docent*)," "they also teach" (AC I, 1; II, 1; III, 1, 4), "We believe, teach and confess (*Wir glauben, lehren and bekennen*)" (FC, Epit. I, 2, 3). And we must not forget the *negativa*: "They condemn," "We reject" (e.g., AC I, 5; FC, Epit. I, 11). The very title "Protestant" which the Reformers adopted for themselves shows that they see the church as a witnessing church. The great emphasis upon doctrine in our Confessions, on the truth of the *doctrina evangelii*, its continual relevance throughout all history (Ap. XII, 53, 73) brings out this same fact that the church has a message to proclaim. Specifically several motifs from our Confessions emphasize this activity of the Church.

1. The Church as a Fellowship

The Lutheran Symbols define the church as the assembly of saints or believers (*congregatio sanctorum, Versammlung aller Gläubigen*) in which the Gospel is taught purely and the sacraments are administered rightly (AC VII, 1). The activity of the church is fellowship, sharing. This is the case whether the *communio sanctorum* of our Creed is taken as the fellowship of the saints, as Luther understood the phrase (*Gemeinde*, congregation, LC II, 47ff.), or as the fellowship in the sacraments. In this community or fellowship the prime activity centers in the obtaining of the forgiveness of sins (LC II, 55) through the means of Word and Sacraments. It consists also of sanctification which in this life is never complete (LC II, 67) and is wrought also through the Word of forgiveness. Such activity is brought about and made possible by the Spirit of God—this is His work (*Amt und Werk*)—who works in and through the church by means of the Word of the Gospel (LC II, 59).

The clear implication of what we have said is that the work of the church is the work of the Spirit; and anything which is not clearly the Spirit's work is not the work of the church. Luther likens the church to "the mother that begets and bears every Christian through the Word of God." This is the work of the church. But Luther goes on immediately to say, "The Holy Spirit reveals and preaches that Word, and by it He illu-mincs and kindles hearts so that they grasp and accept it, cling to it, and persevere in it" (LC II, 42; Ap. IV, 132). Needless to say the preaching of Christ is fundamental to the Spirit's (and church's) activity (*ibid.* 45; FC, SD 56). Luther is most explicit on this point: that the church as commu-nity, as fellowship, is both the creation of the Spirit and His locus for activity, and that His activity in and through the church is the only activity worthy of the church.

> This, then, is the article which must always remain in force. Creation is past and redemption is accomplished, but the Holy Spirit carries on his work unceasingly until the last day. For this purpose he has appointed a community on earth, through which he speaks and does all his work. For he has not yet gathered together all his Christian people, nor has he completed the granting of forgiveness. Therefore we believe in him who daily brings us into this community through the same Word and the forgiveness of sins. Then when his work has been finished and we abide in it, having died to the world and all evil, he will finally make us perfectly and eternally holy. We now wait in faith for this to be accom-plished through the Word (LC II, 61–62; cf. AC XVIII, 2; FC, SD 35–40).

How far are we to press this statement of Luther's? Not a word about social action here, building hospitals, schools, etc., etc. Is such action, then, not the work of the Spirit, and therefore of the church, for Luther? It would appear not, in the present context.[3] Once we see the church in fel-lowship and action as the vehicle of the Spirit's activity we perceive why the church as a fellowship lives by and extends the means of grace, that is, works the works of the Spirit, indulges in soteriological pursuits and is completely involved in this activity.

The church, then, is a spiritual fellowship, held together through the proclamation of the Word and administration of the sacraments. Gospel and sacraments are the external means whereby Christ exercises His spir-itual dominion—and they reveal where the church is (Ap. VII, 10 *passim*). In this sense the church is the *regnum Christi* (Ap. VII, 26).

---

3 Corporate social action and political concerns have to do with an outward and temporal mode of existence (*ein äusserlich, zeitlich Wesen*) and, according to our Confessions (AC XVI, 4), are the work of the civil government which, like the church, is an institution of God under the category of creation and law (fourth commandment), not Gospel. It is the Creed that distinguishes Christians from Turks and Jews, who can also raise armies, build schools and hospitals, and attain a degree of civil righteousness.

2. THE MINISTRY

The doctrine in our Confessions concerning the ministry sheds much light on what our Symbols consider to be the mission of the church. The key passage in our Confessions to speak of the ministry of the church is AC V:

In order that we may obtain this faith, the ministry of teaching the Gospel and administering the sacraments was instituted. For through the Word and the sacraments, as through instruments, the Holy Spirit is given, and the Holy Spirit produces faith, where and when it pleases God, in those who hear the Gospel.

Notice that in this passage no mention of the office of pastor is made, no mention of man, of rank, of *ordo*. Rather an activity is spoken of, a function, a preaching activity (*ministerium docendi evangelii*). This is the means whereby faith is created and nourished, the means whereby the church is born and nourished. And thus this ministry becomes the essential work of the church. Notice the prominent place given this ministry by Melanchthon. The article on this ministry of the Word follows directly upon his presentation of the work of Christ and justification by faith, and it precedes the articles on the new obedience and the church (Art. VI–VIII), for there can be no new obedience or church without this ministry.

It is important to note the functional, non-institutional, nature of this ministry. Melanchthon is simply speaking here, as elsewhere, of the preaching of the Gospel Word, or of the work of the Gospel Word.[4] This fact is illustrated clearly in the Schwabach Articles VII as they speak on this point, "To obtain this faith, or to bestow it upon us men God has instituted the ministry or the oral word [*Predigambt oder mundlich Wort*], namely, the Gospel through which He causes this faith and its power and use and fruit to be proclaimed, and through it as through means He gives us faith along with the Holy Spirit, as and where He wills. Apart from this there is neither means nor way, neither mode nor manner to receive faith."[5] There can

---

4 This is brought out in other statements from the Symbols. See Ap. XXVII, 22, which speaks of pious men in cloisters "*qui serviunt ministerio verbi.*" But the German has simply "*frommen Leuten. welche lesen und studieren.*" Tract. 67 speaks of the ministry as the edification of the saints (cf. Eph. 4:12). Ap. XXVIII, 9 uses *ministerium* in the same active sense of carrying out a function. *Ministerium verbi et sacramentorum* is in the German *das Amt der Predig und die Handreichen der heiligen Sacrament.* AC XXVIII, 19, after saying that bishops have the power of the sword only *jure humano*, adds the words: *Haec interim alia functio est quam ministerium evangelii.* Ap. XV, 44 (German text) has the activity of preaching the Gospel when it speaks of the *Predigtamt.* Cf. LC I, 86, where Luther says that the special office (*eigentlich Amt*) of Sunday should be the ministry of preaching (*Predigtamt*) to young, poor, etc.

5 See *Bekenntnisschriften*, p. 61.

be no doubt that this article, like AC V, describes the work of the church, or more properly, God's work through the church in causing His kingdom to come. This conforms to the Confessional notion that God is the author of baptism and of the Sacrament of the Altar. The church's mission, or ministry, is God's mission through the church. And it is a ministry with a completely soteriological and eschatological goal. The kingdom of power (creation, preservation, providence, civil government) is totally in the service of the kingdom of grace, namely, God's Gospel claim upon men.

The Lutheran Confessions see this ministry as the work of the whole church in contrast to a *ministerium leviticum* which still dominated the hierarchical notion of the Romish church (Tr. 26). This functional view of ministry destroys all ranks (Tr. 7–13). What, then, is the office of the pastor? He is simply the public servant of the church, rightly called to teach and preach publicly and administer the sacraments (AC XIV). The pastor does nothing that the church is not commissioned to do. The ministry of the Word today is seen as the continuation of the apostolic ministry which in turn was the continuation of Christ's ministry (Tr. 9), Christ's *opus proprium*, which is to proclaim the Gospel. Fagerberg says,[6] "The Lutheran Confessions present a functional understanding of the ministry. The pastors and bishops of the Church have no other duty than to proclaim the Word of Christ as preserved in Scripture. It is through this Word that God becomes present among men. The Church cannot set forth any new words; it has the one task of mediating the living Word of Christ." The church's ministry, then, is to continue Christ's office of proclaiming the forgiving Word. Again Fagerberg says,[7] "In all the functions of the ministry God's own voice is to be heard and His will done." And God's will is known through His Word. Fagerberg does not speak too strongly or exclusively. According to our Confessions the church's ministry (mission) is confined to the proclamation of the Word of God. This point is made clear in the Apology as it speaks of ecclesiastical power (Ap. XXVIII). In discussing ecclesiastical power the Roman Confutation had maintained that bishops have the power not only of the ministry of the Word but also of ruling and coercive correction in the political and social realm—for salutary ends, of course.[8] Melanchthon replies that bishops have no power to

6 Holsten Fagerberg, *Die Theologie der lutherischen Bekenntnisschriften von 1529 bis 1537*, übersetzung von Gerhard Klose (Göttingen: Vandenhoeck & Ruprecht, 1965), p. 32. See also Leiv Grane, *Confessio Augustana, Infoerelse i den Lutherske Reformations Hovedtanker* (Copenhagen: Gyldendal, 1963), p. 51.

7 *Ibid.*, p. 33.

8 See Michael Reu, *The Augsburg Confession, A Collection of Sources* (Chicago: Wartburg Press, 1930), p. 381.

involve themselves in civil government (AC XXVIII, 2). Nor can they impose secular punishment (AC XXVIII, 19–20). Authority in such realms has nothing to do with the office of the Gospel *(". . . und gehet das Ambt des Evangeliums gar nichts an")*. They have not even the power to judge in secular cases of marriage (AC XXVIII, 29).

It is clear from the foregoing, in the light of the sharp distinction in our Confessions between the secular and the spiritual realms (a subject to which we shall have occasion to return), that the ministry of the church and pastor is definitely limited. It is a spiritual function and ministry which the church has, the ministry of preaching the Word and administering the sacraments. It is the power of the keys, no more and no less. "Our teachers hold that according to the Gospel the power of the keys or the power of bishops is a power or command of God to preach the Gospel, to remit and retain sins, and to administer the sacraments. . . . This power is exercised only [*tantum*] by teaching or preaching the Gospel and by administering the sacraments either to many or to individuals, depending on one's calling. For it is not bodily things that are thus given, but rather such eternal things as eternal righteousness, the Holy Spirit, and eternal life. These things cannot come about except through the ministry of the Word and sacraments" (AC XXVIII, 5, 8, 9. Cf. 21; Ap. XXVIII, 19, 9). The means of grace and salvation, the proclamation of the Gospel and administration of the sacraments: these are the power through which the Spirit of Christ creates the church, these are the marks which identify the church and unify it, and these are the *ministerium* which occupy the church in mission. And it is to preach the Gospel and administer the sacraments that pastors are called.

3. THE GOSPEL

As a fellowship of believers in Christ, the church shares and ministers with the Gospel. This is the central theme and concern of our Confessions. It is essential therefore that we understand precisely what our Confessions mean by the Gospel. The term "Gospel" is used in our Confessions in both a broad and a narrow sense. And our Confessions recognize this fact (FC, SD V, 5). In the broad and loose sense the term may refer to the New Testament, to parts of the New Testament, to the content of Scripture, or even to the Scripture itself (AC XXVIII, 5; Tr. 60; LC I, 65, 182, 276, 285; Ap. XI, 4).[9] At times the term is used inter-

---

9 For a thorough discussion of the various nuances in which the term is used see Fagerberg, pp. 90–106. Also Ralph Bohlmann, "Our Commitment to the Gospel," a paper prepared for the Intersynodical Commission of the Lutheran Church— Missouri Synod and the American Lutheran Church, 1969, pp. 1–2, 8.

changeably with Scripture: Melanchthon may say either *scriptura docet* (Ap. XII, 157) or *evangelium docet* (Ap. XV, 5). The term is even used synonymously with doctrine (Ap. VII, 8).

Our concern, however, is with the meaning of the term "Gospel" in the narrow, or proper, sense. In its form the Gospel is an external, oral proclamation (LC IV, 30; SA III, IV). Often the Gospel is simply called "the promises" (*promissiones, Verheissung Gottes, Zusage*). The promises are concerning free remission of sin and concerning reconciliation through faith in Christ (Ap. IV, 188. See also Ap. IV, 60, 388; XII, 53; SA III, 3, 4). The Gospel offers us God's own promises that He will be gracious to us and justify us for Christ's sake (Ap. IV, 43), or that He will no longer be angry with us (*Deum nobis propitium esse*) for Christ's sake (Ap. IV, 345), so that He forgives us for Christ's sake (Ap. VII, 35),

So there is a very explicit and definite content to this Gospel proclamation. Throughout our Confessions (especially in Ap. IV and FC V and SA II, I) we observe the burning desire to retain and proclaim this Gospel content unimpaired and unadulterated. Perhaps the best definition of the Gospel content is found in FC, SD V, 21:

> The content of the Gospel is this, that the Son of God, Christ our Lord, himself assumed and bore the curse of the law and expiated and paid for all our sins, that through him alone we re-enter the good graces of God, obtain forgiveness of sins through faith, are freed from death and all the punishments of sin, and are saved eternally [cf. FC, Epit. V, 5].

One easily perceives the Christological burden in the Gospel content. The Gospel proclamation centers on the saving work of Christ and in the results of this saving work for the world and the individual. As Melanchthon says, the Gospel compels us to make use of Christ. It teaches that through Him we have access to God, reconciliation with God, and victory over sin and death (Ap. IV, 291). And the Formula tells us that the Gospel "directs" sinners "solely to the merit of Christ, and raises them up again by the delightful proclamation of God's grace and favor acquired through the merits of Christ" (FC, Epit. V, 7).

Because the Gospel centers "in those articles which pertain to the office and work of Jesus Christ, or to our redemption" (SA II, intro.), it is considered throughout our Confessions to be "the first [in the sense of priority] and chief article" (*der erste und Hauhtartikel*) of the Christian faith (SA II, I, 1).

> Nothing in this article can be given up or compromised, even if heaven and earth and things temporal should be destroyed. For as St. Peter

says, "There is no other name under heaven given among men by which we must be saved" (Acts 4:12). "And with his stripes we are healed" (Isa. 53:5).

On this article rests all that we teach and practice against the pope, the devil, and the world. Therefore we must be quite certain and have no doubts about it. Otherwise all is lost, and the pope, the devil, and all our adversaries will gain the victory (SA II, I, 5).

The Gospel voice not only tells us all that Christ has clone for us but how we may appropriate reconciliation and justification through His death and blood, namely, by faith. And this is the *res maxima* and the *praecipuus locus* which becomes the very reason for the existence of the Confessions themselves. Therefore Melanchthon at times will call the article of forgiveness the most important point of the Gospel (*praecipuus evangelii locus*) or he will call the article of justification the fundamental theme of Christian doctrine (*praecipuus locus doctrinae Christianae*), for this is the result of Christ's office and work.

The Gospel as the proclamation of Christ's saving work is a divine dynamic; it has a function, an office, an activity.[10] It effectively teaches me concerning Christ (LC II, 38), creates faith in my heart, brings me the Holy Spirit and comforts me with the treasure of salvation (AC V, 2; Ap. IV, 73; LC III, 38). It also functions to open up to me an understanding and appreciation of all the articles of faith. It powerfully teaches me to make use of Christ as mediator and propitiator (Ap. IV, 299) and to set Him against the wrath of God (Ap. IV, 291). It offers and confers consolation and continual forgiveness (SA III, III, 8). Without this divine power, therefore, all is lost: there is no Christ, no Holy Spirit, no Christian Church (LC II, 44–45; Ap. II, 10; IV, 298). And so it is Christ's *opus proprium* and the church's *opus proprium* (LC II, 31–33; Ap. XII, 50ff.). Our Confessions see this Gospel as preached to the whole world (SA III, IV). And the fundamental office of the church is to propagate this Word "that alone brings salvation" (Preface to the Book of Concord, Tappert, p. 13).

We must bear in mind that the Gospel as understood by our Confessions is more than a mere divine dynamic. It is a cognitive, dianoetic message, a doctrine. The entire fourth article of the Apology of the Augsburg Confession struggles to articulate this Gospel of justification. True, the Gospel is no mere theoretical statement, but it is a true cognitive doctrine, nevertheless. Thus our Confessions speak of the *ministerium docendi evan-*

---

10 Fagerberg, pp. 99ff.; Edmund Schlink, *Theology of the Lutheran Confessions*, trans. by Paul F. Koehneke and Herbert J. A. Bouman (Philadelphia: Muhlenberg Press, 1961), p. 103.

gelii (AC V, 1). The church whose burden is to preach the Gospel is a *teaching* church: *Ecclesiae magno consensu apud nos docent* (AC I, 1). The church *teaches* the Gospel of Christ (Ap. IV, 400). The marks of the church are the *pure doctrine of the Gospel* (*pura evangelii doctrina*) and administration of the Sacraments (Ap. VII, 5). And so the church is called the pillar of truth (I Tim. 3:15) because it retains the "pure Gospel" (Ap. VII, 20). Without the true doctrine (*die reine Lehre*) concerning Christ and the righteousness of faith there can be no church at all (Ap. IV, 377 German). Doctrine is stressed all through the Confessions; and the church of the Lutheran Confession with its burden to proclaim Christ's Gospel believes, teaches (*lehren*), and confesses the true doctrine (*Lehre*). In fact, the Gospel is doctrine (Ap. XII, 10); the *doctrina evangelii* is the *doctrina apostolorum* (Ap. VII, 38).[11] And so he who teaches opinions contrary to the Gospel teaches contrary to the truth and to the church (Ap. IV, 400).[12]

B. THE CHURCH AS A SERVING CHURCH

THE CHURCH'S MINISTRATION OF WORKS

It is the activity (or mission) of the church to be a serving church. What is the meaning of this idea in our Confessions, the basis, nature, and

---

11 Fagerberg is most insistent that, according to the Confessions, the Gospel Word is based upon the Word of Scripture and normed by it (*op. cit.*, p. 21; cf. SA II, II, 2; Ap. XII, 173; AC XXVIII, 5; Ap. XV, 16). Fagerberg's thesis is proved most clearly in Ap. IV which operates with the Scripture principle throughout its effort to formulate and defend the nature and function of the Gospel in the life of the church. Fagerberg sees the proclamation of the church, according to the Confessions, as assuming various applications at times, but having a content which is always that of the written Word. Thus, the Bible, as it were, is "brought to life" through preaching. Preaching, in the meantime, must conform to the Scriptures. He says (p. 32): "The spoken Word in no sense becomes a critical authority to be used against the Word of Scripture but it is God's active Word in the present precisely because it is grounded in the Holy Scripture. The Scripture Word, brought to life in preaching and in the administration of the Sacraments, mediates the very activity of God."

12 Since the Gospel is doctrine and the teaching ministry of the church is to propagate and apply and formulate and defend the Gospel, it goes without saying that our Lutheran Symbols never pooh-pooh or depreciate Christian doctrine. A deep concern for the purity of the *doctrina evangelii* is evident throughout the Confessions and was clearly an impetus for the writing of the Confessions. One is therefore alarmed and ashamed to witness modern Lutherans who pledge their loyalty to our Confessions making light of such a concern for pure doctrine and contrasting the Gospel to doctrine. This is the most disappointing feature of a recent article by Martin L. Kretzmann, "What on Earth Does the Gospel Change?" *Lutheran World*, XVI, 4 (Oct. 1969), pp. 311, 313, 315, 316, 321. Such an antithesis is never found in our Confessions and would be considered false and a contradiction in terms by the writers of the Confessions.

scope of the church's service? In a crucial passage in the Apology, Melanchthon speaks of the two-fold service or worship in the church of Christ (Ap. IV, 310):

> Thus the service and worship of the Gospel [*cultus et latreia evangelii*] is to receive good things from God, while the worship of the law is to offer and present our goods to God. We cannot offer anything to God unless we have first been reconciled and reborn. The greatest possible comfort comes from this doctrine that the highest worship in the Gospel is the desire to receive forgiveness of sins, grace, and righteousness (cf. Ap. IV, 49, 154; AC XXI, 3).

This statement of Melanchthon's offers the proper perspective for understanding the church's ministration of works. What does Melanchthon mean by a *cultus legis* whereby we offer and present our goods to God? He is obviously referring to the good works of Christians, the fruits of faith, which is the burden of the entire second part of his discussion in Apology IV (entitled, "Love and the Keeping of the Law," cf. AC VI). There are many points which we must bear in mind if we wish to understand the church's ministration of good works as the matter is understood and presented in our Confessions.

1. *It is a service only of those who have been reconciled and reborn*, as Melanchthon's statement put it. It is never called a ministry (*ministerium*). The ministry of the church, strictly speaking, has to do with the Spirit's work in the church through the means of salvation. It is a *cultus*, a service, an activity of response to the Gospel, an activity which is made possible only by the power of the Gospel.

Our Confessions never tire of maintaining that the service of works, acts of love, is the fruit of faith in the Gospel and is therefore unique to Christians. Melanchthon says, "After we have been justified and regenerated by faith, therefore, we begin to fear and love God, to pray and expect help from him, to thank and praise him, and to submit to him in our affliction. Then also we begin to love our neighbor because our hearts have spiritual and holy impulses" (Ap. IV, 111. Cf. 129, 270). Before faith there can be no true obedience to the law by which we serve God and men (Ap. IV, 128–9). Certain *civilia opera* can be managed; but this does not please God and often does not get very far. It is the righteousness of the heart which bears the fruits of righteousness which please God and are the proper office of the Christian (Ap. IV, 375). And these fruits please God only because of faith and the mediator Christ (*propter fidem et mediatorum Christum*). Here is the right use of the *propter fidem*. (See Ap. IV, 166, 172, 181, 355, 177: *Inchoata impletio legis placeat propter fidem.*)

Faith always produces love and good works, according to our Confessions. It absolutely must do so (Ap. IV, 141; FC, SD 8). Not only because it is never the Christian's option not to do good works (FC, SD IV, 20). Not only because works are commanded as a testimony of our faith (Ap. IV, 184, 189). Not only because our works glorify Christ (Ap. IV, 269, 189). But because the Spirit has transformed us by bringing us to faith, and "faith is a living, busy, active, mighty thing, so that it is impossible for it not to be constantly doing what is good" (FC, SD IV, 10). And so faith in the Gospel is joined inseparably to the service of good works in Lutheran theology. Listen to Melanchthon: "We are justified for this very purpose, that, being righteous, we might begin to do good works and obey God's law. For this purpose we are reborn and receive the Holy Spirit, that this new life might have new works, new impulses, the fear and love of God, hatred of lust, etc." (Ap. IV, 348–9).

2. This service of works which marks the "new life" of every true Christian is not a dumb and blind service, normed by some vague and nebulous notion of love. *It is an obedience of God's law*, says Melanchthon (*ibid.*). Good works are only those which have been commanded by God (AC VI, 1). And God's "immutable will according to which man is to conduct himself in this life" (FC, SD VI, 15) is found epitomized in the Decalogue (Ap. IV. 22; FC, SD VI, 12). The Ten Commandments are the norm for our life, the only norm for our service to God or our neighbor; they are the fountain through which all good works must spring, and apart from these Commandments no deed is pleasing to God, no matter how precious it may be in the eyes of the world (LC I, 311).[13] And the Commandments are set forth and applied most beautifully in the Scriptures. Therefore no one will serve God or man with his works without support in God's Word (Ap. XV, 14, 17, 29). And the Christian in his behavior in the world and in relation to the world seeks guidance from the Scriptures.

3. As the Christian seeks to live a life of service in good works he discovers that his activities often correspond to those of unbelievers or of the state. This leads us to the notion of civil righteousness (*justitia rationis, opera rationis, justitia civilis, justitia philosophica, civilia opera, justitia legis, justitia propria, äusserliche Frömmigkeit*) so often mentioned in our Confessions. This is the outward obedience to natural law (*ex naturae*).[14] The

---

13 Unlike Melanchthon in the Augustana and Apology and the Formula of Concord, Luther never calls God's positive will for our life "law," but rather *Gebot, mandatum, praeceptum*. For Luther, who owed so much to Paul, "law" was too closely related to God's wrath.

14 The concept of natural law in the early Luther, a concept which is fundamental to an appreciation of his treatment of the Ten Commandments in the Large Cate-

concept of civil righteousness in our Confessions is a difficult but important concept. It is a righteousness, to be sure, and yet it does not really serve God because it is wrought by those who are carnal and cannot serve God (Ap. IV, 35). In fact it is sin in God's eyes, even though it may be most praiseworthy according to human judgment. Dialectically, then, it is a *justitia* and at the same time sin. Why? Because it is done without Christ and the Holy Spirit (Ap. IV, 124, 130, 181).

And yet the correspondence exists between the good works of Christians and the *justitia civilis* (mere outward good works: Ap. II, 43; IV, 12ff.) of the world. Both are normed by natural law and both promote and are able to achieve some order in society and improvement of human relationships. Is the Christian's ministry of works, then, simply to do what others do, but perhaps better and from totally different motives? According to Fagerberg, there is in this sense no necessity for speaking of a unique Christian ethic.[15] And Melanchthon appears to support him, for he says that the commandments of the second table "contain the civil righteousness that reason understands" (Ap. IV, 34; cf. also XVIII, 4).

4. All this would certainly imply that *the Christian in the world will work in and with the secular realm and will thus serve according to his calling* (AC XVI; LC I, 150–154; SC IX, 4–5). Melanchthon's understanding of civil righteousness and his strong emphasis upon its importance in the secular and civil realm would suggest, moreover, that the Christian will not only support the works of civil righteousness where in good conscience he can do so, but that the works of civil righteousness supported by Christians will actually accomplish the optimum of justice and order in the civil realm (*Regiment, officia*; see AC XXVIII, 12, 18).

To clarify the nature of Christian service in the present context two observations must be made from our Confessions. First, we must bear in mind the rather strong emphasis in Luther and the Confessions on the notion of vocation. This notion was developed in opposition to the Roman view which confined vocation to the clergy only. The Lutheran position was that the individual Christian serves by doing good works according to the Ten Commandments (Ap. XII, 174 German), each obeying according to his station or calling (LC I, 120). Parents have one station, children another; rulers one station, subjects another, etc. The commands are not the same to all, and so the service of the different Christians in their vari-

chism is treated by Fagerberg, pp. 69ff. See also Lauri Haikola, *Usus Legis* (Uppsala, A. B. Lundequistska Bokhandeln, 1958), p. 95, *passim*. The best presentation of the matter is by Paul Peters, "Luther on the Form and Scope of Mosaic Law," *Quartalschrift*, 45, 2 (April, 1948), pp. 98–113.

15 Fagerberg, p. 70.

ous offices will vary (SC V, 20), as Luther's table of duties makes clear (SC IX). This service which each Christian carries out in his own vocation is not merely the response to a command but is directed according to the very creation and order of God (*creatio et ordinatio Dei, Gottes Geschöpf and Ordnung*; AC XXVII, 20). God's commands are the commands of Him who is the preserver of nature, and that is a reason why they are so important as we carry out our different vocations. The rationale behind this concept is that we receive everything from God (LC I, 26) and we are the channels through which God bestows blessings. Therefore as His means we take and give only as He has commanded. In practice this means carrying out our calling where God has placed us and serving people in our calling. Doing this and practicing all the virtues of Christian piety will keep us more than busy (LC I, 311–314).

The second corollary observation is that the service or ministration to which we have been referring is, according to our Confessions, always the ministration of the individual Christians in their several callings, not the service of the church as such. There is no mention and, it would seem, no place for corporate ecclesiastical action in the sphere of civil and secular affairs (*weltlich Regiment, politica administratio*, AC XXVIII, 11 *passim*). Why is this so? We might speculate that such action was impossible when our Confessions were written. Church and civil government were so merged in many ways that the very idea of corporate ecclesiastical action in social and civil matters, which today seems so fundamental to some, could not even have been envisaged, even though the Lutherans clearly distinguished between the spiritual and civil realms. Such an answer would, however, be superficial and not entirely true. There are several *theological* reasons why our Confessions do not and really could not advocate corporate, institutional, ecclesiastical activity in the sphere of social and civil affairs, what we today would call social or political action.

First, the clear distinction between the two authorities (*regnum Christi et regnum civilis*, Ap. XXVIII, 2) definitely limits the church in its labors and functions. "Therefore, ecclesiastical and civil power are not to be confused" (AC XXVIII, 12). "Let it [the ecclesiastical power, the church] not invade the other's function, nor transfer the kingdoms of the world, nor abrogate the laws of civil rulers, nor abolish lawful obedience, nor interfere with judgments concerning any civil ordinances or contracts, nor prescribe to civil rulers laws about the forms of government that should be established" (*ibid.* 13). The spiritual kingdom (*regnum spiritualis*) does not change civil or world government (*status civilis, Weltregiment*), but there is government redress for righting various wrongs (cf. Ap. XVI, 7; cf. also 2, 3, 6). As representatives of the church, bishops and pastors are to exercise only a spiritual function to preach the Gospel and administer the sacraments (AC XXVIII, 2, 3; Tr. 31; Ap. XXVIII, 19; Ap. XIII, 9). And this is the one function also of the church of Christ itself (AC XXVIII, 9; Ap. VII, 28).

Second, the very nature of the church precludes corporate ecclesiastical invasion of the social and political realm. For the church as the *regnum Christi* (Ap. VII, 16, 17) is not a mere association of outward rites like other political entities (*aliae politiae*), but is an association of faith and the Holy Spirit in men's hearts (*ibid.* 5), a "fellowship of saints who share the association of the same Gospel or teaching and of the same Holy Spirit, who renews, consecrates, and governs their hearts" (*ibid.* 8). As the *regnum Christi*, ruled by the Spirit of Christ, the church's activity is spiritual, always linked with the Spirit's work in and through the church. In Luther's beautiful description of the Spirit's work in the Large Catechism all the church's life and activity is centered in what the Spirit accomplishes spiritually through the Word and Sacraments (LC II). "Where He does not cause the Word to be preached and does not awaken understanding in the heart all is lost" (LC II, 43). Where the Spirit is not present with the Word there is no Christian church (LC II, 44), "for where Christ is not preached, there is no Holy Spirit to create, call, and gather the Christian church, and outside it no one can come to the Lord Christ" (LC II, 45). Neither in this discussion of Luther's which is a sort of epitome of the Spirit's and the church's work and mission nor anywhere in our Confessions do we find any mention of the ministry or function of the church as church to engage in purely social or civil activities—this is the activity of the individual Christian in his calling.

All this does not imply that the church does not have a deep interest and stake in affairs of the social order. Not only does the church pray for the civil order and honor it and urge the Christians to support and obey it (AC XXVIII, 18; LC I, 141; III, 75), but the church also expresses itself on matters (like education) which affect both church and state and encourages its young to prepare for service in the secular government (*weltlichem Regiment*) and other occupations (SA II, III, 1). Nor does the church hesitate to advise the highest rulers of state concerning their responsibilities and duties (Ap. XXI, 44). However it is as members of the church (*praecipua membra ecclesiae*) who have their specific calling that rulers are given such counsel (Tr. 54).

We are now prepared to answer this question: What is the church's mission? According to all the evidence offered above, it is the single ministry of being the Spirit's instrument in proclaiming the Gospel and administering the sacraments. Meanwhile every Christian in his calling has the "ministry" of service both in the church and in the world. That the church's mission is single and confined to the proclamation of the Gospel and administration of the sacraments is clear from three great emphases in our Confessions, and these must be mentioned to improve our perspective to see how fundamental this mission is and must be for the church.

1. *Soteriology.* Werner Elert speaks often[16] of the notion of "Heilsego-ismus," the personal concern for one's salvation, which is typified by the "for me" in Luther's works and in our Confessions. This notion, so often cast into the teeth of Lutheranism, is of the very essence of the evangelical faith, according to Elert. For it is a result of the soteriological burden of Lutheranism, a burden made clear in our Confessions with their stress upon the centrality of the Gospel in the church's theology and worship and life (Ap. IV, 310). Structurally the Augsburg Confession is built around Articles III and IV on Christology and justification through faith. The same is true of the Smalcald Articles. The whole purpose of the Confessions was to set forth and confess the Gospel in its purity, and this in order that troubled consciences could have peace and forgiveness and salvation (FC, SD V, 9, 12, 20; cf. also Preface to the Book of Concord, Tappert, pp. 5, 13). And Melanchthon in his great discussion of justification by faith constantly urges the Christian as he lives out his life of faith to "make use" of Christ who is the content of the Gospel and the only mediator and propitiator against God's wrath (Ap. IV, 40, 45, 46, 80, 154, 213, 214, 221, 222, 291, 299, 300). This alone offers the believer hope against the monster of uncertainty (Ap. IV, 346, 118). The soteriological concern dominates and pervades our Lutheran Confessions. This is true even when the most peripheral concerns are discussed (see, e.g., SA II, II, III, IV). Thus, we see our Symbols as an act of confession carrying out the mission of the church to proclaim the Gospel.

2. *Eschatology.* There is no special article on eschatology in our Symbols except for the brief presentation in Augustana XVII on Christ's return to judgment (which interestingly follows the article on civil government). And this article merely sums up what was found in the catholic creeds. But eschatology, too, permeates our Confessions. The Confessions were written consciously and deliberately in anticipation of Christ's imminent return to judge and to vindicate (Ap. Preface, 19; SA II, IV, 15). The subscribers of the Book of Concord preface their confession with these words, "By the help of God's grace we, too, intend to persist in this confession until our blessed end and to appear before the judgment seat of our Lord Jesus

---

16 *The Structure of Lutheranism*, trans. by Walter A. Hansen (St. Louis: Concordia Publishing House, 1962), p. 68ff.

Christ with joyful and fearless hearts and consciences" (Preface to the Book of Concord, p. 9). And the last words of the Formula of Concord repeat that confident declaration (FC, SD XII, 40, 6). Such is the certainty of Christ's return and of victory in Him which marks the Lutheran fathers as they confess the Gospel in their day and for all posterity.

The Confessions reflect the conviction that we live in the last times. Antichrist is raging and all the signs of the end time are revealed. Meanwhile our life here has the goal of eternal life. Our regeneration and justification through faith make us partakers now of that life (Ap. IV, 352). And the Gospel brings us all the eternal, eschatological blessings of God (Ap. VII, 15; SC VI, 6; LC II, 31; LC III, 53–4). The Christian has eternal life now. And so our life here is lived in anticipation of the eternal life to come (LC II, 61–62). This is what the central soteriological emphasis of our Confessions is all about (see, e.g., Ap. IV, 291; LC II, 28–32; FC, Epit. VI, 5): as justification and faith belong together, so faith and eternal life belong together (*Sicut autem iustificatio ad fidem pertinet, ita pertinet ad fidem vita aeterna*, Ap. IV, 354). One can easily perceive how such a dominant eschatology will effect the church as it engages in its ministry. All is done *sub specie aeternitatis*, with the urgency of eternity about it.

3. *Satanology.* The eschatological emphasis is intensified by the Satanology in our Confessions. The realistic demonology of our Confessions is linked with the teaching concerning the two kingdoms[17] and is extremely important in seeing the work of the church according to the Confessions and the apparent lack of "social concern." The devil's reign in Lutheran theology is not some vague demonic "unauthentic existence," a sort of theology of failure or discontinuity in a Tillichian sense, but a non-mythical, real kingdom governed in direct enmity against God. The reign of Christ in turn is not a sort of beachhead for ultimately conquering the world (note how chiliasm is rejected in AC XVII, 5) by reforming it or changing it. It is rather a fellowship with Christ the Lord (SC II, 4), a spiritual kingdom of righteousness in the heart and the gift of the Spirit (Ap. VII, 13, 18; XXVII, 27). The two kingdoms are not static, but in constant opposition with no neutral ground between them. All men are by nature slaves of the devil and his prisoners (Ap. II, 47) and can be brought into Christ's kingdom only by a gracious act of the Spirit (SC II, 4; LC II, 27). Thus, the church's work is not to "reform" the devil's kingdom which is the fallen world, but to call men out of darkness. And Christ will destroy that kingdom at His coming.

---

17 Schlink, p. 194.

The intensity of the conflict between the two kingdoms is portrayed in most graphic detail by our Confessions. The devil is God's enemy on earth (AC XX, 25). He badgers the church from all sides and tears us from faith, hope and love, inspires false security in our hearts and draws us into unbelief and abominable sins. We spend our lives striving against his darts (LC III, 104). It is always against the church that he lies and fumes day and night. And we must count on this. "For where God's Word is preached, accepted and believed, and bears fruit, there the blessed holy cross will not be far away" (LC III, 65). The devil's whole purpose is to take from us what we have received from God (LC III, 80). He not only obstructs and overthrows spiritual order, but also "prevents and hinders the establishment of any kind of government or honorable and peaceful relations on earth." This means that the devil reigns on earth. Luther blames everything on him: war, sedition, injustice, crop failure, even air pollution (*die Luft zu vergiften*). If it were in his power, and our prayers did not restrain him, we should not have a straw in the field, a penny in the house, or even our lives (LC III, 82; cf. Ap. IV, 47ff.). World history shows the power of the devil's rule. Blasphemy and wicked doctrines fill the world. Only the church which follows Christ, who is Lord and Victor, can win the victory over Satan. And she does so with the weapons of the Spirit which He has given her, with baptism (SC IV, 6; LC IV, 41, 83) and the Word (LC Preface 10; I, 100; FC, SD XI, 76).

Such a demonology will certainly support an eschatological viewpoint and recall the church constantly to her true ministry. But does such a theology, such preoccupation with salvation and victory over sin and Satan, such emphatic hope in the life to come imply an escape from this life, from love of life, appreciation for God's created world, and social concern? Our brief studies above concerning the emphasis in our Confessions upon the home, civil government, the Christian life, love and good works, and also the great appreciation for God's creation which we observe in Luther's catechisms would indicate that Lutheran theology is not escapist and unconcerned about the issues of life in this world. It is just that our theology is balanced and realistic. Lutheranism knows that the church on earth is a militant church, engaged in a dreadful and deadly battle. At the same time she believes and lives by the words of Jesus, "Be of good cheer; I have overcome the world" (John 16:33). And as she lives in a hostile world and awaits ultimate victory at the coming of her Lord she knows what are the weapons of her warfare: truth, the Gospel, faith, salvation, the Holy Spirit (Eph. 6:10; cf. 1 Pet. 5:6–11). All this is reflected in our Lutheran Confessions. And we as Lutherans today will do well to emulate this spirit of our great Confessions which are truly missionary affirmations also for our day.

Two questions remain to be answered, questions which must be broached in any contemporary study of the mission of the church in confessional Lutheran theology.

1. Do historic Lutheranism and our Lutheran Confessions support the sending of missionaries throughout the world? Put more strongly, is the sending of missionaries an imperative of the Lutheran understanding of the Gospel and the ministry of the church? In spite of the many failures of the Lutheran churches throughout the years to respond to the need and challenge of sending missionaries into foreign lands, Werner Elert and others have responded to our question with a resounding yes. The lack of specific directives in our Confessions for the sending of foreign missionaries is due not to any truncated doctrine of the Gospel or the mission of the church but to the situation in which our Confessions were written and to which they responded.[18] In this regard we must bear in mind that there was at the time of the Reformation no distinction between foreign and home missions. Whether the apostolic message sweeps through the ancient heathen world or the same message of the Reformation sweeps through its world, the same ministry and mission of the church is in operation. That the Reformation came for the most part to lands and people who were nominally Christian does not negate its missionary character. After all, freeing the Gospel from works is opening the door for all missions. And moving the church and its ministry away from being on one level with Caesar's realm is freeing it for mission in the true sense, not with the sword, but with the Word of the Holy Spirit. The passion for the Gospel is the passion for souls, and this is the essence of the spirit of mission. Therefore we have in our Lutheran Confessions with their burden for the teaching and proclamation of the Gospel the authentic Lutheran mission affirmations.

2. What implications do our findings concerning the ministry of the church in the Lutheran Confessions have for our relation to the ecumenical movement today? Our relations to the modern ecumenical movement, and specifically the World Council of Churches, must be determined by a

---

18 Elert, *The Structure of Lutheranism*, pp. 385–402. See also Paul Peters, "Luthers Weltweiter Missionssinn," *Lutherischer Rundblick*, XVII, pp. 3–4 (1969), pp. 162–175. Both Elert and Peters bring up numerous examples of mission work in the narrow sense which was carried out by the early Lutherans wherever they had opportunity. They both explain the lack of opportunity for foreign mission work in the case of most Lutherans, except in Lapland and Greenland and similar limited fields. Earlier efforts to bring the Gospel to the Arab world were abortive, but both contend rightly that the impetus and inherent dynamic for foreign mission work are basic to Lutheran theology. And the fervor to go to heathen lands was always explicitly present.

large number of concerns with which our Confessions deal and not by the Confessional position on the church's ministry alone. However, we can at least help to determine our stance toward this movement today by examining briefly the modern ecumenical attitude toward the mission of the church, specifically as seen in the "Report on Renewal in Mission," adopted by the WCC assembly in Uppsala in 1968.[19] An analysis of this Report, which is the result of years of study and preparation (since the WCC assembly in New Delhi) by theologians and member churches of the WCC, reveals that the WCC in its official statement has virtually missed and passed over the great evangelical themes and concerns which dominated the Reformation and our historic Lutheran Confessions. The Report has little in common with either the New Testament teaching on the church's mission or that of our Confessions. This severe judgment is not mine only but that of practically all those many evangelical Lutherans and Christian theologians who were present at the assembly and who struggled to understand and grapple critically with the contents of the Report and who publicly aired their views.[20] It is a well known fact that both Scandinavian and German substitute drafts, both of which were far more Biblical and evangelical than the Report, were submitted to the assembly. In one case a committee from the Norwegian Mission Society from the Church of Norway could not accept the Uppsala draft and considered it so poor and unbiblical that, if accepted by the assembly, it recommended that "the Church of Norway seek new instruments for its continued ecumenical engagements."[21] The changes between the draft and final Report were not very many or formative. Specifically and in the light of our present study from the Lutheran Confessions the following must be said by way of comment and criticism of the "Report on Renewal and Mission."

a. The Report scarcely touches the great soteriological and eschatological themes so fundamental to historic Christianity and to our Lutheran Confessions as they lay a background for the ministry of the church. One might perhaps respond that such criticism is picayunish and such themes

---

19 See *The Uppsala Report 1968: Message, Section Reports and Proceedings of the Assembly* (no place, no date), pp. 27–36.

20 See "Discussion of the Report on Renewal in Mission" in *The Uppsala Report 1968*, pp. 25–27, where the remarks of such Lutherans as Per Loenning and K. E. Skydsgaard are noted. More severe is the critique of Haakon Haus, Rektor of the Misjonsskolen in Stavanger, Norway in *Fornyelse i Misjonen.* See *Konsultasjonen "Misjonstenkningen Idag—og Imorgen,"* Stavanger, 1968, no. 17. Cf. *ibid.*, nos. 20, 22. Cf. also "Uppsala 1968" in *Christianity Today*, August 16, 1968, pp. 1067–71; also June 21, 1968, pp. 937–8.

21 *Konsultasjonen*, no. 20, p. 7.

are taken for granted in the Report. One very favorable commentator says just this and then strangely commends the document for presenting a structure that is "classical and comprehensive."[22] But can the very content of the Gospel, the great themes of salvation, reconciliation, justification, the work of Christ, to say nothing of the eschatological themes of Christ's return, judgment, resurrection and eternal life—can the content of the Gospel be ignored when Christians band together to speak of the mission of the church? The urgency for proclaiming the Gospel is simply not apparent in the Uppsala Report. And this is inexcusable.[23]

b. The Report makes the goal of the church's mission not reconciliation with God, not conversion in the New Testament sense, but a vague humanization, "the new humanity." This serious fault has been criticized more than any other by Lutheran and evangelical theologians.[24] Not a

---

22 Harold Ditmanson, "Doors Opened to a World: a North American Reaction to Uppsala," *Lutheran World*, XVI (1969), pp. 159ff.

23 Cf. the explicit and warm statement of the Alternative Draft from Scandinavia (*Konsultasjonen*, 22, pp. 5–6): "We pray that as Christian churches committed to God's mission, we may have the vivifying vision of that unsurpassed gift from God: the sacrifice of His Christ to save the world from all its horrors and all its sinful corruption. In the apostolic proclamation this rings through the world for generations: Christ died for our sins, in accordance with the Scriptures, he was buried, he was raised to life on the third day in accordance with the Scriptures, and he appeared to his disciples and apostles and was present with them and is present with us always to the end of the world. As ministers of reconciliation we have to be restored to our high calling by a new grasp of that basic truth that God in Christ has reconciled the world unto himself. When anyone is united to Christ, the new creation is here, the old has gone, and the new has already begun. From first to last this has been the work of God, and he has enlisted us in this service entrusting us with the message of reconciliation. We come therefore as Christ's ambassadors, sharing in God's work, participating in His mission." Other modern mission affirmations are equally explicit concerning the content of the Gospel. Cf. the *Wheaton Declaration*, Subscribed by the Delegates to The Congress on the Church's Worldwide Mission, April 9–16, 1966. Cf. also *The Frankfurt Declaration* in *Christianity Today*, June 19, 1970, pp. 844–846. Cf. also "One Race, One Gospel, One Task," Closing Statement of the World Congress on Evangelism (Minneapolis: World Wide Publications, 1967). All these statements are very explicit on what the Gospel is and on what the soteriological aim of the mission of the church is. In this respect our own Mission Affirmations are disappointing. They come far short of *The Frankfurt Declaration* in its explicit articulations of the Gospel in the language of Scripture. Obfuscation in this urgent matter, such as we observe especially in the Report of the Uppsala Assembly, is never a virtue in a theological declaration of this kind, but a great fault.

24 See *Konsultasjonen*, Summary of Critical Comments to Section II, "Renewal in Mission," no. 22, p. 4: "*Reconciliation* is primarily understood as man's reconciliation, not to God, but to his fellow-man. The horizontal dimension of the Christian life is emphasized at the cost of its vertical dimension. Humanization, not Christianization, it is stated, must be the chief concern of the missionary congregation today."

word about repentance, faith, salvation, rescue from sin and the wrath of God as the great object and goal of mission work. Rather the few vague allusions to this great soteriological burden of the New Testament are turned into a mere sort of *terminus a quo* for the church's mission in community (social action) toward the proximate goal of "justice, freedom and dignity as a part of the restoration of true manhood in Christ." These goals which are humanitarian and not specifically Christian become the means for humanization. Thus the mission of the church has been secularized. This fact is illustrated by a later statement in the Report which suggests revolution against injustice in the struggle "for a just society without which the new humanity cannot fully come."

c. The Report confuses or fuses the ministry of the church, the ministry of proclaiming the Gospel and administering the sacraments, with the service of Christians (*cultis legis*, good works). The Gospel in the narrow, proper sense cannot be confused with good works which are the fruit of the Gospel. Any such confusion results in a disastrous commingling of Law and Gospel and prevents the church from carrying out its mission.

d. The Report does not offer any Biblical basis for its conclusions regarding renewal in mission. One might respond that here, too, a Biblical basis is taken for granted. But this would beg the question. For the confu-

---

The goal of mission should be the new humanity in Christ, i.e. leading men and women for the sake of greater justice and freedom, etc. Humanization no doubt is a legitimate aim of the church's mission, but as an *aspect* of and a *result* of Christianization, i.e. the reconciliation of man to God through Christ and his church. Christianization (in the sense just indicated) is and must be the dominant purpose of mission, cf. 2 Cor. 5:20; 1 John 2:2, Rev. 1:5; 5:9; 7:13f" (O. G. Myklebust). One gets the impression that Myklebust for similar reasons might object to the strange and weak terminology used in Martin Kretzmann's article mentioned above, "What on Earth Does the Gospel Change?" Kretzmann's contention and refrain is that the Gospel changes "man's self-understanding." Like "humanization," "self-understanding" is a very vague notion which is secular in origin (Martin Heidegger) and ordinarily has no vertical dimension, to use Myklebust's jargon, no reference to God and His work of regeneration and quickening. One wishes that a more Christocentric and soteriological stress might have been made, although one does at times detect this as Kretzmann answers the question posed. Cf. the statement of P. Andrè Seumois, pp. 4–5: "Ne peut etre accepté tel qu'ici présenté. Le but de l'Eglise restela christianisation de l'humanité, non pas, directement du moins, son humanisation. L'Eglise cependant est appelée á un role indirect dans ce secteur séculier du progrés ou développement humain, ainsi qu'il est dit plus haut. Si l'on veut insister sur cet role, il faut alors parler de l'humanisme intégral qui comporte également et avat tout l'aspect du développement religieux et chrétien: le développement/spirituel, et c'est ici que s'insère le role de l'Eglise . . . Par ailleurs les chrétiens, en tant qu'appartenant á la société séculière, ont le devoir comme chrétiens, d'etre des ardents promoteurs du développement humain; mais le role de l'Eglise comme telle reste de caractére directement spirituel, si non on sécularise l'Eglise et la mission du Christ."

sion and gaps in this study concerning the basis, nature, and goal of the church's mission reveal the Report to be glaringly unbiblical.

What, then, can be our relation today, as Lutherans who have a Lutheran and Biblical doctrine of the church's ministry, to the ecumenical movement? To identify with a great movement which so tragically buries the Gospel and misses the crucial mission of the church would constitute a compromise and denial of our understanding of the Gospel and the work of Christ's church. This is a dogmatic and negative judgment, to be sure, and suggests that the WCC as viewed from its approach to the church's mission must he regarded as unevangelical and even heretical. It is my conviction that just such a judgment must be made against the WCC not merely by those of us who wish to remain loyal to the Lutheran doctrine of the Gospel but by all Christians who desire to keep and spread the Gospel. There is simply no future for a movement such as the present ecumenical movement, if the "Report on Renewal in Mission" is to be its banner and standard for action. We can and we should converse with those Christians and member churches who find themselves in this movement. Many of these Christians are deeply committed to the Gospel and evangelical in their approach to the ministry of the church. But to identify with the movement as such or make common cause with it by aligning ourselves with it, cooperating with it, supporting it, joining it, would constitute a denial of the Gospel.

The Influence of the Formula of Concord on the Later Lutheran Orthodoxy

"The Influence of the Formula of Concord on the Later Lutheran Orthodoxy" is historical in nature. It distinguishes those articles in the Formula that had a strong influence on later seventeenth-century Lutheran luminaries and those that did not. It first appeared in *Discord, Dialog and Concord: Studies in the Lutheran Reformation's Formula of Concord*, edited by Lewis Spitz and Wenzel Lohff, copyright © 1977 Fortress Press. Used by permission of Augsburg Fortress.

THE INFLUENCE OF THE FORMULA OF CONCORD on the Later Lutheran Orthodoxy is an interesting and instructive topic. The title might better be stated: The Influence of the Theology of the Formula of Concord on the Most Fruitful of the Following Generations of Orthodox Theologians. For then we could easily demonstrate the way in which Quenstedt and others of his era, often without any originality, followed at points Chemnitz or Chytraeus, or Selnecker in many of their theological discussions.[1] I believe the matter of the influence of the Formula of Concord and its theology on later Lutheran theologians of the seventeenth century will be convincingly settled to the reader's satisfaction by a simple sampling of how later seventeenth century orthodoxy was affected by the Formula of

---

1 One need only compare the Christology of John Andrew Quenstedt in his *Theologie Didactico-Polemica sive Systema Theologiae* with that of John Gerhard's *Loci Theologici* and particularly Martin Chemnitz's *De Duabus Naturis* to note an almost utter dependence upon not only the thought but even the terminology. In many cases Quenstedt simply quotes verbatim at great length without even mentioning the fact or giving references, a practice not uncommon in those days.

Concord and its authors. A massive assembling of evidence (or nonevidence) which very assuredly exists in abundance is hardly necessary. We can see where the later orthodox theologians follow Chemnitz, Selnecker, Chytraeus, and, to a lesser degree, the other authors of the Formula of Concord, again where they went back to the earlier confessions and more commonly to Luther and in some cases to Melanchthon, and then in some instances where they launched out on their own and showed almost no dependence upon the Formula of Concord or sometimes any of the confessions.[2]

In this essay I propose to comment on the subject of the relationship between the theology of the Formula of Concord and the later orthodox theology with, I trust, sufficient evidence, to show just how deeply the Formula of Concord itself affected the orthodox theologians of the following century. The conclusions drawn are significant if for no other reason because the seventeenth century theologians, with their giant tomes in dogmatical and exegetical theology, have exerted a strong influence on nineteenth and twentieth century theologians, who in turn have left their mark on the theology and on entire church bodies of our day.

---

2 Not only authors of the Formula of Concord such as Chytraeus and Selnecker wrote books on the confessions, but later orthodox Lutherans of all succeeding generations did the same. Most were written on the Augsburg Confession; but several were devoted to the theology of the Formula of Concord, most notable of which were Nikolaus Selnecker, *Erklärung etlicher streitiger Artikel aus der Concordienformel* (Leipzig, 1582); Leonard Hutter, *Concordia Concors, de Origine et Progressu Formulae Concordiae Ecclesiarum Confessionis Augustanae* (Wittenberg, 1614); and Sebastian Schmidt, *Articulorum Formulae Concordiae Repetitio* (Strasbourg, 1696). It is interesting that the seventeenth century dogmaticians in their dogmatical or exegetical works seldom cite the confessions; even less do nineteenth and twentieth century confessional Lutherans, e.g., Gisle Johnson, *Den Systematiske Teologi* (Oslo: Dybwad, 1897) and K. Krogh-Tonning, *Den Christelige Dogmatik* (Christiania: P. T. Mallings Boghandel, 1885) among the Norwegians; Friedrich A. Philippi, *Kirchliche Glaubenslehre* (Stuttgart: Samuel Gottlieb Liesching, 1854) among the Germans; and Francis Pieper, *Christian Dogmatics*, trans. Theodore Engelder, John T. Mueller, and Walter W. F. Albrecht (St. Louis: Concordia Publishing House, 1951–) and Adolph Hoenecke, *Evangelish-Lutherische Dogmatik* (Milwaukee: Northwestern Publishing House, 1909) among the American. Why? Perhaps it is because they were writing to some extent for non-Lutheran readers, but more likely because of their convictions, conscious or unconscious, that exegesis just does not require a confessional basis of any kind. This is not to say that later Lutherans were not guilty of dogmatic exegesis (see John Gerhard, *Annotationes Posthumae in Evangelium D. Matthaei* [Jena, 1663] and many of the shorter exegetical treatises of the day). Friedrich Balduin's *Commentarius in Omnes Epistolas Beati Apostoli Pauli* (Frankfurt on the Main, 1710) is a good example of the better quality of the dogmatic exegesis of that day. But all this does not mean that the "dogmatic exegesis of that day" (which I suppose is common also to our day) was based on the confessions *per se*. It was not.

STRONG INFLUENCE — ARTICLES I, II, AND III

In their discussions of original sin the theologians of the late sixteenth and seventeenth centuries follow very closely the treatment of the Formula of Concord which in turn defines original sin in terms identical with the Augsburg Confession. The same is true of their discussions of the freedom of the human will; and here, too, the Formula of Concord consciously follows Luther.

The Formula of Concord, in treating the doctrine of original sin, is combating two opposite errors: that of Flacius, which made sin the very substance of man and thus opened up a Pandora's box of misunderstandings and aberrations; and that of Viktor Strigel who was a synergist. I regard Article I of the Formula of Concord as a commentary on the history, not so much the text, of Genesis 3, with rather little regard to Romans 5 and other evidence for the fact of original sin. Thus, the article takes for granted an historical Fall (SD I, 6, 9, 11, 23, 27, 28; cf. SA III, II, 1; AC II, 1) whereby Adam, the progenitor of the entire human race, brought sin, guilt, and eternal punishment upon the entire human race. The definition of original sin as inherited, propagated sin (*Erbsünde*), which consists of a lack of fear and trust in God and of concupiscence, is simply taken from the Augsburg Confession. The polemic is almost exclusively against the Flacian error and its impossible consequences. The context of the entire discussion is a certain Pauline understanding of the image of God. Man in his state of integrity possessed this image which consisted in righteousness and knowledge of God. The loss of the image was not the loss of man's humanity, nature, or essence (Epit. I, 17ff.), much less a mere "external impediment" of some kind but a corruption of man's nature and a "complete deprivation or loss" of all his spiritual powers (Epit. I, 15).

This doctrine, with all its details, is completely taken over by the later Lutheran dogmaticians.[3] But a great mass of biblical evidence is assembled to press certain points, particularly that original sin is a total corruption, that it is propagated, and that it is an active and dynamic concupiscence. Quenstedt says that original sin encompasses and controls all our powers, our members, indeed, the total man. Like a garment original sin encircles and clings to us and hinders us in our course toward true piety. It produces its own germs or fruits. It is the "root," as Luther puts it in SA III, II, 1–2, of all vices and is the common source of all sin. And what is of paramount

---

3 See, for instance Abraham Calov, *Socinismus Profligatus, hoc est, Errorum Socinianorum Luculenta Confutatio* (Wittenberg, 1668), pp. 259ff., and John Andrew Quenstedt, *Theologia Didactico-Polemica sive Systema Theologiae* (Leipzig, 1702), part II, chap. II, sec. II (1:914–1076).

importance, original sin is an active following after hostile attitudes and wicked traits (*positio pravae concupiscentiae & successio contrarii habitus & vitiosae qualitatis*), and active rebellion, a desire for all that is base, a hatred of God.[4] This active nature of original sin, so commonly emphasized by the early reformers and the Formula of Concord, is stressed with the same vigor by the dogmaticians. Speaking of man's habitual inclination toward evil (Matt. 15:19; Mk. 7:21), Quenstedt remarks that even such initial and involuntary movements of our concupiscence are truly sin (Romans 7). And when Jesus says that evil thoughts proceed from the heart and Paul says we will what is evil, they are not speaking metonymically, but of an actual warring against the law of the mind, a sinful willing of evil even in the regenerated man (Rom. 7:13).[5]

The soteriological backdrop out of which Article I of the Formula of Concord is written is also shared by the later Lutherans, sometimes as they follow closely the Formula's discussions of the consequences of the Flacian error,[6] but also at times out of an evangelical concern of their own. Erik Adhelius[7] insists that the correct understanding of the human situation is so important because it alone shows a sinner his need for a savior. The fact to be stressed is that all sin (and this includes at the outset man's sinful condition) is against God's law and therefore against God. And man's tragic situation can only be remedied by Christ. Thus, original sin must be taught out of such a soteriological concern.[8] Only if a proper understanding of sin is preached in the church will a proper understanding of Christ

---

4 Quenstedt, *Theologia Didactio-Polemica*, sec. I, thesis 34 (1:918). Cf. Melanchthon's statement in his *Loci Communes* of 1521 in *Melanchthons Werke in Auswahl*, 2:1, ed. Hans Engelland (Gütersloh: C. Bertelsmann Verlag, 1952), p. 21: "Original sin is a sort of living power (*vivax quaedam energia*) in no way and at no time bringing forth any other fruit than vice. For when does the soul of man not burn with evil desires, desires in which the most base and offensive things are not checked? Avarice, ambition, hatred, jealousy, rivalry, the flame of lust, wrath; and who does not feel these things? Pride, scorn, Pharisaic big-headedness, contempt of God, distrust of God, blasphemy. . . ." Such language is typical of the Formula of Concord and the later Lutheran theologians.

5 Quenstedt, *Theologia Didactio-Polemica*, thesis 35 (1:119).

6 Ibid., sec. II, ques. 10 (1:1021). Cf. Martin Chemnitz, *Loci Theologici* (Frankfurt and Wittenberg, 1653), 1:244–45.

7 Erik Adhelius, *Disputationum Homologeticarum in Augustanam Confessionem prima— sexta* (Uppsala, 1653), p. 83: "*Sed nihilominus sincera hujus peccati agnitio valde necessaria nobis peccatoribus, ut eo avidius medicinam per Christum amplectamur. Necque enim potest intelligi magnitudo gratiae Christi, nisi morbis nostris cognitio. Tota hominis justitia mera est hypocrisis coram Deo, nisi agnoverimus cor naturaliter vacare amore, timore, fiducia Dei.*"

8 Ibid., pp. 92–95.

and his work result in the church, One repents of "propagated" sin and turns to Christ.[9]

Very little is made in the Formula of Concord about the imputation of Adam's sin or guilt to the entire human race, probably because the concern was primarily centered in the anthropological aspect of the doctrine, the nature of man's sin as propagated. The imputation of course is implied when the Formula describes original sin as involving guilt (*reatus, Schuld*) and brings God's wrath and damnation (SD I, 13–19; cf. AC II, 2). The dogmaticians are more explicit about the imputation of Adam's sin, or guilt, to all posterity. When Rom. 5:12ff says that all men sinned in Adam, it does not mean that all did precisely as Adam did, but that all "participated in his guilt," and thus in God's reckoning.[10] Because all participated in Adam's sin, the two notions, inherited sin and imputed guilt, go together.[11] The reason that this matter, barely touched upon by our confessions, was stressed by the later dogmaticians was due to the Socinian threat. Quenstedt devotes one entire question to the forensic imputation of Adam's sin and guilt to the entire human race, using almost exclusively Rom. 5:12–19 as his exegetical basis.[12] The exegetical works of the late orthodox Lutherans take up the matter in greater detail, again at least in part for polemical reasons, also against papists and Arminians.[13]

One would suppose that with such close dependence upon the theology of the Formula of Concord in its doctrine of original sin, the later Lutherans would also lean heavily upon the same source as they treat the subject of Article II of the Formula of Concord, that is, freedom of the will. This is true, particularly among the earlier post-Reformation theologians (e.g.,

---

9 Ibid., pp. 1, 4, 5.

10 Calov, *Socinismus Profligatus*, p. 243.

11 Ibid.

12 Quenstedt, *Theologia Didactico-Polemica*, sec. II, ques. 7 (1:993–98).

13 E.g., see Calov, *Biblia Novi Testamenti Illustrata* (Dresden and Leipzig, 1719), vol. I, book II, p. 99: "*Uti enim hic peccatores constituti sunt imputatione in obedientiae Adami, sic justi nos constitutimur imputatione vel justitiae Christi.*" Again Calov says, "*Quomodo autem poena esset in posteris peccati primi, nisi posteris primum illud peccatum imputaretur?*" Calov, in such typical statements, is polemicizing against Bellarmine, Becan, and other papists, but his soteriological concern is clearly apparent. Cf. also Balduin, *Commentarius*, p. 183, *passim*. Aegidius Hunnius, in his *Thesaurus Apostolicus Complectens Commentarios in omnes Novi Testamenti Epistolas* (Wittenberg, 1705), pp. 51–52 is more careful to relate the inherited nature of original sin with God's imputation of guilt. "*Non solum reatus alieni peccati imputatur posteris, sed ipsum quoque vitium in illos propagatur. . . .*" Also: "*Peccatum originis non definitur imputatione nuda lapsus alieni primorum parentum, sine vitio & corruptione propria; sicut Scholastici Theologi censuerunt: sed ea ratione & peccatum, & cum peccato mors in nos propagata scribitur, quatenus ipsi quoque peccavimus. Hoc palam affirmat Apostolus.*"

Leonard Hutter, John Gerhard) and all the Scandinavians (e.g., Jesper Brochmand, Kort Aslaksøn, and Olav Laurelius). Aslaksøn simply and unabashedly takes over the doctrine of the Formula of Concord,[14] as does Laurelius, although the latter subsumes the subject under the doctrine of original sin.[15] At times, however, later theologians tend to depart from the theology of the Formula of Concord on the matter of the freedom of the will. They accepted Luther's strong emphasis upon man's utter passivity in conversion and his "block," "stone," "log," "pillar of salt" imagery (SD II, 19, 20, 24), although God works in man as in a rational creature (SD II, 49, 50). But in the discussion of other subjects synergism definitely crops up. Hollaz,[16] for instance, poses the question why God does not grant all men saving faith, and finds the answer in the theory that all unregenerated men do not resist the work of the Holy Spirit with the same intensity.

Article III of the Formula of Concord is a masterful discussion on the nature of justification, just as Melanchthon's treatment of justification by faith in the Apology is one of the finest ever written on the subject. The two notable discussions complement each other and afford a total picture of the doctrine of justification. Earlier Lutheran orthodoxy, taking its cue from these two great sections of our Book of Concord, combine the work of Christ, his obedience of doing and suffering, his life and death (SD III, 15–16, 55–88), later called active and passive obedience, under one heading, namely justification (Chemnitz and Gerhard). This is in keeping with both the intent of Melanchthon and the Formula of Concord. For Melanchthon offers his most explicit treatment of the work of Christ in his discussions of justification. In a sense this procedure of Gerhard and Chemnitz retains justification as the center and chief theme (*praecipuus locus*) of Melanchthon in the Apology (IV, 2) and at the same time retains Luther's strong emphasis in the Smalcald Articles that "the first and chief article" of Christian doctrine is the article of Christ and his saving work. This procedure by the earlier dogmaticians retains the atoning work of Christ not simply as the basis of a sinner's justification, but also as an element and form of the very declaration of justification itself. Like the

---

14 Kort Aslaksøn, *De Libero Hominis Arbitrio* (Copenhagen, 1612), p. Blv.

15 Olav Laurelius, *Syntagma Theologicum* (Uppsala, 1641), pp. 149ff. Cf. also Abraham Calov, *Historica Syncretistica* (Wittenberg, 1682), p. 663.

16 David Hollaz, *Examen Theologicum Acromaticum* (Rostock and Leipzig, 1718), part III, sec. I, chap. I, quest. 9 (p. 602): "*Dist. inter resistentiam naturalem, & malitiosam. Illam Spiritus S. per gratiam praevenientem frangit & refrenat: ahec in aliis hominibus minor, in aliis maior & ferocior est, quae saepe impedit, quo minus vera fides in corde hominis irregeniri accendatur.*"

Formula of Concord and Luther and Melanchthon, the dogmaticians make much of the imputation of Christ's righteousness (his obedience) to the believer (Apol. IV, 305, 307; in fact, this is Melanchthon's definition of justification!).[17]

A statement by Balthasar Mentzer may serve to show the dependence of later Lutherans on the theology of the confessions and particularly the Formula of Concord as they work out their Christocentric doctrine of justification.

> The basis which merits our justification is Jesus Christ the God-man who in both of his natures is the one mediator and redeemer of the entire human race. Although he was Lord over the law for our sake he was made under the law to redeem those who were under the law, that we might receive the adoption of children (Gal. 4:4, 5). He not only observed the whole divine law, but fulfilled it completely and exactly (Matt. 5:17, 18). Thus he is called the end (*telos*) and the perfection of the law (Rom. 10:4). But he also sustained the punishment which we deserved by our sins, he suffered and died in our place, as the whole gospel history abundantly testifies. This entire obedience of his, both in what he did and what he suffered (which is commonly termed active and passive obedience) is called the righteousness of Christ, i.e., the righteousness which is revealed in the gospel, and the righteousness of faith, i.e., the righteousness which is apprehended by faith and counted for righteousness to us who believe.[18]

Lutheran orthodoxy almost slavishly, but albeit with great vigor and real warmth, adheres to the Reformation doctrine of justification, to its centrality in the theological enterprise, to the reality of the imputation of Christ's righteousness to the believer, to the *sola fide* and the *sola gratia*, to Luther's understanding of faith directed always toward Christ.[19] But exactly here at the point of justification *propter Christum* it takes much from the masterful treatment of the Formula of Concord.

---

17 Cf. SD III, 4, 9. Perhaps more than any of the other of the dogmaticians Gerhard emphasizes this fact in his lengthy discussion of the meritorious cause of our justification (*Loci Theologici*, 7:30–72) and again in his treatment of the nature of justification (*causa formalis justificationis*) as the nonimputation of our sin for Christ's sake and the gracious imputation of Christ's righteousness to us through faith (ibid., 257–315). This definition of the nature of justification is clearly taken from the Formula of Concord and Chemnitz, although, as shown above, it can be traced back to Luther and the earlier confessions.

18 Balthasar Mentzer, *Opera Latina* (Frankfurt, 1669), 1:60.

19 I believe I have clearly demonstrated this fact in my article "The Doctrine of Justification in the Theology of the Classical Lutheran Orthodoxy," in *The Springfielder* 29:1 (Spring 1965): 24–39.

NO APPRECIABLE INFLUENCE—ARTICLES IV–X

After Luther's emphases upon the necessity of good works in so many treatises and after Melanchthon's excellent discussion of the subject of "Love and the Keeping of the Law" in the Apology (IV, 122–400), by far the longest discussion in all the Lutheran confessions, one can only marvel that the theologians who wrote the Formula of Concord would be compelled to treat the matter again and marvel still more that Roman theology persistently misunderstood the Lutheran position, thus compelling the later Lutheran dogmaticians to address themselves to this issue at great length, not merely for the sake of the subject itself, but for the sake of clarifying their position. Because Majorism did not persist with its various subtleties long after the Formula of Concord, the subjects of good works, love, and the fruits of faith (of the Spirit) were handled by the later Lutherans primarily on the basis of Scripture and earlier Lutheran theologians. Jesper Brochmand wrote a commentary on the book of James simply to prove that the Lutherans took the theology of James and good works seriously.[20] A perusal of the great dogmatical works of the era, with their sections on the law, repentance, confession, good works, prayer, and the cross (sections not found in many modern dogmatics) should indicate the seriousness of Lutheran orthodoxy to maintain a proper emphasis upon the Christian life. But the theology of the Formula of Concord had little influence upon their work. Luther in his several discussions of the Ten Commandments did influence the later Lutheran orthodox theologians, and so did Melanchthon in his treatment of the subject in Apology IV.

Articles V and VI of the Formula of Concord, which belong together, had little influence upon later Lutheran orthodoxy, although the dogmaticians treated the subjects of the proper distinction between law and gospel and the Third Use of the law. Once again the immediate occasion for the articles was no longer an issue. The theologians of the seventeenth century simply went back to Luther, Melanchthon, and to the Bible itself as they addressed themselves to the issue of distinguishing the law from the gospel and the threefold function of the law. Hollaz,[21] for instance, never cites Luther or the confessions as he delineates the word of the law and the word of the gospel. Chemnitz first discusses the law at great length and

---

20 Jesper Rasmus Brochmand, *In Canonicam et Catholicam Jacobi Epistolam Commentarius* (Copenhagen, 1706).

21 Hollaz, *Examen*, part III, sec. II, chap. I, quest. 6–chap. II, quest. 10 (pp. 996–1039). Cf. also Gerhard's section on the subject (*Loci Theologici*, 6:132–42) which makes no use of the confessions and little of Luther. He cites a few Bible passages, and is not particularly heartwarming.

then the gospel under his section on justification, but does not treat the distinction *per se*.[22] He treats the threefold use of the law on only two pages of his immense *Loci Theologici*.[23] This is significant because Chemnitz is one of the authors of the Formula of Concord. Apparently the theologians after the Formula of Concord, indeed even its authors, did not think that the subject matter of Articles V and VI merited extended discussions in their theological works, perhaps because they believed the matter had been settled once and for all by the Formula itself.

Once again the later theologians simply pass over Articles VII and VIII of the Formula to Luther and the Scriptures in the case of the Lord's Supper, and to the Church Fathers and the Scriptures in the case of the Person of Christ. This was only natural. The Formula of Concord, while settling the two issues for Lutherans, simply did not do so in respect to the Lutheran and Reformed controversy. To us today the two articles in the Formula might appear quite thorough and conclusive, but they were hardly adequate to use as a basis to carry on the controversy with the Reformed who immediately attacked both articles on biblical and patristic grounds.[24] Searching the Scriptures and Luther's interpretation of them on the points of difference and a thorough study of the patristic doctrine of the Person of Christ was the only way the Lutherans, beginning with Chemnitz, could go.

A couple of observations might be made, however, before leaving these two articles. First, the intensity of the debate between the Lutherans and the Reformed in many cases tended to freeze further biblical research on the subject of the Lord's Supper to the point where little more than the doctrine of the real presence and what appeared immediately adjunct to it was ever discussed. This unbalanced treatment of the subject is already discernible in the Formula of Concord itself which limits its discussion to the doctrine of the real presence (which under the peculiar circumstances obtaining at the time was justified) except for a short discussion on worthy participation and the comfort offered in the Supper to poor and weak sinners who need God's grace and encouragement (SD VII, 68–71). The memorial aspect of the Supper is indeed mentioned by the later theolo-

---

22 Chemnitz, *Loci Theologici*, 2:202–15.

23 Ibid., 2:99–100. Cf. also Laurelius, *Systagma Theologicum*, who presents a rather edifying discourse on the threefold use of the law.

24 It is not necessary and would be fruitless to trace all the Reformed and Lutheran polemics which followed the signing of the Formula of Concord. Rudolph Hospinian's *Concordia Discors* (Zurich, 1611) was only the beginning of the vast discussion that ensued, centering on the articles of the Sacrament of the Altar and the Person of Christ and never settled anything.

gians. And the emphasis upon the "whole action" (words of institution, distribution, and consumption) found in the Formula itself is marked. But the soteriological purpose of the sacrament (SD VII, 62, 68–71) does not receive the emphasis in the later theologians that one would wish for, except often in a rather perfunctory manner.[25] And the relationship between the real presence and the blessing it brings (as expressed in the *huper humon* of 1 Cor. 11:24) is scarcely mentioned. This is not the case with the earlier Lutherans.

Johann Brenz closely relates the real presence of Christ's body and blood in the sacrament with the blessings which Christ has secured for us by his body and blood. I would like to quote some of his presentation to illustrate its uniqueness when compared with that of the later theologians.[26] He asks,

> What has Christ therefore bequeathed to us here? That which he had as his very own and his most precious possession, namely his own body and his own blood. Do not think that this is just an ordinary bequest! He could not have left his church anything greater or more beneficial. For in his body and blood which he expended to God the Father to pay for our sins he has bequeathed to us the remission of sins. And what greater, more marvelous thing can happen to us than that? Where there is remission of sins, we have also a gracious God, righteousness, life, eternal salvation. What then can harm us? Poverty, shame, sickness, death, hell? But where there is no remission of sins, nothing does any good, not wealth nor power nor health nor anything else which this world esteems admires. Wherefore, since Christ in his testament has left to the church his body and blood, and thereby also the remission of sins which was procured through the sacrifice of his body and blood, we must see that he has left it the highest, finest, most useful and by far the most necessary things for our salvation.

The theologians after the Formula seldom talked this way. To Brenz the presence of Christ's body and blood in the sacrament conveys to us what he accomplished for us by his body and blood. The sacrament is the way in which the objective work of Christ is made ours. Sacramentology is the arm or vehicle of Christology.

Brenz proceeds:

---

25 Hollaz, *Examen*, part III, sec. II, chap. V, quest. 22 (pp. 1137–39). Quenstedt is hardly better, *Theologia Didactico-Polemica*, part IV, chap. VI, sec. II, quest. 10 (2:1282–89).

26 Johann Brenz, *De Majestate Domini Nostri Jesu Christ ad Dextram Dei Patris et Vera Praesentia Corporis & Sanguinis ejus in Coena* (Frankfurt, 1562), pp. 177ff.

Now all these things are said that we might make use of this testament, just as we are wont to make use of mundane wills and testaments. For if a person has been made an heir in a testament of this world, but is prevented from receiving his bequest because of the injustice of coheirs or other parties he will straightway appeal to the terms of the testament, bring them to the fore, inspect and weigh them, throw them in the face of his adversaries, and consider all the objects according to these terms, in order that he might finally be permitted to receive his portion. Now we make use of the New Testament of Christ in much the same way. Remission of sins and an inheritance of eternal life have been promised for the sake of Christ our Lord. Now the terms of this testament were executed at the institution of the Lord's Supper. Satan, our adversary, tries to keep us from receiving this inheritance. He throws up at us the multitude and enormity of our sins. Our sins which are to be remitted by God are so great and so many, he says. Then he seeks to deny that we will inherit the kingdom of heaven. Oh, he concedes that God is forebearing and merciful, but only if we love him (as the law prescribes) and observe his commandments. But then he says, you have not loved God with your whole heart, you have not observed even the least of his commandments perfectly. Why should you expect or hope for eternal life. These are the fiery darts of the adversary. What can we do about it? We can produce the terms of our testament, we can partake of the Lord's Supper, and then we are made certain of our inheritance, of the remission of sins and of eternal life. Of course, we do not deny that our sins are great and many; on the contrary, we frankly confess them before God. Nor do we deny that we have never perfectly followed God's law. But we have the terms of the Lord's testament, we have the Lord's Supper. And since he has there committed unto us his body and blood, he has *eo ipso* bequeathed to us also the remission of sins and life eternal. What about this? Will Christ revoke the truth of his testament because our sins are many and great? Will he become a liar because I have been disobedient? Never! Heaven and earth will pass away, he says, but my Word will not pass away. Therefore let us see from the word "testament" what a broad application the Lord's Supper has. As Christ has called this Supper his testament, our great divines have called it, not inappropriately or without purpose, a viaticum. . . . What then is that viaticum through which we can extricate ourselves from destruction? We know of course that Christ is our *hilasmos*, that is, the price of our redemption. But because he has given himself to us to be eaten and drunk along with his body and blood in the Supper, we can correctly say that the Lord's Supper is the viaticum which pays our way on our pilgrimage and protects us from the attacks of thieves and the tyranny of Satan. You see, if Satan, in the hostel of poverty or of sicknesses or of death, exacts the claim he has over us because of our sins and threatens us with eternal destruction, then we have the Lord's Supper in which Christ's body and blood, the price of our redemption, are given us to feed upon with the bread and wine. . . . When we partake of the body and blood of Christ, who has conquered death and risen from the dead and enjoys eternal blessedness, then it can only follow that we too conquer death in him; and when death is defeated, we have reached eternal happiness.

I have found nothing on the real presence and purpose of the Lord's Supper like this quotation from Brenz in those theologians who wrote after the Formula of Concord.

The post-Reformation Lutheran theologians almost totally bypass the Formula of Concord as they present their doctrine of Christology. This is to be expected. Chemnitz, himself one of the authors of the Formula of Concord, had written a great and definitive work on the subject of the two natures of Christ.[27] And Chemnitz supplied the "Catalog of Testimonies" which supported the Formula of Concord on this subject. The later theologians of the seventeenth century, notably Gerhard, Calov, and Quenstedt, follow the theology of Chemnitz who leaned heavily upon the early Church Fathers (especially John of Damascus), except that they reverse the second and third genus (classification) of the communication of attributes. Their theology is that of the Formula of Concord at every point, but it is to Chemnitz, the Church Fathers, and ultimately to the Scriptures that they repair as they work out their Christology.

The occasions for Article X of the Formula of Concord were long gone even at the time of its writing. For this reason little attention is given this article by later Lutheran orthodoxy, except that their doctrine of church fellowship (*concordia*) is based upon agreement in the gospel and all its articles (SD X, 31), like the Formula itself. In the seventeenth century, controversies, not unlike those that followed Luther's death, arose, and the same *modus operandi* was employed by Lutherans to overcome them and reach unanimity. That such efforts failed, even among Lutherans as in the case of Calov's *Consensus Repetitus*,[28] indicates not a departure from the

---

27 Martin Chemnitz, *De Duabus Naturis in Christo* (Frankfurt and Wittenberg, 1653). English translation by J. A. O. Preus, *Martin Chemnitz on the Two Natures of Christ* (St. Louis: Concordia Publishing House, 1971).

28 Abraham Calov, *Consensus Repetitus Fide vere Lutheranae* (Wittenberg, 1666). Calov, Dannhauer, and other theologians of the day wrote dozens of books and pamphlets on the subject of syncretism, in every case following the principles of the Formula of Concord on what constituted adiaphora and what was necessary for harmony and fellowship in the church. Calov himself wrote some twenty books. But the Roman menace and the Augsburg and Leipzig Interims were in no sense the context of their discussions. Rather, it was the negotiations with more liberal

position of the confessions concerning adiaphora, but an adherence to a position which demanded only agreement in the doctrine of the gospel for unity and concord in the church.

DEPARTURE FROM THE FORMULA OF CONCORD— ARTICLE XI

In only one article is there clearly a departure from the theology of the Formula of Concord on the part of seventeenth century Lutheranism: the doctrine of predestination and election. The Formula of Concord presents the doctrine of the election of grace as a great mystery. God in his grace has elected a certain number to faith and eternal life (SD XI, 24, 45, 82). This choosing must not be viewed *nude* to search out God's hidden will apart from God's giving Christ to be the savior of all men. And it must be distinguished from God's foreknowledge in the ecclesiastical sense of knowing all things in advance of their occurrence. But this choosing is a decree (SD XI, 5), which pertains to all who believe in Christ; it offers gospel comfort (SD XI, 26); it particularizes the universal grace of God, just as absolution particularizes the universal grace of God (SD XI, 27–28, 33). Especially is it to be taught and urged to support and affirm the *sola gratia* (SD XI, 43, 44). It is *propter Christum*. And with such an evangelical treatment our confessions stop: there can be no probing of the secret will of God, no asking why he does not convert all. Such questions must remain a mystery (SD XI, 53–59). With perfect justice God could damn all men (SD XI, 60).

I think the dogmaticians honestly try to follow the Formula of Concord as they develop a new approach and doctrine. In their discussions of election they cite the Formula more than in almost any other article they treat. But beginning with Aegidius Hunnius[29] the *intuitu Christi meriti fide apprehendendi* and the simple *intuitu fidei* formulae are brought into the picture; and in the end the election *eis uiothesian* (Eph. 1:5) is denied; speculation replaces simple biblical theology, and the purpose of the doctrine to comfort and lead one to the *sola gratia* is vitiated. We have already seen the synergistic error into which Hollaz fell as he sought to answer the question of why all are not chosen. Hunnius and his successors sincerely tried to combat with their formulae the supralapsarian or sublapsarian doctrines of

Lutherans, such as Georg Calixtus, and the Reformed that prompted their discussions. See Robert Preus, *The Theology of Post-Reformation Lutheranism* (St. Louis: Concordia Publishing House, 1970–72), 1:117–54.

29 Aegidius Hunnius, *Articulus de Providentia Dei et Aeterna Praedestinatione Filiorium Dei ad Salutem* (Frankfurt, 1596).

the Calvinists and the bizarre doctrine of Samuel Huber that all human beings were elect. But they succeeded only in muddying the waters. Hunnius's position is almost impossible to understand. Does he or does he not include the eight points in the Formula of Concord (SD XI, 15–22) as a part of election or as an evangelical context in which the doctrine must always be treated? Gerhard, the systematician, and his followers make the matter quite clear. The eight points are a part of election itself; and thus in effect election becomes no more than God's decree (the dogmaticians do not hesitate to call election a decree, as did the Calvinists) to save those who he already knows will believe, a clear misunderstanding of Paul's use of *proorizo* and of the theology of the Formula on this point.[30] It is significant that Gerhard and those after him treated the decrees of election and reprobation as parallel, both contingent upon God's foreknowledge. Like Calvin, he treats the doctrine prior to the work of Christ or justification and in the context of divine providence, fate, and the cause of sin, thus depriving his treatment of the evangelical context he thought he was offering, and falling into a position radically different, but parallel to Calvinism. All the dogmaticians of the seventeenth century follow Gerhard's doctrine of election.

Striking Out on Their Own — Article XII

Article XII of the Formula of Concord is no doubt the least noticed and studied of all the articles offered there. This article touches topics not under debate among the Lutherans, and therefore one wonders whether it is needed at all. Ironically the only other article not debated by Lutherans at the time was Article XI, and at just this point alone the later dogmaticians departed from the theology of the Formula of Concord. Article XII deals with "Other Factions and Sects Which Never Embraced the Augsburg Confession." Looking back, one observes that it was most propitious that the three items discussed in this final article were included. For the theologies of the Anabaptists, the Schwenkfelder (*Schwärmer*), and the "new anti-Trinitarians" are very contemporary indeed, and it is well that Lutheranism spoke on these issues in the final pages of the Book of Concord.

The theology of later Lutheranism followed closely the polemics and the entire approach of Luther and the early reformers when they addressed themselves to the threats of the Anabaptists and *Schwärmer*, and thus they offered little new on the subjects of baptism and the means of grace. But in

---

30 Chemnitz, *Loci Theologici*, 3:145ff.

reference to the doctrine of the Trinity they did something which had never been done before. Never had the doctrine of the Trinity been given the amount of attention in terms of its biblical basis as during the time of the post-Reformation era.[31] The early Church Fathers and creeds articulated the doctrine and defended it against all kinds of heresies. But somehow they were hampered from presenting a total and convincing biblical and exegetical basis for the doctrine. Luther and the early reformers were apparently too busy with other concerns. They wrote commentaries on the creeds; they included mention of the Trinity in their confessions (AC I; Apol. I; SA I); and Luther's presentation in the catechisms of God as Triune as seen by his external works (*opera ad extra*) is an original and masterful exposition. But they never found time to expend the arduous exegetical labors necessary to nail down the biblical basis for the doctrine, as for instance Luther did in his presentations of justification, or the Lord's Supper. It remained for Lutheran orthodoxy to do this, and this stands as one of the great accomplishments of the age. Perhaps they could not add much to what our confessions and the Formula of Concord have stated on the other articles of faith. But here was an area where the confessions had merely assumed what had been taught so many years by the church catholic and had reiterated the theology of the creeds and to some extent that of the medieval scholastic theologians (AC I). It remained for Lutheran orthodoxy to furnish the fullest exegetical basis for the doctrine yet provided. It was more the Socinian menace than the concern for catholicity or thoroughness that inspired such arduous labors. But the fact remains that John Gerhard, Abraham Calov, John Dorsch, John Quenstedt, Jacob Martini, Leonard Hutter, Martin Chemnitz, and a host of other Lutheran divines, including some exegetes, did a job that had never been achieved before. They followed faithfully the leads, the arguments, and the nomenclature of the great Church Fathers; but the biblical basis, especially for the deity and person of the Holy Spirit, they dug out of Scripture itself. If modern theology does not like their exegesis, contemporary theologians will need to do the job all over again; for no one has so thoroughly presented the doctrine of the Trinity from an exegetical basis since that time.

CONCLUSION

Our study has been brief and perhaps not apparently very productive. Possibly the reader has experienced something of the frustration of the writer

---

31 See Werner Elert, *The Structure of Lutheranism*, trans. Walter A. Hansen (St. Louis: Concordia Publishing House, 1962), pp. 219–20. Cf. also Preus, *The Theology of Post-Reformation Lutheranism*, 2:113–63.

as he pursued the subject. For we seem to have proved a negative thesis. The Formula of Concord as such did not exert a formative influence upon the theological works of classical Lutheran orthodoxy which immediately followed. The rest of the Book of Concord exerted more influence.

But we have not emerged from the study empty-handed. The *theology* of the Formula of Concord clearly corresponds to that of later orthodoxy on every point of doctrine except the doctrine of election. Perhaps we might have expected this agreement, for the Lutherans had the highest respect for their confessional heritage and their forebears.[32] But the facts assembled are, I believe, still significant evidence for the close continuity and agreement in doctrine which prevailed among Lutherans from 1577 until almost the turn of the eighteenth century. And this is a remarkable fact indeed.

---

32 The allegation of Edmund Schlink, *Theology of the Lutheran Confessions*, trans. Paul F. Koehneke and Herbert J. A. Bouman (Philadelphia: Fortress Press, 1961), pp. xxi–xxii, is utterly without foundation. Perhaps Schlink follows Friedrich A. Nitzch, *Lehrbuch der evangelischen Dogmatik*, 3d ed. (Tübingen: J. C. B. Mohr, 1912), p. 26 or Ernst Ludwig Th. Henke, *Georg Calixtus und eine Zeit* (Halle: Buchhandlung des Waisenhauses, 1853), vol. II, part 2, p. 182, or some other secondary sources. Modern historians such as Jörg Baur in *Die Vernunft zwischen Ontologie und Evangelium* (Gütersloh: Gerd Mohn, 1962) and Johannes Wallmann in *Der Theologiebegriff bis Johann Gerhard und Georg Calixt* (Tübingen: J. C. B. Mohr [Paul Siebeck], 1961) have come to the exact opposite conclusions.

Can the Lutheran Confessions Have Any Meaning 450 Years Later?

"Can the Lutheran Confessions Have Any Meaning 450 Years Later?" was published in observance of the 450th anniversary of the Augsburg Confession. It is a brief defense of the timeless nature of Christian confession and of the Lutheran Confessions in particular. It was published by *Concordia Theological Quarterly* in 1980. (Permission has been granted for reproduction in this collection.)

THIS IS A SIMPLE QUESTION, but momentous and inescapable for every Lutheran today. The answer to the question, directed as it is to the president of a Lutheran seminary, is supposed to be yes. And such an answer is surely expected at a congress which has not merely a scholarly and historical purpose, but a confessional one as well. The question and similar questions have, of course, been asked hundreds of times during the last four centuries. And the resounding answer, from the time of Leonhard Hutter's *Concordia Concors* to Hermann Sasse's *Here We Stand*, has seldom varied. Yes, yes, we wish to remain Lutherans, faithful to our confessional heritage, and we can. Yes, our confessions have meaning also today.

But if the question seems simple, the answer is not. A pietist, a Bultmannian, a synergist, a Barthian, a charismatic, a Marxist, a millennialist, a positivist may all claim to be Lutheran and faithful to the Book of Concord according to their understanding of it. And in some sense they will maintain that our confessions convey meaning also today. I suppose that few subjects are more controverted today among Lutherans than the nature of confessional subscription, the force of our symbols' biblical basis, the hermeneutics of the Lutheran Confessions and their validity, the nature of

Lutheranism, and even the truth and relevance and meaning of basic Lutheran doctrine.

Since I cannot in such a short time settle or even clarify any of these problems related to our basic question, may I simply answer our question once more with a resounding yes, and then list some reasons why, also in our secular day when religion and theology have lost their hold on millions who still may call themselves Christian and Lutheran, it is possible and right to affirm that the Lutheran Confessions have meaning today.

1. *The language of the Lutheran Confessions is cognitive and conveys meaning and knowledge about God, man, sin, grace, and salvation.* I make this assertion against all forms of neo-orthodoxy and so-called "biblical theology" which advance the theory that God reveals Himself and man experiences his presence and power through "acts" of history (G. Ernest Wright and Reginald Fuller) or "encounter" (Emil Brunner) and not at all through the Word of God (Scripture, preaching) and doctrine (teaching) as cognitive discourse. I also reject the claims of linguistic analysts and positivists that biblical language is not in any sense cognitive and bears no meaning, but is only emotive (Herman Randall, Jr.) or merely "metaphysical" (Carnap) or expresses merely man's thoughts about God—in other words anthropology (Bultmann *et al.*).[1] I cannot refute all these claims on biblical, empirical, or rational grounds here. But suffice it to say, I agree with Sidney Hook,[2] an atheist, that such theories concerning the nature of theological language in the Bible or in Christian confessions repudiates Christianity in the historic or confessional sense at its very root.

2. *The meaning of the Confessions has remained and will remain constantly the same.* I make this assertion against the curious option of Krister Stendahl and others[3] that the meaning of a given biblical pericope and thus also *a fortiori* of all theological language (e.g. in our creeds and confessions), changes through the years—has a history, as it were. The historian, or interpreter, thus must seek the "meaning then" and the "meaning now" of theological assertions, terms, and doctrine found in the Bible and other theological literature of the past. This bizarre, Prometheian attempt to be

---

1 John Herman Randall, *The Meaning of Religion for Men* (New York: Harper and Row, 1968). John Herman Randall, *The Role of Knowledge in Western Religion* (Boston: Starr King Press, 1958). See Morton White, ed., *The Age of Analysis* (New York: George Braziller, 1957), pp. 209ff. Rudolph Bultmann, *Theology of the New Testament*, tr. Kendrick Grobel (London: SCM Press, 1955), II, p. 239, *passim.*

2 "The Atheism of Paul Tillich," in *Religious Experience and Truth*, ed. Sidney Hook (Edinburgh: Oliver and Boyd, 1961), pp. 59–64.

3 Krister Stendahl, "Contemporary Biblical Theology," in *The Interpreter's Dictionary of the Bible*, ed. George Arthur Butterick *et al.* (New York: Abingdon Press, 1962), I, pp. 419ff.

true to the descriptive tasks of historical criticism and at the same time to apply the text today is based on the assumption that the text as it stands, its *sensus literalis* and *sensus unus*, is either untrue, inapplicable, or irrelevant today. I encountered a classical example of this method of approaching a text not long ago at a LCUSA meeting. A professor quoted I Corinthians 14:34; he granted that Paul's prohibition concerning women speaking in the church included in his day the forbidding of women to enter the office of the public ministry, but he maintained that today the text teaches and demands that women be ordained into the public ministry. Against such a sophistic hermeneutic our confessions speak of the "*unalterable* truth of the divine Word," "the pure, infallible, unalterable Word of God," and "the infallible truth of the divine Word" (*Introduction to the Book of Concord*).[4]

3. *The meaning of our Confessions as they draw their doctrine from Scripture's divine truth cannot be overthrown, falsified, or mitigated.* By this statement I wish to reject the Barthian presupposition concerning the finitude of language in the sense that it cannot once and for all and infallibly speak the truth about God. And I wish to assert that human language can be and is used by the Holy Spirit in Scripture to express infallibly His will and mind to human beings. And I also wish to assert that our ecumenical creeds and Lutheran Symbols, as they articulate the articles of faith, adequately express the mind of God Himself, as He has, of course, only partially revealed it, in Scripture. *Theologia ectypos* in our Confessions and drawn from Scripture is identical, as far as it goes, with the *theologia archectypos* in God. By way of illustration, a confessional Lutheran who affirms that the Confessions have meaning today will side with the Jesuit John Courtney Murray who contends for the immutability of the Nicene dogma concerning the consubstantiality of the Son with the Father against Warren Quanbeck, a Lutheran who can only concede, "Our confession of the Nicene Creed is our recognition that given the fourth century situation we stand with Athanasius against Arius on Trinitarian and Christological issues."[5]

4. *After four hundred and fifty years the confessional Lutheran will affirm that the Confessions are today, as then, a correct exposition of Scripture.* The Confessions exhibit a representation of the heavenly doctrine, "the truth of God" (FC SD, Rule and Norm, 5). We deny exegetical relativism. We also deny that only with the advent of historical-criticism and other

---

4 Theodore G. Tappert, tr. and ed., *The Book of Concord: The Confessions of the Evangelical Lutheran Church* (Philadelphia: Fortress Press, 1958), pp. 5, 8, 12.

5 Warren A. Quanbeck, "Some Questions from Lutherans to Roman Catholics" in *The Status of the Nicene Creed as Dogma of the Church* (Washington: National Catholic Welfare Conference, 1965), p. 9; cf. *passim*.

methods of approaching Scripture and other ancient documents can we be certain of our historical and exegetical conclusions. I recall an incident years ago where I met for the first time the president of a very large non-denominational seminary. His first words in our mixed theological company were, "There is no passage in the Old or New Testament where modern, theological, and exegetical scholarship has not found deeper meaning than Luther could have found in his day." I replied by asking him to illustrate how this was true in the case of Romans 3:28. I do not recall that he had any answer. To me it is remarkable that the exegetical conclusions of Luther (e.g. concerning the church, justification, faith, grace, the Lord's Supper, baptism, etc.) are not only still tenable and cogent, but supported solidly by the most thorough studies of contemporary exegetes. All this is important when we consider that a Lutheran, although he may not accept every detail of exegesis in the Confessions, does subscribe to the exegetical conclusions (the doctrine) of the Confessions. Today, four hundred and fifty years later, the Lutheran can subscribe the Lutheran Confessions in reference to their cognitive content *because* they agree with Scripture.

5. *The Gospel center of all Christian theology according to the Lutheran Confessions is the article of Christ and His work, which we accept by faith* (LC II; Apol. IV, 2, German text, *passim*; SA II, II, 1). This is so today too as Christians preach, teach, and confess the faith and proclaim the Gospel.

In conclusion, it occurs to me that I may not have understood the intention of the question to which I was requested to address myself. Perhaps the question was not clear and not even meant to be. Are we merely asking whether the sixteenth century Confessions have a cognitive content today? Or are we concerned about the contemporaneity and relevance of the Lutheran Confessions after 450 years? Or is the issue of confessional authority and confessional subscription? If any or all of these concerns constitute the intention of the question, then I submit that all five points I have made are most germane and valid.

In Robert Nisbet's latest book, *Twilight of Authority*, the statement is made, "In most ages of history some one institution—kinship, religion, economy, state—is ascendant in human loyalties. Other institutions, without being necessarily obliterated, retreat to the background in terms of function and authority. History is, basically, the account of the succession of institutional authorities; or rather we should say succession and repetition, for if we look at any given area long enough over a period of time we cannot help but be struck by the fact of recurrence."[6] I think we must

---

6 Robert Nisbet, *The Twilight of Authority* (New York: Oxford University Press, 1975), p. 24.

concede that nowhere in western civilization today is religion, much less Lutheranism and Lutheran theology, ascendant in human loyalties, not even in any subculture! If such loyalty, or commitment, to Christ and the Gospel and the evangelical Lutheran confession is ever to recur and gain ascendancy, even in synods or congregations or individuals, the five points I have made will need, I believe, to obtain.

Confessional Lutheranism in Today's World

"Confessional Lutheranism in Today's World" applies the theology and practice of the Lutheran Confessions to issues confronting the church in the final decade of the twentieth century. Preus first bemoans the cleavage wrongly placed between doctrine and practice by some churchmen of his day. Then he applies confessional theology to questions of church fellowship, open Communion, "lay ministers," and women's ordination. This article was published in *Concordia Theological Quarterly* in 1990. (Permission has been granted for reproduction in this collection.)

THE SITUATION IN AMERICAN LUTHERANISM today, and to varying degrees within our synods, is not unlike the situation of the Lutheran Church at the time of the Leipzig Interim. We blatantly quarrel over ethical issues (not to be confused with the subject of "good works" or the meaning of the Ten Commandments), moral principles and their application, social ethics, church polity (i.e., politics), the vagaries and casuistries of pastoral practice—matters which most of us might not call doctrine *per se*, but which nevertheless affect Christian doctrine, impinge upon it, and in certain cases attack it. We need only consult journals and magazines like the provocative *Religion and Society Report*, formerly edited by Lutheran Richard Neuhaus, and note the scores of books written about the above topics to see how society has imposed an "interim," so to speak, upon our Lutheran Church today, as confusing and oppressive as the Romanist Interim after the death of Luther. And these issues which are debated in our church as much as in secular society are having as much impact upon our doctrine and church life as did the Leipzig Interim in the sixteenth century. Furthermore, the discussions of such issues are uncovering deep-seated doctrinal differences within and between church bodies, differences on the third use of the law, the relationship between law and gospel, creation and the orders of creation, hermeneutics, church and ministry, and many other points of doctrine.

Can we classify in some helpful way these issues—world hunger, ecology, Marxism and other economic theories, feminism, planned parenthood and abortion, gun control, discrimination, genetic engineering, church polity, and so on? If so, how? Can we classify these issues under the philosophical category of ethics—or in a kind of interimist way under the heading of adiaphoria? Can we classify them as aspects of Christian life, or "good works," or application of "the evangelical imperative"? Probably none of these attempts at classification will gain a great deal of acceptance among us. Our culture has caused chaos. It has influenced our doctrine as well as our church life and liturgy and practice, so that in all these areas we are at sea. On this point I suspect that there would be little debate among Lutherans today.

In the light of this situation I address myself to the question, "Can we remain confessional Lutherans in today's world?" Of course, the answer in principle is "Yes." One could give much sage advice on how to go about the present and continuing struggle by remaining faithful to the *sola scriptura*, the *sola fide*, and the *sola gratia*, fundamental principles we all know well, and end the discussion there. But one can deal, I think, with the question before us in a more helpful and relevant fashion by centering our attention briefly on a cluster of issues, spawned and cultivated in our culture, issues revolving around two closely related and hotly debated articles of faith, namely, church and ministry. The issues are (1) church (pulpit and altar) fellowship, (2) open communion, (3) the office of the ministry and "lay ministry," and (4) women pastors.

But first I feel compelled to address myself in a prefatory way to a very common, unclear, and bothersome theological distinction which has tended to obfuscate fruitful discussion on the aforementioned issues, the distinction between doctrine, or faith (*fides quae creditur*), and practice.[1]

---

1 The 1938 Sandusky Declaration speaks of the Scriptures being the source, rule, and norm for "faith and life." See *Documents of Lutheran Unity in America*, ed. by Richard C. Wolf (Philadelphia: Fortress Press, 1966), p. 395. The constitution of the ULC of 1918 has "faith and practice" (*ibid.*, p. 273). See also the Minneapolis Theses of 1925 (*ibid.*, p. 340). The Chicago Theses of 1925–1928 has "doctrine and faith." The United Testimony of Faith and Life (1952) speaks of "doctrine and life" (*ibid.*, p. 501). Obviously there is no uniform terminology in respect to this distinction. Pieper uses the term "Doctrine and Practice." See *Unsere Stellung in Lehre und Praxis* (St. Louis: Concordia Publishing House, 1896). Under practice Pieper mentions church discipline, church fellowship, stewardship within the church, lodgery, and the actual public preaching of the Gospel.

Where did the distinction originate? It is not found in the Lutheran Confessions and is only adumbrated in Luther's writings.[2] It originates in the seventeenth century when Lutherans debated Romanists and Reformed on the question whether theology was a theoretical discipline or a practical activity and aptitude (*habitus practicus*). The term "practice" in a different sense came into vogue at about the same time as programs and courses in universities were offered in pastoral theology, or pastoral practice, and books on the subject were written (Dannhauer).

Our confessions use the word "practice," or rather words which can be translated by "practice" (*üben, treiben, leben, tun*), not to distinguish something from doctrine, but in the generic sense in which the New Testament occasionally uses the terms *praxis* and *prasso*. The word "practice" is linked to doctrine, worship, the sacraments, prayer, good works, confession (SA II, II, 1; Tr. 27), the Ten Commandments (LC I, 319), and the Lord's day (by using God's word; LC I, 90). The Large Catechism (90) joins preaching and practice (*predigen* and *üben*) and teaching and life (*lehren* and *leben*; *doctrina* and *vita*), thus hinting at our modern distinction. Later on the Large Catechism (333) extols the Ten Commandments above all other commandments and works which we can teach and practice (*lehrt und treibt*; *docere consueverunt*). At times the term is used merely for a daily practice (*Übung*) or reading and practicing God's word (*zu lesen und zu üben*) (SD II, 16). Often what we would call practice today is called doctrine or considered a matter of doctrine in our confessions. For instance, the "doctrine [*Teil, doctrina*] of penance is taught and practiced [*gehandelt sie*]" by the Lutherans (AC XXV, 6). Now penance is obviously a practice, or activity, like baptism and the Lord's Supper, as well as doctrine. In fact, penance, like baptism and the Lord's Supper, does not exist *extra usum*.

The condemnations of our confessions indiscriminately reject false doctrine and false practice (AC VIII, 3; IX, 3), and at times the formulation "our churches teach" introduces matters of practice rather than doctrine

---

2 This seems to be the case. Note what Luther says in his Galatians commentary (*WA*, 40 II, p. 51): "For this reason, as I often advise, doctrine must be carefully distinguished from life. Doctrine is heaven; life is earth. In life there is sin, error, impurity, and misery—with vinegar, as men are wont to say. There love should close an eye, should tolerate, should be deceived, believe, hope, and bear everything; there the forgiveness of sins should mean most, if only sin and error are not defended. But in doctrine there is no error, and hence no need for any forgiveness of sins. Therefore there is no similarity at all between doctrine and life. One point of doctrine is worth more than heaven and earth. This is why we cannot bear to have it violated in the least." In this passage Luther by the term "life" does not mean practice as the term was later understood, but the Christian's life of love and good works. In antithesis to Luther's position is the modernistic aphorism of a few years ago, "Not creeds, but deeds."

(AC XXI, 1; XXV, 7; XXVII, 1; XXVIII, 34). The veneration of relics and invocation of saints are articles which conflict with the chief article of salvation (SA II, II, 22, 25), and in the case of the Anabaptists not only their doctrine is hereticized, but their refusal to serve their government and even appeal to the government for justice and help when they have been wronged by wicked people (SD XII, 9, 10). When the Formula of Concord condemns the Leipzig Interim in Article X, it condemns not merely the doctrine of the interim but also the application and false liturgical practices of the provisions of the interim, as well as submission to it by many Lutherans (Epit. X, 8–12).

Luther introduces his Large Catechism as a doctrinal summary of the entire Scripture and urges all Christians and pastors to exercise themselves daily (*sich wohl üben*) and always practice (*treiben*) the same. In the Augsburg Confession both articles of faith (I–XXI) and articles on abuses (XXIII–XXVIII) are called *praecipui articuli*. The list includes not only the doctrines of God, sin, and justification, but also indulgences, pilgrimages, abuses of excommunication, and the like, thus showing the inextricable connection between doctrine and what we call practice. They involve each other like two sides of a coin.

Another term used often in our confessions which bears on the idea of practice is "good order" or "ecclesiastical order" (*ordo, Kirchenregiment*). Clearly practice is a wider concept than church order. But church order is practiced and it bridges upon doctrine.[3] It is clear that in the Lutheran Confessions doctrine and practice according to our modern distinction are so intertwined and intermingled in their discussions as to be virtually indistinguishable.[4]

The same might be said for the relation between doctrine and worship (*cultus, Gottesdienst*) in the confessions. The two are linked in our confessions, but integrally so that they involve and entail each other (Tr. 44, 45, 72; SA II, IV, 9), so that they are neither separated from each other nor confused, but in a kind of Chalcedonian pattern joined inextricably together like the two natures in the personal union of Christ. By worship our confessions do not usually have in mind the ordinary church service with or without communion, but the continual service of God in prayer, confession of the gospel, formal worship, partaking of the sacrament, and the entire Christian life, all *practiced* in *faith* which receives the gospel and

---

3 AC XVI, 1: "Of ecclesiastical order they teach (*docent*)," just as they do concerning doctrine and the articles of faith.

4 In his pastoral epistle St. Paul at times includes both doctrine and practice as he uses the term *didaskalia* (Titus 2:1, 7, 10; 1 Timothy 1:10; 4:1, 6; 6:1).

the forgiveness of sins and is therefore the highest form of all worship (Ap. IV, 154, 228, 309).

In recent generations there has arisen a queer dichotomy and divorce, alien to the Lutheran Confessions, between doctrine on the one hand and practice and worship on the other. Since the Enlightenment worship and practice (life, experience, etc.) have been extolled at the expense of doctrine. Such a view obscures the marks of the church (AC VII) and the very gospel itself (Ap. IV). This indifference toward pure doctrine has been the course of classical liberalism, modernism, and at times even pietism. And, of course, neither practice nor worship is God-pleasing without the confession of pure doctrine. On the other hand, those who wish to be touted confessional Lutherans have mouthed the pure doctrine of the confessions, but sometimes abandoned or rejected a practice or worship which conforms with the pure Lutheran doctrine. Pastors, conferences, conventions, and even church bodies fall into this quasi-docetic self-delusion when they give lip-service to the creeds, *pro forma* subscription to the confessions, and reaffirmation of orthodox doctrinal statements, while their practice and worship lapse into Reformed or sectarian or generic forms, disconnected from their high doctrinal assertions. Formal confession (*Bekenntnis*) obtains, but confessing (*bekennen*) the faith wanes.

Years ago an old lady in northern Minnesota, who had little education and had probably never heard of the Book of Concord, said, *"Laere er liv."* Doctrine is life! The Danish hymnwriter, Thomas Kingo, writing during the age of orthodoxy, spoke in the same vein and put it this way:

> 'Tis all in vain that you profess
> The doctrines of the church, unless
> You live according to your creed,
> And show your faith by word and deed. . .

The lady was right and so was Kingo. Doctrine without life (i.e., practice and worship) is a theory, nothing more. Our confessions are as concerned for orthopraxis and pure worship as they are for pure doctrine. For the three are a trinity—doctrine, practice, and worship—which ought not be confused or divided. With this understanding we can now proceed to the four instances where bad and unsound practice today is threatening to undermine the pure doctrine and practice of confessional Lutheranism, also in the Lutheran Church—Missouri Synod.

I. Church Fellowship

In the Lutheran Confessions the term "fellowship" is used in a variety of ways. First and foremost, the church itself is called and is a fellowship.

When not employing the creedal *communio sanctorum*, or other descriptions, the confessions call the church itself a fellowship (*Gemeinschaft, societas*) of believers. According to the well-known passage in the Apology (VII, 5), the church is outwardly a fellowship (*Gesellschaft, societas*) of eternal signs, or marks of the church, the pure teaching of the gospel and the pure administration of the sacraments according to the gospel. In this outward fellowship hypocrites are mingled with the church, as well as evil pastors whose ministry of the means of grace is nevertheless efficacious. But, strictly speaking, the church is the spiritual fellowship (*Gemeinschaft, societas*) "of faith and of the Holy Spirit in the hearts." This is a definition of the church corresponding to others in the Lutheran Confessions (*communio sanctorum*: AC VII, 1; LC II, 49–52; SA III, XII, 2).

A second way in which the term "fellowship" is used in our confessions is for the divine service or Holy Communion. For instance, Luther (SA II, II, 9) speaks of fellowship (*communio, Gemeinschaft*) as the congregation's service of the Lord's Supper (LC V, 87). And elsewhere he speaks of such fellowship as identical with the divine service without the Lord's Supper.[5]

By far the most common usage of the term "fellowship" derives from the first two meanings. We refer to the outward fellowship which exists on the basis of a common agreement (*concordia, consensus*) in doctrine and practice and worship. I shall delineate the position of our confessions on this issue which arose out of controversy and was most pressing. Melanchthon (AC, Preface, 4) teaches that living in doctrinal concord and unity (*concordia, unitas*) involves fellowship. He warns (Tr. 41) that we must beware and not participate (Romans 16:17) with those who adhere to godless doctrine and not have fellowship (*Gemeinschaft, societas*) with them (Matthew 7:15; Galatians 1:8; Titus 1:10; 2 Corinthians 6:14). He is referring to the papacy and to the avoidance of such practices as the papistic practice of confession, masses, penance, indulgences, celibacy, and the invocation of the saints which obscure the glory of Christ and the gospel (Tr. 44ff.). He goes on to point out that the papacy will not allow religious matters (*Religionssachen*) to be judged in the proper way (*rite, ordentlicheweise*), thus frustrating attempts to arrive at God-pleasing consensus. For errors must be rejected and true doctrine embraced (Tr. 52) "for the glory of God and the salvation of souls." By "error" Melanchthon refers to "godless dogmas" and "godless services" (Tr. 51, 59); and those who agree with such false doctrine and worship pollute themselves, detract from the glory of God, and hinder the welfare of the church (Tr. 59).

---

5 The Formula of Concord (SD VII, 57) speaks of *Gemeinschaft* or *communicatio* with Christ through eating His body and drinking His blood, obviously in Holy Communion.

Luther in his confessional writings takes the same position as Melanchthon. Warning against the papacy, he says (SA II, IV, 9) that the church is best governed when all are "diligently joined in unity of doctrine, faith, sacraments, prayer, and works of love." Again, speaking of the papacy he says (LC I, 84) we must avoid (*meiden*) open sinners and testify openly against them and reprove them. He is more vociferous against Zwingli and the Sacramentarians (SD VII, 33): "I rate as one concoction, namely, as Sacramentarians and fanatics, which they also are, all who will not believe that the Lord's bread in the Supper is His true natural body, which the godless or Judas received with the mouth, as well as did St. Peter and all saints; he who will not believe this should let me alone, and hope for no fellowship [*Gemeinschaft; amicitiam aut familiaritatem*] with me. This is final."

The writers of the Formula of Concord, struggling under the many controversies which ensued after Luther's death and were aggravated by the interim, spoke often about the subject of external church fellowship, the basis for it, and the importance of having no fellowship with papists, Calvinists, or other sectarians and errorists. The basis for fellowship is agreement (*consensus, concordia, Einigkeit*) in the doctrine and all its articles (SD X, 31). Without this unity fellowship is broken, idolatry is confirmed, and believers are grieved, offended, and weakened in their faith (SD X, 16). For the sake of the gospel and dear Christians, therefore, false doctrine, injurious to the faith, must be avoided with all diligence (SD IV, 39) for their very soul's welfare and salvation (SD X, 16). Furthermore, there can be no fellowship (*communio, Gemeinschaft*) with errorists or their followers since there is no way to come to agreement (*vergleichen, conciliari*) with them. Furthermore, Christians are "to reject and condemn" whatever is contrary to the true doctrine (SD XI, 93) and are to have neither part nor fellowship (*wider Teil noch Gemeinschaft*) with errorists and their errors, be they great or small, but to reject and condemn them one and all as against Scripture and the Augsburg Confession and ask godly Christians to "beware" (*hüten*) of them (SD XII, 8).

It is clear from the citations above that external church fellowship involves mutual consensus and confession of the doctrine and all its articles, agreement in practice, and full and uninhibited participation in all worship. It also involves the condemnation of error. Where these factors do not obtain, external fellowship is a capitulation and mockery which obscures the gospel and imperils faith. The refusal to enter into fellowship with false teachers and those who follow them springs from a concern for purity of doctrine and the glory of Christ and the eschatological concern for the salvation of souls.

It seems to me that the pressure of our pluralistic society, of contemporary doctrinal indifferentism, of the welter of religions in our country, and the confusion within American Lutheranism concerning the doctrine and practice of church fellowship make it very difficult for us who wish to remain confessional Lutherans today to retain our identity. In the LCMS the discussions concerning pulpit and altar fellowship, prayer fellowship, unionism, levels of fellowship (relationship), and interminable casuistic questions have now gone on *ad nauseam*, so that, wearied by all discussion of the issues, each does what is right in his own eyes, a fact which, if true, indicates the imminent breakdown of our confessional position on this point. This leads me to my second point, intimately related to the doctrine and practice of church fellowship.

II. Open Communion

Within the Lutheran Church in America there have been three positions taken by congregations, groups, and synods relative to open and closed communion. The first is that of the old General Synod, which recognized Christians in both Lutheran and Calvinistic and Reformed communions and offered the Sacrament of the Altar to those from both groups who desired it (open communion). The second was the position of other American synods in the nineteenth century, the General Council, and later those synods belonging to the American Lutheran Conference in our country. This position recognized that there are dear Christians in Reformed congregations but ordinarily refused them communion because they were identified with a different "religion," with a church body which had a different and false doctrinal position. Those who held this position also at times refused to give communion to those Christians who were members of congregations of the synods belonging to the General Council, and while recognizing, more or less, the so-called Galesburg Rule of 1875, eventually communed indiscriminately all who called themselves Lutherans. The third position was that of C. F. W. Walther and the Synodical Conference: communion was, like much of worship, a confessional act, and should not be offered to those, although sincere Christians, who belonged to Reformed and Roman Catholic communions or who belonged to Lutheran congregations holding membership in un-Lutheran and therefore heterodox church bodies. This position is set forth definitively by Walther in his 1870 essay to the Western District Convention entitled "Communion Fellowship with Those Who Believe Differently."[6]

---

6 Translation by Laurence L. White, 1980.

He bases his position on Scripture, the confessions, and citations from Luther and other post-Reformation theologians. It is obvious that he is setting forth a position which repristinates Reformation practice, but was not the practice of his day among Lutherans in his fatherland.

His starting point in defense of the correct Lutheran practice is specifically the doctrine of ecclesiology, namely, that there is a true visible church or fellowship which preaches, according to Augustana VII, the Word of God purely and administers the sacraments according to the gospel, and is thus distinguished by its marks. Those who will not identify with the true confessing church are, after due admonition, to be avoided,[7] and if they remain in a false "fellowship" are not be communed. Rather their errors are to be condemned. Walther then goes on to argue as follows: "The main purpose of the holy sacraments is to be a tool and means through which the promises of grace are offered, communicated, and appropriated, as a seal, guarantee, and pledge through which these promises are confirmed. However, within this major purpose, as a secondary goal, the sacrament is to be a distinguishing sign of confession and a bond of fellowship and worship. Therefore fellowship in the Lord's Supper is church fellowship."[8] Walther then asserts that the sacrament is a mark of pure confession. And if anyone comes to our altar, we must ask him, "Do you believe and confess what we

---

7 Walther cites Luther (*LW*, 38, p. 304): "Because so many of God's warnings and admonitions have simply had no effect upon them [the Sacramentarians, etc.]. . . therefore I must leave them to their devices and avoid them as *autokatakritoi* (self-condemned), Titus 3:11, who knowingly and intentionally want to be condemned. I must not have any kind of fellowship with them, neither by letters, writings, and words, nor in works, as the Lord commands in Matthew 18, whether he be called Stenkefeld, Zwingli, or whatever he is called. I regard them all as being cut from the same piece of cloth, as indeed they are. For they do not want to believe that the Lord's bread in the Supper is His true natural body which the godless person or Judas receives orally just as well as St. Peter and all the saints. Whoever does not want to believe that, let him not trouble me with letters, writings, or words and let him not expect to have fellowship with me. This is final." Compare the Preface to the Book of Concord, Tappert, p. 23.

8 Again Walther quotes Luther (*LW*, 41, p. 152): "Now we shall speak of the proper manner of communicating the people. . . .Here one should follow the same usage as with baptism, namely, that the bishop be informed of those who want to commune. They should request in person to receive the Lord's Supper so that he may be able to know both their names and their manner of life. And let him not admit the applicants unless they can give a reason for their faith, and can answer questions about what the Lord's Supper is, what its benefits are, and what they expect to derive from it. . . .Those, therefore, who are not able to answer in the manner described above should be excluded and banished from the communion of the Supper since they are without the wedding garment (Matthew 22:11–12). . . .For participation in the Supper is part of the confession by which they confess before God, angels, and men that they are Christians. Care must therefore be taken lest any as it were take the Supper on the sly and disappear in the crowd. . . ."

Lutherans believe and confess?"; and if he should answer equivocally, Walther concludes, "It should be known that he is either an unworthy hypocrite or an Epicurean skeptic. We for our part know that we Lutherans alone have the correctly administered communion."

Walther's position, as unpopular today as then, is certainly in accord with our confessional doctrine of fellowship, including Holy Communion, but also with the confessional position in regard to confessing the truth and condemning falsehood and with the concern for the salvation of souls. Never did Luther commune Zwinglians or Sacramentarians, but condemned them. The Formula of Concord concurs with Luther (SD VII, 29–31), quotes him, and with heart and mouth condemns and refuses fellowship to those Romanists, Calvinists, Zwinglians, and *Schwaermer* who do not teach the correct doctrine of the Lord's Supper *and the other articles of faith* (Ep. VII, 21–42; X, 8–12).

Historically the LCMS from its inception has held with the Confessions and Walther on the doctrine of church fellowship and on the issue of open communion. Our pastors and congregations have not communed members of Lutheran congregations belonging to heterodox synods, that is, synods not adhering faithfully to the Lutheran Confessions (e.g., the Anti-Missourian Brotherhood, the General Synod, the ULC, the Augustana Synod, the NLCA, et al.). This was the practice of pastors and congregations belonging to other synods of the Synodical Conference as well. In our circles the practice was adhered to until about World War II. The Galesburg Rule was more or less operative in those synods belonging to the Old American Lutheran Conference, but it was never acceptable to Missouri or the Synodical Conference, inasmuch as it allowed for indiscriminate communing of anyone who called himself a Lutheran.

Today a large number of pastors in the LCMS, ignoring Formula VII and X and Walther's admonitions, have gradually drifted from the position of our confessions to the middle ground of the American Lutheran Conference with its Galesburg Rule. This poses a very vexing problem for our synod, which is itself a fellowship, as congregations, pastors, and officials oppose those pastors who insist on observing confessional Lutheran practice and their God-given right as called pastors to admit or not communicants to the Lord's table. Meanwhile, the synods making up ELCA have officially shifted to the interimist ground and syncretism of the old General Synod, further confusing the fellowship issue among Lutherans.[9]

---

9 See *Lutheran Perspective*, September 8, 1986, p. 12. Also James E. Andrews and Joseph A. Burgess, eds., *An Invitation to the Lutheran-Reformed Dialogue, Series II, 1981–1983*. Because of this action of the ALC, now accepted by ELCA, Concordia Theological Seminary at two synodical conventions has tried to clarify the issue and

III. THE OFFICE OF THE MINISTRY
AND "LAY MINISTRY"

The article of the office of the ministry is considered by Melanchthon in Augustana V where he discusses the work of the Holy Spirit to engender faith through the means of grace. He discusses the call into the public ministry in Augustana XIV. He sets forth the doctrine of the office of minister in the Treatise. I shall describe briefly his discussion there.

A. The public office of the minister (*Predigtamt*) "proceeds from the general call of the apostles," not from any other source, not another apostle (Peter), certainly not the laity (Tr. 10, German text).

B. All ministers (*ministri*; only those who have the *Predigtamt* are called ministers in the confessions) are equal and the church is more than (*supra ministros, mehr sei denn*) the ministers (Tr. 11).

C. Thus, in the church no one rules; only the word rules and has authority (Tr. 11).

D. The keys belong (*pertineant*) to the church, not to some individuals (Matthew 18:18). They have been given and belong (*habet*) immediately (*ohne Mittel*) to the whole church, to all who desire and receive the promises of the gospel (Tr. 24).

E. Final jurisdiction (*Gericht*) is given the church (Matthew 18:17). The pastors "teach" and "rule" with the word (Tr. 30).

F. The office of the ministry (*minister, der Diener des Amts*) is restricted to the public "confession" (*Bekenntnis*; Tr. 25), namely, "teaching the gospel and administering the sacraments" (AC V, 1; Tr. 31), but also including excommunication and absolution. For all this there is a divine *mandatum* (Tr. 60).

G. Pastors, elders, and bishops are equated and hold the same office of minister (Tr. 61ff.).

H. The church as the authority (*jus, jure divino*, Tr. 65, 67) to call, elect, and ordain ministers (SA III, X, 3), since it alone has the "priesthood" (Tr. 69). No human power (*autoritas*) can snatch this authority from the church (SA III, X, 3). According to Ephesians 4:8 ministers are a gift from Christ to the church.

I. The "people" in the early church elected "pastors and bishops." Then a "bishop" confirmed such a call by the laying on of hands. Ordination is "nothing else than such a ratification" (Tr. 70).

---

our own synodical stance vis-a-vis ELCA and open communion, but to no avail. (See *Convention Workbook*, 1989, Memorials 3-33 and 3-50.)

J. The *public* preaching of the word and administration of the sacraments is carried out by the "ministers and pastors" (*pii pastores: Pfarrherren*). They also carry out public absolution and excommunication; but the latter only according to due process (*ordine judiciali*).

The data reviewed above merits some comment. It is clear that Melanchthon does not recognize the chasm between clergy (priests, bishops, pastors) and laity which obtained in the Roman Catholic Church. His use of the terms "priest" and "clergy" occurs almost always in the context of false Roman understandings—that priests should not be married, that priests alone should receive Christ's blood in the Lord's Supper, and the like; and Melanchthon believed there should be no difference between clergy and laity in such matters. Only once, according to my findings, does Melanchthon call Lutheran pastors "priests" (Ap. XXIV, 48). On the other hand, Melanchthon's writings and the other confessions hardly ever use the word "laity," except in the aforementioned polemical context. Rather he and Luther use the term "people" (*populus, vulgus, simplex, der Gemeine Mann, das Volk*). The concept of the "universal priesthood of all believers," emphasized in our day in contrast to the clergy, or pastors, is unknown in our confessions.[10]

One clear conclusion emerges from the confessional discussion of the pastoral office: it is a unique office, conferred upon some men by Christ. The term "minister" is applied only to pastors with a divine call (*Pfarrherr, Prediger*). According to the theology of our confessions, the idea of a "lay-minister" is an inconceivable oxymoron, like sheep being shepherds.

This pattern of church order, or practice, has been that of the LCMS until very recently. Just a couple of years ago the *Lutheran Annual* designated as ministers—"commissioned" ministers, whatever that means!—all kinds of people who are not ministers at all in either the biblical or confessional understanding, people such as schoolteachers, directors of Christian education, and those in other categories of full-time church work outside the holy ministry. Such a development is confusing, to say the least. At the Wichita Convention a more serious error compounded this confusion.[11] Laymen were permitted publicly and on a regular basis to preach the gospel and publicly to administer the Sacrament of the Altar, something never before condoned in the LCMS. This was to be done in emergency situations, it was said, a practice never approved or

---

10 The one exception may be Tractatus 69 cited above, but it cannot be a conclusive reference to the priesthood of all believers in any technical sense.

11 See Resolution 3-05B, *Convention Proceedings*, pp. 111ff.

even suggested in our confessions.[12] However, emergencies, in the nature of the case, cannot be regularized. Wichita also decided for the congregations of our synod that such a contradiction of Augustana XIV was justified because the lay preachers were to receive supervision. But there is nothing whatever in our confessions about supervision of this kind. If a layman of any age or background desires the office of minister, he should do what he has always done, study theology and then be rightly called. The Treatise and Augustana XIV make it abundantly clear that only ministers are to be called and ministers are always to be called.[13]

IV. WOMEN PASTORS

The question of women clergy was an unthinkable notion in the sixteenth century just as in the first century for St. Paul or our Lord. There are two reasons for this, the same reasons we bring against the calling and ordination of women into the pastoral ministry today. First, the very idea conflicts with God's order of creation, or the natural order. Luther (SA III, XI) bases his polemics opposing the anti-Christian prohibition of the marriage of priests (pastors) upon the divine ordination of the two sexes, male and female. He argues that such a prohibition is like making a man into a woman or a woman into a man. The same argument would hold, I think, against women ministers.

---

12 An emergency situation (*casus necessitatis*) is mentioned only once in our confessions as an example to justify the *necessary* right of the church to call pastors. Augustine is cited as narrating the story of two Christians in a ship, one of whom baptized the catechumen, who after baptism absolved the baptizer (Tr. 67). Notice that this casuistic example cited by Melanchthon speaks neither of the public preaching of the word or the public administration of the sacrament.

13 Much of the confusion on this issue springs from the crisis in the spring of 1974 when graduates and candidates approved by Christ Seminary Seminex were prevented from entering the LCMS ministry because they were not, according to the LCMS *Handbook*, qualified by one of the LCMS seminaries. Subsequently four district presidents, duly elected by their districts in convention, were deposed for allowing these candidates to be called and ordained contrary to the *Handbook* of the synod. Ironically Wichita Resolution 3-05B allows for district presidents again to send into the ministry men who are not approved by either of the two seminaries (against the synodical *Handbook*) but, more seriously, who have no call and are not ratified by ordination. The majority of delegates at Wichita seemed to think it proper that, if a leading theologian stated qualifiedly that a resolution allowing lay ministers was not *per se* false doctrine, the resolution could be adopted, even if it flew in the face of the doctrine, practice, and church order of the Lutheran Confessions. Thus, by one grand, highly-motivated step, the LCMS changed its practice and church order and became in this issue Methodist, although stubbornly resisting in principle such a practice for over a hundred and fifty years.

The second reason why the confessors did not even envisage women ministers was their doctrine of the ministry, which we have just outlined. The ministry is an office which derives from the call and mandate to the apostles and from Christ, who is not only true man, but true God, begotten of the Father. So, although the confessions do not speak explicitly against the false doctrine and practice of calling and ordaining female ministers—just as it does not condemn abortion and other contemporary social aberrations—their entire theology is a malediction against feminist theology and the modern feminist movement.

At this point I might mention that the notion of "equal rights" for women is not some new idea which was first propounded and observed in our enlightened age and country. I cite the words of Jacob Burckhardt,[14] written in 1860 concerning the most enlightened, and also pagan, country in Christian Europe before and at the time of the Reformation, namely, Italy: "To understand the higher forms of social intercourse at this period, we must keep before our minds the fact that women stood on a footing of perfect equality with men." Later he says, "There was no question of 'women's rights' or female emancipation, simply because the thing itself was a matter of course." And then Burckhardt supplies copious illustrations of women excelling in all the works and arts of men including not only literature and politics, but at times even warfare, using the eminent Vittoria Colonna as his prime example. But, though she was living in the most nepotistic of all ages and hers was a noble and influential family, neither she nor any other competent woman became a priest or pastor.

Feminism as we know it today did not exist in the open society of Renaissance Italy or in the more closed and primitive culture of northern Europe whence Lutheranism sprang. But today in our Western culture it represents the most powerful and baneful influence of modern society upon the Lutheran Church in America—and also our Missouri Synod. It is a result of pluralism and reflects an ideologically fractured society. This ideology as it enters the thinking and life of our church automatically threatens its confessional character. With its pressure to change the very text of Scripture and our liturgy so as to speak only in inclusive, "non-sexist" language, it attacks not only the *sola scriptura* principle, not only the confessional Lutheran understanding of the doctrine of the ministry and of ecclesiastical order, but also the very doctrine of God as articulated in the creeds.[15]

14 *The Civilization of the Renaissance in Italy*, trans. by S. G. C. Middlemore (London: Phaidon Press, 1950), p. 240.

15 For further discussion on this point and some of the others considered above, see the Opinion of the Faculty of Concordia Theological Seminary (February 11, 1987) rendered to questions from the Alexandria (Minnesota) Circuit Pastors' Con-

V. CONCLUSION

This then is my humble description and analysis of four controversial issues having to do with the doctrine of church and ministry, issues which immerge from practice and spill over into doctrine, issues which, if they are not faced boldly by those in the LCMS who wish to retain their confessional Lutheran identity, threaten to overwhelm us, like a great flood, and reduce confessional Lutheranism in our midst to a few little islands peeping out in a great ocean and at the same time reduce the LCMS, like ELCA, to a nondescript mainline church body.

How do we respond to this cultural interim of our day, this onslaught which has engulfed entire denominations? We must respond as our confessions responded to the Leipzig Interim, not by closing our eyes to facts, not by *pro forma* reaffirmations of old and neglected synodical resolutions which may or may not speak to the issues, but by confession and teaching the whole counsel of God and, like the confessors, bearing in mind always that the gospel and the salvation of souls are at stake. And we must respond, like our confessions, by rejecting error at every point, whether it be false practices of fellowship, open communion, lay ministry, or the ordination of women pastors. All this requires wisdom, courage, and much humility.

I shall conclude with a little story. When my wife and I were traveling in Scotland shortly after World War II, we found ourselves on a train bound for Edinburgh which took a wrong turn and we wound up stopping at a bombed-out bridge. There was only one way to get back on track: back up! Backing up involves admitting that we took a wrong turn in the first place. I pray that God in His infinite mercy may graciously give to us all the wisdom and courage and humility to back up, to return in repentance to the "old paths, where is the good way [the way of the Lutheran Confessions]; and walk therein, and find rest for our souls" (Jeremiah 16:16).

---

ference, which concludes on the subject of women ministers as follows: "At its last convention the LCMS once more reaffirmed 'its conviction that the Scriptures prohibit women from holding the pastoral office or carrying out the distinctive functions of this office (1 Corinthians 11:11; 1 Corinthians 14; 1 Timothy 2)' (1986 *Proceedings*, Resolution 3-10, p. 144). Since the attempt to place women into the public ministry of the Gospel and Sacraments is contrary to the express Word of God, all such attempts should be regarded as null and void, and of no effect. Such women are not pastors. Their public 'ministerial' acts are in fact the acts of private persons, although, of course, the means of grace are in and of themselves valid even when administered improperly."

To Join or Not to Join

(A Study of Some of the Issues Involved in the Question of Joining with the American Lutheran Church in Pulpit and Altar Fellowship)

The doctrine of the formal confessions of the church must be applied to concrete situations. Preus applied the necessity of doctrinal unity and purity to the pressing question of interchurch fellowship that arose in the Missouri Synod in the late 1960s when a formal declaration of fellowship with the American Lutheran Church was proposed and then effected. The same principles also can be applied to the Church Growth Movement.

"To Join or Not to Join" is a study of some of the issues in the question of joining with the American Lutheran Church in pulpit and altar fellowship. It was presented to the 1968 convention of the North Dakota District of the LCMS, about eighteen months before the Missouri Synod declared fellowship with the American Lutheran Church. In this essay, Preus presents the case that fellowship between church bodies must be based upon agreement in all the articles of evangelical doctrine. As he applies these principles to the pending fellowship, Preus strongly cautions against such fellowship. (Permission has been granted for reproduction in this collection.)

One of the most crucial resolutions placed before the Missouri Synod at its forty-seventh regular convention in New York last summer was brought to the floor by Committee 3 on Church Relations. It was numbered Resolution 3-22 and it urged an immediate decision to instruct President Harms in consultation with the Council of Presidents and preferably also with the president of the American Lutheran Church, after the ALC has taken favorable action on the "Joint Statement and Declaration", officially to declare pulpit and altar fellowship between the Missouri Synod and the ALC, and this prior to our Denver convention in 1969. The Convention was not prepared for such a premature and unexpected decision, and so it determined in a subsequent resolution (No. 3-23) to take certain definite steps toward declaration of Altar and Pulpit fellowship with the American Lutheran Church (See 1967 Convention Proceedings, p. 102). The main point of the resolution was quite clear. The entire matter is to be studied throughout our Synod and the President of the Synod in conjunction with the Council of Presidents will make the appropriate recommendations to the 1969 convention in Denver. In Denver our Synod could then possibly vote to decide whether to join the American Lutheran Church in pulpit and altar fellowship.

There was, however, something in the resolution passed which was not quite clear. The resolution several times spoke of a consensus between the two bodies, a consensus revealed by three "essays adopted by the Commissioners of the American Lutheran Church and the Lutheran Church—Missouri Synod" (See 1967 Convention Workbook, pp. 405–419). According to a "Joint Statement and Declaration" of representatives of the Missouri Synod and the American Lutheran Church and the Synod of Evangelical Lutheran Churches to their respective bodies this was a consensus on the following: "What commitment to the 'Sola Gratia' of the Lutheran Confession involves; the Lutheran Confessions and 'Sola Scriptura'; on the doctrine of the church in the Lutheran Confessions." Now just how is this word "consensus" to be understood? Is it merely an agreement between the representatives of the church bodies concerning the theology of our Confessions on three important issues? Is it to be understood as a consensus of both the Missouri Synod and the American Lutheran Church as a whole on these three issues? Is it supposed to mean complete doctrinal agreement between the two churches? Or does it mean something still different?

A similar ambiguity obtains in the case of the word "basis" which is used in the second resolve of Resolution 3-23. The resolve reads as follows: "*Resolved*, that the Synod recognize that the Scriptural and confessional basis for altar and pulpit fellowship between the Lutheran Church—Missouri Synod and the American Lutheran Church exists, that the Synod proceed to take the necessary steps toward full realization of altar and pulpit fellowship with the American Lutheran Church, and that the Synod invite the Synod of the Evangelical Lutheran Churches to join with us in the same." What does the term "basis" refer to in this resolve? Does it refer to an actual agreement which exists between the ALC and the Missouri Synod, agreement in the Gospel and the administration of the sacraments? Or does the term denote merely the Scriptures and the Lutheran Confessions themselves as the continuing existing basis for all pulpit and altar fellowship?

The brochure "Toward Fellowship" which recently was sent from the president's office to all the pastors of our Synod does not resolve this ambiguity in the resolution. In speaking of the second resolve of Resolution 3-23 the brochure states the following, and we quote in full:

> The second resolve declares that there exists the Scriptural and confessional basis for altar and pulpit fellowship between the participating church bodies. This is the basis described by Article VII of the Augsburg Confession as necessary for the unity of the church. Through the process of intensive study and discussion the joint commissioners recognized that this Scriptural and confessional basis exists in the participating churches. The Commission on Theology and Church Relations and the convention committee by their recommendations and the convention by its resolution affirmed this recognition. A fuller explanation of this basis follows in a subsequent presentation. Clarity is essential, however, on the task to which the Synod is committed by virtue of this resolution. The task is not to create or fashion a basis for unity. This Scriptural and confessional basis exists. From this basis the Synod now seeks to move forward with whatever steps are necessary for a full realization of altar and pulpit fellowship.

It would seem that when the brochure says that the "Scriptural and confessional basis [for church fellowship] exists *in* the participating churches," something more than simply the Scriptures and the Lutheran Confessions as the basis for all fellowship is implied. The brochure seems to say that a doctrinal unity, a unity in the Gospel and the administration of the sacraments, actually exists between the ALC and the Missouri Synod. But then when the brochure proceeds to cite the agreement of our Synod's Commission on Theology and Church Relations on this matter, one wonders. For when the Commission in its report to the Synod on relations with the ALC speaks of "doctrinal consensus" it is clearly not speaking of doctrinal agreement between the ALC and the Missouri Synod, but of a "unity" which was "manifested" *among the commissioners from both synods* on the teachings of our Lutheran Confessions "in the fundamental areas of grace, the Holy Scriptures, and the Church." (See 1967 *Convention Workbook*, p. 47.)

The ambiguity of both Resolution 3-23 and of the brochure "Toward Fellowship" is further aggravated by the fact that neither document specifically states that complete doctrinal unity actually exists between the ALC and the Missouri Synod.

Now how are we to react to all this? The assumption throughout the brochure is that doctrinal unity exists between the ALC and the Missouri Synod, although this is never expressly stated. The assumption throughout the brochure is that we should and will declare pulpit and altar fellowship with the ALC at our Denver Convention.

Does this mean that the declaration of fellowship in Denver is a foregone conclusion to which the convention in New York has committed us all? Does it mean that the question of fellowship with the ALC was really decided at New York? Does it mean that we cannot viably opt against fellowship at Denver? Does it mean that one who cautions against fellowship with the ALC at this time or urges our Synod to wait with the decision beyond Denver is somehow out of harmony with the decision of our Synod in New York? Does it mean that all the doctrinal discussion with the ALC prior to Denver is merely to increase understanding between the members of the Missouri Synod and the ALC and not to establish whether doctrinal unity really exists? Does it mean that we in the Missouri Synod have no choice but to take Resolution 3-23 of the New York Convention as "instruction" whereby "all members" of our Synod "proceed together toward the actualization of full altar and pulpit fellowship" with the ALC (*Lutheran Witness*, February 1968, p. 18)?

Surely no fair minded person would wish to answer affirmatively to any of the questions posed above. And so it devolves upon all of us in our Missouri Synod to study and learn before our next convention whether doctrinal unity really exists between the American Lutheran Church and our Synod. Surely we will want to do this before our next convention! Just as we all sincerely long for pulpit and altar fellowship with *all* Lutherans, we sincerely desire that such fellowship rest upon the proper basis, viz. agreement in the doctrine of the Gospel and the administration of the Sacraments, i.e. full agreement in Christian doctrine.

And so if there is to be any outward church fellowship which is pleasing to God, we of the Missouri Synod must know what the theology of the American Lutheran Church really is. We cannot afford simply to drift or be swept into fellowship without knowing what is actually believed and taught in the American Lutheran Church. We cannot act on the basis of wishful thinking, assuming what we would like to believe. And for such a momentous move which will affect some five million Lutherans we cannot be content to use as our only basis the three essays by representatives from both churches, essays which tell us nothing about the actual teaching in the American Lutheran Church but whose aim was simply to "explicate the content of the Lutheran Confessions." No, our concern for the truth and for the purity of the Gospel will compel us to approach this important issue seriously, determined to discover on the basis of facts, not wishful thinking or assurances, whether and how much doctrinal unity exists between our Synod and the American Lutheran Church.

If in our studies and in our meetings with representatives and members of the American Lutheran Church we discover a full doctrinal agreement between our Church and the ALC and if in our dealings with the members of the ALC we are able to achieve a "unified evangelical position and practice in areas of church life" (Resolution 3-23), then we can open our arms to the members of the ALC and enter with them into pulpit and altar fellowship with joy and thanksgiving.

But *if* we should find that the one God-pleasing basis for such fellowship does not exist, we must as honest Christians stand up and speak and vote against pulpit and altar fellowship with the American Lutheran Church. Such an action may be considered unpopular and narrow in our day of friendliness and cooperation across denominational lines. It may make us appear like obstructionists and separatists to those who do not understand our doctrinal commitment. But isn't it just this spirit of cooperation and friendliness and ecumenism so apparent today which should warn us not to be hurried into a relationship without first counting the cost, without first knowing all that is involved?

So let us try to acquaint ourselves with the ALC, first by studying briefly its origins and its past, and second by examining its doctrine and practice today.

A. The Background
of the American Lutheran Church

The present American Lutheran Church is made up of a number of former smaller synods of various national origins (German, Norwegian and Danish). With the one exception of the Lutheran Free Church all of these synods were similar to our own Missouri Synod in many respects. They began in our country with a strong missionary zeal, seeking to follow the German and Scandinavian immigrants wherever they settled; and often the pastors served the scattered Lutheran people at great personal sacrifice. The leadership of the synods was for the most part conservative theologically and confessionally. The pastors and teachers had reacted against the rationalism and liberalism of European theology; in many cases they were the products of evangelical awakenings which were occurring throughout the Lutheran countries of Europe.

The synods of German background which are now merged in the ALC date from the time of the beginnings of the Missouri Synod or before. The Buffalo Synod under the leadership of J. A. A. Grabau served immigrants scattered from New York to Milwaukee. Many of the leaders of this synod had fled the Prussian Union and were strongly confessional in their outlook. However, Grabau had a very high view of the ministry: he insisted that ordination existed by divine command, that the ministry gave validity to the sacraments, and only the minister could exercise the office of the keys. He took issue with the more democratic church polity of Walther and the Missouri Synod and described it as "anabaptistic, democratic stupidity." The differences between Buffalo and Missouri on this question gave rise to a violent controversy during which many pastors and congregations of the Buffalo Synod came over to the Missouri Synod.

The Iowa Synod which was located in Iowa and parts of surrounding states was to a large extent the product of the great German mission societies which contributed much also to the growth and prosperity of the Missouri Synod in its earlier years. The Iowa Synod too had a doctrine of the Church which seemed hierarchial to the Missourians; but it was primarily a somewhat lax confessional position which kept Iowa and Missouri apart in the nineteenth century. The Iowans believed that whatever was not taught in our confessions explicitly and introduced with a phrase like "We believe, teach and confess," could be considered an "open question" and not binding upon a Lutheran pastor. Such "open questions" were the doctrines of the church and ministry, the Antichrist, chiliasm and others. The Missouri Synod believed that nothing which was taught either in Scripture or in the Lutheran Confessions could be considered an open question by any Lutheran pastor. Many meetings were held between the Iowans and members of the Missouri Synod to settle these differences and a good deal of headway was made; but internal difficulties in the Iowa Synod and other problems cut short these negotiations before unanimity was achieved. Later members of the Iowa Synod accused our teachers of false doctrine when we taught that God has justified the whole world for the sake of the obedience and death and resurrection of Christ (objective justification).

The Ohio Synod was older than either the Buffalo or Iowa Synods, dating back to 1818. It began as a rather mild and unionistic synod. But in the 1840s a new conservative trend gradually set in until a minority of pastors who held more liberal views finally left the synod in 1854 and joined the old General Synod (now a part of the Lutheran Church in America).

After a number of internal controversies the Ohio Synod saw fit to join the Synodical Conference, and for several years complete unanimity of doctrine prevailed between the Ohio and Missouri Synods. But at the time of the predestination controversy in the 1880s a majority of the pastors and congregations in the Ohio Synod sided against Prof. Walther and the Missouri Synod; and so the Ohio Synod withdrew from the Conference (1881) and broke off fellowship with our Synod.

In 1930, after discussions and conferences dating back to 1883, the Buffalo, Iowa and Ohio Synods merged into the American Lutheran Church (not to be confused with the present American Lutheran Church). It appears that there was very close agreement between the three merging bodies. For some time there had been misgivings concerning the position of Iowa on the plenary inspiration and inerrancy of Scripture, but in the end that too was cleared up to everyone's satisfaction.

The same year, 1930, the American Lutheran Church joined the so-called American Lutheran Conference, a loosely-knit, co-operative fellowship consisting of the American Lutheran Church, the Norwegian Lutheran Church in America, the Lutheran Free Church (Norwegian), and Augustana Synod (Swedish), and United Evangelical Lutheran Church (Danish). All of these synods except the Augustana Synod are now in the present American Lutheran Church.

The synods which make up the majority of the present American Lutheran Church were of Norwegian origin. With the exception of the Lutheran Free Church they all merged in 1917 to form the Norwegian Lutheran Church in America (later the Evangelical Lutheran Church). Three synods, formerly divided by doctrine and practice, joined to form the Norwegian Lutheran Church in America.

The first Synod to join in forming the Norwegian Lutheran Church in America (ELC) was the Norwegian Synod. This body was organized in 1853. The clergy were a group of highly trained and dedicated young pastors who were the products of a spiritual and confessional awakening in Norway. The Norwegian Synod gravitated almost immediately toward the Missouri Synod in spite of the language barrier, and for twenty-five years educated its clergymen at our seminary in St. Louis. During the controversy over the doctrines of conversion and election in the 1880s the Norwegian Synod split and about one-third of the pastors and congregations left the Synod to form the Anti-Missourian Brotherhood. Four years prior to this split the Norwegian Synod had withdrawn from the Synodical Conference in order to settle, if possible, its own internal problems. The Norwegian Synod was in pulpit and altar fellowship with the Missouri Synod until 1917.

The second synod which joined to form the Norwegian Lutheran Church in America (ELC) in 1917 was the Hauge's Synod. This synod was established by pastors and laymen who were deeply influenced by the great lay awakening in Norway initiated by Hans Nielsen Hauge. Protesting against worldliness and deadness in the Church of Norway in the early nineteenth century, Hauge, a layman, gained a large following, in spite of persecution and great personal sacrifice. His followers in this country were pietists, preferring a simple Christianity, a simple worship, personal experience of God's grace and pious behavior. They criticized the Norwegian Synod with its clergy leadership and stressed lay leadership in the Church, also lay preaching. They were also known to criticize the strong confessionalism of the Norwegian Synod, although they were by no means doctrinally indifferent themselves.

The third synod which joined to form the Norwegian Lutheran Church in America (ELC) in 1917 was the United Norwegian Lutheran Church. This synod was a merger of three smaller Norwegian groups, the Norwegian Augustana Synod, the Norwegian-Danish Conference (which veered toward the Haugeaners and against the Synod) and the Anti-Missourian Brotherhood.

The Lutheran Free Church which also joined the present ALC in 1961 was an outgrowth of the Norwegian-Danish Conference. It was typified by its emphasis upon congregational autonomy, lay participation in the church, and an anti-dogmatic bias. The United Evangelical Lutheran Church which also joined the present ALC in 1961 consisted originally of a group of Danish pastors who left the Norwegian-Danish Conference for reasons of doctrine and practice.

And so the American Lutheran Church which came into being in 1961 is the result of several previous mergers of smaller synods with somewhat different backgrounds and theologies.

With some of the previous synods now making up the ALC the Missouri Synod had rather close contacts and associations, with others we had little or no contact at all. Together with representatives of the Buffalo, Iowa and Ohio Synods members of our Synod produced the "Inter-Synodical (Chicago) Theses" in 1925 which were to serve as a basis for church fellowship. However, the Missouri Synod under the leadership of Franz Pieper never accepted these theses as satisfactory. Rather the "Brief Statement" was accepted in 1932 as a statement of our doctrinal position and as basis for negotiating fellowship with other Lutheran bodies in this country. After the old American Lutheran Church came into being further efforts toward doctrinal unity and fellowship were attempted with that body. In 1941 our Synod instructed its Committee on Doctrinal Unity to produce one document for acceptance by both the Missouri and the former ALC as a basis for fellowship. This document was not to supersede the Brief Statement but to clarify and explain what might not have been clear there. The document called the "Doctrinal Affirmation" stuck rather close to the wording of the Brief Statement, but departed from it in a few crucial points. The document never accomplished its aim. Later in 1949 and 1953 another document prepared by commissioners of both church bodies was prepared. This statement called the "Common Confession" was in its Part I ultimately adopted by both synods, but because the old American Lutheran Church was already then deeply involved in union negotiations with the synods of the American Lutheran Conference this document too did not help to bring about the desired fellowship.

With the several Scandinavian Synods which merged into the American Lutheran Church in 1961 our Synod had no official dealings at all. The only negotiations toward fellowship, therefore, with the majority of the present ALC were initiated in 1964, just four years ago. And the first broad attempt to acquaint our entire church first hand with the entire present ALC was initiated by Resolution 3-23 of our New York Convention. So there may be differences in doctrine and practice between our Synod and the ALC, real roadblocks in the way of true pulpit and altar fellowship, which our representatives might not have caught in their discussions with official representatives of the ALC. Furthermore, by discussing only the teachings of our Lutheran Confessions on just three important articles of faith our representatives may have overlooked some actual affairs and developments in the ALC which indeed constitute a barrier to fellowship.

B. It is in the conviction that such real and serious roadblocks do in fact exist that the second and longer section of this essay is submitted. We shall attempt to investigate in some depth what is the actual practice and doctrine of the ALC on certain crucial issues. We have no desire and no intention of passing any overall judgment upon the ALC. It is our hope and our belief that there are thousands of pious and faithful pastors and Christians in that Church. We have often joyfully observed a deep evangelical concern, a deep piety and a deep interest in the purity of the Gospel in many members of that Church. We trust that it is not necessary to dwell on these things which are apparent and a source of joy to all of us. Our intention is rather in all charity and honesty to present facts, clear and open facts, which indicate that we of the Missouri Synod are not ready for fellowship with the American Lutheran Church. What are these problems which should be solved before fellowship is established with the American Lutheran Church?

1. The Problem of Lodge Practice

It is a well-known fact that our Synod has had a different practice dealing with lodge members from the American Lutheran Church which in the overwhelming majority of its congregations allows lodge members to be members in good standing in local congregations. Should we enter into fellowship without settling this fundamental difference in practice? Resolution 3-23 of the New York Convention urges representatives and officers of our Synod "to work earnestly and sincerely toward a unified evangelical position and practice" in this matter. That is all it says. But what does this mean? Is this "unified evangelical position and practice" to be achieved before or after Denver? What if the matter were not settled before Denver and we declared fellowship there with the American Lutheran Church and this would appear to be perfectly consistent with the import of Resolution 3-23. Would a pastor of our synod then be obligated to accept in transfer or at communion Masons and other lodge members from the American Lutheran Church? And if not, what becomes of altar fellowship? Surely we cannot enter into fellowship with the American Lutheran Church without first settling such a practical concern with its serious doctrinal implications; it would not be fair to the pastors and laymen of either church.

We should point out that the ALC has a very fine position on lodgery *in principle*. The constitution of the old American Lutheran Church of 1930 (Art. II, Sec. 4) said the following regarding secret societies which are un-Christian in nature:

> The synod is earnestly opposed to all organizations or societies, secret or open, which, without confessing faith in the Triune God and in Jesus Christ as the eternal Savior from sin, are avowedly religious or practise forms of religion, teaching salvation by works. It declares such organizations and societies to be anti-Christian, and rejects any fellowship with them. (Richard C. Wolf, *Documents of Lutheran Unity in America*. Philadelphia: Fortress Press, 1966. p. 336.)

The *Common Confession* (Part II, Art. IX) which the old American Lutheran Church accepted in 1954 makes much the same judgment. An even stronger statement is made in the Minneapolis Theses which were approved not only by the old American Lutheran Church but by all the member synods of the old American Lutheran Conference (including the Norwegian Lutheran Church in America) in 1926 and 1930. The statement reads:

> These synods agree that all such organizations or societies, secret or open, as are either avowedly religious or practice the forms of religion

without confessing as a matter of principle the Triune God or Jesus Christ as the Son of God, come into the flesh, and our Savior from sin, or teach, instead of the Gospel, salvation by human works or morality, are anti-Christian and destructive of the best interests of the Church and the individual soul, and that, therefore, the Church of Christ and its congregations can have no fellowship with them. (Gustav M. Bruce, ed. *The Union Documents of the Evangelical Lutheran Church*. Minneapolis: Augsburg Publishing House, 1948. p. 82.)[1]

These are all fine statements about the anti-Christian nature of lodgism. But what about the practice within the ALC? It is significant that none of the historical statements concerning lodgery say anything about dealing with and disciplining individual members who may be lodge members. In no statement are members of anti-Christian societies forbidden to belong to congregations. And what is of highest significance, there is, so far as anyone can determine, no noticeable effort within the ALC today to cope with the lodge problem. These fine old venerable statements of principle have simply not been put into practice. This fact presents a serious difficulty for those who would establish pulpit and altar fellowship with the American Lutheran Church and still carry on a responsible evangelical church practice.

It might be conjectured that the difference between the Missouri Synod and the American Lutheran Church in the matter of lodgery is a mere difference in method, and therefore not divisive. But this is a fallacious argument. The American Lutheran Church has *no* method in dealing with lodge members who are in her fellowship. Nothing perceptible is being done synodically about the problem. Would it not be the part of brotherly love for the American Lutheran Church before offering the hand of fellowship to our Synod to promise that she will try to cope with this difficult situation in her midst and then actually set about to deal with the lodge problem? We in turn should be willing to make every effort to improve our practice in this or in other matters if the ALC should find us to be lax or unevangelical.[2]

---

1 Although E. Clifford Nelson (*Op. cit.*, II, 322) says that the Minneapolis Theses are an unalterable part of the ALC constitution, there is no evidence in the constitution itself to indicate this.

2 We should add that it is a most questionable procedure to separate principle from practice (method), also in the matter of lodgery. A doctrinally based position or principle, if it is sincerely held, ought to be put into practice where possible. This seems to be the position of Resolution 3-23 when it says: "*Resolved*, That the Synod urge all its representatives and officials to work earnestly and sincerely toward a unified evangelical *position and practice* in areas of church life where disturbing diversities still exist, particularly in reference to unchristian and anti-Christian

2. THE ECUMENICAL MOVEMENT

The American Lutheran Church is deeply involved in the ecumenical movement, holding membership in the Lutheran World Federation and the World Council of Churches. At present the American Lutheran Church is not a member of the National Council of Churches, but the Church Council of the American Lutheran Church is recommending membership in 1970. Thus far we have disapproved of membership in these organizations. If we should join in fellowship with the American Lutheran Church, would her involvement in these organizations be a matter of indifference to us? The World Council of Churches is dominated in many of its commissions by theological liberals and political radicals (e.g. the 1966 Conference on Church and Society held by the World Council of

---

societies. . ." In this connection a very perceptive letter was written to the *Lutheran Witness Reporter* by Prof. Ralph Bohlmann, former member of the Commission on Fraternal Organizations of our Synod (*Lutheran Witness Reporter*, IV, 5 [March 3, 1968], p. 4). Prof. Bohlmann says:

First, it is extremely doubtful whether we can or should distinguish sharply between position and method of approach in any situation that divides Christians. It is to be remembered that Article VII of the Augsburg Confession speaks about the *activity* of preaching the Gospel and administering the sacraments and not merely about correctly stated doctrinal positions. In the lodge situation, as in many others, the method of dealing with it is a fair indication of one's own position.

Second, it is not entirely accurate to state that "both church bodies take the same position" on lodges. Both are indeed agreed in recognizing that membership in such societies is in conflict with the Gospel, and for this we should be grateful. But our own position includes more than this.

Not only does it avoid the questionable distinction between clergy and lay membership in such societies but states: "it is and shall be the practice of the congregations of the Synod not to administer Holy Communion to members of such lodges nor to admit such persons to communicant membership, since Holy Communion expresses an exclusive spiritual relationship of the communicant to his Lord and to his brethren."

Both the position and its rationale expressed in this statement are doctrinal. On that account the statement cannot simply be regarded as an optional method for dealing with the problem.

This last point is especially crucial for our proposed fellowship with the American Lutheran Church, for such fellowship will be established on the basis of agreement in the doctrine of the Gospel and the administration of the sacraments. Because our differing lodge positions reveal that we are not yet fully agreed on the proper administration of the sacraments, it appears to me that this matter should be satisfactorily resolved *before* fellowship is established.

I firmly believe that it can be resolved if we follow the advice of the President's office and "work together. . . on the basis of the Gospel and in loving concern."

It would be unrealistic to tolerate the position of a sister church without allowing it to be followed within our own synod.

Churches in Geneva advocated planned economy on a world basis, total redistribution of land and wealth throughout the world, and all this by a system of international taxation, i.e. by force).[3] Shall we ignore the membership of the American Lutheran Church in this council when we ourselves decline membership because of the compromise and unionism involved in such membership? Should not the entire matter of involvement and fellowship in such ecumenical organizations as the WCC and the LWF be settled in a brotherly manner and honestly in one way or the other by church bodies planning to enter into fellowship *before* these bodies establish such fellowship? Such brotherly action which avoids later strife and misunderstanding has been the practice in the past of church bodies entering into fellowship and merger. When the Evangelical Lutheran Church of Australia and the United Evangelical Lutheran Church of Australia recently merged into one Lutheran Church, the latter discontinued membership in the LWF out of deference to the consciences of those in the ELCA who believed that membership in the LWF was unionistic. The same thoughtful action was carried out prior to the formation of the ALC itself. At that time the old American Lutheran Church was a member of the WCC, the Evangelical Lutheran Church was not. But at the strong recommendation of Dr. Schiotz, then president of the Evangelical Lutheran Church, the reverse was suggested, and the ELC joined the WCC, so that there might be no complications on this matter after the merger had been effected. Today too, there must be a clear settlement between the American Lutheran Church and the Missouri Synod on the crucial matter of ecumenical involvement, if there is to be a happy fellowship between the two church bodies.

3. The Lutheran Church in America

The American Lutheran Church practices *de facto* pulpit and altar fellowship with the Lutheran Church in America—at least on a selective basis. The bodies now constituting the American Lutheran Church have never broken their former relation of full fellowship with the former Augustana Lutheran Church which is now a part of the Lutheran Church in America. The American Lutheran Church and the Lutheran Church in America are already practicing full fellowship in their campus ministries, even having

---

3 See *Barron's Magazine*, Jan. 9, 1967. In commenting on this conference of the WCC in response to certain objections, Dr. Frederick Schiotz, president of the ALC, does not even mention this invasion of the Church into the province of the state. His only criticism was a mild stricture against the WCC's condemnation of the American policy in Viet Nam (*Lutheran Standard*, Oct. 4, 1966, p. 19).

joint ministries, and in other activities. Assuming that such pulpit and altar fellowship would not be broken off, would our joining in fellowship at this time with the American Lutheran Church not involve us immediately in virtual fellowship (*de facto*) with the Lutheran Church in America, although we are perhaps assuring ourselves—unconvincingly—that this would not be and that we have no intention of fellowshipping with the Lutheran Church in America? Those who are in favor of immediate fellowship with the American Lutheran Church see the situation just this way. The *Lutheran Forum* (June, 1967, p. 17), for instance, believes that the problem of pulpit and altar fellowship will not be solved until the Lutheran Church in America is totally involved in fellowship moves. Those who try to see the future at all see that fellowship with the American Lutheran Church will result quickly in fellowship also with the Lutheran Church in America. The American Lutheran Church would have it no other way. Right now this body is negotiating with the Lutheran Church in America in the interest of full official fellowship. And it is highly probable, according to good authority, that the American Lutheran Church at its convention this summer prior to our Denver Convention will offer the hand of fellowship officially to the Lutheran Church in America.

A recent issue of the *Lutheran Standard*, official organ of the American Lutheran Church, said (*Lutheran Standard*, VIII, I [Jan. 9, 1968], p. 23): "As a consequence of this [the statements of the Missouri Synod and ALC commissioners on *sola gratia, sola Scriptura* and the Church], the ALC Church Council will submit for approval to the 1968 convention a declaration of pulpit and altar fellowship with the bodies in the LCUSA." This would include the Lutheran Church in America as a member of the LCUSA.

4. Unresolved Doctrinal Differences

As we have pointed out the present American Lutheran Church is a comparatively new Church body, made up of a number of former Lutheran synods which were historically separated from our Synod by doctrinal differences. Although our synod carried on with some success rather extensive doctrinal discussions with the former American Lutheran Church and the three bodies which constituted it, we had no negotiations with the other synods (ELC, Lutheran Free Church, U.E.L.C.) which now make up a majority of the present American Lutheran Church. And our only official conversations with the *present* ALC were in 1964 and led to the three essays referred to above. These essays which dealt only with the theology of the Lutheran Confessions make no study and offer no information on what is actually believed and taught in the American Lutheran Church today. Therefore the essays cannot tell us whether the serious doctrinal differences which once existed between those bodies (at least those of Scandinavian origin) now constituting the American Lutheran Church and our Synod have in fact disappeared.

We have no desire at this point to rehearse all the ancient doctrinal disputes which may have taken place between the synods now constituting the ALC and our own synod. Many of these controversies may well have been settled or are now forgotten. And to dredge them up anew would serve no good purpose.

There was, however, one crucial issue which divided the Missouri Synod from the bodies now constituting the American Lutheran Church, an issue which cannot now or ever be ignored by those who wish to be true evangelical Lutherans. The issue centered in the doctrine of conversion, of how the lost sinner is brought to faith through the Gospel. The issue is really quite simple. Is the Spirit of God working through the means of grace *alone* responsible for the conversion of a sinner? Or is the cause of a man's coming to faith *in part* his own self-determination, his own cooperation, his own lesser guilt as compared with others, his own refraining from wilful resistance, or his own decision to use powers imparted by grace? This issue of man's freedom or bondage before coming to faith, of his capacities prior to conversion, is not academic but vital. It was the issue which threatened to split the church in the days of St. Augustine. It was the crucial issue between Luther, the evangelical, and Erasmus, the humanist, at the time of the Reformation. Synergism, the teaching that man is in some way responsible for his conversion, threatened the Lutheran Church again in the late sixteenth century and gave rise to the second article of our *Formula of Concord*. Again in the seventeenth century the Lutheran Church was engaged in a controversy on this matter. And in the nineteenth century it was this same issue which split Lutheranism in our country so tragically.

So let us examine just this one issue which is unavoidable to determine precisely what were the differences so devisive in the past and to learn if possible whether these differences have been resolved.

The Missouri Synod, claiming to be in harmony with Scripture and the Lutheran Confessions, taught that the unconverted man was dead in sin, that he could not convert or help to convert himself, that his will was not free to accept the Gospel and the grace of God but totally bound to sin. Only by the gracious power of the Spirit of God working through the Gospel could he be born anew and converted. This position which strips sinful man of any responsibility for his conversion and salvation and attributes everything to the gracious work of the Holy Spirit is unequivocally and emphatically set forth in our *Formula of Concord* (SD, II, 6–7):

> We believe that in spiritual and divine things the intellect, heart, and will of unregenerated man cannot by any native or natural powers in any way understand, believe, accept, imagine, will, begin, accomplish, do, effect, or cooperate, but that man is entirely and completely dead and corrupted as far as anything good is concerned. Accordingly, we believe that after the Fall and prior to his conversion not a spark of spiritual powers has remained or exists in man by which he could make himself ready for the grace of God or to accept the proferred grace, nor that he has any capacity for grace by and for himself or can apply himself to it or prepare himself for it, or help, do, effect, or cooperate toward his conversion by his own powers, either altogether or half-way or in the tiniest or smallest degree, "of himself as coming from himself," but is a slave of sin (John 8:34), the captive of the devil who drives him (Eph. 2:2; 2 Tim. 2:26). Hence according to its perverse disposition and and nature the natural free will is mighty and active only in the direction of that which is displeasing and contrary to God.

Now what of the American Lutheran Church? Is this also the position of that body? In some of the bodies constituting the present American Lutheran Church certain aspects of this Lutheran doctrine were in the past denied. It was taught, for instance, that the unconverted man who has been exposed to the Law and the Gospel experiences a period of awakening during which by his own powers of will he can decide to believe and come to Christ. An example of this teaching is found in a book by J. N. Kildahl entitled *The Holy Spirit and our Faith* (Minneapolis: Augsburg Publishing House, 1960). Kildahl was a member of the "Anti-Missourian Brotherhood" of the 1880s; but his little book is still published which indicates that his beliefs are not dead.

The position of those who opposed the Missouri Synod in its doctrine of conversion may perhaps be summed up in a rather famous statement of Professor Fritschel of the former Iowa Synod; a statement not defended always by the Iowa Synod:

> The fact that in the case of the two men who hear the Gospel resistence and death is taken away for the one but not for the other, finds its explanation in man's free self-determination, although this itself is first made possible by grace. (See F. W. Stellhorn and F. A. Schmidt, *The Error of Modern Missouri*, ed. by George H. Schodde, Columbus: Lutheran Book Concern, 1897, p. 68 and *passim*.)

This statement and others like it were condemned by Dr. Walther and other theologians of our Missouri Synod as synergistic. And indeed it expresses an opinion strikingly similar to that condemned in our Lutheran Confessions as synergistic. Describing the position of the synergists the Formula of Concord (SD, II, 3) says the following:

> The one party held and taught that, although by his own powers and without the gift of the Holy Spirit man is unable to fulfill the commandment of God, to trust God truly, to fear and to love him, man nevertheless still has so much of his natural powers prior to his conversion that he can to some extent prepare himself for grace and give his assent to it, though weakly, but that without the gift of the Holy Spirit he could accomplish nothing with these powers but would succumb in the conflict.

There was nothing unique about the statement of Fritschel's cited above. Dr. F. A. Schmidt, the leader of the Anti-Missourian Brotherhood, held the same position according to which there is something in man, in his attitude or will, which accounts for his being converted whereas another remains unconverted. He said, for instance,

> When only one of two ungodly men is converted there must have been a difference in their resistence; if not, both would have been converted—or else God doesn't will equally the salvation of all. (*Lutherske Vidnesbyrd, Gamle og Nye*, I, 3 Feb. 1882, p. 60).

Again Schmidt said,

> Whether a man comes to a decision in the one way or in the other, he always keeps his full freedom and his own power of choice to come to some other determination. All have their free, personal independent choice between the two usable possibilities: either to follow the drawing of grace or to resist it. (*Lutherske Vidnesbyrd*, 1886, p. 552).

Dr. F. A. Schmidt's synergistic doctrine of conversion represented a large segment of the Norwegian American Lutherans (the United Norwegian Lutheran Church) which united to become the Norwegian Lutheran Church in America (later the ELC) in 1917. The union document, called the Madison Agreement, which brought the different Norwegian synods together at that time was clearly a compromise document which allowed Dr. Schmidt's synergism to remain side by side with the doctrine of the Formula of Concord.[4] This fact was brought out twenty years after the

---

4 The compromise nature of the union statement is affirmed by Rev. S. Gunderson, one of the Framers of the Madison Agreement, who said in 1913, "The United Church has not changed a tittle of its doctrine, neither has the Synod. The Madison Settlement is a compromise." (See *Lutheran Herald*, May 18, 1948, p. 504). This position is reiterated by the *Lutheran Herald* (*ibid.*) thirty-five years later: "When our Union Documents are termed 'compromises,' the expression is apt: one

merger by Rev. J. E. Jorgenson, one of the men who took part in the doctrinal negotiations prior to the merger (See "Memories of 1912" in
Lutheran Herald, May 18, 1948, p. 509):

> During the discussion, it was revealed that the opinion was held by
> some that man's spiritual condition before conversion is that he is spir-
> itually dead in trespasses and sins; and by others that he is not exactly
> dead but rather in a kind of neutral state, so that he is yet able to make
> his choice by his own power, between the way of life and the way of
> eternal damnation. . .

In short, the Evangelical Lutheran Church, the largest of the former synods making up the present American Lutheran Church, taught and
allowed two doctrines of conversion side by side: the one that the unconverted man was dead in his sins and could contribute nothing toward his
conversion, and the other that the unconverted man was not exactly dead
but was able of his own powers to make a choice for the Gospel of Christ.

Now what has all this relatively ancient history to do with us today?
Perhaps little—except that there persists the nagging question: is synergism allowed and taught in the American Lutheran Church today? There
has never been any repudiation of the position taught by Schmidt and
now much later (after the ELC accepted the Minneapolis Theses)
explained by Rev. Jorgenson. And in fact the Missouri Synod is still being
accused of Calvinism in its doctrine of conversion by former ELC theologians now in the American Lutheran Church. E. Clifford Nelson says,

> The Calvinistic error of the Missourians, despite their loud denials, was
> most apparent in their theological method. In place of giving the Mate-
> rial principle of the Reformation (justification by faith) the pivotal
> position over against which all other doctrines were to be judged, they
> had made the fatal mistake of introducing the doctrine of divine sover-
> eignty as the major premise in their theological system. (*The Lutheran
> Church among Norwegian Americans*. Minneapolis: Augsburg Publishing
> House, 1960, II, 163).[5]

---

will search the record in vain to find that one part or another 'gave in.' The nego-
tiators simply learned that the differences were not breaches of the unity of the
faith, that a unity of faith had, in fact, been present all the time." Within just this
last year the compromise nature of the Madison Agreement has again been pointed
out by a leader of the American Lutheran Church, this time Dr. O. G. Malmin,
former editor of the *Lutheran Herald*: "Admittedly, a compromise (Madison Agreement) it yet established the fact which should not have been lost sight of during the
controversy, that the doctrine of election can be stated in more than one way, and
that both ways current in Lutheranism are acceptable" (*Lutheran Standard*, VII, 26
[Dec. 26, 1967], p. 6).

5 There can be no doubt that F. W. Stellhorn and F. A. Schmidt (See *The Error of*

In short, there seems to be no evidence that the former differences concerning the doctrine of conversion between the Missouri Synod and bodies constituting the American Lutheran Church have been resolved.

But would it not be the part of charity to try to forget all this past history in our present negotiations and not make an issue of it?

Surely no serious Lutheran could propose such a cynical *modus operandi*. We are not dealing with minor issues here. What a person teaches concerning the Spirit's mighty work of creating faith in the heart of those who hear the Gospel has the profoundest relationship to the Gospel itself, as every student of Scripture and of history knows. The opinion that man could cooperate in his conversion, even in the minutest degree, was condemned by Luther and our Luther Confessions as a denial of the *sola gratia* principle (salvation by grace alone) and of the Gospel itself.[6]

Modern Missouri, p. 602) and now also in our latter day Dr. E. Clifford Nelson misunderstood the Missourian doctrine of election and attributed to our synod the horrible doctrine identified with Calvinism that God did not earnestly desire to save all men. But on the basis of this caricature they said, "Yours is another Gospel!" After all these years it seems strange that our synod is still accused of Calvinism. And it is of course possible that we found within the groups making up the American Lutheran Church synergism where it was not always intended (See *The Error of Modern Missouri*, p. 688).

6 The opinion attacked by Luther and our Confessions was not always the crass Pelagianism and Semi-Pelagianism of the Middle Ages, but a much more subtle thing, what Theodore Schmauk has called "subtle synergism" which means that "man's will is able to decide for salvation through new powers bestowed by God." (*The Confessional Principle and the Confessions of the Lutheran Church*. Philadelphia: General Council Publication Board, 1911, p. 752). Schmauk goes on to say: "This is the subtle Synergism which has infected nearly the whole of modern Evangelical Protestantism, and which is or has been taught in institutions bearing the name of our own Church." We might just examine some of the statements of Erasmus which were most offensive to Luther. He tried to steer a course clearly to the right of Pelagianism. "Those, therefore, who are farthest apart from the views of Pelagius ascribe to grace the most, but to free will almost nothing; yet they do not abolish it entirely. They say that man cannot will anything good without special grace, cannot begin anything good, cannot continue in it, cannot complete anything without the chief thing, the constant help of divine grace. This opinion seems to be pretty probable, because it leaves to man a striving and an effort, and yet does not admit that he is to ascribe even the least to his own powers" (W2, 18, 1619). This statement which appears no more heterodox than those of Fritschel and Schmidt was roundly condemned by Luther. Luther also objected to Erasmus' synergism when he said the following: "I am pleased with the opinion of those who ascribe to free will something, but to grace by far the most." Also at the time of the Formula of Concord it was not a brazen Semi-Pelagianism which was attacked, but the more subtle kind which sought to give to man only a modicum of responsibility in his conversion. Compare, for instance, the statements of F. A. Schmidt cited above with the following statements by Victorine Strigel: "I do not say that the will is able to assent to the Word without the Holy Spirit, but that, being moved and assisted by the Spirit, it assents with trepidation. If we were unable to do this, we would not

At this particular point I am forced to say that our commissioners who represented our Church with representatives of the American Lutheran Church have let us down. It is significant that the essay on the subject of *sola gratia* adopted by the commissioners of the Missouri Synod and the American Lutheran Church never even mentions the question of synergism (the heresy that man cooperates in his conversion) or the question of the freedom of the will of the unconverted man, the two very issues which Luther and our Confessions consider the greatest threats to the doctrine of salvation *sola gratia*, two issues which our Confessions deal with at great length. And so we have no way of knowing that the members of the bodies now constituting the American Lutheran Church have changed their convictions on this matter or what their convictions are. Are we simply to assume that things are now all right and we are now all one on this matter? It is true that there have been very few overt statements made against the Biblical doctrine of conversion *sola gratia* within the new American Lutheran Church. And this is reason for encouragement. In fact there have been no books or articles on this subject printed at all of late.[7]

---

be responsible for not having received the Word." The logic of Strigel is: since the man who rejects the Gospel is responsible for his action, the man who accepts the Gospel is also somehow responsible, the same logic of Schmidt. Again Strigel says: "If the will is not able to assent in some way even when assisted, then we cannot be responsible for rejecting the Word, but the blame must be transferred to another, and others may judge how religious this is" (F. Bente, *Historical Introductions to the Book of Concord*. St. Louis: Concordia Publishing House, 1965, p. 135). The point to be made is: Luther and the Lutheran Confessions took very seriously any form, even the most subtle, of synergism as an undermining of the Gospel. And this has been the position of the fathers of our synod also. Franz Pieper says the following: "Theologians of the modernist wing and not a few from within the American Lutheran Church came to us and made bold to ask that we subscribe to the doctrine that conversion and salvation are the result not only of the grace of God but also, in part, of man's own decision, different conduct, and smaller guilt. The consequence of any yielding on our part would have been intrinsic loss of faith. The attack was directed against our soul. By changing our *doctrine* in this direction we should have surrendered the fundamental article of the Christian religion, and we could no longer lay claim to being an orthodox Lutheran synod. By such preaching men would not be led to trust alone in the grace of God in Jesus Christ but rather in themselves; men would not be led to salvation but to damnation. For this reason we reject any union with individuals or denominations which teach that conversion and salvation are not dependent solely upon the grace of God, but also in part upon man himself, i.e. upon his proper conduct or smaller guilt, as compared with others." (*Unionism, What Does the Bible Say about Church-Union?* St. Louis: Concordia Publishing House, 1925, p. 21).

7 Passing statements made by leaders of the American Lutheran Church do, however, point to a new doctrine of man emerging, a doctrine which if it does not endorse the older synergistic nomenclature, is even more disturbing than the older synergism. For instance, Dr. Warren Quanbeck has the following to say about the new approach of theology to our modern culture: "The development of modern histor-

Although not definitive or foolproof, perhaps the best method open to us for discerning what is really believed and taught within the ALC is to study a recent poll of the doctrinal position within mainline Protestant denominations. This poll taken by Jeffrey K. Hadden (*Trans-Action*, St. Louis: Washington University, 1967, July-August, pp. 63–69) reveals that 73% of those polled within the American Lutheran Church affirmed that "man by himself is incapable of anything but sin." This would indicate that about one-fourth of the pastors of the American Lutheran Church favor a synergistic doctrine of conversion. This is perhaps a lower percentage than we might have expected, and this is gratifying. But can we allow ourselves to be drawn into fellowship with a church body which might harbor synergism on such a scale? Should we not have some assurance that the issue of synergism which plagued Luther and the Church at the time of the Formula of Concord and which split the Church in the days of Walther is really settled among the Lutheran Churches in America and not simply ignored?

5. The Doctrine of Scripture (Authority, Inspiration, Inerrancy)

No church body stands still theologically. Twenty-five years ago there would have been good reason to assume that in the bodies now constituting the American Lutheran Church the absolute authority, infallibility and

---

ical science has given us a new way of apprehending both past and present. Whereas an older way of thought saw the world and man himself as something given, complete and essentially unchanging, we today see our experience in developmental terms. We see the world not as a static essence, but as a process of development. . ." ("Confessional Integrity and Ecumenical Dialogue" in *A Reexamination of Lutheran and Reformed Traditions—IV*, National Lutheran Council, New York, 1967, p. 42). This statement disturbs us by what it denies. Is there something false about seeing man "as something given, complete and essentially unchanging"? Is this not precisely the picture of man presented in Scripture and our Lutheran Confessions with their emphasis upon man's sinful nature, his fallenness? Is it not the terrible law preachment of Scripture that man is a "static essence," that he is in a tragic state of sin? Process philosophy which Dr. Quanbeck seems to be advocating is a denial of the biblical doctrine of man. According to process philosophy "freedom" constitutes the human differentia. Man is not, for instance, a *res cogitans*—to be human means to make "decisions" within a context of "openness to the future." Synergism is no longer discussed because it reflects an anthropology which is no longer relevant. The world picture within which the question of synergism in its *old form* could even rise at all has been discarded. Silence on the question of synergism represents in this case a *theological decision* determined by a new philosophical anthropology. Within the framework of a process philosophy, according to which man exists by making decisions, the question of synergism, the bondage of the human will in spiritual matters, in the old terms has no place.

inerrancy of the Scriptures was taught and believed.[8] This is no longer true. Teachers and leaders in the American Lutheran Church have moved from their former position, sometimes very far. Furthermore, we are today not dealing many cases with the same ALC theologians or even ALC itself as we knew them several years ago. Again this fact is not reflected in the essay of the representatives of the Missouri Synod and the American Lutheran Church on *sola scriptura*: the essay, in spite of its many excellent features, does not even touch the really sensitive and crucial issues of our present day. It shall now be our purpose to point out some of the changes which have taken place within the American Lutheran Church on the subject of the sacred Scriptures. The facts we shall present will illustrate that a false and pernicious doctrine concerning Scripture is now commonly taught within the American Lutheran Church, a doctrine which makes it utterly impossible for us of the Missouri Synod to have fellowship and make common cause with the American Lutheran Church at this time.

Before we present our facts, however, we hasten to point out that we do not imply any wholesale condemnation of all the pastors and teachers in the American Lutheran Church. Thousands of them no doubt believe as we do concerning the Scriptures. Older teachers like Dr. John Lavik, now retired (*The Bible is the Word of God.* Minneapolis: Augsburg Publishing House, 1959), have given clear testimony to the doctrine of the inspiration and reliability of Scripture. In fact, the United Testimony of Faith and Life which is the union document of the present American Lutheran Church and the constitution of the American Lutheran Church speak of the inerrancy of Scripture. But the teachers in many of the schools of the American Lutheran Church pay no attention to this and teach a new doctrine utterly foreign to the old position.

Let us now offer the facts which will indicate the seriousness of the situation. We will refer only to what has been put in writing by those who teach at terminal schools of the American Lutheran Church. And bear in mind that these schools produce the pastors and laymen of tomorrow. And when we mention names along with the positions of those who teach what we sincerely consider to be false and dangerous doctrine, we do so not to condemn personalities, but only to nail down facts.

---

8 There were exceptions in those days, as one might expect. See e.g. *Folkebladet*, Oct. 3, 1945 where it is stated: "On the contrary, there may well be errors in certain portions of Scripture, where purely unessential things are concerned, without having your faith in the revelation weakened thereby; it will then become a matter of historical research to clear up such problems." But these exceptions were isolated and were usually limited to outbursts of frustration (Cf. e.g. *The Lutheran Outlook*, June, 1953, p. 181.).

At Luther College, one of the oldest and most venerable schools of the ALC, the entire religion department appears to be committed to a denial of the verbal inspiration and truthfulness of Scripture. Dr. Robert Jensen (*Dialog*, I, IV, 58) claims that the inerrancy of Scripture is not necessary for its authority which is only to testify to Christ. And he rejects inerrancy as a kind of "dream-authority."

Prof. Harris Kaasa (*Theological Perspectives, A Discussion of Contemporary Issues in Lutheran Theology*, by members of the department of religion, Luther College. Luther College Press, no date, pp. 14–23), head of the religion department, agrees with Prof. Jensen. The inerrancy of Scripture as taught by past orthodox Lutherans must be rejected, according to Dr. Kaasa. It is the result of a "fearful and fundamental legalism" which entered into Lutheran theology, and it has no basis in Scripture. The Missouri Synod is described by Prof. Kaasa as trying to "repristinate" the Lutheran theology of the seventeenth century; and he says, "Particularly significant is the fact that in this school, the monistic-intellectualistic concept of revelation and the inerrancy of Scripture were preserved intact."

Dr. Wilfred Bunge of Luther College continues the theme, but in a slightly different vein. Applying rigorously what he calls "the historical-critical method" to the New Testament, a method which presupposes errors in Scripture, and assuming that the New Testament was "conditioned by the historical and cultural setting in which it was produced," he arrives at the most remarkable conclusions. In the book of Acts "Luke undoubtedly idealizes the history of the early church by making it appear to have been more harmonious than it actually was." For instance, Luke represents Paul as agreeing (Acts 15:28–29) to abstain from meat sacrificed to idols and from what was unclean. But "it is unthinkable that Paul could ever have agreed to any such a thing," says Prof. Bunge: Luke is just interested in harmonizing things, not in facts. Luke has in fact distorted facts for the sake of harmonization. Turning to the Gospel of Mark and the story of Jesus' baptism, Prof. Bunge assures us that "the opening of the heavens, the descent of the Spirit, and the voice from heaven are not objective events accessible to the eyes and ears of the observer. They are the theological interpretation of the meaning of Jesus' baptism by John. Those present saw Jesus baptized by John in the same way that many others were baptized by John. But the church, as it looked back on this event after the death and resurrection of Jesus interpreted the event theologically." What is regarded as fact and represented as fact by Matthew and Mark and Luke, Prof. Bunge regards as interpretation, pure fiction. Take still another example, the temptation of Jesus. None of the details or even the main elements of the account happened, according to Prof. Bunge. "A straight-forward objective account of this incident would have said: After his baptism, Jesus went alone to a deserted place to meditate for a considerable time." That is all that happened, according to Prof. Bunge. "That the Spirit drove Him into the wilderness, that He was tempted by Satan, and that the angels ministered to Him—these are all theological interpretations." If one were to complain that this is all a very arbitrary way of doing exegesis, the easy answer is offered: The Gospel writers are not so interested in history or facts as in interpretation. This is the sort of exegesis which results from the abandonment of Scriptural inerrancy. Prof. Bunge even contends that such "remarkable" sayings of our Lord as "I am the bread of life. . ." (John 6:35), "I am the light of the world. . ." (John 8:12) and "I am the resurrection and the life. . ." (John 11:25) were never spoken by Jesus at all.

This is the doctrine of Scripture which dominates one of the leading and most venerable terminal schools of the American Lutheran Church. And we are not here just listing a few crackpot remarks of younger theologians (including the head of the religion department) who write before they think. This is the position of Luther College today; this is what is taught there. In the college bulletin of Luther College (*Luther*, IV, 2, Spring, 1967, p. 6) Dr. Paul Jersild writes an article entitled "What are those Theologians Saying". He begins with a hypothetical letter from a student to her parents in which she says, among other things, "In regard to the inspiration of the Bible, I've always thought that the Bible doesn't have any mistakes in it because it is God's Word, but my professor doesn't agree with this. I'm beginning to wonder just what I can believe about the Bible, or what I really do believe. I guess you'd have to say I'm kind of confused. . ." Dr. Jersild maintains that the college is concerned to produce just such a reaction which is not uncommon. For the function of the religion department is not to defend and protect the students' faith, but to challenge it. Speaking specifically to the question of Scripture's inerrancy, he says that the American Lutheran Church is today "rather obviously divided" on the issue. But in the religion department at Luther College there is no question on the point: the doctrine of inerrancy is rejected. "We who teach at Luther College cannot subscribe to Scriptural inerrancy because our knowledge of Scriptures prevents us from making such a claim" This is Jersild's conclusion. And to those who would affirm the complete truthfulness and reliability of Scripture he has this to say: "To simply affirm that every statement is inerrant, therefore impervious to critical examination, is not only an obscurantist attitude but fails to recognize that God used human beings to bring us His Word."

Luther College is not some strange island of liberalism in the American Lutheran Church, cut off from the main stream of theological development in the Church. Dr. William Hordern, Prof. at Luther Seminary in Saskatoon, Saskatchewan and a member of the American Lutheran Church (*The Case for a New Reformation Theology*. Philadelphia: Westminster Press, 1959. pp. 59–60), rejects the inerrancy of Scripture because he cannot see that it matters, inasmuch as we are not inerrant in our reading and interpretation. "An objective revelation is not inerrant until it is inerrantly received" is his argument. This sounds very much like saying that a statement cannot be true until it is understood correctly. Was Jesus subject to error until His disciples understood and interpreted his message correctly? Can we never know the truth because one may never know precisely and infallibly what another says? To Hordern the inerrancy of Scripture is "a purely emotive reaction to the Bible." To him the statements of Scripture are neither revelation or infallible.

At Luther Theological Seminary, St. Paul, the largest seminary of the American Lutheran Church and the second largest seminary in our country, the same denial of the truthfulness and infallibility of Scripture is explicit and outspoken. Prof. Warren Quanbeck, teacher of systematic theology and ofttime representative of President Schiotz of the American Lutheran Church, rejects the doctrine of verbal inspiration as the result of an "intellectualistic epistemology" drawn from Aristotle and foisted upon the Scriptures (in "The Bible" in *Theology in the Life of the Church*. Ed. by Robert W. Bertram. Philadelphia: Fortress Press, 1963, p. 22ff.). This approach which reads "the Bible as a collection of revealed propositions unfolding the truth about God, the world, and man" and considers Scripture as "infallible and inerrant" Dr. Quanbeck also rejects. In contrast to this caricature of the orthodox doctrine of Scripture Dr. Quanbeck projects the view that truth has nothing to do with statements or beliefs about God. "There can be no absolute expression of truth in the language of theology," he says, "not even in the language of Scripture." The doctrine that "the Holy Spirit was the real author of Scripture" and that therefore "every proposition in it was guaranteed infallible and inerrant" has been crushed by the blows struck by studies in historical and scientific matters. Those old Lutherans who "absolutized the Scriptures by a theory of inspiration. . . have been rightly reproached for substituting a paper pope for the Roman Pontiff" (See *Academic Involvement in the on-going Reformation*. Papers and proceedings of the fifty-third Annual Convention of the National Lutheran Educational Conference. Washington, 1967, p. 50). Truth is possessed not in statements of Scripture, but only in relationship to Christ. And so to Prof. Quanbeck the authority of Scripture is not due to Scripture's divine origin (nowhere does he identify Scripture with God's Word), but its authority consists in the fact that God uses Scripture and speaks authoritatively through it ("The Bible", p. 33).

Another example of a weak and inadequate doctrine of Scripture is presented in a book written for laymen by Prof. Charles Anderson of Luther Theological Seminary in St. Paul. Stressing the necessity of using modern language in our theology Dr. Anderson says the following about the Scriptures (*The Reformation, Then and Now*. Minneapolis: Augsburg Publishing House, 1966. p. 104): "This is not the first century, nor is it the sixteenth. We add to the offense of the Gospel when we insist on presenting it in ancient dress. For example, the biblical writers, inspired by God to present his Word, his answer, wrote against the background of *their* view of the world. Their ideas of science, i.e. geography, are not essential to the Christian answer; they are not relevant; in some instances they are not even correct. . . This means a scrapping of the view that God dictated the Scriptures; it means a return to the understanding that he conveys his message through human means and human limitations." Now we do not wish to misrepresent Dr. Anderson. The words we have quoted are from a context in which he urges presenting the Christian Gospel in modern and relevant terms. And to this enterprise we are most sympathetic. But it is also clear that, out of fear perhaps of some strange, unknown adversary who seems to believe that the Scriptures are to be used as a sourcebook for science, Prof. Anderson rejects the verbal inspiration and the full inerrancy of Scripture. It is significant that Prof. Anderson is one of the two ALC commissioners who participated in the writing of the essay "The Lutheran Confessions and 'Sola Scriptura' ".

Prof. Gerhard Forde, professor of Church History at Luther Theological Seminary, is more explicit in his rejection of the inspiration and inerrancy of Scripture. He begins a discussion of the subject with a total misrepresentation of the orthodox doctrine by charging that the Church of the past has simply assumed *a priori* that Scripture is inspired and inerrant (See "Law and Gospel as the Methodological Principle of Theology" *Theological Perspectives*, p. 50ff.). Prof. Forde, also of Luther Theological Seminary, charges Franz Pieper with just such a strange view: "According to Francis Pieper, the celebrated Missouri Synod theologian of the turn of the century, it is so [verbal inspiration] because it is a position which is established *a priori*." In the context Pieper is not speaking of verbal inspiration or inerrancy at all, but of God's providence in preserving the Scriptures over the centuries. We know this *a priori*, Pieper says, because of Christ's promise that His Word will remain until the end of time (See John 17:20; 8:31). Pieper is speaking only of the transmission of Scriptures, not of inspiration. But Prof. Forde, without the slightest evidence, has charged that the historic Church has not derived its doctrine of the inspiration and truthfulness of Scripture exegetically, but rather has simply assumed that thus it must be. "The verbal inspiration method is based on a theory—a human theory about the nature of the Word of God." And this theory, Forde contends, like Holmes' "One-Hoss-Shay", has simply gone to pieces under the onslaught of two hundred years of "scientific and historic research." "In the face of the mounting knowledge of the world, the verbal inspiration method has had no constructive counsel to give, but can only advise one to retreat from the world and refuse to face those things which one finds uncomfortable."

This ought to make it crystal clear what is taught in the largest seminary of the American Lutheran Church. To Prof. Forde the Bible can be called the Word of God only "because and in so far as it witnesses to Christ." It is no more inspired than any good Sunday sermon. "There is qualitatively no difference between the inspiration of the Bible and the inspiration of the preaching in the Church." The Bible is our authority only because "it is closer to the original events."

The theological situation which has just been traced is not confined to the terminal schools of the American Lutheran Church. The new views concerning Scripture's inspiration and reliability have filtered down to the Sunday School level of the Synod and are freely expressed in some of the Sunday School and adult education materials, particularly in the teachers' manuals. For instance, the manual to the student book, *God's Word and My Faith* (Minneapolis: Augsburg Publishing House, 1965, p. 31 and *passim*), after stressing the very human qualities of the Bible and the fact that God chose sinful men as His instruments, tells us that "some of their wrong or inadequate ideas also got into the Scripture." Then alleged discrepancies or contradictions are brought in to show that the inspiration of the Bible has nothing to do with "infallibility or inerrancy." Inspiration is granted, but it refers more to the message than to the words (*ibid.* p. 34). Again in a textbook for High School students, *Questions about the Bible* (Minneapolis: Augsburg Publishing House, 1965, p. 9) it is simply assumed that there are "mistakes" in the Bible. And the question is asked: "How do we explain the mistakes in the Bible?" (Cf. also p. 45 which again makes verbal inspiration an open question.) In the teachers' manual of this same book (p. 43) the inerrancy of Scripture is denied. The Bible is said to be "true" in the sense of being consistent with Christ who makes Himself known there; but it is not true in the sense that it tells the truth, that it is without error. Furthermore, the manual states, "The authority of the Bible does not rest on its errorlessness or its historicity, but upon the fact that God reveals himself in and through the Bible." This statement which utterly confuses the authority of Scripture with the power of Scripture attributes to the Scriptures no more authority than may be attributed to any Gospel-centered book through which God reveals Himself.

The developments here illustrated in some of the Sunday School literature of the American Lutheran Church is by no means discernible in all the literature, some of which is quite acceptable and evangelical. But a trend is clearly perceptible, a trend which has disturbed many in the American Lutheran Church.

The facts we have been reviewing concerning the theological development in the American Lutheran Church as it touches just one article of faith, the authority of Scripture, reveals a deplorable situation in that Church body. Twenty-five years ago such things could not have been taught in the church bodies now constituting the American Lutheran Church. Today doctrinal discipline has broken down. Terminal schools are now captive to a theology which the rank and file of pastors and laymen in the American Lutheran Church do not believe and do not want taught. But these Christians are helpless to do anything about it. And they have tried to do something about it. At the Convention of the American Lutheran Church in 1964 protests were leveled against a book published by the Board for Parish Education of the American Lutheran Church entitled *The Bible: Book of Faith*. This book which was to be used in conjunction with the Sunday School literature was not so brash in its statements as the materials we have cited, but it rejected the authenticity of many books of the Old and New Testaments. It questioned whether Paul really wrote certain epistles which clearly purport to have been written by him; and in such ways the book appeared to threaten the reliability of the Scriptures. And the absolute authority of Scripture derived from its divine origin was denied (p. 142). The best resolution which could be extracted from the synod was to let the other side be heard, if possible. After a highly questionable whereas which said, "Not only in hermeneutics, but also in other areas *of doctrine* our Confessions allow for more than one theory or point of view," it was resolved to thank the professors who participated in writing *The Bible: Book of Faith*; and then the following resolution was offered: "Resolved, that we exhort the Department of Parish Education to be continually aware of points of view held by large segments of the church and seek, where possible, to allow for the expression of these points of view." What an abject failure to cope with a pressing emergency!

Dr. Schiotz, President of the American Lutheran Church, was also approached to intervene in this matter and to insist that a high doctrine of Scripture be once again taught in the terminal schools. Dr. Schiotz responded with a rather lengthy article entitled "The Church's Confessional Stand Relative to the Scriptures". Commenting in this article on the statement in the constitution of the American Lutheran Church that the Scriptures are "the divinely inspired, revealed, and inerrant word of God. . . and the only infallible authority in all matters of life," Dr. Schiotz re-marks that the document, "United Testimony of Faith and Life," which brought together the bodies now constituting the American Lutheran Church does not speak of inerrancy "in the absolute sense, but calls the Bible 'the only inerrant and completely adequate source and norm of Christian doctrine and life.' " He then commits the American Lutheran Church to the position that inerrancy does not pertain to the text of Scripture (that is, the Scriptures as such) but only "to the truths revealed for our faith, doctrine and life." When Dr. Schiotz speaks of the inerrancy of the "truths" of Scripture he is saying nothing, he is uttering pure redundancy. The question is: are the Scriptures inerrant? Dr. Schiotz, speaking on behalf of his church, does not wish to affirm the inerrancy and infallibility of all the utterances of Scripture which is what the inerrancy of Scripture has meant historically. And so it would appear that the President of the American Lutheran Church has no intention of settling the doctrinal confusion in his church body by urging a return to the historic doctrine of Scripture's authority and truthfulness.

Conclusion

How are we to react to all this? We must certainly recognize the state of affairs which now exists in the American Lutheran Church and we must sympathize with the Christians in that church body. But we must also ask ourselves some forthright questions. Can we join in pulpit and altar fellowship with a church body which is so clearly uncommitted on such a crucial issue as the formal principle of theology? Is it right and Christian to have fellowship with theologians who clearly and boldly deny the inerrancy and sometimes even the verbal inspiration of the sacred Scriptures and with a church body which promotes this theology? Is there a valid basis for fellowship between the two bodies in the light of such circumstances? And would such fellowship not be a doctrinal compromise for us, a clear and undeniable case of what our synod has always called sinful unionism, that is, "Church fellowship with the adherents of false doctrine" (*Brief Statement*, par. 28)? Surely we must seriously ask ourselves these questions before committing ourselves and the hundreds and thousands of faithful Christians in our Synod to such a momentous (and we might add, humanly speaking, irrevocable) decision.

And the answer to the questions can only be, No! No fellowship until the inescapable roadblocks to fellowship are removed. We did not create the roadblocks. They are simply there, and we cannot ignore them.

Perhaps this appears to be a negative platform to introduce at this late date when things seem to be moving almost inexorably toward better understanding and closer relations between the denominations of Christendom and especially between the Missouri Synod and the American Lutheran Church. But what we are advocating is nothing of the kind. It is rather an honest platform and a healthy one for both Missouri Synod and the American Lutheran Church. For this platform strives to maintain the true doctrine of the Gospel. And this cannot be done if we condone or ignore false doctrine.

One of the great Lutheran theologians of our day, Dr. Hermann Sasse, who was a participant in the union discussions of the Lutheran Churches of Australia and who is a recognized church historian and authority on the Ecumenical Movement, has said, "Just as there is no struggle for true doctrine which is not at the same time a battle against the false, just so there is no project for the true unity of the Church which does not include the warding off of false union" ("On the problem of the Union of Lutheran Churches", *Letters Addressed to Lutheran Pastors*, no. 10 [*Quartalschrift*, 47, 4 (October, 1950), p. 276]).

Should not the roadblocks to fellowship between the American Lutheran Church and our Synod be settled forthrightly *before* any declaration of pulpit and altar fellowship? After a declaration of fellowship these issues would be far more difficult to resolve, and we might be plagued with controversies and factions. Furthermore, with patience, with prayer, with complete dependence upon God and faithfulness to His written Word on the part of all, these roadblocks *can* be removed. We have a right to believe this, we who believe in the unifying power of the Word of God. True, the program of patiently *removing* these obstacles to pulpit and altar fellowship may be a slow and at times trying and difficult undertaking; but it is the only approach to achieve what we so sincerely desire and what we are committed to as Lutherans, viz. a fellowship built on the one proper basis, the unconditioned Gospel of God. It is well to recall that the last of the Lutheran Confessions, the Formula of Concord, is the result of just such an honest and patient program which insisted on agreement in all the articles of faith in settling the many serious and aggravating doctrinal controversies which plagued Lutheranism after Luther's death.

In the minds of many who have attempted to follow these long discussions there may be a number of questions or even objections to what has been said. Let us in conclusion try to anticipate and offer answers to some of these.

1. One often hears the observation made that the Church today is simply moving inevitably in the direction of more cooperation, understanding and dialogue. The Missouri Synod also finds herself swept along in this movement. And so the argument goes: fellowship is coming among the Lutherans and we had best be aware of this, anticipate it, and assume a positive attitude toward it, even if we should have some misgivings about the whole development. It is correctly pointed out that we are already having fellowship of sorts in many activities with the American Lutheran Church: prayer fellowship on many occasions, cooperation in armed service work, social welfare work; members are often transferred within the two synods and communion offered to those of different synodical affiliation. Furthermore, LCUSA which we have recently joined is an organization which promotes just this sort of cooperation. Why not go the next step and consistently do what we are practicing now in part?

Apart from the fallacy of claiming that a historical development is necessary and inevitable, there appears to be a certain cogency in this argument. Are we not already *virtually* in fellowship with the American Lutheran Church? When we are able to work with the members of this body on so many levels, pray with them, invite them to lecture and even teach at our institutions, recommend their institutions to our young people, even invite them to the Lord's Table in our Churches on occasion, why not make this a consistent and regular practice?

A fourfold reply might be given to this argument. 1) There is no cogent reason to believe that if a person is travelling at a certain rate of speed, he will therefore do well to travel at a greater rate of speed, or that a large degree of cooperation calls for a larger degree of cooperation. 2) Although the Church will want to keep abreast of historical trends, it is not always a virtue or advantage to attempt to keep in step with what may seem to be the march of history. 3) Some of the cooperative activities of the past have not been according to the directives of our Synod or our synodical officials. 4) There is quite a bit more involved in the present plan to enter pulpit and altar fellowship than immediately meets the eye. The brochure emanating from our president's office has clarified this issue. According to the brochure (p. 13) pulpit and altar fellowship mean the following:

1. Congregations of the synods may hold joint worship services.

2. Pastors of one synod may preach from the pulpits of congregations in the other synod.

3. Members in good standing in one synod may commune as guests at the altar of congregations in the other synod.

4. Members may transfer their membership from congregations of one synod to congregations of the other synod.

5. Congregations of one synod may call as their pastors those who are on the clergy roster of the other synod.

6. Students may prepare for the holy ministry in the seminaries of either synod.

We might add that joint mission work, particularly on the foreign field, would very likely also result from any declaration of fellowship. One immediately perceives that a much more unrestrained fellowship is being contemplated than that which now prevails, a fellowship like that which we now enjoy with the Synod of Evangelical Lutheran Churches or our sister Free Churches abroad.

2. One hears it said that the same theological development and the same problems which we have traced in the American Lutheran Church are present also in our own Synod. Who are we then to cast stones? Why not join with the American Lutheran Church and face these issues jointly, strengthening and edifying each other? First of all, in response we wish to make it very clear that we are not and have no desire to cast stones at the American Lutheran Church. Our resume of some of the doctrinal problem areas in the American Lutheran Church is not the result of digging into obscure sources or of fault finding, but reflects what anyone would discover who honestly attempts to learn what is going on in the ALC today. If we feel that we must point out false doctrine or practice in the American Lutheran Church it is only in the spirit of Paul in Gal. 6:1: "Brethren, if a man be overtaken in a fault, ye which are spiritual, restore such an one in the spirit of meekness; considering thyself, lest thou also be tempted." We love the Christians in the American Lutheran Church, and this is the way we bear one another's burdens. Second, we recognize frankly our own problems, serious problems. Who would wish to claim that the theology or practice in our Synod is perfect? But really can one liken the theology taught in our schools and in our literature with that which we have just surveyed in the American Lutheran Church? Clearly the situation in the American Lutheran Church is out of hand.

3. One hears it said repeatedly that the Scriptural and confessional basis for pulpit and altar fellowship is "that the Gospel be preached in conformity with a pure understanding of it and that the sacraments be administered in accordance with the divine Word," (AC, VII, 2), and that on this basis spelled out in our Lutheran Confessions there is agreement between the Missouri Synod and the American Lutheran Church. That is to say, there is agreement between the two churches in their understanding

of the Gospel and in their administration of the sacraments. Therefore nothing should hinder pulpit and altar fellowship.

Two things must be said in reply to this rather simplistic solution to the problem of fellowship which has become popular of late.

a) The article of the Augsburg Confession which is appealed to at this point was never meant to be any kind of formula for reunion of disunited or separated churches or synods. Melanchthon in this article is not speaking of denominations and their problems of getting together, but of the *una sancta ecclesia*, the one holy Christian Church, the congregation of saints, which has and always will have a unity, a spiritual unity wrought by the Spirit of God, a unity and fellowship enjoyed right now by Missourians, ALC Lutherans, Roman Catholics, Presbyterians and all who believe in Christ as Lord and are thus members of this Church (Apol. VII, 20–21). For this unity, Melanchthon says, "it is enough to agree [*satis est consentire*] concerning the doctrine of the Gospel and the administration of the sacraments." Melanchthon is concerned to say that human traditions, rites and ceremonies are not necessary for this unity, as the papists insisted. What Melanchthon meant by unity in this article of the Augsburg Confession is made crystal clear by a statement in the Apology of the Augsburg Confession (VII, 31): "We are talking about true spiritual unity, without which there can be no faith in the heart nor righteousness in the heart before God. For this unity, we say, a similarity of *human rites*, whether universal or particular, is not necessary." Therefore Leif Grane is quite confessional and Lutheran when he says, "The one condition for the existence of this spiritual unity is proclamation and sacraments" (Leif Grane, *Confessio Augustana*, København: S. L. Møllers Bogtrykkeri, 1963. p. 74). And Sasse is in perfect harmony with our Confessions, then, when he says that the unity of the Church is neither a lost paradise or some unworkable future ideal (surely not something which will take place if and when we commence pulpit and altar fellowship with another Church body). This would be either Romanism or Romanticism, according to Sasse. No! "The unity of the Church, the fact of one Church, is a reality and we know this in faith. This one Church is present just as surely as Jesus Christ is present with us always even to the end of the world" (*In Statu Confessionis*. Berlin und Hamburg: Lutherisches Verlagshaus, 1966. p. 166).[9]

---

9 This is precisely the position of the "Theology of Fellowship", a document accepted by our Convention in New York and in this instance cited by the brochure sent from our president's office (*ibid.*, p. 14; Cf. *Convention Workbook*, p. 369): "Those who have fellowship with God through faith in Christ are also in fellowship with one another (1 John 1:3). As faith makes all men children of God, so it also makes them all brethren in Christ (Gal. 3:26 and 27). This fellowship transcends

b) Granted that the Augsburg Confession, Art. VII, speaks of the true unity (*vera unitas*) and fellowship which already exists in the Church Universal (the communion of saints), is not the agreement in the doctrine of the Gospel and in the administration of the sacraments, properly understood, nevertheless, a correct and useful basis for establishing fellowship between formerly divided church body?

The understanding of the Missouri Synod has been that the agreement concerning the doctrine of the Gospel spoken of in the Augsburg Confession is complete doctrinal agreement, agreement in *all the articles* of the Christian faith.[10] And this is the only possible interpretation of our

---

every barrier created by God or set up by man and brings about the highest unity possible among men, the unity in Christ Jesus (Gal. 3:28). This transcending of all barriers is beautifully described in Eph. 2:11–22)."

10 This position is made clear in the "Theology of Fellowship" (See *Convention Workbook*, p. 380. Cf. President's *Brochure*, p. 14):

The subject of pulpit and altar fellowship is not discussed *expressis verbis* in the Lutheran Confessions. However, the basis for pulpit and altar fellowship, as it has been understood in the Lutheran Church where it was loyal to its confessions, is set forth in Augustana, Art. VII:

And to the true unity of the Church it is enough to agree concerning the doctrine of the Gospel and the administration of the sacraments.

The doctrine of the Gospel is not here to be understood as one doctrine among many, or as a bare recital of John 3:16, but rather as a doctrine composed of a number of articles of faith. For the doctrine of the Gospel cannot be understood or preached without the Article of God, which the Lutheran confessors say they teach *magno consensu* (AC, I), the Article of Original Sin, which shows man's need for the Gospel, the Article of the Son of God, who became incarnate and redeemed man. The true understanding of Article VII of the Augsburg Confession is correctly set forth by Herbert J. A. Bouman as follows:

This does not mean that the specific *locus "de justificatione"* considered by itself is all that the Lutherans consider indispensable. Rather they regard the entire *corpus doctrinae* as bound up inextricably with justification. All doctrines have their place in this doctrine. All doctrines stand or fall with the doctrine of justification.

This is also the meaning of the Formula of Concord when it says, Epitome, Art. X:

We believe, teach, and confess that no church should condemn another because it has fewer or more external ceremonies not commanded by God, *as long as there is mutual agreement in [the]* doctrine and in all its articles. . .

This was not the position of the former Iowa Synod with its opinion on open questions, viz. that differences on peripheral doctrines revealed in Scripture were not disruptive of church fellowship, an opinion condemned by Walther and the Missouri Synod (See *Lehre und Wehre*, XIV, 2 [1868], p. 66):

This theory we can by no means make our own. We must rather reject it most decidely as one which is syncretistic, unionistic, and indifferentistic, and one which violates the majesty of God's Word. We can regard and

Confessions on this point.[11] This means that to us the inspiration and authority and truthfulness of the Scriptures are not unrelated to Christ and the Gospel. The *sola scriptura* is not unrelated to the *sola fide* and the *sola gratia*. We have no intention of substituting Scripture for Christ; but we are sure of this: the Christ in whom we believe and the Gospel we preach are the Christ and the Gospel of Scripture. It was from the Scriptures

treat as an open question no doctrine which is clearly taught in God's Word or which contradicts God's clear Word, may the same appear to be or actually be one ever so subordinate, and lying ever so far off from the center of the doctrine of salvation, in its periphery.

It is not clear from the *United Testimony of Faith and Life* or from the *Minneapolis Theses* which might represent the position of the present ALC whether the American Lutheran Church today teaches that agreement on all articles of faith is necessary for church fellowship. It is highly significant that the official representatives of the ALC (Warren Quanbeck and Harold Ditmanson) who took part in the recent dialogues with the Presbyterian and Reformed Churches have found no obstacle to fellowship with these churches and even advocate altar fellowship. They believe that there is agreement between Lutherans and Presbyterians on the doctrine of the Gospel and on this basis urge intercommunion. The official statement says: "Intercommunion between the churches, giving a mobile population greater access to the Lord's table, is not only permissible but demanded wherever there is agreement in the Gospel" (*Lutheran Standard*, VI, 8 [March 6, 1967], p. 18). The editor of the *Lutheran Standard* concurs in this opinion but urges caution. This all indicates a strong official voice in the ALC advocating a quite different basis for pulpit and altar fellowship than that traditionally based upon AC VII.

11 There have been various interpretations of what is meant in AC VII by the right teaching of the Gospel (*evangelium pure docetur*), F. J. Stahl thought that it must be understood in relation to the faith of those who believe the Gospel; and therefore the unity referred to is one of faith in the Gospel (*Die Kirchenverfassung nach Lehre und Recht der Protestanten*. Erlangen, 1862. p. 42). Certain Scandinavians, on the other hand, take the *pure docetur* to denote the very act of preaching and nothing else, in line with their functional idea of the Christian ministry (See Grane, *op. cit.*, p. 74). Holsten Fagerberg (*Die Theologie der lutherischen Bekenntnisschriften von 1529 bis 1537*, trans. Gerhard Klose. Göttingen: Vandenhoeck & Ruprecht, 1965, p. 284) takes the only really tenable view, that *de doctrina evangelii* denotes merely the proclamation of the Gospel; but in one concept it includes both proclamation and doctrine. He says the following:

"Für diese geistliche Einheit wird Übereinstimmung in bezug auf das Wort, das Evangelium und die Sakramente gefordert (Apol 7, 31). Bei dieser Einigkeit geht es also nicht nur darum, *dass* das Wort verkündigt wird und dass die Sakramente verwaltet werden, sondern auch darum, *was* verkündigt und verwaltet wird, oder mit einem Zitat aus Nikolaus von Lyra: 'Darum stehet die Kirche auf denjenigen, in welchen ist ein recht Erkenntnis Christi, ein rechte Confession und Bekenntnis des Glaubens und der Wahrheit.' " (Apol 7, 22).

He points out that *docere* and *predigen* are indeed often used in speaking of the marks of the Church, but so are the nouns (CA 20, 22 also Apol. 12, 98), and that more often "doctrine" and "preaching" are used interchangeably (SA II, 4, 9) and without distinction (LC III, 40; Apol 7, 22).

that Paul and Apollos mightily convinced the Jews that Jesus was the Christ, and it is from the witness of the prophets and apostles that we do the same today.

What we are advocating as a condition for fellowship with the American Lutheran Church is not some legalistically imposed, monolithic uniformity, some slavish adherence to dogmatic formulae, the result of someone's chiliastic dream. Nor are we implying that the casual intrusion of error in a church body is disruptive of church fellowship; we agree with Walther (*ibid.*) that such a view would be a "terrible fanaticism, destructive of the unity of the Church" (Cf. *Brief Statement*, par. 29). We are asking only for the unity of which the apostle Paul speaks (1 Cor. 1:10) when he urges us to speak the same thing (τὸ αὐτό) and be joined together in the same mind (ἐν τῇ αὐτῇ γνιόμῃ), the unity of which our confessions speak when they talk of agreement "in doctrine and in all its articles" (FC SD, X, 31).

Dr. Hermann Sasse has said somewhere, "The most important question facing the Lutheran Church today is: Do we want to remain Lutheran?" This is a vital and highly relevant question today for us in the Missouri Synod and also for the American Lutheran Church. If our earnest answer to this question is yes, we wish to remain Lutheran, then in all our efforts toward unity and fellowship among Lutherans we will make every effort to resolve past differences in the doctrine of the Gospel, we will conscientiously warn against false doctrine today, and we will work patiently for agreement "in the doctrine and all its articles" before entering into outward fellowship.

Fellowship Reconsidered

An Assessment of Fellowship between the LCMS and the ALC in the Light of Past, Present and Future

"Fellowship Reconsidered" continues the discussion and argues that the recently established fellowship between the LCMS and the ALC was wrong. This paper, originally presented to the 1971 convention of the Wyoming District of the LCMS, along with "To Join," provides little-known historical details surrounding the declarations of fellowship between the America Lutheran churches of the mid-twentieth century. These articles also rearticulate the historic Lutheran position regarding the necessity of doctrinal purity and unity as marks of orthodox church bodies. (Permission has been granted for reproduction in this collection.)

A GREAT SHOUT WENT UP in the Denver Armory. It was during the 1969 Convention of the Missouri Synod. And although I was outside the meeting, having coffee with friends in the basement, I knew instinctively what that sound meant. Or I thought I did. Only one thing could give rise to that sudden, spontaneous shout of joy—or, in the case of some, of dismay! Fellowship with the American Lutheran Church had been formally declared. "Resolved, that with joy and praise to God the Synod herewith formally declare itself to be in altar and pulpit fellowship with the American Lutheran Church . . ." That was the way the resolution went (Denver Proceedings, Resolution 3-15, p. 98).

Yes, that was the reason for the shout. But I am not at all sure that most of us understood what fellowship meant, or what it would mean—or that we even understand today!

To many who at Denver voted for the proposal the meaning of a declaration of altar and pulpit fellowship was quite clear and unambiguous. Pres. Harms had said it all in his brochure, *Toward Fellowship*, sent out before the Denver Convention to assist delegates and others to understand what was involved in such a declaration. Pres. Harms had said there that union and merger with the ALC were not contemplated in the slightest, not even the union or amalgamation of service groups, boards or commissions (e.g. young people's work, campus work, etc.). The proposal meant simply that Missouri and ALC people could now commune at each other's altars and preachers could be invited into the pulpits of the other synod. That was it in a nutshell: pulpit and altar fellowship. This was a first for Missouri—a change of position, a new step—but for the ALC it was the result and the vindication of years of consistent conviction, concern and effort.

But to many of us who opposed the declaration of fellowship between the two synods a great deal more was involved. Our concern was not merely whether ALC Lutherans in good standing could now commune at Missouri Synod altars. It was not merely whether transfers of members could now take place within the two synods. It was not merely whether on occasion union services could now happen or an occasional ALC pastor might occupy a Missouri Synod pulpit.

Our concerns went deeper. A declaration of fellowship between these two church bodies assumed doctrinal consensus between them and therefore also a *recognition* by the Missouri Synod that the *prevailing theology of the ALC was genuinely Lutheran*. From such a recognition of the Lutheran character of the prevailing theology of the ALC two irrefragable conclusions must be drawn. 1. A new kind of ecumenism which ignores the biblical doctrine of the *spiritual* unity of Christ's church through faith in Christ and makes the unity of the church depend upon outward structures was now recognized in our synod as being on a par with the historic Lutheran idea of ecumenicity which recognized the unity of the church of Christ as a given made outward Christian concord contingent upon agreement in the Gospel and all its articles (Augsburg Confession, Formula of Concord). 2. A new notion of biblical authority which undermines the historic Lutheran doctrine of the divine origin, absolute truthfulness and normative authority of Scripture was now put on a par with the historic position of the Missouri Synod. These two points will be brought out often in the course of this study. At present I merely wish to say that I see these two clear developments as a compromise of the biblical and evangelical theology of our synod, a denial of our past and a jeopardizing of our future as a genuine confessional and confessing church of the Augsburg Confession.

A number of questions arise as one seeks evangelically and objectively to assess the present fellowship between the LCMS and the ALC. Has fellowship turned out as expected? Has it strengthened our synod and the ALC in faithfulness to Christ and His Gospel? Has our theology become more evangelical by our new association, our evangelism more fervent and effective? Have the doubts and fears of 46% of the delegates at Denver who voted against fellowship because they thought it unwise been substantiated? Or have these doubts and fears proved to be groundless?

It is my conviction that the declaration of fellowship with the ALC at Denver was wrong and continues to be wrong. This is not to sit in judgment of those who longed and strived for true Christian concord and doctrinal unity between Lutherans in our country. I longed for such concord too, and continue to long for it; and I strive for it. Nor is this to sit in judgment of those earnest Christians who believed at Denver that such Christian concord and doctrinal unity had been achieved between the LCMS and the ALC. I am persuaded that those who favored as well as those who opposed fellowship were sincere and earnest. I believe also, however, that there was much ignorance and confusion among delegates there as they voted on the fellowship issue. Our church papers such as the *Lutheran Witness Reporter* and the *Concordia Theological Monthly* did not generally offer the concrete and cogent arguments against fellowship that had been advanced, and the Harms brochure, *Toward Fellowship*, mentioned nothing against fellowship but simply assumed as a foregone conclusion that it would be declared. And I believe there was much irrelevant argument and pietistic bombast and outright pressure before and during the convention in favor of fellowship, and this not merely in speeches by Dr. Schiotz or some of the young people who were given the floor.

And so I wish to re-examine the fellowship issue and the action of our synod. And I wish to do so by addressing myself to two kinds of questions. A. What were the issues that were supposed to hinder fellowship between the LCMS and the ALC and make it impossible? Have these issues been resolved? Or are they in the process of being resolved according to the Denver Resolution 3-15 which directed the synod "to seek a unified evangelical position and practice [with the ALC] on the basis of our commitment to the Gospel?" B. Are there problems or roadblocks to fellowship with the ALC which were not known at Denver or clearly seen there, problems that are now apparent? Have new hindrances, even offenses, arisen which make a truly Lutheran and God-pleasing fellowship between the two synods impossible?

A. HINDRANCES TO FELLOWSHIP WITH THE ALC WHICH HAVE NOT BEEN REMOVED

1. THE DOCTRINE OF CONVERSION (SYNERGISM)

Historically the critical issue that divided the Missouri Synod from many of the synods now making up the ALC centered in the doctrine of conversion. Was conversion entirely the Holy Spirit's work in man, wrought through the Word of the Gospel? Or did the self-determination of man play some part in his coming to faith and in his salvation? This second view, condemned by our Lutheran Confessions (FC II), was taught in some of the synods now constituting the ALC. This fact was not considered recently to be very serious in our synod as we approached fellowship with the ALC, probably because most thought that this old controversy, serious in a former day, no longer obtained. And it is true that modern writings on justification and conversion within the ALC do not overtly teach a synergistic doctrine, namely that man cooperates in his conversion, although it may be implied at times.[1] But that a synergistic view of conversion dominates the theology within the ALC is clearly shown from the recent Kersten Report which found that *only one-third* (1/3) of the clergy in the ALC agree with the statement: "Man plays no part whatsoever in his own salvation or conversion." To disagree with such a statement is synergism, pure and simple.[2]

It is synergism, pure and simply—but not of the same brand as that which was a cause of earlier controversies. In a theological system which

---

1 See Joseph M. Shaw, *If God Be for Us* (Minneapolis: Augsburg Publishing House, 1966), p. 20: "Everyone *can* be justified; it depends on man's willingness to receive the gift of justification if in fact everyone *will* be justified." *Ibid*. "The title of this chapter [Everyone Can Be Justified] . . . declares, through the inclusion of the little world 'can,' that men are asked to open themselves to the gift of justification." This statement might appear quite innocuous, were it not for the fact that the author does not believe in any kind of world justification or objective justification (Rom. 5; 2 Cor. 5:19ff.), but makes justification a possibility which does not take place until man believes. In fairness we must add that the author (p. 12) makes as "error" the notion "of regarding the faith which justifies as stemming from self."

2 73% of the Missouri Synod clergy in the poll agreed with the statement. See Lawrence L. Kersten, *The Lutheran Ethic* (Detroit: Wayne State University Press, 1970), p. 153. The Kersten poll, taken in the Detroit area, "shows that widely varying belief patterns exist among the branches of Lutheranism" (p. 33). It is in essential agreement with other major polls taken during the past years (p. 139), e.g. the Glock Study and that of Geffrey K. Hadden (p. 224).

no longer thinks of faith in terms of reliance upon what God has done *for* us, but in terms of "openness" to what God does now *to* us, the question of human cooperation in the bestowal of faith in the sense of receptivity (through which Christ's alien righteousness is imputed to us) cannot arise at all. The whole framework within which the old synergistic controversy arose has been discarded. The "synergism" advocated by Lutheran theologians today does not pertain to a natural capacity of man to accept God's grace, but pertains rather to human capacity to attain to "authentic existence" (new being) by theonomous decision making which promotes the eschaton.

2. THE LODGE PROBLEM

The pressing practical problem most severely threatening true and honest fellowship between the LCMS and the ALC apparently centered in the different way in which the two church bodies dealt with antichristian societies and lodge members. This difference in practice has long been well known: Missouri Synod congregations, in accord with the constitution of our synod, have not generally allowed their members to belong to antichristian organizations, and when Christian church members joined such antichristian organizations our pastors and congregations have generally sought evangelically to help such people to leave such organizations. The ALC, on the other hand, although its constitution condemns antichristian organizations and lodges and warns against joining them, has done little or nothing to encourage and convince its people to quit such organizations. And the more consistent practice of the Missouri Synod has often been labeled unevangelical by members of the ALC.

Has anything been done after our declaration of fellowship to solve this difference in practice and to establish "a united evangelical position and practice" in this matter? Yes and no.

a. On the one hand, a fine statement has been adopted "On United Witness with Regard to Membership in Antichristian Organizations" by a consultative group of LCUSA, including of course representatives from the Missouri Synod and the ALC. This statement comes out loud and clear in regard to principles involved in membership in antichristian organizations. The statement says:

> Any practice—ritualistic or ethical—which involves a denial or at least a blunting of our commitment or witness to this one and only Gospel, must be avoided by pastors and laymen alike.

> As Lutheran Christians we therefore recognize and acknowledge that any organization is an anti-Christian organization which in its basic documents or in its rites, ceremonies, and practices explicitly contra-

dicts the Christian Gospel of salvation, or which in any way conflicts with the obedience to the Word of God.

Other organizations which may not overtly deny or repudiate the Christian Gospel, but by life-style, objectives, ceremonies, or literature implicitly compromise or negate that Gospel are inimical to the faith and witness of the Christian Church and must therefore be considered anti-Christian.

Such statements regarding principles and criteria for judging and belonging to antichristian organizations, however, do not vouch for any change in actual practice within the ALC or LCA, where even some clergy are members of antichristian lodges, and in fact do not carry us a step further toward solving our differences in practice on the issue of lodgery. Some ALC congregations not only have welcomed LCMS members who refused to leave a lodge, but most of these people are still active members of the lodge.

b. On the other hand, a frank but disturbing editorial on this entire issue appeared in a recent issue of *Dialog* magazine (Winter, 1971, Vol. 10, No. 1). Disturbing, I say, because it was written by an ALC participant in the discussions which gave rise to the adoption of the fine LCUSA statement, Prof. Charles Anderson. Anderson pooh-poohs the traditional Missouri Synod position and practice toward membership in antichristian societies as outmoded, passé and unimportant. His feeling over such discussions as took place under the auspices of LCUSA is one, he says, of "quiet despair, the feeling that, to paraphrase the hymn title, 'We gather together—to gather together,' the feeling that the speakers should perhaps number their stock speeches, such as the 'No Other Gospel' declaration of a Missouri Synod man, and then simply hold up the proper number of fingers at the plenary session instead of going over the whole thing again, and again, and again . . ."

What can we make of such a reaction? Is it merely an example of one man having the obvious poor taste and unbrotherly gall to belittle a serious statement publicly on a serious issue? I think not. There is a crucial issue here, a fundamentally different way in the ALC of adopting and accepting official statements on doctrine or practice in the church. When a commission or person representing the Missouri Synod adopts or subscribes a statement on doctrine or church practice, such a commission or person actually approves and stands behind such a statement. Representatives of the ALC do not necessarily (as we see in this case) take such a stance.[3] This

---

3 Pres. Kent Knutson of the ALC, commenting on the nature of the action of the Standing Committee of the Division of Theological Studies of LCUSA points out

is very important. The Missouri Synod representatives who voted to adopt the LCUSA statement on antichristian organizations agreed with what they adopted and seriously supported it. Dr. Anderson and possibly other ALC representatives who voted to adopt the statement did not necessarily agree with it, or he would not have sarcastically attacked it as he did. I say this not in judgment of anybody's ethics, but simply to make clear something that is quite fundamental: the adoption of a statement, whether it deals with lodgery or whether it be the "Joint Statement and Declaration" of the official representatives of the ALC and the LCMS which led to the allegation that there was doctrinal consensus between the two synods (New York Proceedings, Resolution 2-23, p. 102), does not imply that ALC representatives actually agree with the statement or that they or their synod is bound to it.

3. THE PROBLEM OF PURE DOCTRINE

This leads us to the next issue that many felt hindered true Christian fellowship between the Missouri Synod and the ALC, namely the clear tendency in the ALC to deny the possibility of pure doctrine in the church, the immutability or dogma, the "absolute expression of truth, even in the language of theology."[4]

The most serious statement, expressing such a tendency, to appear in ALC circles before the Denver Convention was a statement of the ALC Church Council, entitled "Statement on Doctrinal Concerns" in which the following was said, "His [the believer's] best efforts to formulate a theology in terms of propositions and statements will fall short. To assume that the church can arrive at human concepts or expressions that are in every respect correct is as much a symptom of pride as to assume that the church or its members can achieve sinlessness in their daily lives." This statement

---

that there are several ways in which a committee may adopt a statement. Adoption may simply mean that a statement is worthy of perusal and consideration by another group. Adoption may mean at other times that a committee makes the statement its own, and if it were unanimous, every member would be implicated. On the other hand, a member of a committee may vote to adopt a statement, although disagreeing with it, because he believes it worthy of further consideration and debate. Such an interpretation by Dr. Knutson makes personal and committee adoption of a statement ambiguous or even meaningless, unless properly defined.

4 See Dr. Warren Quanbeck in *Theology in the Life of the Church*, ed. by Robert Bertram (Philadelphia: Fortress Press, 1963), p. 25. Also in *The Status of the Nicene Creed as Dogma of the Church*. Baltimore, Md., 1965. See also *The Lutheran Teacher*, Nov. 1965, p. 31: "We must make some changes in our beliefs to keep them speaking to the world." Again, "Theology can help, not because it is a final and absolute proclamation of the truth of God for all times and places, but because it is a useful statement of our belief as we now hold it."

was given official sanction when it was endorsed by the 1966 Convention of the ALC. Many in the Missouri Synod were troubled by this statement, and after the Denver declaration of fellowship our Commission on Theology and Church Relations, following a synodical directive (Denver Proceedings, Resolution 2-37, p. 93), requested a clarification of the statement. The ALC Church Council asked Dr. E. C. Fendt to prepare such a response on behalf of the ALC. The response in part said,

> The words "in every respect correct" refer to the inadequate and incomplete doctrinal formulations by the church in every question over against the adequate and complete character of these doctrines in God's Word in the Holy Scriptures. The church's formulation on doctrine is "in every respect correct" only if it is in harmony with every reference to this doctrine in the Scriptures and incorporated fully every essential detail in these Biblical references.

> An example to illustrate: When a church document explains the Atonement wholly in terms of propitiation, such a statement is not "in every respect correct" since it has omitted the equally important Biblical references to reconciliation and victory so abundantly found in the Scriptures.

> The word "correct" is to be understood as the equivalent of complete. In fact when complete is substituted for "correct" no violence is done to the meaning and thrust of the entire paragraph.

Dr. Fendt's response which really explained nothing was adopted by the Church Council of the ALC in June, 1970. Thus the original complaint that the ALC does not in fact believe in the immutability of dogma and the possibility of pure doctrine (i.e. absolute and final theological assertions) stands. And this is indeed terribly serious! "Take away assertions," Luther says, "and you have taken away Christianity." This is what the ALC has done by refusing to teach that the church can on the basis of Scripture make absolute, objective theological assertions. The Church Council has confused Christian life which is never perfect with Christian doctrine which can and must be correct in the church, and that because it is *"drawn from and conformed to the Word of God"* (FC SD Rule and Norm 5,10). In all this the ALC is flatly in opposition to Luther and our Confessions. Luther says,

> The great difference between doctrine and life is obvious, even as the difference between heaven and earth. Life may be unclear, sinful and inconsistent; but doctrine must be pure, holy, sound, unchanging . . . not a title or letter may be omitted, however much life may fail to meet the requirements of doctrine. This is so because doctrine is God's

Word, and God's truth alone, whereas life is partly our own doing . . . God will have patience with men's moral failings and imperfections and forgive them. But he cannot, will not, and shall not tolerate a man's altering or abolishing doctrine itself. For doctrine involves His exalted, divine Majesty itself. (WA 40, II, 51).

Such uncertainty concerning pure doctrine, concerning the possibility of dogmatic and authoritative assertions in theology, can only lead a church to doctrinal latitudinarianism, which is incapable of settling doctrinal issues, incapable of proclaiming the doctrine of the Gospel in an incisive and authoritative manner.

4. The Sacred Scriptures

Perhaps the uncertainty with which the theological enterprise is carried out in the ALC is due at least in part to an uncertainty in the ALC concerning the source of theology, the sacred Scriptures, their divine origin and absolute authority. This was the gravest concern which troubled Missouri Synod clergy and laity as they contemplated a declaration of fellowship with the ALC. Is the divine inspiration, authority and absolute truthfulness of Scripture maintained in the ALC? Prior to our Denver Convention some of us researched this question thoroughly and proved that a tremendous change had taken place within the theological leadership of the ALC and throughout that body concerning the doctrine of Scripture.[5] Whereas 25 years ago verbal inspiration and the inerrancy of Scripture were generally affirmed throughout the bodies now making up the ALC, today one can hardly find a leading theologian or teacher who would admit holding in the original and strict sense to these two doctrines of historic Lutheranism. True, inspiration and inerrancy are spoken of in the Constitution of the ALC and in the "United Testimony of Faith and Life" which ostensibly brought the synods together in the ALC under a doctrinal platform. But former Pres. Schiotz in a statement explaining these terms officially divested them of their original meaning, and theologians of the ALC were and are free to reject these terms or accept them according to a new "meaning."[6] One thing was certain to all who examined

---

5 See Robert Preus, *To Join or Not to Join*, A Study of Some of the Issues in the Question of Joining with the ALC in Pulpit and Altar Fellowship. North Dakota District Convention, 1968. See also Waldo J. Werning, *Issues in Deciding the Lutheran Church—Missouri Synod American Lutheran Church Fellowship Matter*. Milwaukee, 1969.

6 See Schiotz, article, "The Church's Confessional Stand Relative to the Scriptures," in which he states that inerrancy does not pertain to the text of Scripture (that is, to the Sacred Scriptures themselves) but to the truth contained therein, a purely redundant statement which never really answers whether the Scriptures are inerrant or not.

the facts: committing themselves to higher criticism, leading scholars and theologians of the ALC abandoned frankly and openly the verbal inspiration and inerrancy of Scripture; and thus the *sola scriptura* principle of the Reformation was lost.

When queried about this development, Dr. Schiotz and others denied that certain sources used to show the rapid and radical deterioration of confidence within the ALC in the inspiration and authority of Scripture were really pertinent or typical of ALC sentiment. For instance, the book, *Theological Perspectives* (Decorah, Iowa: Luther College Press, no date), issued by members of the Religion Department of Luther College, called the Missouri Synod position on Scripture a "fearful and fundamental legalism," denied categorically the inspiration and inerrancy of Scripture because allegedly these doctrines had gone to pieces under the onslaught of two hundred years of "scientific and historic research," and in accord with the higher critical method denied all details pertaining to Christ's baptism and taught that such utterances of Jesus' as "I am the bread of life" (John 6:35), "I am the light of the world" (John 8:12) and "I am the resurrection and the life . . ." (John 11:25) were never spoken by Him at all. Dr. Schiotz said that there was really very little attention paid to this book in the ALC, and thus he gave the impression that such a theology was not representative of the ALC. He also said at our Denver convention that the term "inerrancy" as used in the "United Testimony of Faith and Life" is similar in meaning to our Missouri Synod usage (Denver Proceedings, p. 64), giving the impression in this case that the ALC actually teaches according to the "United Testimony" on the matter of inerrancy and agrees with the LCMS.

Now is this correct? I believe it is completely misleading. The book, *Theological Perspectives*, is not a theological dud which represents a bunch of young ALC theologians cutting their theological teeth. It is rather quite typical of what is taught throughout the leadership of the ALC.

Let me prove this point. Dr. Warren Quanbeck, professor of Luther Theological Seminary and offtimes representative of former Pres. Schiotz, rejects the verbal inspiration of Scripture as an "intellectualistic epistemology" drawn from Aristotle and foisted on the Scriptures ("The Bible" in *Theology in the Life of the Church*, p. 22ff.), and he claims that the doctrine of inerrancy has been crushed by the blows of the scientific historical method.

Dr. Charles Anderson, professor at the same institution, rejects biblical inerrancy, claiming that when Scripture speaks on matters not directly theological, it says things that are not relevant and in some cases not even correct (*The Reformation . . . Then and Now*, Minneapolis: Augsburg Publishing House, 1966, p. 104).

Dr. Philip Quanbeck in a book forwarded by Dr. Kent Knutson, now president of the ALC, asserts that the biblical "writers or editors or assemblers of those books which are presently in the Bible" "wrote or edited the books without an awareness of writing Scripture." This means that "only at a later time did the church decide that there should be a group of books recalling the events of the time of Jesus which should be regarded as having special value" (*When God Speaks*. Minneapolis: Augsburg Publishing House, 1968, p. 29ff). Here is a complete denial of the divine origin of Scripture. Furthermore, according to Quanbeck, the writers of Scripture were like their contemporaries, subject to the same limitations (p. 30). They could not know more than their age allowed them to know (p. 31). For the Bible "comes out of the historical process and is conditioned by that process." (p. 38). Yes, the Bible can be called "revelation" in a sense, but it is not perfect revelation in that it is "either without error or unambiguous or unequivocal." (p. 39). "How did we get the Bible?" Quanbeck asks. "In the historic process," is the answer. Direct divine revelation, inspiration, prevention from error are not even a part of this process, but contrary to it.

Dr. Terence Fretheim, another professor at Luther Theological Seminary, echoes the same assumption that the Bible is the "product of history" and therefore "in every respect a human book" (*Creation, Fall and Flood*. Minneapolis: Augsburg Publishing House, 1969, p. 5ff.). This presumption of the so-called historico-critical method of interpretation leads him not only to the conclusion that the first books of the Bible were the result of many confused traditions and sources, but also to the proposition "that we today (as historians) cannot consider as factual some of the things which they [the biblical writers] thought had actually happened" (p. 31). "This is the case with much of the material which we find in Genesis 1–11," he says. Thus, we cannot accept the creation account as it was originally intended to be understood. The "probings" of the book of Genesis into such matters as "the beginnings of man, sin, death" reflect only "Israel's understanding," "Israel's structure of belief, her faith" (p. 40). Such probings may be called "didactic legend" which relate stories which were not factual or historical but merely present "certain basic truths" about men in his relation to God and the world (p. 41). But even these basic truths represent only "Israel's understanding." Thus, the garden, the trees, Adam and Eve, the serpent and the Fall into sin recorded in the creation and Fall narrative did not actually exist as recorded in Scripture, but only point to certain "basic truths." The same is the case with the flood narrative. "There is," Fretheim asserts, "no doubt that the authors of the flood story in Genesis believed that the flood had actually occurred at some time in the past. The story was composed and transmitted in an age when such was considered a possibility. Such a point of view is impossible for us today, however, at least as far as the details of the flood story are concerned" (p. 107). For instance, it was impossible to get all the animals on the ark, archeological evidence fails to show a universal flood, etc., etc. Now Prof. Fretheim does not explicitly deny the divine origin or inerrancy of Scripture. His entire approach to Scripture as a book "in every respect human" and his calculated rejection of what Scripture plainly says offers screaming evidence that he totally ignores the historic Lutheran doctrine concerning the divine authority of Scripture.

There is no need for me to go on to prove the point from minor publications and other evidence.[7] The ALC in its theological leadership, including its new president, Kent Knutson, as we shall see, is committed to a higher critical approach to Scripture which makes anything more than lip service to such important articles as the inspiration, inerrancy and divine authority of Scripture simply impossible. (I believe that I am being entirely fair to these many theological leaders of the ALC when I say they would agree with me in this judgment.) And the rank and file of the ALC assents to this leadership. The recent Kersten poll (p. 34) bears out this fact with clarity and pathos; the poll reveals that less than one-fifth (1/5) of the pastors in the ALC can subscribe to the statement: "The Bible is God's word and all it says is true." It is significant that the four meetings between representatives of the LCMS and ALC did not produce any "unified evangelical position" on the doctrine of Scripture; the representatives never really wrestled with the problem.

And so the fears before Denver that there were real and valid hindrances to true fellowship with the ALC were well grounded. The synergistic doctrine on conversion, the unevangelical lodge practice, the indifference to doctrine and the Confessions, the denial of the inspiration and authority of Scripture—these hindrances to true Christian concord and fellowship existed before Denver, and they have not been removed.

---

7 E.g. Prof. Ronald M. Hals essay, *The Authority of the Text Today*, delivered at a pastoral conference in Austin, Texas, Jan. 22–24, 1969, which denies the raising of Lazarus; Prof. Paul Jersild's statement in the bulletin of Luther College (*Luther*, IV, 2, Spring, 1967, p. 6) in which he states, "We who teach at Luther College cannot subscribe to Scriptural inerrancy because our knowledge of Scriptures prevents us from making such a claim;" Claus Westermann, *Our Controversial Bible*, Minneapolis: Augsburg Publishing House, 1969.

B. New Issues and Hindrances to Fellowship

We must now ask whether the climate for true Christian concord and fellowship with the ALC has improved since our Denver convention or whether new problems and roadblocks to fellowship have arisen. I believe that the latter is the case. It had to be so: the ALC has for some time been taking a different course from our synod both in its ecumenical interests and involvements and in its doctrinal turn and development. This is of course not what any of us wanted, and I know that many leaders in our synod have tried to prevent this obvious growing apart of the two synods so recently come together in a relation of external fellowship. But so it is. And the evidence which I shall show, with precious little evidence to the contrary, shall prove that the tragedy some of us feared is now swiftly and dramatically taking place.

1. There has been very little interest in the ALC to solve in actual practice the several problems which we in the Missouri Synod thought needed solution for amicable and real fellowship, e.g. the lodge issue, the ecumenical involvement, the inspiration of Scripture, etc. A part of our declaration of fellowship in Denver resolved, "That the Synod reiterate the pledge made in the 'Joint Statement and Declaration' to seek a unified evangelical position and practice on the basis of our commitment to the Gospel." To facilitate this resolution the presidents of the two church bodies appointed representatives to meet and discuss and settle the differences in doctrine and practice which existed between the synods. In two years only four such meetings have been held, two more than Pres. Schiotz originally wished. As I have learned, the ALC representatives in these meetings did not take very kindly to brotherly correction and admonition from our Missouri representatives; they thought that such criticism pertained to internal affairs which belonged to the ALC alone. Similar attempts within districts to come together to iron out differences were similarly unsuccessful or abortive. It would appear that the ALC does not consider brotherly admonition to be an implication of fellowship between the two church bodies. Yet we were led to believe at Denver that our Synod would influence the ALC to take constructive steps toward correcting some of the serious offenses.

In this connection I might just add that some very fundamental aspects of Christian fellowship, as usually understood, have been generally lacking between the two synods, and this not merely because of the reluctance of many Missouri Synod pastors and churches which were originally negative to the fellowship declaration. In a little poll I took in preparing this study I found that in those districts of our synod where the ALC is most heavily represented the actual amount of pulpit and altar fellowship between congregations' of the two synods has been negligible. Apart from services celebrating the declaration of fellowship itself and joint Reformation services, often loudly touted in the press—and as often as not initiated by men of the Missouri Synod (See *Lutheran Witness Reporter*, Nov. 16, 1969, p. 16) little actual manifestation of fellowship is apparent, e.g. continued cooperation between congregations, mutual admonition and consolation of the brethren, etc. It appears that the ALC goes its way and we go ours without consulting each other, except on the more official and higher echelon level usually under the auspices of LCUSA which has all sorts of plans for more united structure and participation of all member synods in many church activities.

Of course, it is possible that the members of the ALC did not generally envisage fellowship with the LCMS to be of the same intimate kind as is espoused in the New Testament. And from reading the issues of the *Lutheran Standard* as it discusses fellowship with the LCMS I rather suspect this is the case. The ALC saw the declaration of fellowship as the formal and official recognition by each of the two synods of the authentic Lutheran character of the other, a recognition which was undergirded by the practice of sharing pulpit and altar if and when this was desired. To us in the Missouri Synod it implied more than this: namely everything the New Testament means about Christian fellowship (Acts 2:24; 1 Cor. 1:10 *passim*; Gal. 2:9; Eph. 4:3).

2. At its last convention in 1970 the ALC formally approved *the ordination of women*. Shortly thereafter the first woman pastor was ordained into the ministry in the ALC. This did not happen without some forewarning. Pres. Schiotz was informed in 1968 that women candidates at Luther Theological Seminary in St. Paul would seek ordination and he brought this matter before the Church Council, which is the governing body of that synod and includes all District Presidents. The Church Council, after overwhelming endorsement, brought the entire matter to the attention of LCUSA. LCUSA assigned the matter to the Standing Committee of the Division of Theological Studies. This committee appointed a sub-committee to work on the problem and on March 7–8, 1969 adopted a statement of the sub-committee (see *The Ordination of Women*, Minneapolis: Augsburg Publishing House, 1970, Condensed by Ratmond Tiemeyer. Appendix). One Missouri Synod member of the Standing Committee, Dr. Theodore Nickel, registered his negative vote. This statement, along with a summary of other studies undertaken by LCUSA, was submitted to the clergy of the member churches of LCUSA. In response to the statement and studies the ALC resolved to admit women into the

office of the holy ministry. Both Pres. Harms and Pres. Preus of our Synod had informed Pres. Schiotz that such a decision by the ALC would be considered disruptive of fellowship with the LCMS, but apparently the ALC president did not take such urging seriously. Pres. Schiotz and the ALC were also surely aware of the report of our Commission on Theology and Church Relations, adopted at our Denver Convention, opposing women ordination as contrary to Scripture.[8] But this too was ignored by our new sister synod. Clearly the concern even to consider the convictions and urgings of fellow Lutherans is not one of the implications of fellowship to the ALC. This is not said out of bitterness, but simply to confirm what was already said about the ALC concept of church fellowship.

But more is involved in the decision to ordain women than merely an unbrotherly act toward the Missouri Synod. The ALC has formally acted against the clear teachings of Scripture (1 Cor. 14:34–36; 1 Tim. 2:11–15). Of course, this would be denied by those who favor the ordination of women. They would argue that the Pauline passages appealed to in this connection apply only to that day and situation, not to our radically changed society. But I repeat; a different attitude toward Scripture is manifested in this action, an approach which rejects its divine authority.

The same approach relativizes the biblical implications concerning abortion and Paul's judgments against homosexuality and other sins against the sixth commandment (Rom. 1:26ff.). Principles of ethics, orders of creation are denied, and a sort of ethical relativism and quasi-antinomianism come to ascendancy. The LCA has already clearly taken this turn. At its last convention in Minneapolis, July 1970, the LCA adopted a policy on the subject "Sex, Marriage, and Family" in which homosexuality was not considered sin and "on the basis of the evangelical ethic [sic], a woman or couple may decide responsibly [sic] to seek an abortion" (*Social Statements of the LCA*, Board of Social Ministry Lutheran Church in America, 1970). According to reports, the convention was barely able to secure a majority vote to restate the church's traditional blanket condemnation of sexual intercourse outside of marriage (Betty Medsger, *Kitchener-Waterloo Record*, July 6, 1970).

Now the ALC made no such liberal judgments at its convention later in the year. But it is significant that its Commission on Research and Social action in a report to the convention entitled "Abortion, Christian Counsel,

---

8 See Denver Proceedings, Resolution 2-17, p. 88: "Those statements of Scripture which direct women to keep silent in the church and which prohibit them to teach and to exercise authority over men, we understand to mean that women ought not to hold the pastoral office or serve in any other capacity involving the distinctive functions of this office."

326 DOCTRINE IS LIFE

and the Law" advocated a very similar position and platform. True to its more cautious posture, the ALC tabled the matter, but the report still stands as an official report of an official commission. And the synod took no action on two of the most pressing moral issues facing Christians in our modern society.

Meanwhile official organs of the synod such as *Event* magazine brand the church's traditional views on sex as "nonscriptural;" uphold without qualification the decisions of the LCA at its recent convention ("Sex, Marriage, and Family") as "forthrightly biblical," "thoroughly evangelical" and "gospel-centered;" relativize sexual behavior for Christians, deny that there is any Christian platform or "pattern of family life or marriage" ("no legal provisions for those human relationships could be sanctified as Christian"), deny that sexual relations prior to marriage are sinful, and defend homosexuality (*Event*, Feb. 1971, XI, II, p. 1ff.). It is significant that the ALC at its last convention formally resolved to "commend the staff of *Event* magazine for its contribution and encourage the maximum distribution and use of this publication" (*ibid.*). Clearly we see the direction the ALC is taking in ethical matters, and this because the authority of Scripture has been denied or ignored.

3. A third disturbing development threatening fellowship between the LCMS and the ALC to emerge since our Denver Convention is the increasingly apparent determination of ALC leadership to lead all American Lutheranism toward *structural coordination and union.* This does not necessarily mean organic union or merger of the three large synods in the United States. Such a move would be contrary to the express aims of our synod which consistently has sought doctrinal consensus as a priority above church union and as an end in itself. But it does involve what could well be a substitute for such union, namely common "structures" for all Lutheranism now in LCUSA.

Let me offer some background for this master plan which has been endorsed officially by the ALC.

Last year the executive committee of the Lutheran Council in the USA submitted a statement "Regarding Lutheran Unity" to all member synods in the Council. This statement, prepared by seven representatives of the synods belonging to LCUSA, was highly significant. It began by saying, "The goal of Lutheran unity is that the oneness of those who are committed to the fulfillment of the will of God shall be evidenced by their oneness of understanding, activity, *and structure.*" Mark this well! Lutheran unity (whatever may be implied by the term) fulfills God's will only when it leads to "oneness in structure." Again the statement says, "We affirm that *organizational oneness* is a more effective testimony of His [Christ's] church's mission than fragmentation." It is quite clear that more than unity in the Gospel and pulpit and altar fellowship is envisaged here. The plan of the LCUSA statement is to "develop common styles, forms, *and structures*, whether they be geographic or programmatic." This will involve "transfer to their common agency, the Lutheran Council in the USA . . . many things which they now do separately, when they can do them *as effectively or more effectively together*." Mark well! This is not necessarily a platform for organic church union which would involve the complete dissolution of our present synods, a spectre our present Missouri Synod people fear and would never support. It is however a substitute platform which would accomplish the same goal. The present synods would remain, but the structured activities (e.g. youth work, university work, Armed Services work, education, missions, etc.) would be united under the auspices and virtual control of the Lutheran Council in the USA, probably along geographical lines. At this very time efforts are active in promoting just such a program in several areas of church work, e.g. youth work, Armed Forces work, campus ministries, and world missions. The ALC and LCA seminaries in St. Paul and Minneapolis are now engaged in plans to unite the two schools structurally by Sept. 1, 1975.

Now this statement submitted by LCUSA was adopted by the ALC at its San Antonio Convention and the ALC invited the LCA and Missouri Synod to do the same. The ALC takes the lead in this program for change and structural union and the LCA is following suit: its Executive Council has also endorsed the plan, virtually assuring adoption by the LCA next year. What is the significance of this?

The Missouri Synod, when it was urged by Pres. Harms and others to declare fellowship with the ALC, was assured again and again that nothing was contemplated further than the simple and frank declaration of pulpit and altar fellowship (See *Toward Fellowship*, p. 13). Merger or organic union or structural union of boards and commissions were not contemplated. Not even fellowship with the LCA was considered an adjunct of the fellowship declaration. Prior to Denver, however, the ALC at its Omaha Convention (1968) had resolved, "That the American Lutheran Church declare itself ready to participate *in union discussions* with the *three* Lutheran churches with which it cooperates in the Lutheran Council in the USA, namely, The Lutheran Church—Missouri Synod, the Synod of Evangelical Lutheran Churches and the Lutheran Church in America as soon as these churches find it desirable." The statement prepared by LCUSA's committee is now clearly the ALC blueprint to accomplish its goals in this regard. Goals which are clearly against the more modest, but Scriptural goals which Missouri had as it joined in fellowship with the ALC.

Goals which were not made clear to Missouri Synod delegates who voted on fellowship with the ALC at Denver. In other words, when the Missouri Synod declared fellowship with the ALC, this fellowship was a goal in itself to us. The ALC, however, saw the declaration of fellowship with Missouri only as a means to a much larger goal: the new vision of Lutheran Union in the form of "organizational oneness."

If this grand LCUSA and now ALC scheme prevails, we can perhaps expect the Missouri Synod to remain intact. But it will become a puppet synod, serving the aims of LCUSA and its planners. It will continue to exist, but like a great cathedral in secularist Western Europe today, a monument to past greatness.

This goal in the thinking of ALC and LCUSA leadership may well reach beyond all geographical limits and transcend all present confessional lines. Dr. Kent Knutson, newly elected president of the ALC, speaking before the LWF at Evian on the subject, "The Response of the Lutheran Churches to the Roman Catholic Church and Theology Today" said the following: "The future holds much promise and much work for Catholics and Lutherans. I believe that we are on a convergent course. If history will permit the time, we shall move more closely together. *Our goal can be nothing less than reunion.*" (See *Sent into the World*, The Proceedings of the Fifth Assembly of the Lutheran World Federation. Evian, France, 1970. Ed. by LaVern. K. Groxc. Minneapolis: Augsburg Publishing House, 1971, p. 51). We are living in an apocalyptic age, Knutson suggests, "in which God is thrusting us forward by leaps and bounds and calling us to break with our past at numerous points." It is clear that such an enthusiastic, apocalyptic notion of history simply ignores the biblical and confessional basis (AC VII; FC SD X, 31 *passim*) for Christian unity and concord, say nothing of reunion. Yet it is such an apocalyptic dream which ignores the whole doctrine of the Gospel that we are involved in as we fellowship with the ALC and support LCUSA with its present non-apocalyptic, hard nosed machinations.

4. The election of Dr. Kent Knutson as the second president of the ALC presents a final indication that the Denver declaration of fellowship with the ALC was premature and wrong. This is a bold statement to make, I know, and in no way implies the slightest *ad hominem* argument or slur against Dr. Knutson's person or ability. He is obviously an extremely competent, intelligent and industrious person, who on such a basis deserves the trust he has been given. I refer merely to the fact that as a leading theologian in the ALC whose position was well known from many writings, his election indicates clearly the theological direction the ALC wishes to take

at the present time. And the direction is straight away from the doctrinal position of the Missouri Synod.

Without going into lengthy detail to prove this point, let me merely summarize Dr. Knutson's theological position on a couple of vital issues; and I think this should be sufficiently convincing.

The March 1969 issue of the *Concordia Theological Monthly* contains a study of Dr. Knutson's entitled "The Authority of Scripture." The study is a curious mixture of Barthian and Lutheran emphases. But on the crucial issues the author comes out on the side of Barth. According to Knutson God's Word is not the Bible, but God's Word comes to us "through" the Bible. Objectively, the Bible (the words, sentences, pericopes, books) is not the Word of God. It must first be interpreted, heard, made kerygmatic (p. 158). "It must *say* what it says to be what it is . . . The Word of God is Christ made present." This is patently the Barthian position: Scripture (or preaching) *becomes* the Word of God as God becomes present through it. That is what is meant by the statement: "*The Bible is the Word of God.*" "The Word of God must be understood as the making-present-of-God," Knutson asserts. Without this taking place, the Bible is "not His [God's] Word in the proper sense at all."

What does such a notion imply in regard to Scripture's authority? Knutson answers: "God's presence is always presence with power; God's presence is always presence with authority. If there is Word of God, there is always power. If the Word of God is God's self-disclosure, God making Himself present, God emerging and communicating Himself, that in itself is already an understanding of authority and power" (p. 159). It is clear here that for Knutson the authority of Scripture is not its canonical authority which inheres in Scripture as such and by which it as God's Word norms all teachings and teachers in the church (FC SD, Rule and Norm, 3; Epitome 1)—it is not a *divine* authority in such a sense; but it is a power, the power of Law and Gospel (power which we would insist obtains in any biblically based writing or preaching of Law or Gospel.) To Knutson the authority of Scripture is actually God's power "conferred upon the Scripture," a power which "*becomes* the medium through which He exercises His authority [power?] to save and to judge" (p. 160). And if this authority of Scripture, newly defined, which is really the power of the Word to Knutson, is infallible, it is not so because the Scriptures are true and binding upon us as God's Word. No! "They're infallible because God, the ultimate source of authority and power, reveals and communicates His power here, and that power is the Gospel" (p. 163).

And what does such a notion of authority and infallibility imply in regard to the Scripture's inspiration? The conclusion is that the inspiration of Scripture is not its inspiredness (*theopneustia*), its formal nature of being God-breathed, the product of His breath, the written Word of God (2 Tim. 3:16), but merely, once again, its capacity to be inspiring. Inspiration "is a way of saying that God speaks through Scripture," says Knutson. This is not what Paul means when he says, "All Scripture is given by inspiration of God . . ." (2 Tim. 3:16). But this is all Knutson means. "To me," he says, "it is the same to say the Scriptures are inspired and to say that God speaks through them" (p. 160).

And so the theology of the new Bishop of the ALC can be summarized as follows as it applies to the sacred Scriptures:

1. The Bible is the Word of God = God becomes present through the Bible

2. The authority of the Bible = the power of Law and Gospel

3. The infallibility of the Bible = God reveals and communicates His power through the Bible

4. The inspiration of the Bible = God speaks through the Bible

Such a theology is not evangelical, it is not Lutheran, it is not biblical. The entire position is heterodox. I do not understand how the staff of our *Concordia Theological Monthly* which favored fellowship would have published such an article. The article should have stopped fellowship. And now the author is elected chief bishop of the ALC.

Dr. Knutson has been asked recently to write a statement on the Scriptures, "A Statement of Reassurance," to us in the Missouri Synod who had misgivings over the doctrine of Scripture in the ALC. In this new statement Dr. Knutson actually offers what he thinks to be in general the stance of the ALC toward Scripture. The discussion is very general and simple, containing strong assurances of loyalty to the Lutheran Confessions and the "United Testimony of Faith and Life" of the ALC. But there is nothing in this brief "Reassurance" to mitigate or qualify the position toward the sacred Scriptures which Dr. Knutson much more clearly and elaborately worked out in the previous *CTM* article.

Now all that has just been summarized does not represent merely some isolated quirk in the theology of the ALC's new president. His position toward the sacred Scriptures affects the rest of his theology, as we might expect. This is seen in his discussion of the person and work of Christ in a book entitled, *His Only Son our Lord* (Minneapolis: Augsburg Publishing House, 1966). In this book Dr. Knutson rejects as docetic the classical Lutheran Christology of our Lutheran Confessions (FC VIII) which taught that Christ from his incarnation according to His human nature possessed—although He did not always use or reveal—all the fulness of the

Godhead (Col. 2:9), including divine power, majesty and omniscience (p. 40–41). And he *denies* that Jesus Christ was *omniscient* (p. 44). Concerning Christ's vicarious atonement, Knutson asserts, "The ransom, of course, was paid to no one." (p. 62). And he goes on to liken the sacrificial death of Jesus to that of a soldier who might have laid down his life at Iwo Jima and who certainly paid his life a ransom to no one. Such notions as sacrifice and ransom in Scripture are, according to Knutson, merely ways of stating that it cost God very much to save us. Thus the substitutionary and propitiatory nature of Christ's death are undermined. But Paul says, "Christ also hath loved us, and hath given himself *for us* an *offering* and a *sacrifice to God* for a sweetsmelling savour" (Eph. 5:1). Again Knutson denies that Christ's descent into hell (as recounted in the Apostles' Creed) was a specific saving event, but affirms that it was merely another way of stating the atonement of Christ. He mistakenly understands Luther's and the Formula of Concord's teaching on the descent into hell as "a symbol for the Victory Picture of the atonement" (p. 85). He says, "Christ has redeemed us from the power of death and evil. The *descensus* (as it is technically called) is therefore repeating a view of the atonement and is inserted into the creed to insure that interpretation." Even Knutson's doctrine of Christ's ascension is not clear. He accepts the ascension "as an integral part of the faith" (p. 94). But he seems to identify the ascension, depicted in Mk. 16:19, Lk. 24:51 and Acts 1:9,11, with Christ's sitting at the right hand of God (Mk. 16:19; Rom. 8:34; Eph. 1:20; Col. 3:1), thus denying what is expressly stated in the New Testament, that Jesus in His body "was taken up; and a cloud received him out of their sight" (Acts 1:11). Knutson says, "Space conditions do not really apply. Jesus ascended into a cloud, that is, into the presence of God" (p. 95). It is quite clear however that the Scriptures and our Confessions make the ascension and the sitting at the right hand of God two different acts.

Why this weak Christology? It is due, at least in part, to the weak position that Dr. Knutson takes toward Scripture. He has yielded to the pressures and claims of modern higher criticism. Never in his entire discussion does he consider God's direction of the apostolic witness to the person and work of Christ. Never does he consider the divine origin of the Christology of the New Testament. For instance, speaking concerning Paul's theology of the resurrection, he says, "Paul applied his great intellect to this whole matter and had great difficulty in finding words to convey meaning. He struggles to find some way of talking about the nature of Jesus after the resurrection and he finally hits upon the strange (for a Jew) phrase 'spiritual body' (1 Cor. 15:44)" (p. 90). But Paul's theology of the resurrection is not the result of an application of his "great intellect." It is as an apostle of

Jesus Christ, Christ's spokesman, that Paul testifies to the resurrection and preaches its meaning, its comfort and its power. The lesson in all this is clear, I believe. A poor bibliology will often result in a poor Christology. A low view of Scripture will often result in a Gospel drained of much of its power, cut from its scriptural roots.

Pres. Knutson's editorship of the *Tower Books* of Augsburg Publishing House also reveals his supporting of unscriptural treatises. Portions of three of these books have already been quoted: *The Reformation . . . Then and Now* by Charles Anderson; *Creation, Fall and Flood* by Terence Fretheim; *When God Speaks* by Philip Quanbeck. Pres. Knutson underwrites theology which opposes clear scriptural doctrines in his foreword to these books: "Committed to the Biblical faith, the various authors . . . open up the Scriptures as honestly and competently as they can . . . Take and read. And joy to you!"

It has been no pleasure for me to criticize the theology of the president of the ALC. I would prefer that it had not been necessary. To tarnish or undermine the reputation for scholarship and integrity of another theologian is not my aim in the slightest. My aim has been only to show with clarity the utterly divergent direction the theological leadership in the ALC is taking from the position of our Missouri Synod. For Dr. Kent Knutson, theologian, was not chosen over all other candidates as leader and bishop of the ALC by mistake. His theological position and posture were known by the delegates. It was the posture, honestly taken, of latitudinarianism toward doctrine and errant church bodies *and* of the historico-critical approach to Scripture, an approach which we have seen at work by all the theological leadership in the ALC, consistently and relentlessly at work.

This is a simple fact which we ought not and cannot and must not ignore in our synod. We are further away from doctrinal consensus and true Christian concord and fellowship with the ALC than we were at Denver. He who has eyes to see cannot fail to perceive this sad fact.

It is highly significant that a recent editorial by Prof. Carl Braaten, teacher at Lutheran School of Theology, Chicago, Ill. and would-be pundit and authority on the development in American Lutheranism, has passed precisely the same judgment on the situation in the ALC, and the direction the ALC has taken theologically. After criticising severely the president of our Synod and mentioning the fact that he left the old ELC because of false doctrine, Prof. Braaten says of the ALC, "If anything, that church has become 180 degrees more liberal since that time." (*Dialog* 10,1, Spring, 1971, p. 86).

CONCLUSION

We cannot ignore the facts. If we wish to retain our integrity and our identity as a confessional and confessing Lutheran church, committed to the Scriptures and our Lutheran Symbols, if we wish to follow these Scriptures and Symbols and do God's will, there is one clear course open to us: suspend fellowship with the ALC until the false theology, the un-Lutheran and unscriptural and unevangelical ecumenism which hold sway in the ALC have been corrected. This is the brotherly thing to do, the honest and scriptural thing to do (Gal. 5:1; Rom. 16:17; 1 Cor. 1:10; 2 Tim. 4:1, Lev. 19:17).

There will of course be objections to what I propose, strenuous and heated objections. Allow me to reply to some of these in advance.

1. We should not terminate or suspend fellowship now because it is only two years old. We have not given fellowship with the ALC a chance. Let us rather work at it harder rather than suspend it.

I reply, if we perceive that the declaration of fellowship was premature and mistaken in the first place and is not even working now—we have not even begun to achieve "a united evangelical position and practice in areas of church life where disturbing diversities still exist" (Denver Proceedings, Resolution 3-15, p. 98)—the ALC will not listen to our admonition—if this is so, should we not simply do now what is right? In our synod fellowship has been likened to marriage. In the ALC it was likened to engagement or "going steady." In any case, the analogy breaks down if we argue that it is now somehow uncharitable or wrong to suspend such fellowship. Pulpit and altar fellowship is based on doctrinal agreement and concord. And if that concord is clearly and objectively lacking, the fellowship (which itself is the public demonstration of such concord) is itself a travesty, a deception that serves only to undermine our witness and to weaken both us and the ALC.

2. If we should suspend fellowship at this time we will disrupt our own synod which is already polarized to a perilous degree.

I reply, the present polarization in our synod is due in great part to the fact that we are in fellowship with the ALC. A polarization which threatens to decimate our synod might well be alleviated were we to reconsider and correct a precipitous action considered by many pastors and congregations in our synod to be unwise and even wrong. Such concern for the brethren would do much to heal the wounds in our synod.

3. How can we suspend fellowship with the ALC, thus sitting in judgment over the theology and actions of that church body, when we have so much difference of opinion and theological confusion in our own synod? A

suspension of fellowship in the light of such facts could only be presumptuous and hypocritical. We ought to solve the problems and right the wrongs in our own church before casting the moat out of our brother's eye and leave a fellowship which has just begun.

I reply, let us turn the argument around. How can we solve the immense problems in our own synod, problems which center in doctrine, and achieve the unified and confessional position (which I believe the majority in our synod want) when we recognize as a sister synod a church body in which less than 20% (1/5) of the pastors believe that "the Bible is God's word and all it says is true" (Kersten, p. 34), in which only one-third (1/3) of the pastors believe that "man plays no part whatsoever in his own salvation or conversion" (Kersten, p. 153), in which barely one-fourth (1/4) believe in a historic Fall into sin (Kersten, p. 36), in which scarcely one-half (1/2) believe that "only those who believe in Jesus Christ as their Savior can go to heaven" (Kersten, p. 36)? Indeed, the attempt to achieve doctrinal unity and discipline in our own synod when we recognize that fellowship with a church body where such a lack of evangelical theology prevails would certainly be considered "presumptuous and hypocritical."

Let me pursue this argument. We shall simply never achieve the concord and doctrinal unity that Scripture and the Lutheran Symbols require of us, never, if we remain in fellowship with the ALC with its convinced and consistent latitudinarianism and indifference to doctrine. How can our church retain the purity of the doctrine of the Gospel, how can false doctrine when it arises in our synod be corrected and those who may lapse into error be helped and led into the truth, when we recognize as genuinely Lutheran a church body in which doctrinal errors are taught and defended?

It has been said that to suspend fellowship when we are trying to set our own house in order (e.g. through the investigation of the doctrine and life of our synodical schools) would be like fighting two wars at one time and tactically unwise. Let us do one thing at a time. But apart from the fact that the Christian is called upon to fight the fight of faith at *every* front at *all* times, the assumption behind such a strategy is false. The problems caused by the fellowship declaration with the ALC and the problems in our synod do not confront our synod with two wars, but one. The connection between the two problems is intimate. We will not solve our internal strife by ignoring one of the main causes for it.

To me the great threat to our synod today is indifference, indifference often born of frustration, but indifference, none the less, indifference to the investigation at our seminary, indifference to what is actually taught in our synodical schools, indifference to what is believed and taught in the

ALC and practiced in a sister synod, indifference to the violent and shameful attacks against the president of our synod, indifference to what our brother pastors believe, teach and confess, yes, and indifference to the Gospel; indifference which will not take a stand on the ethical and doctrinal issues that confront our synod and cry for solution, lukewarm indifference which plays to the "uncommitted middle" and tries to anticipate what this shapeless group will do or not do; indifference which immobilizes us and saps our strength and will ultimately change us into a different kind of people and into a different kind of synod than we formerly were. For we have changed and we are changing. We are unimpressed, indifferent to the Lutheran-Reformed conclusions of *Marburg Revisited* and now more recently the new declaration of the LWF which seeks to commit all Lutherans to a future of open communion with the Reformed although agreement on the Gospel and the Sacraments has never been reached. We are unimpressed, indifferent to the poor theology emanating from LCUSA which undermines the deity of Christ (*Who Can This Be?*) and advocates the ordination of women. We are unimpressed, indifferent to the clear efforts in our synod to break down our historic position on the inerrancy of Scripture (*CTM*, Sept. 1969, p. 527), on Confessional Subscription (*Lutheran Forum*, April, 1969, p. 15), or even abortion (*Lutheran Witness Reporter*, March 21, 1971. p. 7). Think of it! No shock, no protest, no reaction, just massive indifference!

Paul has a word to say about such apathy and unconcern: "Now it is high time to awake out of sleep . . ." Rom. 13:11. We must take a stand on the issues that confront us, even if this be unpopular. We must live and act *coram Deo*, eschatologically. "Now is our salvation nearer than when we believed," Paul says.

I believe that the best and right way for us to act today, to bring about that true Christian concord among Lutherans which was achieved by our Lutheran Confessions, is to suspend the fellowship which now exists *de facto* between the LCMS and the ALC and then work for such concord anew as Lutherans committed to the Gospel of Scripture and the Lutheran Confessions. We must not allow personal non-involvement or some local situation where fellowship may indeed be working well blind us to the larger issues. For there are larger issues than any one pastor or congregation; the Gospel is involved. I believe that the future of our synod depends on such living and acting, the future of Lutheranism, and of course our own future.

THE BASIS FOR CONCORD

> "The Basis for Concord" is a brief presentation of ecclesiology, particularly the relationship between the nature of the church and its quest for doctrinal purity and unity as taught in the Lutheran Confessions. It is, therefore, an apology for the historic Lutheran position that fellowship must be based on agreement in doctrine. It was published in 1977 and was included in *Theologians Convocation: Formula for Concord*, which was published by the LCMS Commission on Theology and Church Relations. (Permission has been granted for reproduction in this collection.)

KARL RAHNER ONCE SAID[1] that if the doctrine of the Trinity were no longer taught in the Roman Catholic Church today, there would probably be no real change in the worship and practice of contemporary Roman Catholics. With some modifications the same might be said of the Lutheran doctrine of the church as it affects modern Lutheran doctrine and practice. For generations now Lutherans all over the world have acted and lived without apparent awareness of the necessary implications of our historic confessional Lutheran ecclesiology on the life and practice of the church. This fact is nowhere more apparent today than in Lutheran discussions and activities relative to the formula for concord in contemporary Lutheranism and in Lutheran ecumenical involvement as a whole. Such activity has often been carried on as though there were no Lutheran doctrine of the church, as though there were no clear and infallible marks of the true church, or as though the church were no more than some sort of external *societas* comparable to a club or lodge or nation.

---

1 Karl Rahner, *The Trinity*. Tr. by Joseph Donceel (London: Burns & Oates, Ltd. 1970), pp. 9–10.

A study of the Lutheran Confessions will reveal with clarity that a close relationship exists between what the church of Jesus Christ is and what its activity will be in its constant efforts toward doctrinal unity and concord. In fact, the nature of the church is a constitutive element, a paradigm, or model, in the church's formula for concord. When the doctrine of the church is ignored or distorted there will accordingly be no effective or God pleasing (Lutheran) efforts toward achieving purity of doctrine and unanimity in the doctrine.

It will be the purpose of this essay to demonstrate from the Confessions this relationship between the nature of the church and its quest for doctrinal purity and unity and to present the position of the Confessions on this issue which is crucial also today.

I. WHAT IS THE CHURCH?

What is the church? Who are members of the church? This is the fundamental question of all ecclesiology, recognized by Melanchthon in the Augsburg Confession and by the Roman Catholics in the Confutation.[2] One cannot speak to the subject of unity, concord, marks or anything else pertaining to the church until one has determined definitely what the church is. Accordingly, Melanchthon begins Article VII of the Augsburg Confession with a definition of the church and repeats the definition in Article VII.

This definition of the church is very simple and straightforward, so much so that a theologian might erroneously conclude that the doctrine of the church was never thought through totally and a finished definition never presented in our confessions.[3] But the doctrine of the church in our confessions is a finished position and well thought through. And the Lutheran stand concerning the right approach to unity is also clear in our confessions, albeit briefly put. And the relationship between the nature of the church and its quest for doctrinal unity, though not explicitly stated, is, I believe, adumbrated with sufficient force and clarity that there should be no question about it.

---

2 CR 27,102ff. Roman Catholics today too acknowledge as much. See Karl Rahner, "Membership in the Church according to the Teaching of Pius XII's Encyclical 'Mystici Corporis Christi' " in *Theological Investigations*, Vol. 11, Tr. Carl-H. Kruger (Baltimore. Helicon Press, 1963), pp. 1–88.

3 This seems to be the position of Arthur Carl Piepkorn, "What the Symbols Have to Say about the Church" in CTM., Oct., 1955 (XXVI, 10), pp. 721–763. Piepkorn's essay does not answer the question posed by its title, but is rather a very thorough, if at times inaccurate, word study of the word *ecclesia* (*Kirche*) as used in the confessions.

The church, according to Melanchthon in the Augsburg Confession, is the assembly of all believers (AC VII, 1; VIII, 1; Ap VII, 1, 8, 28), or communion of saints (*congregatio sanctorum*). That is the simple definition. In the same vein Luther defines the church as "a little holy flock or community of pure saints under one head, Christ" (LC II, 51), a "holy community or Christian people" (LC II, 49–50, 53). Again he defines the church as the "holy believers and sheep who hear the voice of their shepherd" (SA III, XIII, 2; cf. Apol. VII, 14). In every case Melanchthon and Luther in their definition of the church are attempting to be faithful to the catholic creeds, but especially to the Scriptures as they spoke of the ἐκκλησία and likened it to the body of Christ (Apol. VII, 7, 29; LC II, 47–50).

Having *defined* the church as the Christians or community of believers, the confessions more fully *describe* the church, especially in relation to the Holy Spirit and the righteousness of Christ which the church and its members possess through faith. The church is not merely an association (*Gesellschaft*) of outward ties (*rerum*) and rites, like some political organization, although it may resemble something like this externally, but it is *principaliter* a community (*Gemeinschaft*) of faith and of the Holy Spirit in men's hearts (Apol. VII, 5). Christ renews, sanctifies and rules this church through His Spirit (*ibid.* Eph. 1:22,23). The Spirit brings to the church all the blessings that Christ through His obedience has procured for the church, notably forgiveness and the righteousness (obedience) of Christ offered through the Gospel (LC II, 54–59; Apol. VII, 8, 36). Through the Gospel the Spirit creates, calls and gathers the Christian church (LC II, 45, 53). The church is the locus of the Spirit's work; through it He gathers believers and by it creates and increases sanctification (LC II, 53), "and outside it no one can come to the Lord Christ" (LC II, 45, cf. 56).

The church is a "spiritual people, separated from the heathen . . . by being God's true people, reborn by the Holy Spirit" (Apol. VII, 14). Thus we find Melanchthon often calling the church the "kingdom of Christ" or likening it to the kingdom of Christ "which is righteousness of the heart and the gift of the Holy Spirit" (Apol. VII, 13; cf. 16). Obviously the kingdom of Christ is not something external, but is spiritual, something that has not yet been revealed (*ibid.* 17).

Precisely this is the point of debate with the Roman Catholics. And at just this point the Confutation criticizes the Augsburg Confession. According to Roman opinion the church consisted of those who professed the Christian faith, who assembled around the sacraments and who were under the rule of legitimate pastors and especially the Roman Pontiff.[4] This doc-

---

4 This position has remained the doctrine of the Roman Church ever since the

trine which made only the *profession* of dogmatic faith a criterion for membership in the church and which made submission to the juridical authority of the papacy a *sine qua non* for membership meant in effect that the church was essentially a visible, palpable, empirical entity.[5] And it meant as well that unregenerate and wicked people and hypocrites are true members of the church.[6] At every point Melanchthon takes strong exception to the Roman Catholic doctrine, and Apology VII is in fact a polemic against Rome's teaching that the church is a kind of external society *politia* and that therefore hypocrites can be members of it (Apol. VII, 16–19, 22, 29).

II. THE CHURCH *Proprie Dicta* AND *Late Dicta* (INVISIBLE AND VISIBLE)

But if evil men and hypocrites are not the church or a part of it, they must nevertheless not be separated from it and its outward fellowship (*externa societas*) (Apol. VII, 1, 9, 28). And against the ancient Donatists Melanchthon contends that the sacraments performed by evil men and hypocrites are indeed valid and efficacious (Apol. VII, 2, 3).

This contention of Melanchthon's leads to a highly significant distinction in his ecclesiology, the distinction between the church *proprie dicta* and the church *late dicta*. Against the papal doctrine Melanchthon is forced to state over and over again what the church, strictly speaking, really is, namely, the assembly of saints (Apol. VII, 8, 16), the living body of Christ (12, 29), a spiritual people who are God's true people, born again by the Holy Ghost (14). The church properly speaking is that which has the Holy Spirit (22, 28). The term "Church catholic" does not denote an external government (*externa politia*) "but is made up of men scattered

---

Reformation. It was more precisely set forth after the Reformation by Robert Bellarmine "Liber Tertius de Ecclesia Militante" in *Disputationes de Controversiis Christianae*, Paris, 1615, I, 982.

5 See Bellarmine *ibid.* "The church is an assembly of men, an assembly which is visible and perceptible to the senses just like an assembly of the Roman citizenry, or the kingdom of France or the Republic of Venice." This position, with only minor qualifications and modifications, is still held by Roman Catholic theologians. See Rahner *ibid.* p. 17. "Since the visibleness and visible unity of the Church are constituted by the sacramental and juridical authority of the Church (which latter includes in its turn the teaching and ruling authority of the church), all and only those belong to the Church as members who are visibly, i.e. in the external forum, subject to these two powers of the Church. And everyone who, on the social plane, is cut off or has withdrawn himself from one or both of these powers, is not a member of the Church."

6 Henrick Denzinger, *Enchiridion Symbolaram*, Friburg: Herder, 1957, 424; 485ff.; 588; 627; 629; 631; 838; 1522–25; 1515.

throughout the world who agree on the Gospel and have the same Christ, the same Holy Spirit, and the same sacraments, whether they have the same traditions or not" (10).

At the same time Melanchthon is compelled to use the term "church" in a broad sense meaning territorial churches or groups of congregations. This is no doubt the meaning of the oft used phrase in the Augsburg Confession, "Our churches teach with great unanimity . . ." (AC I, 1; II, 1; III, 1 etc.), or "Our churches condemn . . ." (AC I, 5; II, 3; V, 4 etc.; cf. also AC Summary, 1; Ap. IX, 2; Tr. 12, 14, 16; SA II, IV, 4). In such cases the term no doubt denotes an external entity which calls itself church and professes to believe in Christ. This broader meaning of the term which all the Lutheran confessions employ regularly and with a variety of connotations was recognized and in vogue prior to the Reformation, and Melanchthon cites with favor a Decree of Gratian which says that "the church in the larger sense (*late dicta*) includes both the godly and the wicked and that the wicked are part of the church only in name and not in fact, while the godly are part of the church in fact as well as in name" (Apol. VII, 10).

Perhaps the best account of the distinction is found in Apology VII, 12–13 which we quote: "Hypocrites and evil men are indeed associated with the true church according to external rites. But when it comes to defining the church we must define it as the living body of Christ; and this is the church in fact and in name. We must understand what it is that first of all (*principaliter*) makes us members, that is, living members of the church. If we were to define the church as only an external organization of good and evil persons, then men would not understand that the kingdom of Christ is the righteousness of the heart and the gift of the Holy Spirit, but would judge it to be only an external observance of certain forms of worship and rituals." It is important to note throughout Melanchthon's discussion that he never uses the adjective *externa* to describe the church in the proper sense, but rather to describe what the true church is not, or a caricature of the church; or that which mingles with the church *per accidens* (such as evil men and hypocrites, church rites, the papacy, human traditions and adiaphora, cf. AC XXVI; Apol. VII, 34, 37; XXVII, 27; TR 11; SD X, 15, 27). Meanwhile, the church in the strict sense remains the congregation of believers. Thus, Melanchthon speaks of hypocrites and evil men being mingled with the church (*admixti ecclesiae*, Apol. VVII, 47), being in the church (9) and holding office in the church (*in ecclesia*, 17), of wolves and ungodly teachers running rampant in the church (22), and of hypocrites and wicked men sharing with the church an association of outward marks and being members of the church according to such an association of external marks (28). In this latter case it is obvious that hypocrites cannot be members of the church, strictly speaking, but only in the metonymical sense that chaff will be present among wheat (1). The distinction is often made that hypocrites are in the church but not *of* the church.

This clear distinction in the Lutheran Confessions between the *una sancta* (*ecclesia proprie dicta*) and local and territorial churches, entities possessing external empirical order, discipline, rites and membership (*ecclesia late dicta*), conforms precisely with the later Lutheran distinction between the invisible and visible church.[7] And a very useful and necessary distinction it is. Both Walther and Pieper employ the distinction as being confessional and insist on the basis of Apology VII, 14–19 that the adjective

---

7 Actually, Luther himself followed the distinction, although perhaps not always consciously and in an adumbrated form, as we can see even from his writings in the confessions. And he used the adjective invisible to describe the *una sancta*. See WA &, 710: "Just as the rock [Christ] is without sin, invisible and spiritual, so the church which is without sin, must be invisible and spiritual, and is grasped only by faith." Cf. WA 7, 684; 2, 552; 26, 506. Cf. also Jacob Heerbrand, *Compendium Theologiae*, Wittenberg, 1582, p. 761ff. The distinction between the church invisible in which "all members and true and living members, who are known only to God" and the church visible "which outwardly professes [the faith] and assembles to hear the Word", but "in which are many rotten and dead members, and yet among whom there is a [certain] consensus in doctrine" is clearly articulated by Martin Chemnitz, *Loci Theologici*, Frankfurt, 1604, De ecclesia, Cap. III (III, 308). And Chemnitz attributes the distinction to Luther! It is interesting that this distinction is found stated so explicitly among Lutherans, and in the writings of one who helped author the Formula of Concord. The Reformed theologians to whom the general use of the distinction has often been attributed make much less of it than the Lutherans do. For instance, Amandus Polanus, who debated with Cardinal Bellarmine just as John Gerhard and so many Lutherans had done (See Gerhard, *Loci Theologici*, Tuebingen, 1762, IX, S4ff.) does not employ the distinction, although he would have done well if he had (See Polanus, *Systema Theologiae Christianae*, Geneva, 1612, Lib. 7, Cap. 2ff. [II, 506ff.]. Also William Bucan, *Institutiones Theolagicae*, Geneva, 1609, p. 456, who does not use the distinction.). Unlike Luther and Chemnitz, Melanchthon does not use the adjective invisible in speaking of the *una sancta*. Rather, in his later writings he persistently speaks of the church as visible. However, he does so either because against the Enthusiasts he is viewing the church in relation to its marks which are external (CR 24, 365ff.) or, in opposition to the Roman contention that the Lutheran ecclesiology made the church a mere Platonic idea, Melanchthon is denying that the church viewed as the outward assembly gathered around the Word is an invisible fiction or idea (CR, 21, 825). In every case he is speaking of what was commonly referred to as the assembly of the called, later termed the church visible. For instance, he defines this visible church as such: "The visible church is the gathering of those who embrace the Gospel of Christ and rightly use the Sacraments. In this gathering God is at work through the ministry of the Gospel and causes many to be reborn unto eternal life, but in the gathering are also many who have not been reborn but go along with the pure doctrine" (CR 21, 826). Thus, there is no difference between Melanchthon's ecclesiology on this point and the earlier teaching of Luther and the later teaching of Chemnitz, Gerhard, and the later Lutherans.

"invisible" must be attributed to the church *proprie dicta* inasmuch as the church, as the Apology stresses, is a spiritual assembly of believers dispersed over the entire world (Apol. VII, 10) and often hidden under the cross (18) and is known only to God.[8] Lutherans today who call the distinction unconfessional simply because its later formulation is not found in the confessions *expressis verbis* seem not to have grasped the total implications of the Lutheran doctrine of the Church *proprie dicta*. The distinction between the church *proprie dicta* (invisible) and *late dicta* (visible) only helps us to bear in mind at all times what the church really is.

III. THE MARKS OF THE CHURCH

Although the church is invisible and, as the communion of saints, known only to God, it is a reality together with its unity and all its attributes, just as God is real. Its reality and presence are known by certain marks (*notae* Apol. VII, 5, 7, 20; XIV, 3; also IV, 400). These marks are external (*externae*), visible, audible, empirical. If the church were visible, a mere external association (*externa monarchia*, *externa politia*, Apol. VII, 23, 13), there would be no need for external (empirical) marks.

What are the marks of the church? Melanchthon consistently lists two. They are the pure doctrine of the Gospel and the Sacraments through which the Holy Spirit creates and sustains the church in the first place. Melanchthon says (Apol. VII, 5): "And this same church [the *una sancta*] has also external marks whereby one can recognize it, namely, where God's Word is pure, and the Sacraments are administered in conformity with the same, there certainly is the church and there surely are Christians" (German Text). Luther, in speaking of the marks of the church, has mentioned seven: 1) the true preaching of the Gospel, 2) the right administration of the Baptism, 3) the right use of the Sacrament of the Altar, 4) the right use

---

8 See C. F. W. Walther, *Kirche und Amt* (Erlangen: C. A. Ph. Th.Bläsing, 1852), p. 16ff. Francis Peiper, *Christian Dogmatics*, Tr. Walter Albrecht (St. Louis: Concordia Publishing House, 1953), III, 401 *passim*. I do not understand why Schlink, whose understanding of the Confessions' doctrine of the church seems to be quite perceptive, and Piepkorn refuse to call the *una sancta* invisible on the basis of the Lutheran Confessions, especially since the term invisible has been so clearly defined by the vast number of orthodox Lutherans since Chemnitz and identified exactly with the confessional definition of the *una sancta*. See Edmund Schlink, *Theology of the Lutheran Confessions*, Tr. Paul F. Koehneke and Herbert J. A. Bouman (Philadelphia: Muhlenberg Press, 1961), p. 218; Piepkorn, *op. cit.* In the light of history since the Reformation insistance that the adjective "invisible" be ascribed to the church *proprie dicta* illustrates not only a correct understanding of the doctrine of the church against the Roman Catholic heresy, but also indicates that one has not succumbed to the pressures of constant Roman caricaturing of the Lutheran position.

of the keys, 5) the legitimate calling of ministers to teach and administer the sacraments, 6) public prayer, psalmody and instruction, and 7) crosses and tribulations from without and within.[9] There is no difference on this point between Luther and Melanchthon in the Apology. Luther is obviously speaking of both accidental and essential marks. The former indicate that the church is present, but they are not infallible and not always present (Luther's last four), depending as they do on times and conditions. The latter are constant, essential and infallible.[10]

What is the precise function of a mark (*nota*)? According to Melanchthon in the statement previously cited, it is simply an external sign by which something (otherwise not perceived or seen) can be recognized (*agnosci potest*). Since in the present case these marks are the very means through which the Holy Spirit calls, gathers, enlightens and sanctifies the church, they are indeed constant, essential and infallible, as Gerhard had said.[11] The external marks are what indicate to us that the church, for all its dispersion and hiddenness, really exists (*existere*) and is made up of those who truly (*vere*) believe and are justified (*iustos*). It is no mere idea, or Platonic state (Apol. VII, 20). One can see the practical importance of Melanchthon's doctrine and its great comfort in times of trouble

---

9 *Von den Kinziliis und Kirchen*, WA 50, 628.

10 This is Gerhard's explanation and is quite correct. See *Loci Theologici Loc. XXIII*, Cap. X, Par. 126.

11 See also Leonard Hutter, *Systema Universae Theologiae*, Ulm, 1664, II, 557ff. Hutter lists four criteria for a true mark: 1) it must be adequate to denote its object, 2) it must mark off and distinguish its object from everything else, 3) it must be coextensive with its object, neither broader nor narrower, 4) it must be separable from its object which it denotes. See also Olav Laurelius, *Syntagma Theologicum*, Uppsala, 1641, p. 420 who speaks even more extensively about the nature and function of the marks of the church. We know what the church is, he says, from the definition and description given in Scripture. The marks function to inform us that the church does in fact exist, where it is present, and that it is the true church that is being designated. He says, "The church, since it is the company of those who have been called and chosen and who live in the one fellowship of Word and Sacraments will consequently have marks of such a nature that the church can be distinguished from all other gatherings and these marks will proceed from the essential structure of the church itself." Laurelius' is perhaps one of the most perceptive and complete delineations of the confessional Lutheran doctrine of the marks of the church and the implications of this doctrine for external church unity. The marks show us only where and what the church is. They cannot be used to denote sects—although Christians may be outward members of sects—since they are not founded on the Word, but upon human opinion (423). This does not imply that only the Lutheran church is the church *proprie dicta*. And the Word does not cease being a mark when it is for some reason not taught in all its truth and purity. The intrusion of error does not automatically or immediately destroy the marks of the entire congregation. Paul struggled with this situation at Corinth and Galatia (426). This seems to be essentially what Melanchthon is saying throughout Article VII.

and persecution when so many parties cry, "We are the church." For the marks reveal what the church is and that the "foundation" (1 Cor. 3:12) is Christ; and so long as Christ remains the foundation the church exists and stands (20, 21). But when the article that the forgiveness of sins is received by faith is denied the foundation is also overturned.

The marks must not be confused with the church itself, nor are they to be considered mere attributes of the church. Rome made certain marks—not merely doctrine and sacraments, but also papal jurisdiction and certain church rites—a part of the very nature of the church. Thereby they obscured the doctrine of the church denying that it was simply the total assembly of believers, and made its unity and membership in it depend upon submission to the juridical authority of the papacy and other man-made traditions and rites.

IV. THE UNITY OF THE CHURCH

What is the unity of the church? The term "unity" when applied to the church is analogous to its meaning when applied to God who has brought the church into being. As there is only one God, there can be only one Gospel, one way of salvation, one faith, one baptism (Eph. 4:5–6)—one church (AC VII, 4).[12] The church is therefore one and undivided in essence and in number, "without sector schism", as Luther puts it (LC II, 51). There cannot be two or three or four churches of Christ, only one. In analogy with the unity of God, the church is one also in the sense that it is unique, *sui generis*. There is nothing, no *societas* or entity whatever, that is like the church. And it is, like the One who brought it into being, indivisible. No Lutheran would possibly speak of "fracturing" or dividing the church, the body of Christ, although there may well be divisions in its outer manifestations. The church is one "holy flock or community of pure saints under one head, Christ" (*ibid.*). "*Gemeine*" which Luther uses in this context is a very conscious interpretation of the biblical phrase "body of Christ." So as a body has only one head and a head one body, so it is with the church (*Gemeine*) and Christ, its head.

The church has been called together by the one God, the Holy Ghost, into "one faith, mind and understanding" (*ibid.*). Here we have a description of the church's unity. Luther refers here to both objective faith (doctrine) and subjective faith by which one is justified and brought into the church. The means whereby the church is gathered are the Word and

---

12 The unity of God presupposes the unity of the church in Lutheran theology and calls for unity of worship and doctrine in the church. See Abraham Calov, *Systema Locorium Theologicorum*, Wittenberg, 1655–77, II, 290.

Sacraments, and the church (perceived by its signs, or marks) becomes the locus of the Holy Spirit's gathering and sanctifying His church (LC II, 56). One faith, one doctrine, one Gospel, one baptism, one forgiveness of sins, one church, one God. The church's oneness, like the church itself, is monergistically the work of the Spirit who continually sustains, forgives and comforts the church (LC II, 52–5, 57–9) "through God's Word in the unity of the Christian Church" (55), and continually brings to the church all the treasures and blessings Christ has procured for it (54).

Melanchthon in the Apology describes the unity of the church in much the same way. It is a unity consisting of faith and the righteousness of Christ which is received by faith (Apol. VII, 31). This unity is not affected by differences of rites or customs (33, 34, 36), although uniformity of liturgical rites is beneficial for the tranquility in the church. Without faith in Christ and the Gospel and without the imputed righteousness of Christ in the heart there is no unity in the church at all, just as there is no church (31). There is no question that Melanchthon in his entire discussion of the church and its unity relates it all to his previous article in the *Apology* on justification by faith. Thus, what is necessary for the church's unity is simply that which brings about man's justification before God, and that which brings about the unity itself, namely the Gospel Word (*doctrina evangelii*) and the Sacraments (*administratione sacramentorum*, See Apol. VII, 30; cf. 5; AC VII, 2). And the unity of the church is expressed simply by the agreement (*consentire*) in this doctrine of the Gospel and in the administration of the Sacraments (AC VII, 2). Or, to put it differently, the unity of the church consists in the fact that men scattered throughout the whole world have the same Christ, the same Holy Spirit, the same Sacraments (Apol. VII, 10). It is a spiritual unity of faith.

This doctrine of the unity of the church is evangelical. The Gospel creates the unity, and faith in the Gospel constitutes it. Francis Pieper reflects the spirit of the confessions when he says that wherever there is a denial or diminution of the vicarious satisfaction of Christ a false doctrine of the church results and a distortion of what constitutes its unity.[13] The unity is then based upon human jurisdiction and law, not Gospel. This comment faithfully reflects Melanchthon's constant emphasis in his polemic against the Roman doctrine of the church's unity. Melanchthon's concern and question in his discussion of the church's unity is simply: What brings a poor sinner forgiveness and Christ's righteousness (Apol. VII, 31, 34, 36, 39)? How does the Holy Spirit make a sinner righteous before God? It is by the means of grace, the doctrine of the Gospel and nothing else. That is

---

13. *Christian Dogmatics*, III, 405.

how the Spirit gathers the church and that is how He makes it one. Thus, Fagerberg[14] is correct when he says, "The consequences of the Lutheran view of justification, the sacraments, and the ministry are revealed in the doctrine of the church . . . That the church is conceived of at all points as God's direct work through Word and sacrament without itself mediating grace is the basic view of the church's essence and membership, its origins and unity."

Fagerberg is correct in another point as he comments on the confessional position regarding the unity of the church. He points out, as does Schlink,[15] that the Gospel is never *mere* proclamation devoid of doctrinal content but is always doctrine (*doctrina evangelii*). Therefore the church, the true church and *una sancta*, even though it may be dispersed throughout the world, hidden and suffering under persecution and heretical teachers, and thus invisible, will be not only a believing community, but also a confessing community. As Schlink says, "Since the Confession grows out of the unanimity of the preaching of the Gospel and of faith and serves the preservation of the preaching of the Gospel and of faith, the unity of the church is essentially also the unity of Confession." This conclusion must be drawn from the *consentire* of AC VII, 2. The two attributes of unity and apostolicity ascribed to the church are therefore closely connected, if not identified by the Lutheran confessions. For the unity of the church consists in agreement in the apostolic doctrine (Apol. VII, 38–39).

V. Concord in the Church: The Formula for Concord

The formula for concord in the church as worked out so carefully by the later writers of the Lutheran Confessions is based solidly on the ecclesiology of the earlier Lutheran Symbols. The ecclesiology of the earlier Confessions, including the definition of the church, the unity of the church and the marks of the church, becomes the paradigm or pattern for later confessional and faithful Lutherans in their striving under God to achieve God-pleasing doctrinal agreement and unity among the divided and quarreling churches of the Augsburg Confession in their day. This formula for concord in the churches is both biblical and ecumenical (i.e. applying to the universal church, not just a situation in Saxony at a certain time in history). The writers of the Formula of Concord consciously and consistently *apply* the eccle-

---

14 Holsten Fagerberg, *A New Look at the Lutheran Confessions 1529–1537*, Tr. Gene J. Lund (St. Louis. Concordia Publishing House, 1972), p. 251.

15 *Op. cit.*, p. 270. Cf. Schlink, *op. cit.*, p. 206. Cf. Leif Grane, *Confession Augustana* (Copenhagen: Gyldendal, 1903), pp. 74–5 for the contrary opinion.

siology of the earlier confessions as they attempt to solve under God the problem of divided churches (Lutheranism) in their day. They present no basic ecclesiology themselves—there is no need to do so—but they clearly assume the doctrine of the church articulated in the earlier confessions.

The earlier confessions, on the other hand, do not address themselves explicitly to the matter of achieving doctrinal unity and harmony among divided churches, although implicit in their doctrine of the church and throughout the documents themselves is a concern for consensus in doctrine and a program identical to that spelled out expressly by the later symbols. This fact is perceived as these early confessions warn against heretics and false doctrine. Although false teachers are in the church, they are a curse and scourge upon it. Mingled as they are with the church (*admixti ecclesiae*), these false ministers do administer the sacraments efficaciously; nevertheless (*doch*) they are not to be received nor listened to (Apol. VII, 47–48 [Matt. 7:15; Gal. 1:9]. Cf. also Tr. 38, 41–44, 54, 56, 72; SC III, 5; LC I, 551f., III, 47). Melanchthon and Luther are directing such warnings against Romanists and Zwinglians as well as ancient heretics such as Donatists, Pelagians and the like, who are condemned explicitly in the *Augustana*.

Obviously, just as hypocrites and bad ministers (*mali ministri*), mingled with the church are to be avoided (Ap. VII, 22), so also false doctrine. Only the true doctrine should be taught in the church and adhered to. This fact is brought out in the early confessions by their deep concern for purity of doctrine, even in minutiae, but also by the confession making process itself. And the goal of this concern and this process, namely consensus in the doctrine by the evangelical churches, is actually achieved by the Confessions themselves. The catechisms and the Smalcald Articles are witness of this fact. And the *Augustana* too, with its impressive introductory formula, *Ecclesiae magno consensu apud nos docent* . . . (AC I, 1). So the formula for concord, which embraces the avoidance of false doctrine and the consensus in the pure doctrine of the Gospel and all its articles, later explicitly spelled out, is clearly by the grace of God being employed and carried out by that early *Magna Carta* of the Protestant Reformation, the Augsburg Confession.

What precisely is the formula for concord as it is so carefully worked out by the writers of the *Formula*? And how does the church apply this formula (or model for action) in a given situation? As noted before, the writers of the Formula of Concord clearly take the ecclesiology of the earlier confessions, specifically *Augustana VII* (and also Apology VII and perhaps SA II, IV, 9) as their starting point and model.[16]

---

16 See Appendix.

In accordance with this model the formula for concord for churches that are divided is very simply to achieve consensus in the doctrine and administration of the sacraments. This fact is clearly put by the Formula of Concord in its Summary Formulation (SD, Rule and Norm 1): "The primary requirement for the basic and permanent concord within the church is a summary formula and pattern, unanimously approved (*unanimi consensu approbatus*), in which the summarized doctrine commonly confessed by the churches of the pure Christian religion is drawn from the Word of God" (cf. also Preface, Tappert, p. 6). In other words, concord in the church consists of consensus, and this consensus is expressed and represented by a formal confession (Epit. Rule and Norm, 3–4). This confession is drawn always and only from the Word of God, Scripture (Tappert, p. 6; SD Rule and Norm, 5, 9). And it is unanimously, that is, with total commitment and without qualification (*unanimi consensu*), subscribed by the churches (*ibid.* 1, 2, 6, 8). This consensus means that the churches will never depart nor deviate from the formal confessions (Tappert, p. 9; SD XII, 40).

This formula for concord which takes in hand controverted articles in the churches and settles them in a document (the Book of Concord) on the basis of God's Word is clearly delineated in the Preface to the Book of Concord (Tappert, p. 7ff.). We can trace this process as it was concretely carried out by citing at some length the Preface. "In a Christian fashion they [Christian teachers representing the churches] discussed with one another the articles in controversy and also the just cited written agreement composed with reference thereto. Finally, after invoking almighty God to his praise and glory and after mature reflection and careful diligence, they brought together in good order, by the singular grace of the Holy Spirit, everything that pertains to and is necessary for this end and put it down in one book" (p. 7). "As indicated above, our disposition and intention has always been directed toward the goal that no other doctrine be treated and taught in our lands, territories, schools, and churches than that alone which is based on the Holy Scriptures of God and is embodied in the Augsburg Confession and its Apology, correctly understood, and that no doctrine be permitted entrance which is contrary to these" (p. 12). "We desire particularly that the young men who are being trained for service in the church and for the holy ministry be faithfully and diligently instructed therein, so that the pure teaching and confession of the faith may be preserved and perpetuated among our posterity through the help and assistance of the Holy Spirit until the glorious advent of our only Redeemer and Saviour Jesus Christ" (*ibid.*). "Since this is the way things are, and since we are certain of our Christian confession and faith on the basis of the divine, prophetic, and apostolic Scripture and have been adequately assured of this in our hearts and Christian consciences through the grace of the Holy Spirit, the most acute and urgent necessity demands that in the presence of so many intrusive errors, aggravated scandals, dissensions, and long-standing schisms a Christian explanation and reconciliation of all the disputes which have arisen should come into being. Such an explanation must be thoroughly grounded in God's Word so that pure doctrine can be recognised and distinguished from adulterated doctrine . . ." (p. 13). "Therefore, just as from the very beginning of this Christian agreement of ours it was never our disposition or intention—as it is not now—to keep this salutary and most necessary effort toward concord hidden and concealed in darkness, away from everyone's eyes, or to put the light of divine truth under a basket or a table, we ought not suspend or postpone its printing and publication any longer. We do not have the slightest doubt that all pious people who have an upright love for divine truth and for Christian, God-pleasing concord will, together with us, take Christian pleasure in this salutary, most necessary, and Christian effort and will allow nothing to stand in the way of this cause and the promotion of God's glory and the common welfare, both eternal and temporal. In conclusion, we repeat once again that we are not minded to manufacture anything new by this work of agreement or to depart in any way at all, either in content or in formulation, from the divine truth that our pious forebears and we have acknowledged and confessed in the past, for our agreement is based on the prophetic and apostolic Scriptures and is comprehended in the three Creeds as well as in the Augsburg Confession, submitted in the year 1530 to Emperor Charles V, of kindest memory, in the Apology that followed it, and in the Smalcald Articles and the Large and Small Catechisms of that highly enlightened man, Dr. Luther. On the contrary, we are minded by the grace of the Holy Spirit to abide and remain unanimously in this confession of faith and to regulate all religious controversies and their explanations according to it. In addition, we have resolved and purpose to live in genuine peace and concord with our fellow-members, the electors and estates in the Holy Roman Empire, and also with other Christian potentates, according to the content of the ordinances of the Holy Empire and of special treaties into which we have entered with them, and to demonstrate toward everyone, according to his station, all affection, service, and friendship. We likewise purpose to cooperate with one another in the future in the implementation of this effort at concord in our lands, according to our own and each community's circumstances, through diligent visitation of churches and schools, the supervision of printers, and other salutary means. If the current controversies about our Christian religion should continue or new ones arise, we shall see to it that they are settled and composed in timely fashion before they become dangerously widespread in order that all kinds of scandal might be obviated" (pp. 13–14).

I have quoted at length these words from the Preface to the Book of Concord because the entire Lutheran program for concord is clearly spelled out there. Article X of the Formula of Concord simply applies these basic principles as it responds to the controversy concerning adiaphora in the Lutheran churches. A few observations might be made about the basis for concord as the Confessions speak of it in the above citations and elsewhere. 1. Consensus in the church is clearly the work of the Holy Spirit, and it is only by His grace and guidance that confessions are formulated and accepted on the basis of the divine Word. 2. The Confessions which are worked out by the grace of God actually settle doctrine and become the basis, or formula, for concord. 3. Those who identify with these confessions and subscribe them do so without reservation; and they commit these confessions to their posterity and for all times (SD Rule and Norm, 16; cf. SD VII, 30–31). 4. This common and unanimous summary of the churches' faith becomes a rule and judge for all other books and writings for every age (SD, Rule and Norm, 10, 11). 5. A formal confession bringing about concord and exhibiting consensus in the churches will not only present the pure doctrine correctly, but will also accuse adversaries who teach otherwise (1 Tim. 3:9; Titus 1:9; 2 Tim. 2:24; 3:16) and condemn false doctrine (*ibid.* 14ff.). 6. The acceptance of confessions based on Scripture which serve as the basis for concord always entails a *certainty* (*unanimi consensu*, Tappert, p. 9 *passim*) of the doctrine contained therein; thus *Bekenntnis* becomes *bekennen*, a formula for confessing and witness, the confessional church becomes a confessing church. And this is the very burden and mission of the church: to share and witness to the pure doctrine of the Gospel contained in her confessions (Ap. VII, 8), to preach the Gospel according to a pure understanding of it and to administer the Sacraments in accordance with the divine word (AC VII, 2). Thus the marks of the church will be in conformity with the pattern of sound doctrine found in the churches' formal confessions. 7. Although it is the Gospel in the narrow sense that creates the church, the *una sancta*, as we have earlier shown, it is Spirit-wrought agreement in the Gospel in the wide sense ("the doctrine and all its articles") which brings about *concordia* in the visible church. 8. Using the terminology of Chemnitz, the seventeenth century dogmaticians and our Missouri Synod fathers (Walther, Pieper, *et al*), it is quite proper to say that the writers of the Confessions saw the churches of the Augsburg Confession as the true visible church of Christ on earth, and this by virtue of their formal orthodox symbols. If one does not believe that an orthodox visible church is possible, it would appear that one does not consider the consensus (exhibited in a formal confession) in the doctrine and all its articles a possibility either. In such a case one cannot be a truly confessional Lutheran. Again we see the relationship between the ecclesiology of our Confessions and the program for concord in divided churches.

APPENDIX

The similarity between AC VII and SD X, 31 is striking and the writers of the Formula deliberately carry out the implications of AC VII as they address themselves to the problem of church fellowship and consensus in doctrine in Article X and elsewhere in the FC (especially, Rule and Norm and Introduction to the Book of Concord). Both affirm that differences in church customs and adiaphora do not affect that unity. Both refer to the marks of the church and agreement in these marks. But are there differences also between the two statements? Does the statement in the FC at all points correctly understand and interpret AC VII? Does it employ the crucial terms (church, unity, Gospel) precisely as does the AC VII? Let me now compare these two formative statements, pointing to what appear to be parallels, similarities, dissimilarities and difficulties in interpreting the two in harmony. We may then better understand the relationship between the two.

1. The two passages do not speak to the same situation. The AC, though considered to be just as ecumenical as the Creeds, is written as an apology or confession of the doctrinal position and understanding of the Gospel held by the Lutherans. The FC serves to settle doctrinal controversies between a divided Lutheranism. These differences in situation and purpose must not be overemphasized, however. Both confessions are consciously catholic and evangelical (although the FC is not so all-embracing in scope, confining itself to the consideration only of controverted articles). And both are written and considered to be adequate symbols in the strict sense of the Word.

2. The term "church" cannot have the same referent in both statements. Melanchthon defines the church *proprie dicta* in AC VII and no doubt uses the term in that sense throughout the short article. The FC, if not using the term in the usual *late dicta* sense, as the total number of those who outwardly profess to be Christians and gather about the means of grace, is obviously using it as something other than the *una sancta*. It is using the term in the sense of local or territorial churches. The German text has "churches" in the plural and the Latin says that "no church" can

condemn another because of differences in ceremonies. The usage here seems quite the same as the plural in AC I, 1 and similar introductory formulae throughout the AC (cf. Epit. X, 4 *ecclesiae* [*Gemeine*] *in ubivis terrarum*).

3. The terms "Gospel" and "doctrine" seem to be used indiscriminately and interchangeably in the two contexts as the Gospel in the wider sense, and not simply in contrast to the Law (as, e.g., in Apol. IV, 5; SD V, 1, 17–20 *passim*). This definitely is the thinking of the writers of the FC at this point as they try to apply in their day the implications of Apol. VII, 2–4. In Article X they employ indiscriminately and interchangeably such terms as "pure doctrine" (*die reine Lehre; sincera doctrina*, 3, 14), "the pure doctrine of the Gospel" (5, 10; cf. SD Intro. 3), "the doctrine and all that pertains to it" (*die Lehre und was zur ganzen Religion gehöret; pia doctrina iuxta verbum Dei et quicquid omnino ad sinceram religionem pertinet*, 10), simply "doctrine" (16), or "the doctrine and all its articles" (*die Lehre und allen derselben Artikel; doctrina et in omnibus illius partibus*, 31); and in every case they have in mind the Gospel in the wider sense, as the entire Christian doctrine (See SD V, 3–6).

Does Melanchthon mean the same thing by "*doctrina evangelii*" in AC VII, 2? I believe he does. But there are some difficulties in my interpretation which I should mention before making my case. And there are some arguments for taking "doctrine of the Gospel" in VII, 2 in the narrow sense which need to be mentioned first.

If Melanchthon uses the term "*doctrina evangelii*" as the Gospel in the broad sense, then he is making the Gospel in this wider sense a mark of the church; and then the means of grace *per se* cannot be the marks of the church. Otherwise, the law would be a means of grace together with the Gospel, a position utterly unevangelical and contrary to Melanchthon's theology (Apol. IV; XII; Cf. FC IV, V, VI). I suspect that Lutheran scholars have perceived that these are indeed the unpleasant consequences of interpreting Melanchthon's usage of "*doctrina evangelii*" in the broad sense here. Therefore they have jumped at the opportunity of interpreting the term in the narrow (and at time minimalistic, even anti-doctrinal) sense (Grane, *op. cit.*, 74). This might be a neat and consistent explanation if one were dealing only with the AC and not the Apology or Formula of Concord. Melanchthon thus appears consistently evangelical and orthodox in never ascribing to the Gospel in the broad sense (the Christian doctrine) the office of bringing a sinner to faith, something he never would have intentionally done (See AC V, Apol. XII); to ascribe to the Law the function of working faith would be a denial of the Christian faith. Furthermore,

Melanchthon would then be using the term "Gospel" in the same sense he apparently does in AC VII, 1 and most certainly employs in AC V, 1–2.

But against this popular and facile interpretation let me offer a few solid arguments for interpreting *"doctrina evangelii"* in the wide sense in this context.

a) The fact that Melanchthon speaks of the *doctrine* of the Gospel here, whereas he always speaks merely of the Gospel when referring to it in the narrow sense as that through which the Holy Spirit converts the sinner and begets faith might bear weight (see also the German text); although such close exegesis of the usage of terms in the Confessions is often perilous and cannot stand by itself.

b) This interpretation does not ascribe to Melanchthon a slip whereby he ascribes to the law or to the Christian doctrine as a whole the office of declaring forgiveness or working faith. I am suggesting that *"doctrina evangelii"* should be taken as Gospel in the broad sense in paragraph 2 and "Gospel" in the previous sentence in the strict sense. Paragraph 1 in the German text uses the term *"Evangelium"* twice, obviously in two different senses, so it is not at all strange to find Melanchthon switching meanings suddenly (See AC XXVIII, 5).

c) Melanchthon in all his confessional writings teaches that the Gospel in the strict and narrow sense cannot do its saving and justifying work unless the law has first carried out its *opus alienum*, of showing the sinner his lost condition and driving him to contrition (Apol. XII, 49ff. *passim*). Furthermore, Melanchthon insists, particularly in his monumental discussions of justification and repentance (Apol. IV and XII), that an error concerning the law and its function will *eo ipso* result in an error in one's understanding and application of the Gospel in the narrow sense. This is Luther's emphasis too as he demonstrates in the Smalcald Articles that the Roman aberrations concerning the invocation of the saints, monasteries, the papacy, etc. are contrary to the Gospel in the narrow sense, i.e. the article concerning Christ and His work (SA II, IIff.). Could Melanchthon, who was as anti-Antinomian as Luther or any of the later Lutherans and who saw clearly the organic unity of all Christian doctrine, have excluded all consideration of the Law and all the chief articles of faith which were not part of the Gospel in the narrow sense as he speaks of consensus in the Gospel and the administration of the sacraments as essential for the unity of the church and later calls the doctrine of the Gospel and the correct administration of the sacraments marks of the church? Article II in the AC on original sin was in no sense part of the Gospel in the narrow sense. And yet it is clear that Melanchthon thinks that a denial of this doctrine or aberration concerning it is disruptive of the unity of the church and under-

mines the Gospel itself (Apol. II, 33. Cf. SA III, I, 11 and SD I, 34–48 and
SD V, 20, where the preachment of the Law is woven into the definition of
the Gospel in the narrow sense).

d) Both the adversaries in the Confutation and the later Lutherans, so
far as I can determine, understand *"doctrinae evangelii"* in the AC as a designation of the Gospel in the broad sense. Otherwise, the Confutation
would not have let the matter go without comment. And it is incredible
that Chemnitz, Selnecker, Chytraeus and other contributors to the FC
would have deliberately or mistakenly misinterpreted Melanchthon as they
draw from AC VII and in so doing consistently refer to the Gospel in the
broad sense as they speak of consensus in the doctrine and all its articles as
necessary for fellowship and recognition among the churches.

e) Finally, the twelfth article of the Schwabach Articles, the precursor
of AC VII, clearly refers to the invisible church while at the same time
speaking of the unity as embracing faith in the doctrine and all its articles.
The article reads: "This church is none other than the believers in Christ,
who hold, believe, and teach the above named articles, and items, and are on that
account persecuted and martyred in the world." (*Bekenntnisschriften*, p. 61)
(Cf. T. Mueller "notes on the 'Satis Est' in article VII of the Augustana",
CTM, XVIII, 6 (June, 1947), pp. 401–410.)

4. The term "unity" (German: *Einigkeit*; Latin: *unitas* in AC and Apol.,
concordia, consonantia, consensio, consensus in FC) is, I believe, used in essentially the same sense in AC VII and FC X. Surely the *agreement (miteinan-
der einig; concordes firirint)* in the doctrine and its articles is the same in the
intention of the writers of FC X as the agreement (*consentire*) of AC VII.
It is apparent, as Piepkorn points out, that the German *Einigkeit* is rendered by *unitas* in the AC and Apol. and by *concordia, consensus*, etc., never
by *unitas*, in FC X (*op. cit.*, 759). Piepkorn also points out that
Melanchthon usually speaks of *Einigkeit der Kirche*, not *Einigkeit in der
Kirche*. On the basis of these differences in expression he concludes that the
FC is not speaking of the unity of the church at all, but merely of organizational integrity and harmony, external union or inter-communion, external unification which "Christians have a role in". This is a facile and
fascinating theory. But it does not do justice to what the FC actually says
about *Einigkeit (concordia)* in the church. Concord in the FC is not something organizational, not external union at all, but agreement in the doctrine and all its articles, precisely what Melanchthon was talking about in
the AC. I would submit that the difference in expression, if it has any significance at all, is due to the fact that the FC is using the term "church" in
a different sense from Augustana VII, as we have already observed, not that
the concept of unity is different in the two confessions. In the one case (AC

VII) it is the unity of the *una sancta* the spiritual unity of the faith, perceived by the marks of the church, that is referred to; in the other (FC X) it is the same unity (*consentire de doctrina evangelii et de administratione sacramentorum*) *in* the territorial churches and congregations that is referred to.

A WORD
FROM HIS FRIENDS

The Holy Trinity 1996 issue of *Logia: A Journal of Lutheran Theology*, dedicated to the memory of Robert Preus, contains a number of brief articles about Robert Preus. Four of them have been included in this volume to demonstrate the esteem with which Preus was regarded by his peers.

Commemoration Sermon for Dr. Robert D. Preus

David P. Scaer

Then the days of weeping and mourning for Moses were ended
(Dt 34:8).

Two things were remarkable about the funeral orations for Dr. Preus. He was the greatest Lutheran theologian of our time. He also happened to be a sinner—hardly startling information. For a reminder, the Monday edition of the most carefully read newspaper in the Missouri Synod put that fact in headlines six times. "Who's the best" and "who's the worst" at anything, including doing theology or sinning, is an open question, but Robert Preus himself spoke in superlatives.

Four days before he died, Dr. Preus introduced Pastor Gottfried Martens at the Sasse Symposium. He mentioned that Martens's idea for a doctoral dissertation came from his elective on justification. Justification and inspiration were what Preus was all about. He introduced his sermons like this: "The text is taken from the second chapter of St. Paul's letter to the Galatians, which the Holy Ghost caused to be recorded by inspiration." It was like the first course in dogmatics, but better. Then he would recite a hymn which had to do with faith, fear of sin, the inevitability of death, and salvation in Christ. He was the ablest of dogmaticians, but he never preached doctrinal essays. That was not his style. He preached Jesus Christ.

Preus's introductions were full of hyperboles. Fort Wayne had the best students, faculty and campus. Some squirmed with feigned modesty. The 1980s have already become legendary as the best of times. Ask the students. History may in these next years again prove his exaggerations right. Preus encouraged when we were depressed.

Exile from his own church and seminary brought on a depression of his soul that only a few experience and from which nearly all flee. Some still shout, "If this man were not an evildoer, we would not have handed him over." Let these voices be forever silent. Abandonment by friends and desertion by brothers, by those whom you love, is God's ultimate approval, though it does not seem that way at the time. "A man's enemies are those of his own household." Luther called it *Anfechtungen*, God's masks. In the Psalms it's *eli eli lama sabachthani*. For Jesus it was: "So persecuted they the prophets which were before you." Divine affliction perfects the saint. Robert Preus in his last years was perfected with a divine vengeance. He bore those marks in his body and soul. Friend and foe watched him age.

Preus's introduction of Dr. Martens was full of his customary compliments. In his Erlangen University dissertation Martens showed that the Lutheran World Federation was not able to define the chief doctrine of faith. Justification is not an existential experience, something within the believer, but it happens in Christ and gives faith its certainty. Paul said Christ is our justification. Preus was about to say Martens had been his best student. He caught himself in mid-sentence. With so many other students present, he couldn't do it. A father cannot say he loves one child more than another. His students were his sons. If the last seven years had been kinder to him, as many prayed, and had he lived another decade, as he had planned, the thousands of students who counted him as their father would have increased. A veritable Abraham. Put Preus in the commons after chapel and it was jammed. Put Preus in the Lone Star State in a hot August and the pastors gave up their vacations. "Where the body is, there the eagles gather," and they gathered and kept gathering and they are gathering in this place today. Like a Lutheran John Wesley, he had more students outside locked classrooms than we had inside. If the doors of one pulpit were shut, a world opened to him. Students are here today because of him and they will still come.

On the night before Preus died, an emeritus colleague said we had to let the past go. The next morning the past actually refused to go away. He was on the phone with Bill Weinrich with plans for his place at the seminary. The hands of the clock were being turned back, so it seemed. Twice banished like Jacob, he was returning from Egypt to join Israel in her march. In hours God rendered nostalgia useless. From Nebo he saw the future of a seminary which reflected who he was, but to which God did not permit him to return. "So Moses the servant of the Lord died in the land of Moab." An era in the synod had ended. The bell had tolled on his generation. Preus more than anyone else set the tone of the age and determined its character. The top half of the hour glass had discharged its sands. The silver cord was snapped. The golden bowl was broken. The dust returned to the earth. And we watched.

Some said it was only his charisma. They were right. His person, piety, theology, call, and ministry were his charisma from God. If the seminary students are now discouraged from hammering out theological differences, Preus talked theology all the time—as much with his family as with his students. Since he was what he believed, he could no more let his call be taken from him than he could let the charge of false doctrine against him stand, especially a charge that it was wrong to hold that Christ permeates theology in all its parts. Unanswered false doctrine would let lies masquerade as God's truth. He fought. He was vindicated. He paid a price. We are paying that price without him.

My classmates are agreed to a man that dogmatics in the mid-1950s was a completely undistinguished enterprise. That's a polite way of saying it was dull. You read the book. The highlight of the day was a poorly worded quiz. When Preus came to St. Louis in 1957, the change was radical. He had the intellectual capacity to recognize where the church was going and the conviction and courage to do something about it. And he did. Around him gathered a generation of students who caught the contagion of his convictions. From this confessional revival we were born. When students are talking theology outside the classrooms, you know the enterprise is alive. Authoritarianism kills theology. Now his students are found in the pulpits and classrooms everywhere. They are still doing theology at this symposium, which was his brainchild. Luther disputed the church councils. Preus questioned a synod's direction. Lutherans cannot surrender that right. Edicts, decrees, resolutions, opinions, and policies cannot take the place of theology. Church councils can and do err and will. That's Luther.

Unattended on the desk rests the pen of the scholar of classical Lutheranism. The popular young dogmatics teacher of the 1950s and 1960s is gone. Death has removed the lonely champion of the St. Louis seminary of the early 1970s. Where would St. Louis, St. Catharines, and Fort Wayne be without him? But life denied him the honors which men with safely concealed courage and fractional intellectual ability continue to receive in abundance. If no seminary honored him with *doctor divinitatis honoris causa*, a grateful church may recognize him as *doctor ecclesiae*. He was a teacher of our church in a sense that only a few men in our 150 years are. He encapsulated a theological generation within himself. He has departed. Honors given in death can never compensate for the recognition life was embarrassed to give.

Robert Preus fought his first battle for the Bible: "us conservatives versus those moderates." Issues were clear, or at least clearer than they are now. We are in another conflict whose first battle was Preus's last. When he was tried for the alleged christological heresy, he responded at his trial with the hymn: "Jesus, Jesus, only Jesus / Can my heartfelt longing still." St. Paul had a similar problem: to live was Christ and to die was gain. Preus has gained. We must content ourselves with Christ alone. If the demythologizing of the 1970s was a twentieth-century form of Rationalism, then a neo-evangelicalism of spiritual self-advancement, rapacious self-analysis, financial self-promotion, and emotional self-satisfaction is only another form of self-centered Pietism where Christ again is pushed to the side and our weak faith is put in the center.

"[Preus] was a witness for the truth, the truth of the biblical gospel, a real teacher of the church. He was a confessional Lutheran who confessed that faith all through his life. He did not waver; he did not compromise the Lutheran Confessions. He followed his mentor, Luther, and taught the theology of the cross. And he lived the theology of the cross, which is never easy. That was his accomplishment in life, the glory of his ministry, and his legacy to the church, all by grace alone." Not my words but his.

Our ensign is lowered, but God shall raise another Gideon for us around whom banners shall fly. On the bottom of Robert Preus's funeral folder was Revelation 14:13, "Then I heard a voice from heaven say, 'Write: Blessed are the dead who die in the Lord from now on.' 'Yes,' says the Spirit, 'they will rest from their labor.' " The last words of that verse were left out: "For their works follow them." For Robert Preus these words may have been the least important, but for us they are the most important. For the greatest work of faith is restoring the foundations, preserving the pure doctrine, and preaching the gospel. This he did!

Those who die in the Lord are absorbed into his wounds and are safely hidden under his altar on which he offers himself as an eternal sacrifice to God. As God's priests they are not silent, but they join Jesus, our High Priest, in praying to the eternal Father that he would deliver us from sin, death, and all evil. To their prayers for us we respond with our hymns so that only one song of praise rises in the power of the Holy Spirit from earth and heaven to the Father of all mercies and to him who washed us by his blood. In the poverty of sin, but in the conviction of faith, we salute that soldier who fought for the faith and won.

All hail mighty legions! You toiled in tears and pain.
Farewell! Sing salvation's glad refrain!
Swing high your palms. Lift up your voice.
Eternal praise belongs to God and the Lamb.
Farewell, dear friend, farewell.

Robert Preus, Historian of Theology

John Stephenson

When Robert and Donna Preus, holidaying in England with Steve and Katy Briel, treated my wife and me to dinner along with Ron and Carol Feuerhahn, Bonnie and I approached their Cambridge hotel with no little trepidation. Just married and fresh from passing my Ph.D. oral exam, in the summer of 1983 I was a Lutheran of less than five years' standing, greatly curious to learn more of the ELCE's big sister across the ocean. Several Americans passing through Cambridge had chilled my spine with horror stories of a humorless, nay downright fulminating Torquemada figure responsible for turning the Fort Wayne seminary into a training school for guards at the dead orthodox concentration camps that Missouri's parishes had allegedly become.

The real Robert Preus swiftly exorcised the caricature assembled by many unkind tongues, whose owners took the easy route of substituting scornful satire for reasoned engagement. Over a twelve-year period, mention of Dr. Preus in the Stephenson household conjured up memories of his infectious smile and unbounded generosity. Already by the time we left Fort Wayne after my year of colloquy study (1984) and oftentimes thereafter, my wife would voice her strong impression that Robert Preus wanted the best for the church, whether in the parish, the classroom, or the mission field. This gifted man lived for things other than his own reputation or comfort.

As a professor I have observed the dire burden invariably placed on a seminary president, who must be pastor, churchman, theologian, administrator, diplomat, and much else besides. With the Oxbridge model of academic life still dominating my mind, back in 1984 I had little sense of the pressures then borne by Dr. Preus in his North American context, but was hugely impressed by the quality of the conversations he would initiate when I stopped by his office in connection with the nuts and bolts of my colloquy program. This Midwesterner was cosmopolitan, *au fait* with the churchly, theological, and cultural goings-on of several continents. His reading ranged far beyond theology—at some juncture in 1984 he returned from his Minnesota cottage eager to discuss a volume on English society under the later Stuarts. Preus's theological learning, worn lightly, was profound, and his vocabulary, though never shown off, was immense. As we later corresponded about the progress of his dogmatics series, I discovered how unparochial was this deep-dyed Synodical Conference Lutheran, who entertained considerable respect for Joseph Cardinal Ratzinger, whom he once labeled "more Catholic—in the best sense of the word—than the pope."

The many tributes recently paid to Robert Preus as this generation's premier dogmatician of the Missouri Synod have over-looked the remarkable yet widely forgotten fact that his major full-length works rank under the heading of historical theology. Along with his Edinburgh dissertation *The Inspiration of Scripture*, the two volumes of *The Theology of Post-Reformation Lutheran Theology* are, properly speaking, historical studies clearing a path for systematics. A winsome raconteur in the classroom and at the dinner table, Preus delighted to tell the story of the epochs, personalities, and issues of Lutheran Orthodoxy, authoring the only major study of this chapter of theological history available in the English language. The historical dimension remained prominent in the writings which, notwithstanding his increased administrative duties, Preus devoted to the Formula and Book of Concord in the late 1970s. Significant contributions to recent church history can be found in the elderly Preus's review of John Tietjen's memoirs, and in his obituary remarks on his brother. The planned third volume of *The Theology of Post-Reformation Lutheranism* ended abruptly in the locus of angelology to leave the discipline of historical theology the loser. Preus once explained to me that systematics has no subsistence of its own, but exists as an alloy of exegetical and historical theology.

Preus's love of the past was not the flip side of a hatred of the present; respect for former practitioners of Lutheran Orthodoxy did not lead him to practice a blinkered repristinationism insensitive to the needs of the present. In the first volume of *The Theology of Post-Reformation Lutheranism*, he related how John Gerhard added philosophy to exegesis and history as a third strand to be woven into the texture of systematic theology. While not uncritical of Gerhard's innovation, Preus was himself an attentive student of modern thought; he strove for an updated confessionalism that would address today's issues in contemporary language.

If a fanatic is one who can't change his mind and won't change the subject, Robert Preus must be spared this epithet on both counts. As Kurt Marquart noted in his Preface to *A Lively Legacy*, Preus's theological career was not spent "riding pet hobbyhorses," but involved "a creative, not uncritical, appropriation of the tradition." As ecclesiastical trends shifted his attention from *sola Scriptura* to *sola gratia* while his devotion remained focused on *solus Christus*—his only criticism of the Sasse Symposium papers was that they did not contain enough Christology for his taste— Preus went out of his way to encourage and enter into the work of other, especially younger, scholars. The Robert Preus of liberal caricature would have hit the roof when presented with Gottfried Martens's mammoth term paper on the understanding of the *ex opere operato* principle in the early Lutheran Confessions. Martens instead received an A+ grade fortified with more than a decade of high praise. This teacher could be persuaded by a student that classical Lutheranism had misrepresented Roman sacramentology. Preus thus exercised the chief cardinal virtue of prudence under the aspect of *docilitas*. It is the mark of a great teacher to be himself teachable.

Robert Preus's scripturally and confessionally bounded open-mindedness on disputed historical and systematic issues was apt to be accompanied by superabundant graciousness. As in the case of the *ex opere operato* principle, so also on the matter of the Consecration in the Lord's Supper Preus allowed the cumulative weight of evidence to overrule long-standing opinion. While he never became an ardent "consecrationist," Preus conceded that later Lutheran Orthodoxy departed from the fullness of Luther's and Chemnitz's confession as embodied in FC SD VII. Whenever the Consecration came up for discussion, he would point out that the issue was settled by Luther's quotation of Augustine in the Large Catechism to the effect that "The Word is added to the element, and it becomes a sacrament." Almost a decade ago a virulently polemical *ad hominem* article of mine on this issue generated at least as much heat as it did light. Though this unmannerly blast occasioned Preus great embarrassment, he never rebuked me for the substance of what I wrote, even though he certainly regretted my tone.

As we lunched together three days before his death, I was struck by the contrast between the youthful zest of his ongoing passion for good theology on the one hand, and the painful evidence of how the vendetta of officialdom against him had both outwardly aged and inwardly hurt Preus on the other. Lunch turned into a tutorial on the methodology of orthodox Lutheran systematics given with an eye to future work on the dogmatics series. While Preus spoke of the progress of volume three of *The Theology of Post-Reformation Lutheranism* and announced his intention to get down in earnest to his fascicle on justification, his chief concern lay in encouraging the labors of younger scholars. This modest man had no greed for fame, wishing simply that God be glorified for the monergism of grace in the second and third articles of the Creed. Yet with the passing of both Preus brothers, who has the requisite fluency in Latin to undertake the historical scholarship that would allow the seventeenth century to speak to our present?

In recent years Preus had several times signed his letters with "Robert," thus granting permission for me to address him by his Christian name. The contempt heaped on him by his enemies reinforced my old-world inclination to stick with the respectful, but not obsequious, vocative "Dr. Preus," but I was both moved and delighted to return from the Maple Grove funeral to find on my desk a handwritten letter on the day before his death, expressing his enjoyment of the Sasse Symposium ("a great conference"), and ending with "Yours, in Christ, Robert." Looking back on last October, I rejoice to have been permitted to say a personal thank you to the yet living Dr. Preus at the symposium banquet before bringing greetings from the St. Catharine's seminary over his mortal remains. Thank you, Robert, for being to me a kind, fatherly friend and mentor. May God grant to your many spiritual sons the grace to continue and complete the work you began for His glory and the Gospel's lively sound and spread.

THE "REALIST PRINCIPLE" OF THEOLOGY

KURT MARQUART

ROBERT PREUS DELIVERED HIS REFORMATION LECTURES at Bethany College and Seminary on the subject "How Is the Lutheran Church to Interpret and Use the Old and New Testaments?" The year was 1973. At that very time Preus was at the center of a fierce struggle that led to the "Seminex" eruption a few months later. Forged in the furnace of that conflict, Preus's hermeneutical theses clearly mark and document the total incompatibility between the theology of the *Book of Concord* and the ideology of historical criticism.

As the fourth of his six theses Preus lists "Luther's Realist Principle." This is nothing to do with any philosophical theory. It means that Luther "was a simple realist in the sense of the early Christians in their antipathy to docetism, Gnosticism and pagan mythologies."[1] The whole scope is theological, not philosophical: "The doctrines revealed in Scripture and the acts of God recounted there have a real basis, a real referent, or there could be no theology at all [for] Luther."[2] Like Luther, the authors of the Confessions "did believe that history and reality underlay the theology of Scripture." Citing election, the sacraments, justification, the virgin birth, miracles, resurrection, and ascension, Preus concludes: "Any theology of non-event is unthinkable to Luther and our Confessions."[3] By contrast historical criticism, with Zwingli as a forerunner, reduces Christianity

> to a religion of ideas or truths which are not based upon historic facts
> or reality (Hegel, Strauss, Troeltsch, Ritschl, Harnack, Idealism, Clas-

---

1 Robert Preus, "How Is the Lutheran Church to Interpret and Use the Old and New Testaments?" *Lutheran Synod Quarterly* 14 (Fall 1973): 31–32.

2 Ibid., 31.

3 Ibid., 32.

sical Liberalism). Or one may retreat into subjectivity (Kierkegaard, Tillich, Bultmann, Kaesemann and the post-Bultmannians), or Schwaermerei (E. Brunner, K. Barth). But in both cases one has departed from historic Christianity which is based upon the reality of a living God acting in real history.[4]

Responding to the essay, Prof. B. W. Teigen saw in this realism "the heart of the difference" between Lutheran and historical-critical hermeneutics.[5]

Preus kept returning to this crucial theme whenever he treated of hermeneutics. So for instance he specified "biblical realism, a presupposition for biblical interpretation," in his discussion of the hermeneutics of the Formula of Concord.[6] There he introduced the word "ontological" in rejecting the historical-critical approach: "These exegetes claim to be faithful to Scripture and even to its *sensus literalis*, although they do not believe often in the historic or ontological reality underlying biblical assertions."

Having pointed out the repeated use of *vere* (verily, truly) in the Augsburg Confession—regarding God, sin, Christ's redemptive suffering and resurrection, and his sacramental presence—Preus concludes:

> The *vere* is added to underline the fact that *est* expresses reality as used in Scripture and theology, even when figurative language is employed. For instance, the right hand of God may indeed be a figurative expression, but it denotes a reality.

Highly significant is this conclusion: "In fact the very doctrine of the real presence of the body and blood is a classical expression of the principle [of realism]."

Elsewhere[7] Robert Preus—in the name of Luther's "Christocentricity . . . always affirmed in a doctrinal and realistic soteriological context"—castigated "modern liberal theologians since the Enlightenment [who] cannot accept the historical or in many cases the theologico-ontological (Incarnation, Trinity, etc.) referents of biblical assertions." Indeed, if Christology is thus reduced to "mere general spiritual truths, religious ideas, symbolic language, eternal truths, experience, myth, anthropology, then the very

---

4 Ibid., 48.

5 Ibid., 59.

6 Robert Preus, "The Hermeneutics of the Formula of Concord," in *No Other Gospel*, ed. Arnold J. Koelpin (Milwaukee: Northwestern Publishing House, 1980), 332.

7 Robert Preus, "A Response to the Unity of the Bible," in *Hermeneutics, Inerrancy, and the Bible*, ed. Earl D. Radmacher and Robert D. Preus (Grand Rapids: Zondervan Publishing House, 1984), 678–679.

term Christocentricity of Scripture is a piece of deceptive theological blather."

In his earlier contributions to Montgomery's *Crisis in Lutheran Theology* in 1967 Preus had not yet defined a "realism principle" as such, or talked about "ontology." But all the same basic concerns are there, as are extensive polemics against non-historical readings of Genesis or the Gospels. One final citation will have to suffice here:

> It is not by accident that the central doctrine of justification is preceded in the AC by the articles on God, Creation, the Fall and Original Sin, Christ and his work of propitiation. All these must be real if there is any reality in the justification of a sinner before God.[8]

Why all this stress on what is "real," or, to give it a fancy name, on "ontology"?

As an experienced combatant in the world-wide theological arena, Robert Preus understood very well the fatal illness at the heart of most contemporary theologizing. It is a fundamental frivolity, which endlessly weaves, unweaves, and reweaves various word-patterns, which, however ingenious, do not ultimately bind anyone to anything. Such a non-committal manipulation of religious verbiage is an academic game, unworthy of the solemn name "theology"—words from and about God! The caricature was exemplified not long ago by the theological faculty of the University of Riga, when it reportedly told the Latvian church authorities that it could only provide academic theology, but was neither able nor willing to prepare pastors for the church!

With the Lutheran fathers, Robert Preus insisted, on the contrary, that theology is a practical, spiritual, God-given fitness for the holy office of administering the saving treasures of God ("stewards of the mysteries of God," 1 Cor 4:1; "able ministers of the New Testament," 2 Cor 3:6). To reduce theology to a *mere* intellectual exercise or to clever conjuring with "cultural" images is to make light of, to profane, holy things. Hence the scarcely concealed scorn in Preus's words: "deceptive theological blather."

A non-referential theology is a theology without content, a discipline without subject matter. That is the ultimate force of Ferdinand Hahn's observation that the "renunciation of the theological relevance of the factual element . . . has meant for exegesis something like a loss of reality."[9] The "post-modern" attempts to gloss over this loss merely create verbose

---

8 John Warwick Montgomery, ed., *Crisis in Lutheran Theology* (Grand Rapids: Baker Book House, 1967), 2:91.

9 Ferdinand Hahn, "Probleme historicher Kritik," *Zeitschift für die neutestamentliche Wissenschaft* 63 (1972): 6.

pretend-theologies: we all tell our favorite "stories" *as if* they were true—but of course we know that none of them is really, ontologically, superior to the others. It is difficult to improve on the biting satire of "The Bishop's Gambit," an episode in the BBC comedy series *Yes, Prime Minister*, in which a cynical bureaucrat instructs a naïve prime minister that "theology's a device for helping agnostics stay within the church"!

A theology worth its salt will hardly gain the world's admiration (1 Cor 1:18–24). But a theology that does not even respect itself invites a double portion of contempt. Take the case of a well-known physicist, Frank Tipler, attending the 1990 meeting of the American Academy of Religion. When a speaker mentioned Thomas Aquinas's treatment of cannibalism as an obstacle to the resurrection of the dead, the "audience, several hundred theologians and religious studies professors, thought this quaint 'problem' hilarious, and laughed loudly." Tipler concluded: "I infer that the typical American theologian/religious studies professor has never seriously thought about the resurrection of the dead."[10] One can at least understand the attraction of Tipler's impossible alternative: "Either theology is pure nonsense, a subject with no content, or else theology must ultimately become a branch of physics."[11] Tipler's own wide-ranging *tour de force*, entitled *The Physics of Immortality*, illustrates the futility of the theology-as-physics project. It purports to demonstrate scientifically the probability that the universe will ultimately converge upon an Omega Point, which will be a personal, omnipotent and omniscient god/goddess, who "loves" us and will cybernetically "emulate" or resurrect us all for a happy eternity! Is it a case of the very stones—or their quantum slates—crying out when theologians are silent or laughing?

The most unlikely stories are now believable if told by "science," whilst the most obvious moral platitudes are suspect if associated with historic Christianity. This catastrophic reversal belongs to the Cultural Revolution, which, accelerated by the social dislocations of several major wars, has now overtaken the western world. For the foreseeable future the mythology of scientism will supply the articles of faith for our cultural elites, who are increasingly impatient with what seem to them the narrow, divisive, and exclusive truth-claims of the Christian creed.

The British science writer Bryan Appleyard has written a thoughtful account of our cultural crisis in his *Understanding the Present: Science and the Soul of Modern Man*. He shows the squalor that results from the confusion

<hr />

10 Frank J. Tipler, *The Physics of Immortality: Modern Cosmology, God, and the Resurrection of the Dead* (New York: Doubleday, 1994), xiii.
11 Ibid., 3.

of technological effectiveness with truth. All ethical issues are ultimately redefined as problems to be solved by an omnicompetent scientific technology. Permanent moral standards are therefore by definition ruled out. "Science begins by saying it can answer only *this* kind of question," writes Appleyard, "and ends by claiming that *these* are the only questions that can be asked."[12] An even more energetic critique is *Reason in the Balance: The Case Against Naturalism in Science, Law, and Education*, by Berkeley law professor Phillip E. Johnson. Johnson actually takes on the sacred cow of Darwinism, something about which the physicist Tipler seems oddly credulous.

The great merit of Johnson in particular is that he differentiates clearly between naturalism and science. Our so-called "chattering classes," that is, the shapers of our public culture, by contrast, see no difference between science and scientism. Yet that distinction is crucial. It is in fact suggested by the recent philosophy of science, especially in the wake of the late Sir Karl Popper, which effectively discredits superstitious notions of science as an all-encompassing infallible dogma. The genuine achievements of relativity theory and quantum mechanics are one thing—and they make the universe a much more mysterious entity than classical physics could imagine. But pontifications about the spontaneous and chance origins of the universe, of life, and of human consciousness are quite another thing. The propaganda for scientistic naturalism deliberately lumps all these together and presents them to a dazzled public as "science." But when the "soft" mythology is cloaked in the prestige of "hard" science and technological success, people become completely skeptical of anything that runs counter to the official mythology.

Since dominant cultural forces are notoriously pervasive, it would be sheer nonsense to pretend that we church people are unaffected by them. Rather, the cultural predisposition acts as a hidden deafness to the Christian proclamation, discounting it with a sort of subliminal definition of faith as "believing what you know to be untrue." Hence the enormous pressures at all levels of church life to waffle, fudge, and smudge.

If there is anything to these musings, it is clearly not enough to respond by crying "faith, faith, faith!"—for it is the very nature and content of faith that is at issue. Of course only the Holy Spirit creates faith, and this only through the gospel (always including the sacraments). But genuine gospel preaching does not skirt issues. Its duty is also to "confute objectors" (Ti 1:9 NEB). Nor may such confutation be restricted to the safely dead mythologies of the past. It is the living dragons of deceit above

---

12 Bryan Appleyard, *Understanding the Present* (London: Picador, 1993), 249.

all that must be unmasked and discredited. If scientistic secularism is indeed the leading mythology of our age, which seeps into our very bones from every blaring radio and every blathering television screen, then the preachers of the gospel need to be able to understand the thing clearly and cope with it competently. That implies much more attention to science and the philosophy of science in seminary curricula, which have traditionally focused instead on the humanities. Luther did not rave ignorantly against scholasticism, but demolished it on the basis of a competent grasp of the subject. Scientism is today's scholasticism.

It is clear that the issue of "realism" in theology is not settled simply by professions of belief in the authority of Holy Writ. The pervasive secularist mythology can emasculate and unnerve theology despite formal assent to Scripture. Two examples come to mind. One is a grim preoccupation, at the behest of "Church Growth," with methods, techniques, and endless statistical surveys and studies. The corresponding disinterest in, if not outright hostility to theology suggests a flight from the intangible realities of faith (2 Cor 4:18) to the firmer ground of sight, measurement, and "scientific" validation. It is just what the ruling culture would predict.

The second example is suggested by Luther's comment in a letter to Spalatin of 9 September 1521 that Erasmus was "far from a knowledge of grace, since he in all his writings looks not to the cross but to peace. He therefore imagines that everything must be treated and handled courteously and with a certain urbane benevolence" (WA Br 2: 387). One thinks at once of a certain formulaic kind of bureaucratic theologizing: Start with a windy list of alternatives, apply philology to show that the Bible does not speak directly to any of them, set out carefully balanced "guidelines" or "biblical principles," conclude inconclusively to ensure that no concrete change in the status quo is required. Theology suffers whenever words are stressed at the expense of realities. In his comments on Genesis 16:12–14 Luther repeatedly stresses the primacy of content over words, philology, and grammar:

> To him who has no knowledge of the subject matter the knowledge of the meaning of the word will be of no help . . . Thus if you have a firm grasp of the subject matter, the language is easy, as Horace also points out. Words, he says, are not reluctant to follow where the subject matter has been discerned well beforehand, understood, and considered. But where there is no knowledge of the subject matter, there a knowledge of the words is worthless . . . Those whose words originate in their mouths are talkative but not eloquent (AE 3:67, 68, 73).

"Realism" simply means taking theology with the utmost seriousness. In doing just that Robert Preus showed himself a true spiritual son of

Martin Luther, who took all the divine treasures at face value, and refused the counterfeits spun from mere mental conceits. Mortimer Adler's *Truth in Religion* cites Josiah Royce's quip "that a liar is a person who willfully misplaces his ontological predicates, putting 'is' where he should put 'is not,' or the reverse."[13]

"Yea, let God be true, but every man a liar" (Rom 3:4).

---

13 Mortimer Adler, *Truth in Religion* (New York: Macmillan, 1990), 116.

Solus Christus: Robert Preus

Daniel Preus

ROBERT PREUS WAS A LUTHERAN—not just in name, but also in confession, in practice, and in faith. Throughout his entire career, as it was for Luther, the article of justification was central to his theology, and Christ was at the center of this article. Those who sat at his feet as students can testify to his love for the "first and chief article." His insistence upon the teaching of objective justification as necessary to a proper understanding of God's saving work testifies to the christocentric nature of his belief with regard to justification and all of theology.

Like Luther, Robert Preus believed that to speak of justification was to speak of Christ, and to speak of Christ was to speak of justification. In 1992 he described Luther's *solus Christus* principle. "It is obvious that justification before God and the work of Christ as Propitiator and Redeemer belong inextricably together and, so far as Luther is concerned, really constitute the same article."[1] He could just as well have been describing his own convictions. And when he continued in the same article to speak of Luther's view that all Scripture is christocentric, he echoed again his own belief. How can it be otherwise? Jesus is our Savior; Jesus is our hope. Without him we have nothing.

Like Luther, Robert Preus also had a heightened appreciation for eschatology during the latter years of his life. His christocentric understanding of the article of justification and of Scripture led him to this greater appreciation when he saw in his own life what Luther had seen in his, namely, that the person and work of Christ will always be the target of all Satan's attacks. If all theology is christocentric, this is how it must be. He saw it as no coincidence that one who so dedicated himself to the study of justification, and whose own faith was so firmly anchored in him

---

1 Robert Preus, "Luther: Word, Doctrine and Confession," *Lutheran Synod Quarterly* 32 (December 1992): 31.

who is at the center of all doctrine, should have suffered so much abuse at the hands of members of his own church body. And if his exile did not seem *to others* to be a direct result of his teaching on justification, Satan's purpose was obvious. For if the teacher is discredited, what will be thought of his teaching? And in the end, this was the primary concern for Robert Preus, as it was for Luther. He did not want vindication for his own sake but for the sake of the gospel and therefore for the sake of the church. He was a pastor to congregations for only about ten years, but he was a pastor to the church from the day of his ordination until he died.

Probably nowhere else can his pastoral heart be discerned more clearly than in the instruction he provided to his own children. He was not content to leave this task to others; catechization was a common feature of the daily family devotions he conducted. And in these devotions the article on justification was central, again with particular emphasis on the person of Christ.

This emphasis was probably seen most easily in his hymn selection. Over the years he and my mother taught us hundreds of hymn verses. A quick review of the verses used most often in family devotions reveals a startlingly heavy emphasis on the christological. The so-called "Praise Hymns" were not his favorites. He apparently wanted his children pointed to Jesus, because over and over again he chose hymns and single stanzas of hymns that were strongly christocentric in their proclamation of salvation. One hymn in particular was typical of the focus of the hymnody in our home. The first verse proclaims:

> Christ alone is our salvation,
> Christ the Rock on which we stand;
> Other than this sure foundation
> Will be found but sinking sand. Christ,
> His cross and resurrection,
> Is alone the sinner's plea;
> At the throne of God's perfection
> Nothing else can set him free.

The third verse with a stronger eschatological flavor is equally christocentric:

> When we perfect joy shall enter,
> 'Tis in Him our bliss will rise;
> He's the essence, soul and center
> Of the glory in the skies;
> In redemption's wondrous story
> Planned before our parents' fall,
> From the cross unto the glory,
> Jesus Christ is all in all.

Another very popular hymn in our home was the well-known hymn "One Thing Needful!" We sang the first verse, skipped the next six, some of which dealt with subjects such as leaving earthly joys behind, the heart of Mary burning with emotion, the faithful following of Jesus, and then sang the eighth verse, which speaks for itself in its christology:

> Jesus, in Thy cross are centered
> All the marvels of Thy grace;
> Thou, my Savior, once hast entered
> Through Thy blood the holy place:
> Thy sacrifice holy there wrought my redemption,
> From Satan's dominion I now have exemption;
> The way is now free to the Father's high throne,
> Where I may approach Him in Thy name alone.

Melodies were never a barrier. Good hymns simply had to he learned, and the christological stanzas had to be sung. One hymn with a particularly difficult melody was "In Jesus' Name." We always sang the first verse of a hymn, but once again we omitted the second verse of this hymn, which deals with our praising of God, and directed our attention to the third verse, which spoke more directly of the work of Christ and his grace. Robert Preus believed that the greatest praise that could be given to God was to speak of the person and work of his Son. Until the day he died, he never tired speaking of Jesus. His love for the gospel and his desire to proclaim it remained undiminished. Thus this third verse of the hymn "In Jesus' Name" was sung in our home not only because it taught us children about Jesus, but also because it so vividly expressed the faith of our mother and father:

> In Jesus' name
> We live and we will die;
> If then we live,
> His love we will proclaim;
> If we die, we gain thereby.
> In Jesus' name,
> Who from heaven to us came,
> We shall again arise
> To meet Him in the skies,
> When at last, saved by His grace,
> We shall see Him face to face,
> Live with Him in Paradise.